STUDIES IN FICTION

STUDIES IN FICTION

(George Orwell, John Steinbeck, Thomas Love Peacock, Anita Desai, Jerome David Salinger, Charles Dickens, Mrs. Elizabeth Gaskell, Anthony Trollope, W.M. Thackeray, George Eliot, Walker Percy, George Meredith and Thomas Hardy)

S.D. SHARMA

ATLANTIC
PUBLISHERS & DISTRIBUTORS

Published by
ATLANTIC PUBLISHERS AND DISTRIBUTORS
B-2, Vishal Enclave, Opp. Rajouri Garden, New Delhi-27
Phones : 5413460, 5429987, 5466842

Sales Office
4215/1, Ansari Road, Darya Ganj, New Delhi-02
Phones : 3273880, 3285873, 3280451
Fax : 91-11-3285873
web : www.atlanticbooks.com
e-mail : info@atlanticbooks.com

ISBN 81-269-0207-8

Typeset at
APD Computer Graphics, Delhi

Printed in India at
Nice Printing Press, Delhi

Dedicated to

My committed and self-abnegating wife
Smt. Chhaya Sharma, with total affection,
endearing love and ever-growing gratitude.

PREFACE

This book is apparently the quintessence of research spirit which I have tried to keep up in my other books too. The novelists included in this volume are George Orwell, John Steinbeck, Thomas Love Peacock, Anita Desai, Jerome David Salinger, Thomas Hardy, Charles Dickens, Mrs. Elizabeth Gaskell, Anthony Trollope, W.M. Thackeray, George Eliot, Walker Percy, and George Meredith. In addition, a number of other novelists belonging to both the Early and the Late Victorian Fiction have also been dealt with. In particular, the three American novelists namely, John Steinbeck, Jerome David Salinger and Walker Percy have also been included as mentioned above.

Readers will certainly find Chapters 7 and 9 as reinterpretation of the Early and the Late Victorian Fiction in the light of the emerging contemporary scientific *isms* such as Uniformitarianism, scientific positivism and Darwinism. Chapter 10 deals with George Meredith and Thomas Hardy with regard to their acceptance of Darwinism.

Narratology and structure of John Steinbeck, Jerome David Salinger and Walker Percy have been dealt with by dwelling upon their major novels. Whereas Cosmic Consciousness and Immanent Will have partly been dealt with in Chapter 6, Anita Desai's feminine sensibility has been studied in her major as well as shorter fiction in Chapter 4. Dehumanization in George Orwell's *Nineteen Eighty-Four* and *Animal Farm* has been dealt with in Chapter 1, and Thomas Love Peacock's *Headlong Hall, Melincourt, Crotchet Castle* and *Gryll Grange* have been probed into from the point of view of novels of ideas class in Chapter 3.

S.D. SHARMA

ACKNOWLEDGMENTS

For critical counsel and discussion, I am grateful to Dr. Amlendu Bose, former Professor and Head, Department of English, Calcutta University, Calcutta; Dr. V.A. Sahane, former Professor and Head, Department of English, Osmania University, Hyderabad; Dr. Ram Bilas Sharma, former Director, K.M. Hindi Institute, Agra University, Agra; Dr. D.D. Sharma, former Professor and Head, Department of English, Lucknow University, Lucknow; Professor A.A. Ansari, former Professor and Head, Aligarh University, Aligarh; Professor W. Sidney Allen, University of Cambridge; besides my colleagues in the Department.

Parts or whole of the Chapters included in this volume have already appeared in different journals/books which have duly been acknowledged. Some parts of the Chapters were also presented at other symposia, seminars, conferences and workshops, which, too, have been duly acknowledged.

I warmly acknowledge the debt I owe to my wife and to my dear children. I am also beholden beyond words in gratitude to my *Almighty Creator,* Who have given me a very fine and perfect life to live by.

With all apologies, notwithstanding, the present book may still have some errors, but adapting Tari Tung's words, "Were I to await perfection, my book would never be finished."

S.D. SHARMA

CONTENTS

1

Marionette and Masquerade : Dehumanization in George Orwell's *Nineteen Eighty-Four* and *Animal Farm*

ERICH FROMM writes in the *Afterword* of *Nineteen Eighty-Four* :

> George Orwell's *1984* is the expression of a mood, and it is a warning. The mood it expresses is that of a near despair about future of man, and the warning is that unless the course of history changes, men all over the world will lose their most human qualities, will become soulless automatons, and will not even be aware of it.[1]

But in a regimented society, it is not possible to have the Tennysonian faith in human progress, despite one's being possessed of incorrigible optimism. In such a society, the Meredithian belief in the spiritual evolution of man is certainly a very difficult proposition. Thomas Hardy had had a profound faith in the physical evolution of man : for, he was greatly influenced by Charles Darwin. But the Hardyian man may evolve in such a regimented society physically but what about his evolution from the viewpoint of soul ? What will happen to his free will, to his intuition and to his spontaneity ? After all, we do no want a man to evolve as "soulless automaton" what Erich Fromm had already predicted. A Winston Smith should evolve not just a *soulless automata;* a Julia should evolve not wholly bereft of human qualities. We do not certainly need a Napolean or a Big Brother or an O'Brien to perpetuate the rein of terror and convert fine, lively, cheerful human beings into just dead corpses, fit to be thrown into prison. In a struggle for power between a Stalin and a Trotsky or between a Napolean and a Snowball, the society should not be converted into a lifeless affair, a mere means to keep the masses busy, and to force them believe in the imagined, unfounded and unbaked untruths as realities of life.

Walter Cronkite writes quite justifiably that George Orwell's denunciation of a regimented society under the superintendence of a cruel dictator will certainly produce soulless men, merely automatons, just cogs in a big machine completely bereft of noble visions and a definite individuality of their own. Such a generation will certainly be the stupid, senseless generation of slaves and mountebanks :

> We've met Big Brother in Stalin and Hitler and Khomeini. We hear Newspeak in every use of language to manipulate, to deceive, to cover harsh realities with the soft snow of euphemism. And every time a political leader expects or demands that we believe the absurd, we experience that mental process Orwell called doublethink. From the show of trials of the pre-war Soviet Union to the dungeon courts of post-revolutionary Iran, *1984*'s vision of justice as foregone conclusion is familiar to us all. As soon as we were introduced to such things, we realized as had always known them.[2]

In 1941, Nazis launched an attack on Russia though a no war pact was negotiated between both the parties. They also did a lot of damage to the Russians till they were finally driven out. Frederick in *Animal Farm* reminds of the forces of Nazi who, notwithstanding the fact that a trade pact had already been negotiated between Napolean and Frederick, attacked the prized windmill and almost ruined it. But unfortunately Frederick and his men were finally pushed back. Both Frederick and Napolean are the champions of a regimented society. The Stalinism is almost synonymous to totalitarianism, where means must totally be subservient to ends; where the total and exclusive atmosphere of fear should always continue. Winston Smith and Julia must confess their great crimes, they have really done to their masters. Napolean must feel happy that his trained dogs have humiliated loyal and faithful pigs; and many hens and ducks must invariably be butchered after confessing horrible offences they have really committed against their master. The *INGSOC PARTY* and its boss *BIG BROTHER* are omnipotent, omnipresent and omniscient, though their sources of strength are mere espionage and telescreen.,.Napolean is all powerful and the Seven Commandments of the Animalism should change as and when he needs their change and interpretation to suit his whims, fads and idiosyncrasies. What a fun of equality and what a strange twist of socialism!

The tales told by Moses of Sugarcandy Mountain in *Animal Farm* have something very absorbing to satirize religion particularly the Church. In fact, in 1944, Stalin allowed the Orthodox Church to continue services in Russia, though initially he was vehemently opposed to it as was Karl Marx who treated religion as opium to induce sleep to the masses. Moses represents the Russian Church, and he is allowed to return after the pigs had consolidated their position as rulers of the farm. Now the question arises as to who fashioned the Russian Church ? Who is Moses? The real prophet or just the creation of a Napolean and a Stalin. In a regimented society, religions are deformed and re-shaped in tune with the whims of the dictator. The bugbear of Emmanuel Goldstein in *Nineteen Eighteen-Four* is created as a Satan, a terror to all those who have any pious feelings left in them. Winston's piety is defiled by O'Brien in a most perverted way :

> Some years ago you had a very serious delusion indeed. You believed that three men, three one-time party members named Jones, Aaronson and Rutherford -- men who were executed for treachery and sabotage after making the fullest possible confession — were not guilty of the crimes they were charged with. You believed that you had seen unmistakable documentary evidence proving that their confessions were false. There was a certain photograph about which you had a hallucination.[3]

Both *Animal Farm* and *Nineteen Eighty-Four* project a society where nightmarish conditions are spawned by effective negative tendencies of control over scientific and technical advancement in communication and other techniques in a totalitarian, regimented society. Philanthropists like Bertrand Russell have also prognosticated that in a regimented society ushered in by abrupt exodus of scientific and technical advancements, soulless men will further infect the society with degeneration of all sorts.[4] In a regimented society, it is very difficult for the persons to develop their inner self : for, they are subjected to all kinds of controls whereby they become oblivious of their conscious self. Despite every effort on the part of an individual, he can never regain his true self. Winston Smith is subjected to all inhuman horrors : he is forced to confess what he earlier never believed. But the constant beating and electric shocks force him to believe in the authority of the Big Brother; in the veracity of the Newspeak and also in the powerful force of the Doublethink. He now fully believes that *IGNORANCE IS STRENGTH*; that *FREEDOM IS SLAVERY*; and that *WAR IS PEACE.* As a defeated man, in the end, he fails to make any quest[5] for his true self : for, he is satisfied with his *Victory Gin* and *Victory Cigarettes* and worn-out overalls.

II

In George Orwell's *Animal Farm,* Old Major symbolises Karl Marx; Nepolean does Stalin and Snowball Trotsky explicitly or implicitly, collectively or severally and often all together at the same time. Marx disliked the exploiters and always sided with the exploited. So does George Orwell as is evidenced by his earlier writings such as *Down and Out Paris and London* and *How the Poor Die* (an essay), wherein he identified himself with the outcasts of the society, trumps, destitute people and other downs and outs, the under-privileged and the exploited. But he hates the regimented system which never guarantees to ensure equality to all those weaker sections of the society. He, therefore, hates any big brotherhood forged to realize such a dream of equality, may be this forged brotherhood includes Karl Marx, Stalin and Lenin. Marx prognosticated that in an industrially advanced country, Communism would invariably usher in earlier than in backward countries, where the proletariat or the common people were always in want of everything. He anticipated Germany to go Communist earlier than Russia, but he was astonished to see the events actually happened otherwise. Jone's amazement is justified to see his animals all up in arms against him. The Old Major has already given his clarion-call of equality to the proletariat against Mr. Jones and his favourites, the bourgeois class of the privileged. The Animalism is propounded with great enthusiasm and avidity on the animal farm and everboy rejoices the herald of a new dawn. The Seven Commandments are vigorously persued to regulate the life of the proletariat, the common masses. *Four legs good, two legs bad* — this dictum makes everybody happy; even sheep which represent the masses are happy; and, they, therefore, bleat out in and out of season. But Napolean and Snowball constitute the bourgeois in due course of time and usurp the masses of their rights.

Marx disapproves of religion and treats it just as the opium to induce sleep to the masses. The Communist Russia crumbed the mighty pillars of the Church and religion was rendered totally and exclusively a private and personal affair. But Stalin rose to such heights that he himself assumed the role of the Church and religion and anybody who ever dared to oppose his dictates was instantly liquidated. Napolean in *Animal Farm* emerges the most powerful leader in the end after the disappearance of Snowball, who was his arch enemy right from the very beginning. His orders are final and absolute, and whenever he appears in the public, he comes in his full glory and a black Cockeral acts as a trumpeter. On his birthday, a gun is fired and whatever little is achieved on the farm is wholly credited to Napolean. For instance, if hens lay five eggs in six days, the credit goes to him. If water tastes well, then again the credit must go to Napolean. Minimus, the famous poet, composes a lengthy poem in his honour so that Napolean may feel flattered and cajoled. Napolean likes the poem and orders that it shall be written in bold letters on the walls of the barn. In order to create fear-psychosis, the cult of confessions continues. With this end in view, Napolean orders all the animals to assemble at the store-house so that he can ascertain whether there exists any dissenter among the masses. On the appointed day, Napolean comes in his full honours before the public surrounded by his cajolers and flatterers. In the way, his trained dogs seize four of the dissenting pigs by ear and drags them to Napolean's feet. Three of the dogs assault Boxer, but he is too strong for the dogs. Then Napolean asks Boxer to let the dogs go. The four ducks confess their conspiracy against Napolean which they have hatched in collusion with Snowball, who is Napolean's arch enemy. They also confess that Snowball is in secret league with Mr. Jones and the windmill was destroyed by them. Napolean, therefore, orders their (duck's) liquidation at once, and accordingly, they are killed. Even the favourite song named the Beasts of England is stopped to be sung by the animals and in its place a new song glorifying Napolean was taught to the animals to be sung compulsorily by them as a mark of respect to him.

Boxer is Stakhanovile, who notwithstanding any hardship in his way will never endure slavery. But Mollie, the white mare finds herself ill at ease, despite the ushering in of a new social order. She leaves the farm in utter frustration and prefers to serve a publican in Willingdon. Moses, the raven, also deserts the rebels as he is loathsome to work. Sugar and ribbons are treated as symbols of bourgeoisie. Jones is regarded as the most corrupt and cruel fellow and all the animals are deadly against his possible return as the master of the animal farm. But in practice, Napolean perpetuates all sorts of cruelty on other animals. For his own self-aggrandisement, even Seven Commandments epitomising the whole philosophy of Animalism are suitably modified by Napolean. He like Stalin himself does everything for his own glorification and gratification.

Orwell learnt in Spain that socialism was certainly different from Communism and he was not convinced with Stalinism as a possible replacement of Socialism. As such, *Animal Farm* articulates the mocking voice of a socialist at the socialist experiment. There is, therefore, an apparent lament for the fate of revolutions that are generally ushered in with great hopes but which usually end in utter despairs. Stalin promised to usher in a golden period of equality in Russia, but when his own deeds came to light in 1953, people in general condemned them as bloody and terrifying acts resembling like those of Napolean and his coterie. Whatever be the form of government, whether Animalism, Communism, Fascism or Nazism, the struggle for power after the revolution is most damnable. The struggle for power that ensured after Jones's removal between the followers of Snowball and Napolean is horrifying. The accusations and counter-accusations, the confessions and revelations are all imagined and fictitious. Napolean's followers accuse Snowball of everything that goes wrong on the farm. The destruction of the windmill is attributed to Snowball's malicious designs. Whenever there is even the remotest possibility of any opposition, the Jones-Snowball boggey becomes as provoking as a red rag to a bull. The ducks which dared to object to Napolean's plans are immediately silenced by his trained dogs.

III

Of all George Orwell's famous novels *viz.*, *Burmese Days* (1934), *A Clergyman's Daughter* (1935), *Keep the Aspidistra Flying* (1936), *Coming Up For Air* (1939), and *Animal Farm* (1945), *Nineteen Eighty-Four* (1949) is the most poignant, the most widely-read and the most criticised novel. It seeks to expose the inherent weaknesses in a politically regimented system : the deep fissures in a society founded on a wholesome utilitarian philosophy of life completely shorn of sensible human values. A despondent forecast of the future awaiting mankind, as *1984* really is, it certainly conveys three messages : that the English Socialism is an incipient totalitarianism; that it robs a man of his heart; and, that it shall breed spiritual corruption by suppressing individuality. A mental perversion the society thus projected may visibly appear to be (George Orwell was dying of consumption when he wrote *1984*), the utopia risks to rouse people to the dangers of human freedom mortgaged to the ruthless hands of politicians rather than to the scientists'.

The hero, Winston Smith, works in the *Ministry of Truth,* where his duty is largely to rewrite, alter, falsify and manipulate historical references, previous records, and the names of persons liquidated to tailor to the needs of the Ingsoc Party. He is a white-collar worker in the Outer Party and lives in a one room apartment in a party workers' hostel in London, now the principal city of Airstrip One, part of Oceania which comprises Britain and North and South America. Oceania is as big a super-power as Eurasia and Eastasia are and is a completely totalitarian police state, rigidly adhering to the principles and policies of *INGSOC* or English Socialism. A fierce war is waged between Oceania and Eurasia plus Eastasia, in which both the belligerent super states claim victory. At lunch time on April 4, 1984, Winston takes time off from his job to go home. He recalls and ruminates over the life he leads; the telescreen fitted in his apartment to report back his activities to the Party bosses. He also hates the shabby and poor life the workers are forced to lead, the poor Victory Gin and Victory Cigarettes; the cheap Party Overalls. He also hates the Party leader — Big Brother. He is also bored of the Two-Minute-Hate session which everybody compulsorily attends to in order to show contempt for Emmanuel Goldstein, the almost legendary enemy of the Party, an alleged counter-revolutionary and scapegoat for all the military, social and economic failings of the Party. As the picture appears on the telescreen, which is fitted there for news, music and entertainment besides, the audience works itself up into a frenzy and anyone who fails to scream curses at the screen is immediately reported to the Thought Police to be '*Vaporized*' and liquidated. Winston records his feelings of revolt against this regimented society in a diary he procures from Mr. Charrington's shop. He does it hiding his actions in a corner from the over-watchful telescreen knowing it fully well that "*Down with big Brother*" or "Down with Ingsoc" are treasonous outbrusts to invite vaporisation and liquidation according to the Party decrees.

While one forenoon the daily Two-Minute-Hate session is at its climax, Winston encounters a lovely, cool, dark-haired young girl named Julia, who he thinks a member of the dreaded Thought Police chasing him. He also mistakes her to be a staunch supporter of the Party whereas the fact is that Julia hates the system as much as Winston himself. Dressed in a regulation overalls with a banner of the Anti-Sex League draped around her, Julia's job is to repair the machines that churn out cheap fiction for the Proles in the Fiction Department of the Ministry of Truth. The Proles constitute the majority of the population who are treated as inconsequential to the Party and power. A lover of promiscuous life as Julia is, she despises the Party's philosophy of love, marriage and children. Julia hates the Party system which robs its workers of love, privacy and simple pleasures of life. Being guided by this secret revolt against the system, one day Julia slips a note reading "I love you" to Winston to his great amazement. Thereafter, Winston and Julia arrange a rendezvous in a secluded nook in the country where the dragnet of telescreen may not net them. They now make love, share confidences, explore black markets run by the Proles, enjoy coffee and chocolate instead of synthetic 'Victory' substitutes that the Outer Party members are supposed to consume.

But Winston dreads the imminent danger in lieu of his contempt for Big Brother and his forbidden love for Julia. He also dreads the efficacy of spying so common even by neighbours like Parsons, who himself is scared of his children, the active spies themselves; and by co-workers like Syme in the Ministry of Truth, who doggedly circumscribes the size of the Newspeak Dictionary aimed to restrict human thought. To avoid all the spying, he hires an accommodation above Mr. Charrington's junk shop to enloy Julia's love. Winston really feels happy in Julia's company and in moments of retrospection thinks of Catherine, his first wife, an active member of the Party, who deserts him because Winston fails to produce children. The room Winston hires is seedy put confortable. In a fit of frenzy, he forgets that the room is equipped with a telescreen and that Mr. Charrington apparently looking an aged shop-keeper is a member of the Police Thought.

Bolstered by love for each other, Winston and Julia intentionally meet O'Brien, a member of the Inner Party, mistaking him to be a rebel against the brotherhood. O'Brien lends them a heretical book to read supposedly written by

Emmanuel Goldstein, the bitterest foe of the Party. In the meantime, Oceania and Eurasia become allies and fight ends against Eastasia, and Winston has to delete and falsify all records to this new situation. Being relieved of the drudgery of the Hate Week, Winston reads the book. To his great surprise, orders are announced on the telescreen for the immediate arrest both of Winston and Julia. Mr. Charrington alongwith other guards invades the room; Julia is instantly kicked in the stomach by one of the guards while Winston is hustled off to a stinking dungeon in the Ministry of Love. There he is kicked, clubbed and bludgeoned for days until he is almost mad and cries in pain just like an animal. O'Brien orders electric shocks to be given to him so that he (Winston) may truly understand how in the struggle for power, it is always the middle class that survives; the masses incapable of capturing power, and the upper class always unable to cling to power. He also realises his folly to have private ideas, to have an independent individuality. Even his pride of Julia's love is shattered when a large cage of revenous rodents (rats) is placed next to him and when O'Brien threatens to open its door. Winston is highly scared of it and in a moment of unreasoning panic, begs him to set the rats on Julia instead, which is, precisely, a great betrayal of love. He is now a completely transformed Winston having practically nothing left to feel proud of. His mind, physique and spirit are completely broken; his teeth knocked out; his hair gone. Not considered worth 'vaporisation' and liquidation, he is now given a very minor job that leaves him plenty of time to sit in a cafe alone and despised, drinking Victory gin and Victory cigarettes. Equally crest-fallen and dejected is Julia, who, took often sits in the workers' canteen contemptuously all alone gazing at Winston. He now truly loves Big Brother; for, the brainwashing and shock treatments have completely overhauled his person. The announcement that Oceania wins a great Victory in Africa appears wholly true to an erstwhile sceptical Winston. His surrender to Big Brother, in a word, is complete and his confession to the Party quite clean and spontaneous. He is ultimately converted into a soulless automaton, a degenerated fellow to be fit to do what his master dictates him to do.

IV

George Orwell is a supporter of right-wing socialism. The *anti-utopia* presented by Orwell projects the future of the negative tendencies of technicality alongwith the dread of collectivism experienced by the bourgeoisie mentality. It is a sharp satire, ridiculing the inhuman social arrangements. It is, among other things, also an anti-Communist voice, since Communism's proclivity with Fascism has been repeated. As the novel appeared in 1949 just after the Second World War, there is no denying the fact that the anti-Communist overtones in it have their origin in violation of Socialist Democracy witnessed before the war. It seems that Orwell's imagination has not gone very far ahead of its time, remembering the nightmarish gas chambers of Hitler's Third Reich that is projected less repugnantly in his anti-utopias concerning a totalitarian regime of Oceania.

In fact, *Nineteen Eighty-Four* is basically a protrayal of a *total organisation,* in which all aspects of life and activity are worked into a single mechanism that follows an established and orchestrated order and is directed by a supreme will; and decidedly becomes an aim in itself. The ruling elite (the mysterious Big Brother and his closest associates) subjects its will and passion to a mystical 'common interest' which, in some inscrutable way, suits the true interests of none. The system is something like *an automatic control unit* built into the machinc, and everybody seems to be slaves of this state machine. Typically, some members of the ruling elite, like O'Brien, have fairly sound views of everything and are aware of the injustices of the established order. But it never occurs to them that something could bc done to alter matters.

The exclusive subordination and the complete subservience of the machine to the goal of maintaining the *status quo* is also seen in other areas of social structures like classes, groups and coteries. In fact, the Orwellian society consists of two classes, namely the controllers and the controlled; and there is no social mobility. But both are condemned to the role of passive performers and are equally estranged from their human essence. The aim of the system is thus reduced to a cyclical reproduction of the conditions of existence. Another significant component of this society is *total control.* The life of people is regimented to a fastidious extent; and each movement is programmed, and any deviation from the well-entrenched pattern is promptly interfered. In every Orwellian home of *1984,* there is a spy, a TV eye that observes everything the inmates indulge in. The two minute love Big Brother campaign and also the two minute hate session against Goldstein are held over TV. Thus the life-style is absolutely controlled : even sex is controlled but with different methods in both the social groups : the managers must view sexual desire as something undersirable forcing to consider marriage to be as necessary evil and extramarital relations as a grave anti-social offence. They even have to become a member of anti-sex league. But the Proles are given sexual freedom in order to reproduce manpower as well as an effective means of filling the few leisure hours. There is even a special *pornosec* of the information department handling the publication of cheap pornobooks. To regulate such controls, agents of the *Thought Police* are present everywhere; and the damned will be the one who defies the existing social order. Control of thought is backed up by control over history. In fact, history is banished from the assortment of knowledge, and the remaining pasts are distorted in ways suiting the needs of the hour. The philosophy of the ruler of the Orwellian society is expressed in the motto : that one who *controls the past controls the future; and one who controls the present controls the past.*

Such a dreadful society does exist but through a *total deception*, which is the third significant component. In the Orwellian society, everything is turned inside out. The permanent war is handled by the Ministry of Peace : the starvation rations are prepared by the Ministry of Plenty : the Ministry of Truth concerns itself with lies : and the Ministry of Love performs the functions of detective and repressive agencies. Equally absurd are the widely advertised slogans and postulates of the prevailing ideology that *freedom is slavery; war is peace,* and *ignorance is strength.*

But this juggling with words and its oft repetitions have their obvious reasons. By deliberately suppressing traditional notions, and by turning the formulas of reason inside out, the governors rob people of their ethical values, and teach them to accept any and all nonsense they may be chosen to be cultivated as an article of faith. But mere deceit is no longer tempting : for, a set of coercive means and incentives is set in motion to turn deceit into *self-deceit,* which is a fourth significant component. Consequently though Big Brother does not actually exist, yet everyone believes in the physical existence of the leader. Moreover, though the three surviving superpowers are occupied with their own concerns and almost never communicate, the people in each of them are convinced that they are in a state of permanent war, and to sustain this self-deceit, the governors drop bombs of *foreign manufacture* on their own cities from time to time. Orwell also deals with the questions of genesis of such a society and its reasons : he makes his leading character ask the question. The answer is that there have been three kinds of people, the high, the middle, and the low : the high were always preoccupied with keeping their place of command; the middle with changing places with the high; while the low, the downdrodden cannot even hope of any change. During the middle of the twentieth century, there emerged an elite that discovered the way of perpetuating its power. For this, it learned that the standard of living must be artificially held back; for, it stimulates political activity and, in addition gets absolute totalitarianism established. In other words, the Orwellian society takes its origin not in some objective circumstances rooted in the conditions of society's economic and political pattern, but in an *exaggerated lust for power.*

Orwell also makes technicality the function of totalitarianism, which is called here an oligarchic collectvism. Totalitarianism is the rein on technical progress or the medium of its use to the detriment of humankind. The responsibility for the ghastly consequences of totalitarianism, Orwell certainly shares out in so many words between Fascism and Communism. In effect, Orwell reflects the fallacious concept of some political philosophers, who ignore the social substance of power; who give power an abstract, self-sufficient meaning, and infer social relations from power.

V

Finally, a word about the soulless automatons, the like of the regimented society just outlined above, readily produces. The Orwellian society in *1984* is a perfectly totalitarian society, an exclusively regimented society which mechanically produces automata like Winston Smith and Julia. The society projected in *Animal Farm* is the same society in which nothing can be said against Napolean and in which a Boxer and a Clover are all soulless automata. Jones, Pilkington and Frederick are the perpetuators of terror psychosis among human beings as senselessly and mercilessly as Napolean, Snowball and Squealor are among animals. They avowedly want to invent a social system of authority which will render every form of administration into a totally regimented system, which should invariably produce soulless automatons; lifeless human beings only fit to be controlled like sheep, pigs and hens or ready to work incessantly without questioning the authority like Boxer and Clover in *Animal Farm*. A case study of a leading character will certainly throw further light on this argument relating to the effect of regimentation on human psyche and conduct. Of all the leading characters *viz.*, Jones, Pilkington, Frederick, Napolean, Moses, Clover, Boxer and Squealor in *Animal Farm*, and Julia, Charrington, Katherine, O'Brien and others in *Nineteen Eighty-Four*, the most representative figure to prove degenerating effect of a regimented society on human psyche and conduct is certainly Winston Smith. In order to understand the theme of relationship between a totalitarian society and its product — soulless automatons, a little bit of deeper probe into Winston Smith's mind and heart and his social environments (where he actually failed) is decidedly a *must*.

Winston Smith is the hero of the novel named *Nineteen Eighty-Four (1984)*. He plays a significant role from the beginning to the end in the novel. The novel opens with the description of his outward features, "*Winston, who was thirty-nine and had a varicose ulcer above his right ankle, went slowly, resting several times on the way.*"[6] The novel also ends with the description of a changed, totally surrendered and psychologically depressed Winston Smith with his struggle for independent ideas fully lost, "*But it was all right, everything was all right, the struggle was finished. He had won the victory over himself. He loved Big Brother.*"[7] His body is small and frail. He wears the blue overalls, the prescribed uniform of the Party. "*His hair (is) very fair, his face naturally sanguine, his skin roughed by coarse soap and blue razor blades and the cold of the winter that had just ended.*"[8] Winston's mother disappeared miraculously when he was ten or eleven years old. His mother was "*a tall, statuesque, rather silent woman with slow movements and magnificent fair hair.*"[9] His father was dark-complexioned and thin, "*dressed always in neat clothes and wearing spectacles.*"[10] Winston's father and mother died in one of the first great purges of the fifties. Winston Smith works in the Ministry of Truth and his job is to alter and falsify historical references and data in accordance with the requirements of the Party. He hates his job as much as he hates the system perpetuated through telcscreen and spying. He hates regimented write-ups, he prepares to befool the masses and to project the party image. The diary he maintains is a symbol of individuality struggling for evolution, but he is finally charged with revolt against the system. Utilitarianism rather than individuality is the objective Winston has been ordered to nurse and develop.

Power corrupts a man and absolute power corrupts a man absolutely. William Smith hates the citadels of power; he sees *Big Brother's* power as a big impediment in any kind of social development worth the name. He treats corridors of power as stinking cells of mental perversity : for, the more the power and pelf, the more will be the deformation of human thought. Power for mere power's sake without any specified mission ahead is simply a source of terror and human degeneration. To strangle a throat crying for truth with the spectre of power is a contemptuous spectacle for Winston Smith. To think deeply about systems one lives in is no crime. He disagrees with Parsons whom he meets in prison that it is indeed a crime to arrest a man for his thought. "Thought crime is a dreadful crime"[11] screams Parsons out in dismay and to disrespect *Big Brother* is still a greater crime. To this Winston shows his ingrained contempt and outbrusts, "Down with *Big Brother*".[12] Winston also hates the extreme methods to perpetuate power. He is horrified to see the extreme physical torture given to Parsons and Bumstead in prison. Parson's stinking cell and Bumstead's hunger remind us of everything inhuman. Winston himself is subjected to great physical torture by O'Brien. With the help of electric shocks and a "hypodermic syringe",[13] Winston is almost reduced to a mere skeleton. He now realises, "Nothing in the world was so bad as physical pain. In the face of pain there are no heroes, he thought over and over as he writhed on the floor, clutching uselessly at his disabled left arm."[14] Five or six men in black uniform used to beat Winston : "Sometimes it was fists, sometimes it was truncheons, sometimes it was steel rods, sometimes it was boots",[15] which were used to beat him. "There were times when he rolled about the floor, as shameless as an animal, writhing his body this way and that in an endless, hopeless effort to dodge the kicks, and simply inviting more and yet more kicks, in his ribs, in his belly, on his elbows, on his shins, in his groin, in his testicles, on the bone at the base of his spine."[16] This is, in fact, the height of physical and mental torture meted out to Winston in a system exclusively devised to perpetuate absolute power of the *Big Brother*. The pillars of the citadel of this power do crumble, but many tiny, helpless men, the likes of Winston, are inevitably crushed by the dragnet of absolute power.

Winston treats love as a lifeless affair, a stale game, in a regimented society, governed by the decrees of the *INGSOC* and the Big Brother. In an atmosphere of distrust and discord, telescreen and spying, love is certainly the first casualty. His first wife named Katherine deserts him for the simple reason that he has failed to produce children. His infertility, his barrenness comes as an utter shock to Katherine, who herself has established the bond of marriage with him merely for the purpose of producing children. Being a member of the Junior Women's Anti Sex League; Katherine treats marriage just as a means to produce children; love as a sin, an evil; for, it is against the postulates of the *INGSOC*. But afterwards, his love affair with Julia is marked with all the freshness and spontaneity that is expected of love in a free atmosphere and unfettered society. He hires a private apartment just above Mr. Charrington's Antique Shop in order to enjoy Julia's love. Julia herself hates the Party's philosophy of love that marriage is a painful process simply to produce children and nothing more. For the first time, Winston finds love-instinct an ever-benign and enjoyable segment of life besides the stinking *Victory Gin* and *Victory Cigarettes* and poor *Victory Ration*. Both of them now feel that the *Big Brother* and the *INGSOC*, all powerful as they are, can never control and regiment such perennial human instincts as love and friendship. But Winston and Julia are not permitted to make love for long. Their activities of love are spied through telescreen fitted behind a calendar and are subsequently reported back to the whole *Brotherhood*. Mr. Charrington arrests them and Mr. O'Brien, a senior member of the Inner Party, who loaned them the book on Party's philosophy, tortures them to their utter shock, because their love-making is visibly an aberration or crime according to the specified Party philosophy. They are finally condemned, vehementally tortured and consequently forced to confess everything the Party wants them to confess. Love-making, they confess, is a crime, even a thought crime and Winston who initially defies confession ultimately does so because he has now no stamina left to bear with O'Brien's beastly tortures.

Winston's arrest alongwith Julia on various charges and the subsequent treatment in prison meted out to them is really a tale of horror. Winston is treated just like an animal; he is thoroughly starved and severely beaten. He rolls about the floor of the prison, writhing his body in an endless effort to dodge the kicks. Often he is beaten till he hardly stands, then flung like a sack of potatoes. Ultimately, he confesses everything the Party wants him to confess — that he is a religious believer; an admirer of capitalism; a sexual pervert; has murdered his wife; has been hobnobbing with Goldstein for years; and even that *Big Brother* must be respected and the *INGSOC* is supreme. The end of the novel is really the end of a Winston Smith now perfectly defeated and surrendered. He now fully understands the message hidden behind the three top slogans that :

'War is Peace'

'Freedom is Slavery'

'Ignorance is strength'

and that he, in Big Brother's regimented and orchestrated regime, is just like a soulless automaton.[17]

REFERENCES

1. Fromm, Erich, *Afterward* to *1984*, p. 257 (New American Library, New York, 1983; referred to as *NAL* below).
2. Cronkite, Walter, *Preface* to *Nineteen Eighty-Four*, *NAL*, pp. 1-2.
3. Orwell, George, *Nineteen Eighty-Four*, *NAL*, p. 203.
4. Russell, Bertrand, *The Impact of Science on Society,* Unwin Paperbacks, London, pp. 34-35; 56 and 61; Herbert Marcuse, likewise, treats scientific rationality and logic of domination as essentially contributory to increasing social control; Barry Barnes (ed.), *Sociology of Science,* Penguin Books, London, pp. 331-51.
5. Alldritt, Keith, *The Making of George Orwell : An Essay in Literary History,* Edward Arnold Pvt. Ltd., London, p. 162.
6. Orwell, George, *Nineteen Eighty-Four*, *NAL*, p. 5.
7. *Ibid.*, p. 304.
8. *Ibid.*, p. 6.
9. *Ibid.*, p. 32.
10. *Ibid.*
11. *Ibid.*, p. 239.
12. *Ibid.*
13. *Ibid.*, p. 245.
14. *Ibid.*

15. *Ibid.*, p. 246.
16. *Ibid.*
17. This was also presented at the 44th AIETC Session at BHU on December 20-22, 1999; also submitted to *POW* for publication.

2

John Steinbeck : *Tortilla Flat* and *The Grapes of Wrath*

THE FIRST part of this chapter deals with John Steinbeck's *Tortilla Flat* and the second one with *The Grapes of Wrath.* Of the famous novels of John Steinbeck, a specific mention must be made of *Cup of Gold, Tortilla Flat, To a God Unknown, Of Mice and Man, The Grapes of Wrath, East of Eden, The Winter of Discontent, The Pearl,* and *Sea of Cortez.* However, for *Tortilla Flat* and *The Grapes of Wrath,* Steinbeck was widely admired. In 1962, he received the covetous Nobel Prize for literature. A contemporary of Faulkner and Hemingway, Steinbeck has vividly delineated social events of his times in his novels. There is a lot of American Trancendentalism, myth and legends in his novels. In fact, he has many claims to be a celebrity as a novelist.

I

Tortilla Flat is one of the well-known novels of John Steinbeck. It was first published in 1935 by Heinemann, London and reprinted in 1967. The novel is divided into seventeen chapters and covers three hundred and seventeen pages. The main objective of writing of this novel has been made sufficiently clear in the *Preface* containing pages nine to fifteen, approximately six pages with three comic photographs of Mr. Danny and his friends exclusively on page thirteen.

Tortilla Flat is an uphill district situated above the town of Monterey, where mostly the paisanos inhabit. The paisanos of Monterey were a mixture of peasants whose ancestors were the Spanish, the Indian, the Mexican and the Caucasian. Danny is a paisano and is the favourite child of all the inhabitants of Tortilla Flat. Danny endears himself amongst the paisanos of Tortilla Flat so much that everybody likes him. Moreover, Danny is fortunate in having a number of relatives in Tortilla Flat. His grandfather was a rich and respectable person of Tortilla Flat, a small town of Monterey. Danny is of dark complexion. He is strongly built and has a very passionate desire to accomplish even adventurous tasks entailing plenty of risk and adventure. Steinbeck himself has projected Danny's personality in the *Preface* in a somewhat dramatic manner. "Danny was," writes Steinbeck, "a paisano, and he grew up in Tortilla Flat and every one likes him, but he did not stand out particularly from the screeching children of Tortilla Flat. He was related to nearly every one in the Flat by blood or romance. His grandfather was an important man who owned two small houses in Tortilla Flat and was respected for his wealth. If the growing Danny preferred to sleep in the forest, to work on rancher and to wrest his wine from an uncoilling world, it was not because he did not have influential relatives. Danny was small and dark and intent. At twenty-five his legs were bent to the exact curves of a horse's sides."[1]

Danny is a pure and perfect paisano; for, his forefathers have lived in California for over two hundred years. He speaks English with a paisano accent. He is also proficient in Spanish and pronounces Spanish words with perfect ease, stress and intonation of a typical paisano of the Monterey origin. He is proud of his pure Spanish race. Steinbeck has graphically drawn his person and personage with a touch of perfection. "He is," writes he, "a mixture of Spanish, Indian, Mexican and assorted Caucasian bloods. His ancestors have lived in California for a hundred or two years. He speaks English with a paisano accent and Spanish with a paisano accent. When questioned concerning his race, he indignantly claims pure Spanish blood and rolls up sleeves to show that the soft insight of his arm is nearly white. His colour, like that of a well-drowned meerschaum pipe, he ascribes to sunburn."[2]

The geographical location of Monterey is on the slope of a

hill on the coast of California with "a blue bay below it and with a forest of tall dark pine trees at its back."[3] Monterey being an old city, surrounded by forests and hills has a special appeal of creative environment for John Steinbeck. Comparing the inhabitants of Monterey with the Ancient Britons for their safe and protected dwellings, Steinbeck has thrown some hints in the *Preface* of the novel itself :

> "...The lower parts of the town (Monterey) are inhabited by Americans, Italians, Catchers and Canners of fish. But on the hill where the forest and the town intermingle, where the streets are innocent of asphalt and the corners free of street lights, the old inhabitants of Monterey are embattled as the Ancient Britons are embattled in Wales. These are the paisanos.
>
> They live in old wooden houses set in weedy yards, and the pine trees from the forest are about the houses. The paisanos are clean of commercialism, free of the complicated systems of American business, and, having nothing that can be stolen, exploited or mortgaged, that system has not attacked them very vigorously."[4]

When Danny was twenty-five years old, the war with Germany was declared. Danny and his friend named Pilon have two gallons of wine when they come to know of the outbreak of the war. Danny and Pilon rest for a while under the cool shade of pine trees. One young man named Big Joe Portagee, somehow, smells of the bottles of wine and he also immediately decides to join the adventures of Danny and Pilon. Now, all the three sit together and drink wine. Like King Arthur and his Knights of the Round Table, Danny and his friends start talking of the patriotism as and when the wine intoxicates them. Boastfully, they make other senseless protestations and vainglorious resolves to fulfil a number of noble deeds under the intoxication of wine.

But the moment the intoxication of wine is weakened, they come again to their senses. They are now worried about their safety : for, in the thick of forests, they were on the brink of their destruction by wild animals and inclement weather. However, finding no way out, they muster up courage and go down the hill arm and arm for comradeship and protection. They go to Monterey in the end and in front of an enlistment station, they raise loud voice of appreciation for America and make vehement protests against Germany. Listening to their cries, the enlistment sergeant is awakened. He puts on his uniform in order to verify the source of noise. It is worthwhile to quote from the novel itself at this juncture to highlight the inherent symmetry of thematic structure in the plot :

> Now when Danny was twenty-five years old, the war with Germany was declared. Danny and his friend Pilon (Pilon, by the way, is something thrown in when a trade is concluded — a boot) had two gallons of wine when they heard about the war. Big Joe Portagee saw the glitter of the bottles among the pines and he joined Danny and Pilon.
>
> As the wine went down in the bottles, patriotism arose in the three men. And when the wine was gone they went down the hill arm in arm for comradeship and safety, and they walked into Monterey. In front of an enlistment station they cheered loudly for America and dared Germany to do her worst. They howled menaces at the German Empire until the enlistment sergeant awakened and put on his uniform and came into the street to silence them. He remained to enlist them.[5]

The sergeant makes some questions from Danny and his friends, and finally, it is decided that Pilon will be employed in the infantry. After making a number of queries from Big Joe, the sergeant decides that he too is fit for employment in the infantry. The sergeant also asks from Danny with regard to his choice of employment. Dany prefers the job of a mule skinner. Pilon marches about Oregon with the infantry and Big Joe goes to jail for many acts of his omission and commission. Danny goes to Texas and breaks mules for the duration of the war. The mock-heroic presentation of the conversation between the Sergeant and Danny and his friends is worth appreciation :

> The Sergeant lined them up in front of his desk. They passed everything but the sobriety test and then the sergeant began his questions with Pilon.

"What branch do you want to go in ?"

"I don't give a god-man," said Pilon jauntily.

"I guess we need men like you in the infantry" and Pilon was written so.

He turned then to Big Joe, and the Portagee was getting sober. "Where do you want to go ?"

"I want to go home," Big Joe said miserably. The sergeant put him in the infantry too. Finally he confronted Danny, who was sleeping on his feet.

"Where do you want to go ?"

"Huh ?"

"I say, what branch ?"

"What you mean branch ?"

"What can you do ?"

"Me ? I can do anything."

"What did you do before ?"

"Me ? I'm a mule skinner."

"Oh, you are ? How many mules can you drive ?"

Danny leaned forward, vaguely and professionally :

"How many you got ?"

"About thirty thousand," said the sergeant.

Danny waved his hand. "String, 'an up'." he said. And so Danny went to Texas and woke mules for duration of war. And Pilon marched about Oregon with the infantry, and Big Joe, as shall be later made clear, went to jail.[6]

If Steinbeck's *Cup of Gold* is heroic, *To a God Unknown* tragic, *The Pastures of Heaven* ironic, *Tortilla Flat* is mock-heroic describing the Arthurian fellowship founded by the illiterate paisanos of *Tortilla Flat.* The sombre mythopoeic of *To a God Unknown* and the reaction of critics led Steinbeck to explain in *Tortilla Flat* : "It is well this cycle be put down on paper so that in future time scholars hearing the legends, may not say as they say of Arthur and Roland and Robinhood — "There was no Danny, nor any group of Danny's friends, nor any house. Danny is a nature god and his friends primitive symbols of the wind, the sky, the sun." This history is designed now and ever to keep the sneers from the lips of sour scholars."[7]

Tortilla Flat became an immediate success : for, the contemporary society felt bored of the economic and political toils of the Great Depression.[8] The paisanos who lived in the Monterey town were illiterate peasants immensely believing in the Arthurian legends. They were "clean of commercialism, free of the complicated systems of American business, and, having nothing that can be stolen, exploited, or mortgaged, that system has not attacked them very vigorously."[9] F.W. Watt, a great scholar of the Steinbeck fiction, is of the view that while dealing with such people the author has placed himself in a position of double advantage : he can exploit the carefree, gay, irresponsible world of the paisano while at the same time criticising, explicitly or implicitly the aspects of respectable society which make the holiday life of those beyond its bounds so attractive.[10]

Tortilla Flat appeared on best-seller lists for several months. It also received the California Commonwealth Club's annual gold medal for the best novel by a Californian writer. It was also produced as a stage play, which obtained for Steinbeck a Hollywood contract and was sold to Paramount Studios. A telegram offered four thousand dollars for *Tortilla,* which the Mexicans must have thought a code word for a race horse. Steinbeck was much amused by the fortunes of *Tortilla Flat* in Hollywood : "A moving-picture company bought *Tortilla Flat....* And when, a few years later, the same company fired its editor, one of the reasons was that he had bought *Tortilla Flat.* So he bought it from the company for the original four thousand dollars and several years later sold it to M-G-M for ninety thousand dollars."[11] The publishers were also surprised at the book's financial success but their doubts about the loose structure were confirmed by book reviewers and subsequent critics.[12]

A number of critics wrote adversely about *Tortilla Flat.* This was not taken kindly by John Steinbeck. In fact, his concept of the Arthurian cycle was not properly understood by the contemporary reviewers like Carlos Baker, who felt greatly infuriated at the publication of *Tortilla Flat* and who did not take it for granted that *Tortilla Flat* was a novel at all. Steinbeck was also unhappy to see negative criticism of *Tortilla Flat* in many leading literary journals. He also felt unhappy to mark that his concept of the immortal characters of Gawaine, Launcelot, Arthur and Galahad was not properly appreciated. Even the incidents of the Sangreal in the search of the forest, he felt, was not understood by the critics. He emphatically propounded about the scheme of actions to take place in *Tortilla Flat,* moulding the form of the Malory version and the comic adventures of Danny imitating them. In his detailed letter to his publishers named McIntosh and Otis, Steinbeck made the actual scheme of *Tortilla Flat* sufficiently clear :

> Perhaps you would care to show this to Mr. Kronen berger. This book has a very definite theme.... I thought it was clear enough. I had expected that the plan of the Arthurian would be recognized, that my Gawaine and Launcelot, that my Arthur and Galahad would be recognized. Even the incident of the Sangreal in the search of the forest is not clear enough I guess. The form is that of the Malory version, the coming of Arthur and the mystic quality of owning a house, the forming of the round table, the adventures of the knights and finally, the mystic adventures of Danny.... What do you think of putting in an interlocutor, who between each incident interprets the incident, morally, aesthetically, historically, but in the manner of the paisanos themselves. This would give the book much the appeal of the Gesta Romonorum, those outrageous tales with monkish morals appended, or of the Song of Soloman in the King James version, with the delightful chapter headings which go to prove that the Shulamite is in reality Christ's Church.... You will remember that the association forms, flowers and dies.[13]

However, despite the above correspondence and his statements made in the *Preface* of *Tortilla Flat,* as explained in the foregoing paragraphs, John Steinbeck could hardly convince critics like Peter Lisca about the Arthurian legends made almost identical in the novel. In fact, it is not possible to identify with certainty and consistency Gawaine, Launcelot and Arthur and Galahad, "If Danny is the Arthur of the saga, since he owns the property which corresponds to the Round Table, his identity is confused when, like Launcelot, he goes mad."[14] Similarly, it is also difficult to identify the episodes related to Pilon, Jesus Maria, Big Joe and Danny himself. The Malory Knights are tempted and seduced : so do many characters in *Tortilla Flat.*

But the resemblance of incidents in *Morte d'Arthur* and *Tortilla Flat* do not tally. Furthermore, Percival and the Pirate do appear in many episodes but they also differ on a number of grounds. The Pirates' dogs see a vision of San Francis : so does Percival sees the Grail. In Malory, the quest for the Grail results in the disbending of the Round Table Knights. The paisanos help the Pirate by a golden candlestick for San Francis. In chapter eight of the novel which is titled as "How Danny's Friends sought Mystic Treasure on St. Andrews Eve. How Pilon found it and later how a pair of serge pants changed ownership twice" despite the Pirate's fulfilling his promise, does not make a convincing resemblance with the Melory episodes for the readers.

Steinbeck himself acknowledges in one of his letters to his publishers, "...curious that this second-rate book (*Tortilla Flat*), written for relaxation, should cause this fuss. People are actually taking it seriously."[15] This acknowledgment by John Steinbeck suggests that he may have exaggerated the book's parallel to Malory in order to impress the publishers. Nevertheless, Steinbeck maintained as late as 1957 that *Tortilla Flat* was actually based on the *Morte d'Arthur.* He also impressed upon his critics that he was well versed with the entire episodes of the *Morte d'Arthur* as well as the complete versions of the Arthurian cycle. In his correspondence to C.V. Wicker, John Steinbeck also made it clear that he had already read the Arthurian cycle through the Oxford three volume edition brought out by one scholar named Dr. Vinaver :

> You can imagine that I was pretty excited in 1936 when the Winchester mss came to light and I could hardly wait until Dr. Vinaver brought out his great Oxford three volume edition.... I think this cycle has had enormous effect not only on our literature but also on our mores and our ways of thinking about things. But over the years I have found that although everyone knows the essence of the stories, very few people have read them.... They are the stuff psychiatry is made of. They are actually the lore on which our attitudes are based and still they have not been read except in saccharine rewritten and cut versions for children.[16]

In June 1936, Steinbeck planned to contact Dr. Vinaver and wanted that his version of the *Morte d'Arthur* in the form of *Tortilla Flat* must be authenticated by him — at least not for the scholars but for the great mass of the readers. Steinbeck disliked the criticism that his novel was not on the models of *Morte d'Arthur* and was just a sketch book.

However, to call *Tortilla Flat* just a sketch book is also not proper : for, the unity of tone and style and the presentment of a philosophic moral system make *Tortilla Flat* a novel of merit in which the tragic comic theme has a mock-epic dimension. In the *Preface* of the novel, Steinbeck has made it clear that there is no Danny nor any house. Danny is a nature god and his friends just primitive symbols of the wind, the sky and the sun.

The mock-epic tone is also obvious in the chapter headings which are seventeen in number and each declaring the synoptic view of the narrative. Moreover, within the narrative itself, John Steinbeck's occasional interruptions deepen the mock-epic tone. One such occasional interruption strengthening the impression of *Tortilla Flat,* being a serious type of mock-epic narrative, is the following, which is quoted with the view to enlarging comprehension of the narrative plan :

> Sometime a historian may write a cold, dry, fungus-like history of the Party. He may refer to the moment when Danny defied and attacked the whole Party, men, women and children, with a table-leg. He may conclude, "A dying organism is often observed to be capable of extraordinary endurance and strength." Referring to Danny's super-human amorous activity that night, this same historian may write with unshaking hand : "When any living organism is attacked, its whole function seems to aim towards reproduction." But I say, and the people of *Tortilla Flat,* would say, "To hell with it. That Danny was a man for you."[17]

The tone and style of the novel are also determined by the occasional interruptions of the author himself as well as by the special mould of the chapter planning. However, a major role for setting the tone and style is played by the paisanos themselves. In the novels of Hemingway, the Italians and the Spaniards often speak. Their speech, full of native idioms, is directly translated into English, whereby special effects and dramatic environment are created in his novels.

Steinbeck adopts, more or less, the same technique of using the native speech with the native accent and intonation of speech in his novels. For example, when Pilon learns of Danny's property, he sadly says to him : "Now the great times are done. Thy friends will mourn, but nothing will come of their mourning.... When one is poor, one thinks, 'If I had money I would share it with my good friends.' But let that money come and Charity flies away. So it is with thee my once — friend. Thou art lifted above thy friends who shared everything with thee, even their brandy."[18]

Another important technique which Steinbeck uses in *Tortilla Flat* in order to heighten the effect of tone and style is "a conscious elevation of stress by the speaker himself."[19] This is an apparently the Hemingwayian technique which Steinbeck has gainfully exploited. *Tortilla Flat* is filled with a number of such illustrations, where a character raises the pitch of his voice rather prominently to give special effect for presenting his point of view.

One such illustration is when Danny is recuperated from his illness of madness and when Pilon profoundly welcomes him : "Where is there a friend like our friend ?.... He takes us into his house out of the cold. He shares his good food with us, and his wine. Once, the good man, the dear friend."[20] In fact, this speech, punctuated with accent of Pilon, reminds us of the special effect of speech of the Twenty-Third Psalm.

One of the major functions of language is that it acts as an idea-crystalliser. Mark Schorer in his well-known essay titled as "Technique as Discovery" has opined that language in itself defines themes and meanings. Peter Lisca is also of the view that critics have failed to recognise this fact in *Tortilla Flat.* And, in fact, it is on the basis of this incomplete approach that some critics like Stanley Edgar Hyman have termed *Tortilla Flat* as a novel dealing with "a primitivistic humanity and society."[21]

Some critics like Woodburn Ross also consider *Tortilla Flat* just "a quaint and curious picture of the dispossessed."[22] This is due to the fact that the language used by Steinbeck in *Tortilla Flat* has not properly been appreciated and evaluated by such critics. A balanced and objective analysis of the language function in *Tortilla Flat* reveals that language not only states and defines themes and meanings but also sets-forth revelation of the philosophical and the moral system of the paisanos.

Steinbeck's language working *at tandem* with plot reveals a system of morals and ethics of the paisanos. An analysis of this system is as essential as the different ramifications of semantic inferences of the language used. There are a number of passages which can thoroughly be analysed, but for the sake of brevity and compendium, it is prudent only to quote just two or three illustrations. One such episode is when Danny escapes from the jail. Despite the fact that he does something wrong, he tries to abide by law. Similarly, when Danny learns that Pilon, Pablo and Jesus Maria have burned down his other house, he is in a dilemma. He realises that as a man of property, he has a certain poise and character to keep up. "He had thought over the ruin of his status as a man with a house to rent; and, all of this clutter of necessary and descent emotion having been swept away, he had finally slipped into his true emotion, one of relief that at least one of his burdens was removed."[23] When the friends show up with their sad news, Danny faithfully goes through the forms of anger and sorrows. He calls them "dogs of dogs," "thieves of descent folk's other house," "Spawn of cuttlefish,"[24] and such other terms. Nonetheless, after his anger is over Danny again welcomes his friend.

The system revealed by the use of language is a system that reflects upon the social convention of the paisanos. Whether the modern society will look upon their social conventions just as frigid and irrelevant is a matter of debate. However, a strict observance of social convention is apparent throughout the novel. Illustrations, full of condenscending observance of social convention, are galore in *Tortilla Flat,* yet to cite one or two such examples will suffice here. When the Pirate gets his golden candle stick for St. Francis, his friends insist that he should buy some decent clothes for the Church service and that he should leave his dogs at home. Even Danny's funeral is respected by his friends as a social form, and they who before gave as much thought to the raiment as do the lilies of the field do not attend the ceremonies because they cannot steel, beg, or even borrow the proper clothes for such an affair. Equally important is the fact to be noted that the paisanos are strictly conservative in their social manners. For example, if Danny sees Pilon going alone with a jug under his coat, he will not ask him for a drink. Instead, he throws his arm about his friend and offers to share some little thing he himself has for friendship's sake.

The group code is also illustrated by the language alongwith the episode in *Tortilla Flat*. For example, the episode of The Pirate's money is an episode where the group code demonstrated by Danny and his friends comes to the fore. Danny and his friends spend much time luring the Pirates to live with them so that they can easily discover where his treasure is hidden. One day, when the Pirate comes home with his treasure and gives it to them for safekeeping, they ask if he will not take some out before putting it in their hands. Later, when the outcast Big Joe Portagee steals some of the Pirates' money, the friends pursue and torture him with the vengeance.

The paisanos are the special peasants of the Monterey town who, of course, have no fascination for wealth. They even look down upon whatever little they have got as inherited property. They want to lead a life which is quite carefree and which is in close proximity with nature. They have, of course, no respect for their own property and also, no respect for the property of those outside their social circle. They subsist by a series of very petty larcenies and divine interventions in the form of miracles. The miracle of the dollar does not only express the paisanos attitude towards property but demonstrate their perfect defence against exploitation : "One night he (Pilon) had a dollar, acquired in a manner so astounding that he tried to forget it immediately for fear the memory might drive him mad. A man in front of the San Carlos hotel had put the dollar in his hand, saying, 'Run down and get four bottles of ginger-ale. The hotel is out.'

"Such things were almost miracles, Pilon thought. One should take them on faith, not worry and question them."[25] With regard to the paisanos' adjustment towards property, their delicate code of manners and their philosophic, moral system as reflected through language, Peter Lisca has made a very pertinent comment, in which he has hinted at George Orwell's *1984*. Whether the comparison is acceptable by critics or not, one vital fact certainly comes to notice that the paisanos' modes of behavour have metamorphosed into a socially acceptable behaviour. In *Tortilla Flat* such a metamorphosis of social conduct appears to have a logical structure. "A psychologist might," comments Lisca, "call it 'rationalisation'; George Orwell's term for it in *1984*, "double think," is perhaps better. In *Tortilla Flat,* this becomes a highly developed technique whereby socially unacceptable modes of behaviour are metamorphosed into socially acceptable, even praiseworthy ones and predatory instincts forms into dictates of moral conscience — all without compromising the original goal. Almost every incident in *Tortilla Flat* has its logical substructure.[26]

Steinbeck never wished that, on the basis of the social morality, as shown in *Tortilla Flat,* paisanos would be considered by some critics, like Edmund Wilson, to be just like animals or the human beings just at the rudimentary level or just as "cunning little living dolls that amuse us like pet guinea pigs or rabbits."[27] He also never expected that the society he had created in *Tortilla Flat,* could be considered by such eminent critics like Freeman Champney just as a society inhabited by "man as animal...without any other pretension."[28] But this type of criticism is not justified : for, it is biased and subjective.

The use of parable is a part of the mythical setting in a novel. In *Tortilla Flat*, there is a famous episode related to the story of the corporal and his son which serves as a parable. This story comes after the story of "Sweets" Ramirez and her vacuum sweeper. It so happens that Marie rescues the young corporal and his baby son from the policeman. They are brought to the paisanos' house. The corporal's wife is taken away by force by a captain while he (corporal) was serving in the Mexican army. The corporal now wants his son to become a general. For this, he gets his son admitted to a good school where he is advised by a psychologist that he could succeed in his venture of grooming his son as a general only when he constantly repeats the sentence — you will become a general — to the child.

But unfortunately the baby dies soon after arriving at the paisanos' house. All feel sorry for the sudden and unfortunate demise of the baby. When the corporal comes to know of it he is profoundly grief-stricken. "What is this ?" he demanded. I have nothing to do with this captain. He is the captain...."[29] In the end, the corporal finding him helpless, develops a positive idea of endurance of the stature of a mythical and legendary character. To his great surprise, the corporal finds himself gradually recovering from grief and happily notices in the end, that he had been saved from developing ulcers and other terminal diseases, if he had not got rid of grief and negative mental thinking.

Tortilla Flat serves as a dwelling place for the characters like Danny and his friends of the Arthurian stem. The paisanos constitute the society where the Arthurian type characters make their round table, the centre of their wild, reckless lives everyday. The wild bacchanalian orgy enjoyed by these characters has specifically been outlined in *Tortilla Flat.* But in the context of North American society, with its reverence for property and the free enterprise system, there is more to this attitude and behaviour than mere quaintness and irresponsible fun. The casual lazy paisanos are satisfied with their wine and food and are too easily distracted in the midst of costly possessions. They hate to build up material empires completely ignoring what is moral and ethical. They are large-hearted resembling, the mythical characters such as Senora Teresina Cortez, who, having born eight children already, cannot stop the astonishing and mysterious processes even though distraction and starvation threaten her overgrowing family.

Ten years after *Tortilla Flat,* Steinbeck wrote the script for a motion picture called "A Model for Benny." In this motion picture, Steinbeck has further defined and elaborated, but with a sense of conviction, the inherent virtues, which the mythical characters of paisanos do certainly possess. Benny, a Danny like character, dies the death of a hero during the World War II. His illiterate father is to receive the posthumous decoration of Danny. The people of the town raise a big statue to mark the memory of Danny. The tourists pay their homage to it.

In due course of time, the father picks up the idea that his son, though now dead, is being exploited for commercial purposes. So in a fit of anger, he says to the publicity manager, "Mister Lovekin — Benny was a wild boy, but even Benny would not do a thing like this.... Never would we use the bravery and a beautiful medal to sell a lot of hot dogs and real estate.... No even Benny would not do that."[30]

However, the all-pervading tone of the ultimate triumph of good is always dominant, despite the boastful and often unrealistic heroic bravadoes of the main characters of the Arthurian mould. In Chapter III of the novel named 'How the poison of possession wrought with Pilon and how evil temporarily triumphed in him', a type of struggle between what is good and what is bad and what is triumphant in the end, occurs in such a way that Pilon, who earlier suffered from vice is now a reformed man. In his arguments with Danny and Pablo, he makes a confession of this fact :

But let us go back to the first mark, which says serious and concentrated conversion, for it was at that place that Pilon made his coup.

"Pablo," he said, "dost thou never get tired of sleeping in ditches, wet and homeless, friendless and alone?"

"No," said Pablo.

Pilon mellowed his voice persuasively. "So I thought, my friend, when I was a dirty gutter dog, I too, was content, for I did not know how sweet a little house is, and a roof, and a garden.

Ah, Pablo, his is indeed living."

"H's pretty nice," Pablo agreed.

Pilon pounced. "See, Pablo, how would you like to rent part of my house ? There would never be the cold ground for you any more. Never the hard sand under the dwarf with crabs getting in your shoes. How would you like to live here with me ?"

"Sure," said Pablo.

"Look, you will pay only fifteen dollars a month! And you may use all the house except my bed, and all the garden. Think of it, Pablo! And if some one should write a letter, he will have some place to send it to."

"Sure," said Pabloo. "That's swell."[31]

The mythical environment in Steinbeck's fiction is all the more heightened by the semiotic use of narration. In Chapter IV of the novel named 'How Jesus Maria Corcoran, a good man, becomes an unwilling vehicle of evil', this use of narration is quite evident :

> Pilon knew he had blundered. "When you lay on that beach at Seaside, God floated the little rowboat to you. Do you think the good God did it so you could buy silk drawers for a Cannery slut ? No! God did it so you would not die from sleeping on ground in the cold. Do you think God is interested in Arabella's breasts. And besides, we will take a two dollar deposit," he went on. "For one dollar you can get one of those things big enough to hold the udders of a cow."
>
> Still Jesus Maria protested.
>
> "I will tell you," Pilon went on, "unless we pay Danny two dollars we shall all be turned into the street, and it will be your fault. You will have it on your soul that we sleep in ditches."
>
> Under so many shots, coming from so many directions, Jesus Maria Corcoran succumbed. He passed two of the crumpled bills to Pilon. And now the tense feeling went out of the room, and peace and quiet and a warm deep comradeship took its

> place. Pilon relaxed. Pablo took the comforter back to his own bed, and conversation sprang up.
>
> "We must take this money to Danny." Their first appetite over, they were sipping the wine out of fruits jars now.
>
> "What is this great need Danny has for two dollars ?" Jesus Maria asked.
>
> Pilon grew confidential. His hands came into play like twin moths, restrained only by his wrists and arms from flying out the door. "Danny, our friend, is taking up with Mrs. Morales. Oh, don't think Danny is a fool. Mrs. Morales has two hundred dollars in the bank. Danny wants to buy a fox of big candy for Mrs. Morales."[32]

In Steinbeck's fiction particularly in *Tortilla Flat,* the dialogues also heighten the mythical element. Often they create horror and often a sense of risk. Often they are broken abruptly and are resumed in such a way that they appear to have been repeated rather mechanically by a person extremely suffering from an intense pain of experiences. In Chapter XV titled as 'How Danny brooded and became mad. How the devil in the shape of Torrelli assaulted Danny's House', the following narrative dialogues are of this nature :

> Jesus Maria paused. He saw with pride that his friends were leaning in toward the story. "That was the way of it," he said.
>
> "But Gracie Montez married that Petey Ravanno," Pilon cried excitedly. "I know her. She is a good woman. She never misses mass, and she goes once a month to confession."
>
> "So it is now," Jesus Maria agreed. "Old man Ravanno was angry. He ran to Gracie's house, and he cried, "See how you murder my boy with your foolishness. He cried to kill himself for you, dung-heap chicken."
>
> "Gracie was afraid, but she was pleased, too, because it is not many women who can make a man go so far. She went to see Petey where he was in bed with a crooked neck. After a little while they were married.
>
> "It turned out the way Petey thought to be good wife, she was a good wife. She didn't laugh to men any more. And she didn't run away so they chased her. Petey went on cutting squids, and pretty soon Chin Kee let him empty the squid boxes. And not long after that he was the mayordoma of the squid yard. You see," said Jesus Maria, "There is a good story. It would be a story for a priest to tell, if it stopped there."[33]

Steinbeck is above the reach of critics with regard to the diversity of themes and styles used in his novels. Almost every novel has a different theme and a different style, and for this reason, Steinbeck cannot be branded as a novelist of some set themes and the same style. In each of his novels, he has made an effort to rediscover truth in his own unique way through his own unique artistic technique.

As such, in each novel, there is always a fresh theme and a virbrant style. In *Tortilla Flat,* the style is often narrative and simple so far as the environmental setting is concerned. But where the specific effect is to be given, he uses dialects in the characters' speeches to capture the mythical element. For instance, in the earlier Chapters in *Tortilla Flat,* a simple but forceful style has been used with words pregnant with appropriate meaning :

> When Danny came home from the army he learned that he was an heir and an owner of property. The vie Jo, that is the grandfather, had died leaving Danny the two small houses on Tortilla Flat.
>
> When Danny heard about it he was a little weighed down with the responsibility of ownership. Before he ever went to look at his property he bought a gallon of red wine and drank most of it himself. The weight of responsibility left him then, and his very worst nature came to the surface. He shouted, he broke a few chairs in a poolroom on Alvarado Street; he had two short but glorious fights. No one paid much attention to Danny. At last his wavering bow-legs took him toward the wharf where, at this early hour in the morning, the Italian fishermen were walking down in rubber boots to go out to sea.
>
> Race antipathy overcame Danny's good sense. He menaced the fisherman. "Sicilian bastards," he called them, and "Scum from the prison island," and "Dogs of dogs of dogs." He cried, "*Chinga tu madre*, Piojo." He thumbed his nose and made obscene gestures below his waist. The fisherman only grinned and shifted their oars and said, "Hello, Danny. When'd you get home ? Come around to-night. We got new wine."[34]

But towards the close of *Tortilla Flat,* the simple, narrative style has grown into a sober and ponderous kind, in which even words have been used rather carelessly and in a somewhat diffused sense :

> Torrelli opened the paper a little bit. "The law will not be interested in that," he said. "And so, my dear little friends, it is my terrible duty to tell you that you must leave my house. I have plans for it." His face. lost its smile, then, and all the cruelty came back into it. "If you are not out by noon, I will send a policeman."
>
> Pilon moved gently toward him. Oh, beware, Torrelli, when Pilon moves smiling on you. Run, hide yourself in some iron room and weld up the door. "I do not understand these things," Pilon said gently. "Of course I am sad that Danny should do a thing like this."
>
> Torrelli gigled again.
>
> "I never had house to sell," Pilon continued.
>
> "Danny signed this paper, is that it ?"
>
> "Yes," Torrelli mimicked him, "Danny signed this paper. That is it." Pilon blundered on, stupidly.
>
> "This is the paper that proves it." Pilon looked puzzled. "I thought you must take it down and have some record made."
>
> Torrelli laughed scornfully. Oh, beware, Torrelli! Do you not see how quietly these snakes are moving ? There is Jesus Maria in front of the door! There is Pablo by the kitchen door. So Big Joe's knuckles white on the pick-handle.[35]

The mock-heroic style of *Tortilla Flat* is to be treated as Steinbeck's great achievement : for, this style was also earlier used by writers both in prose and fiction, poetry and drama by a number of celebrities. But in Steinbeck's mock-heroic style, the touch of great learning is copiously absent : for, he regarded that use of language as the best one which was merely functional and not ornamental. Secondly, the mock-heroic style does not mean to him a direct kind of lampooning and denunciation. For him, the butt of criticism must be only suggestive in nature :

> He started playing a satiric game. He caught a bedbug, squashed it against the wall, drew a circle around it with a pencil and named it "Mayor Clough." Then he cought others and named them after the City Council. In a little while he had one wall decorated with squashed bedbugs, each named for a local dignitary. Hedrew ears and tails on them, gave them big noses and moustaches. Tito Ralph, the jailer, was scandalised;

> but he made no complaint because Danny had not included either the justice of the peace who had sentenced him, nor any of the police force. He had a vast respect for the law.
>
> One night when the jail who lovely, Tito Ralph came into Danny's cell bearing two bottles of wine. An hour later he went out for more wine, and Danny went with him. It was cheerless in the jail. They stayed at Torrelli's, when they bought the wine, until Torrelli threw them out. After that Danny went up among the pines and fell asleep, while Tito Ralph staggered back and reported his escape.
>
> Why the brilliant sun awakened Danny about noon, he determined to hide all day to escape pursuit. He ran and dodged behind bushes. He peered out of the undergrowth like a hunted fox. And, at evening, the rules having been satisfied, he came out and went about his business.[36]

With the above exhaustive treatment of *Tortilla Flat,*[37] let us now come to *The Grapes of Wrath,* another significant novel of Steinbeck, for detailed study and analysis, in the second part of this chapter.

II

The Grapes of Wrath is a novel of protest because the life of the people of Oklahoma and California forms the very basis of this novel. That is why this novel was popularly known as the book on *Okies.* The Emersonian Transcendentalism, which summarily denotes the essential goodness of man, has found a full and forceful play in this novel. Jim Casy, Joad and Rose of Sharon are essentially fine creatures who always wish for the betterment of all human beings. Universal compassion and foregiveness, concerted oneness of mankind and a Christ-like cosmopolitan outlook are the inherent messages of the novel. The texture of human life is woven with the strong thread of joy and suffering. However, pain and suffering are essential to give a sense of fullness in human life. The universal feeling of love and help is obviously reflected in the qualities of Joads and Rose of Sharon. In fact, *The Grapes of Wrath* brings together the proverbial *trio* of American thought namely the Transcendental Oversoul, the Universal Religion of Love and the Philosophy of Pragmatism.

John Steinbeck's *The Grapes of Wrath* was published in 1939 and it contains thirty consecutive chapters with no larger grouping. This novel is John Steinbeck's great fictional achievement and this brought to him a lot of name and fame. The diverse materials used in each chapter makes it difficult to trace a unifying plot in the novel, nevertheless, it does have a structural form. The action progresses through three successive movements, and its significance is revealed by an intricate system of themes and symbols. The novel is basically made up of three major parts — the drought, the journey and California.

The first section ends with chapter ten. It is separated from the second section, the journey, by two interchapters which are termed as intercalary chapters. The first of these chapters presents a picture of the deserted land. The second interchapter is devoted to Highway 66 and is followed by chapter thirteen, which begins Joads' journey. The journey section extends past the geographical California border, across the desert to Bakersfield. This section ends with chapter eighteen. The next chapter begins the Californian section by introducing the reader to labour conditions in that state. Steinbeck had this tripartite division in mind as early as September of 1937, when he told Joseph Henry Jackson that he was working on "the first three related longer novels."[38]

Essentially, *The Grapes of Wrath* is a plea for the landowners of California to be more tolerant. The novel has been told from the viewpoint of a migrant family — the Joads, who are forced off their land in Oklahoma and who seek employment in California. During the course of the novel, the Joads move from a concern only for themselves and their own personal welfare to a concern for all the people of the world. Early in the novel, we meet an itinerant preacher who has been drifting for four years and has arrived at an Emersonian view of the world. He believes that all the people are holy and that his soul is only a little piece of a larger soul.

But the preacher is unable to propound his views effectively until his arrival at California. He goes to jail while defending a person named Tom Joad and sacrifices himself for the welfare of the Joads family. During the course of his stay in the jail, the preacher learns the value of organising the small people. He tries to lead the people on a strike and is killed brutally by some cop in California, but he has had an influence on the Joads.

Like Jim Casy, the preacher, Ma Joad, another significant character in the novel, has a deep-rooted concern for humanity at large. In the very beginning, she appears to be worried only for her family but towards the end of the novel, she becomes a part of the larger human family. In fact, the Joads' journey to the west symbolises a journey from the personal concern to a larger concern for all the humanity. This change is also accompanied by a significant change in the Joads' economic situation.

As the Joads deteriorate economically, they seem to enlarge their view of humanity. At the first camp in California, they do not have enough to feed their own family, but Ma leaves 'a little something' in the bottom of the pot for some strange children, who have been standing around. Thus, the more the decline in economic and pecuniary condition, the more the tolerant the vision for humanity grows.

The novel is full of a number of such characters as fully symbolize and justify their actions and performance in the novel and, in fact, leading to a number of mythical and symbolic inferences. If there are elderly characters full of sympathy and compassion for all such as Pa Joad, Ma Joad, Grampa and Granma, there are such younger characters as Naoh Joad, Tom Joad, Rose of Sharon, Al Joad, Connie, Ruthic, Winfield Joad and Ivy who have either learned the spirit of love, endurance and sympathy from the elderly characters or have met such situations in life where they are compelled to be more tolerant and sincere than before. If there is such violent and sneaky characters such as Muley Graves and Willie Eaton, there are such enduring figures as Tom Joad himself and Jim Casy.

The Grapes of Wrath has been termed as the novel of protest and also as a historical social document. When the novel was published, it was less discussed as a work of art and more as a source of social propaganda. A few serious critics doubted whether the facts presented in the novel were actually based on reality. Some attacked this novel as obscene. The people of Oklahoma and California felt disgraced by this novel. The citizens of Oklahoma resented the fact that the people were depicted as Okies and denied the implications that Oklahoma was a dust bowl, where it was impossible to grow crops.

An Oklahoma Congressman went on record maintaining that the book was a black infernal creation of a twisted and distorted mind. A number of pamphlets appeared in California itself leading to prove that John Steinbeck had filled *The Grapes of Wrath* with big lies. Consequently within a period of about six months or so, the general public reacted to this novel differently — some admired it whereas others deplored its presentation of Okies. In the history of the American fiction, this novel was interpreted more differently and miscellaneously than even Uncle Tom's *Cabin.*

However, Steinbeck was defended by a number of sociologists, university professors and government employees, who vigorously testified to the accuracy of details as were presented by John Steinbeck in *The Grapes of Wrath.* Magazines such as *Life* ran feature stories on the plight of the migrants, and before the novel was made into a movie, the director sent men into the field to verify the accuracy of the details as presented by Steinbeck. In fact, the director got the report that, whatever was presented in the novel, was based on truth.

The social philosophy as propagated by Steinbeck in *The Grapes of the Wrath,* somehow became an issue of controversy between those who believed in Communism and those who loved the Emersonian Transcendentalism. Whether the basic tenants of the Communism are fully obtainable in this novel is yet to be further debated by scholars. Nonetheless, the Emersonian Transcendentalism, which essentially means that every person is divinely tinged, wholly permeats throughout the novel. The concluding intercalary chapters twenty-nine and chapter thirty read like the Emersonian philosophy of Transcendentalism.

The conduct of Jim Casy, Joad and Rose of Sharon is really very superb. Chapter twenty-nine, which is the last intercalary chapter of the novel predicts the rains which will down out the Joads in the next chapter. Its overall appeal and charm lie in the message of 'Oneness.' In fact, the final message of Oneness is spread through the spirit of universal compassion and foregiveness. Women and children know it very deeply that no misfortune is too great to bear if their men were whole and united. On the contrary, if they do not stand united, they cannot achieve the final goal of 'Oneness.' In the quest of Oneness, barriers of the rich and the poor, the high and the low, the healthy and the unhealthy, are rendered inconsequential. Jim Casy, a Christ-like figure in the novel loves the migrants despite their pains and sufferings :

> Then from the tents, from the crowded barns, groups of sodden men went out, their clothes slopping rags, their shoes muddy pulp. They splashed out through the water, to the towns, to the country stores, to the relief offices, to beg for food, to cringe and beg for food, to beg for relief officers, to try to steal, to lie. And under the begging, and under the cringing, a hopeless anger began to smoulder. And in the little towns pity for the sodden men changed to anger, and anger at the hungry people changed to fear of them. Then sheriffs swore in deputies in droves, and orders were rushed for rifles, for tear gas, for ammunition. Then the hungry men crowded the alleys behind the stores to beg for bread, to beg for rotting vegetables, to steal when they could.[39]

In the last chapter thirty, Al takes the tarpaulin down and covers the motor of the car. Then the Wainwrights and the Joads become one family. Rose of Sharon is down with cold and high fever. Pa decides to try to build a bank to keep the water away. Others also help Pa in the construction of the bank throughout the night. They succeed to block out water but a tree is suddenly washed into the embankment and knocks a huge hole in it. The result is that water spreads everywhere submerging even the crank, the truck and the boxcar. Pa, Al and uncle John do their best to keep their dwelling places safe from water the whole night. While the entire family is in confabulation, they find some dry hay in the barn and suddenly see a man lying on his back with a boy hudding close to him. The man was about to die and is helped by Rose of Sharon.

Thus, despite the fact, that the Joads family members were in great financial problem, they have a compassionate and enduring attachment for others. Their approach is constructive and positive, protecting life and its evolving processes. Rose of Sharon gives life to a dying stranger, which symbolises sacrifice for others. The universal feeling of love and help is obviously reflected in the Christ Jesus like qualities of Joads and Rose of Sharon and in others in the following dialogues :

> "Look! In the corner."
>
> Ma looked. There were two fingers in the gloom; a man who lay on his back, and a boy beside him, his eyes wide, Staring at the newcomers. As she looked, the boy got slowly up to his feet and came forward her. His voice croaked.
>
> "You own this here ?"
>
> "No," Ma said. "Jus' come in outa the wet. We got a sick girl. You got a dry blanket we could use an' get her wet clothes off?"
>
> The boy went back to the corner and brought a dirty comforter and held it out to Ma.
>
> "Thank ya," she said. "What's the matter'th that fella ?" The boy spoke in croaking monotone. "Fust he was sick-but now he's starvin'."
>
> "What?"
>
> "Starvin'. Got sick in the cotton. He oin't et for six days." Ma walked to the corner and looked down at the man. He was about fifty, his whiskery face gaunt, and his open eyes were vague and staring. The boy stood beside her. "Your Pa ?" Ma asked.
>
> "Yeah! says he wasn' hungry, or he jus'et. Give me the food. Now he's too weak. Can't hardly move.
>
> The pounding of the man moved his lips. Ma knelt beside him and put her ear close. His lips moved again.[40]

Critics, like Miran, Monroe and Birney are of the opinion that *The Grapes of Wrath* is a novel of social philosophy and promotes hatred of class war. Miran in his book *The Truth About*

John Steinbeck and the Migrants, has suggested that "no other novel which advances the idea of class war and promotes hatred of class against class...more than does *The Grapes of Wrath*."[41] But S.E. Hayman does not agree to this view of Miran. "Actually as a careful reading," writes Hyman, "makes clear, the central message of *The Grapes of Wrath* is an appeal to the owning class to behave to become enlightened, rather than to the working class to change its working conditions."[42]

Peter Lisca also dittoes this point of view. Steinbeck himself writes in *San Francisco News* in October 1936, "California...is gradually building up human structure which will certainly change the State and may, if handled with the inhumanity and stupidity that have characterized the past, destroy the present system of agricultural economy...."[43] A similar issue was raised by Steinbeck at the end of his article in *The Nation* : "It is fervently to be hoped that the great groups of migrant workers so necessary to the harvesting of California's crops must be given the right to live decently, that they may not be so badgered, tormented, and hurt that in the end they become avengers of hundreds of thousands who have been tormented and starved before them."[44]

In his third article of the News Series, he has given another warning that "a continuation of this approach (intimidation and repression) constitutes a criminal endangering of the peace of the State."[45]

In the final article of the series, Steinbeck offers three suggestions : first, that migrant labourers be allotted small subsistence farms on which they can live and work when there is no call from migrant labour; second, that a Migratory Labour Board be created to help allot labour where needed and to determine fair wages; third, that vigilanteism and terrorism be punished.... If, on the one hand, as has been stated by a large grower, our agriculture requires the creation and maintenance of the peon class, than it is submitted that California agriculture is economically unsound under a democracy."[46]

In fact, Steinbeck has himself denied that there is any Marxian class war or Bolchevik Revolutionary Border. But there is certainly a society which must live and die for others.

The likes of the Jim Casy, the Rose of Sharon and the Joads are the creatures with an unusual love and zest for the well-being of others. Their self-ego has completely been sublimated into lofty feelings of compassion and happiness for others.

The *Grapes of Wrath*, brings together, in a word, three specific steins of American thought. First of all, it presents the Transcendental Oversoul. Secondly, it gives a religion of love of all men as was vigorously preached by Walt Whitman. Thirdly, it also combines mythical and poetic ideas with realistic philosophy of pragmatism. But there is a critic named Chester E. Eisinger, who adds a fourth stein of American thought — the agrarianism of Jefferson. "Because he had faith in the common man and thus gave his thinking a broad popular basis, Steinbeck was closer to Jeffersonianism rather than with the Southern Agrarians, who sought to resurrect not only an agricultural way of life but also the traditional cultural values of Europe. Steinbeck was concerned with democracy and looked upon agrarianism as a way of life that would enable us to realise the full potentialities of the creed. Jefferson, of course, held the same creed."[47]

The agrarian issues have also been dealt with by John Steinbeck in his two important novels named *To a God Unknown* and *Of Mice and Men,* but they have been presented in a mystical, symbolic and mythical manner. Whereas "these values persist in *The Grapes of Wrath,* man's identification with the growth cycle is also seen as pragmatic, socially practical in Jeffersonian terms. The human erosion pictured in the book is as much the result of a separation from the land as it is of poverty."[48] But, there remains a moral question attached to the relationship of the land owners, too. The loss of land, in fact, led to a loss of dignity because the migrants suffered from a sense of shame to have deserted their homeland.

The ideas and materials of *The Grapes of Wrath* present Steinbeck with one of the most difficult problems of structure.

Neither the variations on a single line of action and development that he used in *Cup of Gold, To a God Unknown* and *Of Mice and Men,* nor the episodic structure of *The Pastures of Heaven* and the *Tortilla Flat* could handle the scope and diversity of *The Grapes of Wrath.* "His position was," writes Lisca, "not unlike that of Tolstoy in writing *War and Peace.* Tolstoy's materials were roughly the adventures of the Benzukhov, Rostov and Bolkonski families on the one hand, and on the Napoleonic Wars on the other."[49] For Steinbeck, the adventures of the Joads family and the Great Depression provided the thematic material. But as the Napoleonic wars were dealt with in separate philosophic interchapters by Tolstoy, likewise, sufficient material related to the Great Depression was dealt with by Steinbeck in separate philosophic interchapters. In the light of this basic analogy, Percy Lubbock's comments on the structural role of these two elements in *War and Peace* has, of course, become significant for a close analysis of a structural analysis in *The Grapes of Wrath.* "I can discover no angle at which the two stories will appear to unite and merge in a single impression. Neither is subordinated to the other, and there is nothing above them...to which they are both related. Nor are they placed together to illustrate a contrast; nothing results from their juxtaposition. Only from time to time, upon no apparent principle and without a word of warning, one of them is dropped and the other resumed."[50]

If Lubbock's argument is stretched a little further, it can be safely inferred that the intercalary construction and strategies adopted for thematic ramifications give rise to aesthetic conditions in *The Grapes of Wrath.* Exclusively, the number of intercalary chapters describing the drought and the penultimate chapter on the rains is, sixteen, making up a total of just under a hundred pages — almost one-sixth of the book and, of course, in none of the chapters do the Joads, Wilson or Wain Wrights appear. These intercalary chapters present a kind of support for the narrative and provide.a sort of historical information. While the intercalary chapters fulfil the functions of providing a general picture of society and also the essential background, there is still an artistic interweaving between these chapters. Some of them fulfil the symbolic functions also.

Intercalary chapter one, briefly speaking, describes the drought, which compelled the Joads family to leave their homeland. Chapter five is mostly a dialogue between two generalised forces — the banks and the farmers. Chapters seven and nine depict, respectively, the buying of Jalopies and the selling of household goods. Chapter eleven describes at length a decaying and deserted house which is the prototype of all the houses abandoned in the dust bowl. Chapters fourteen, seventeen and twenty all the three present the salient features of the nomadic society which the Joads appear to be trying to form. Chapters nineteen, twenty-one and twenty-five provide such historical information as development of land, ownership in California, the consequent development of migrant labour, and such other economic problems. Curiously enough, there is a general correspondence between the material of each intercalary chapter and that of the current narrative portion. For instance, chapter five deals with the banks' foreclosing of mortgages, which forces the sharecroppers to immigrate. Likewise, Highway 66 is given a chapter as the Joads begin their trap on that historic route.

So far as the Biblical structure of *The Grapes of Wrath* is concerned, it is supported by a continuum of symbols and symbolic actions. Moreover, it has also its roots in the Old Testament. The novel's three sections which correspond to the Oppression in Egypt, the Exodus, and the Sojourn in the land of Canaan, which, in both accounts, is first viewed from the mountains. Peter Lisca argues that "...this parallel is not worked out in detail, but the grant design is there : the plagues (Erosion), the Egyptian (Banks), the Exodus (Journey), and the hostile tribes of Canaan (Californians)."[51] The interchapters or the intercalary chapters have the abundance of such passages which seek semblance from the Old Testament. The symbol of grapes in the novel is highly pervasive and suggestive. The novel's title, taken from "The Battle Hymn of the Republic," ("He is trampling out the vintage where the grapes of wrath are stored") is itself a reference to Revelation : "And the angel thrust in his sickle into the earth, and gathered the vine of the earth, and cast it into the great wine press of the wrath God." Similarly, in Deuteronomy : "Their grapes are grapes of call, their clusters are bitter. Their wine is the poison of serpents...in Jeremiach : "The fathers have eaten sour grapes, and their children's teeth are set on edge." Sometimes, this meaning of the symbol is stated in the novel's interchapters : "in the souls of the people, the grapes of wrath are filling and growing heavy, heavy for the vintage."[52]

Steinbeck also uses grapes for symbols of plenty, as the one huge cluster of grapes, which Joshua and Oshea bring back from their first excursion into the rich land of Canaan is a symbol of plenty, a cluster so huge that they bare it between two on a staff. It is this meaning of grapes that is frequently alluded to by Grampa Joad : "Gonna get me a whole big bunch grapes off a bush, or whatever, an' I'm gonna squash 'em on my face an' let 'em run often my chin." Although Grampa dies long before the Joads get to California, he is symbolically present through the an ominous old man in the barn. Closely associated with this symbolic meaning of grapes and the land of Canaan is Ma Joads's frequent assertion that "we are the people."[53] She has not been reading Carl Sanburg, she has been reading her *Bible.* As she tells Tom while he is looking for suitable value to bury with Gempa, "Turn to Psalms, over further. You kin always get somepin outa Psalms." And, of course, it is from Psalms that she gets her phrase : "For he is our God; and we are the people of his pastures, and the sheep of his hand." Certainly, they are the people who pick up life in Oklahoma (Egypt) and carry it to California (Canaan) as the turtle picks up seeds and as the ants pick up their eggs in "The Leader of the People." These parallels to the Israelites of Exodus are all brought into focus when, near the end of the novel, Uncle John sets Rose of Sharon's still born child in an old apple crate like Moses in the basket, sets the box in a stream among the Willow stems, and floats it toward the town saying, "Go down an' tell 'em".

In fact, as the Israelites received the new Law in their exodus, likewise, the migrants develop new Laws. The families learned as to what rights must be observed — the right of privacy in the tent : the right to keep the past black hidden in the heart : the right to refuse help or accept it, to offer help or to decline it; the right of son to court and the daughter to be courted : the right of the hungry to be fed; the rights of the pregnant and the sick to transcend all other rights. Chapter seventeen can be seen as the Deuteronomy of *The Grapes of Wrath.* It is this context that makes the Joads' journey out west an archetype of mass migration :

> And as the cars moved westward, each member of the family grew into his proper place, grew into duties; so that each member, old and young, had his place in the car; ...each member has his duty and went to it without instruction : ...and this was done without command.... The families, which had been units of which the boundaries were a house at night, a farm by day, changed their boundaries....[54]

Peter Lisca opines that "...Through this supporting Biblical structure and context, there are interwoven two opposing themes which make up the book's 'plot.' One of these, the 'negative' one, concerns itself with the increase in straitened circumstances of the Joads."[55] The Joads begin their journey just with hundred fifty-four dollars, household goods, two barrels of pork, a serviceable truck and, of course, the physical stoutness of the members. With the passage of time, they are impoverished until at the end they are virtually rendered as destitutes. Their economic decline leaves a distinct impact on the morale on the family. With the decline in morals, the basic idea of the unity of family gradually becomes weaker.

Granma is buried as a pauper. Noah deserts the family. Connie gets separation from Rosasharn. Tom becomes a fugitive. Not only this that the misfortune stops here, there are other similar happenings which heavily tell upon the strong fibre of the family unity. Casy is killed. The Joads are compelled to abandon the Wilsons. But these two negative movements are balanced by two positive movements. The family unity is replaced by the community unity : for, the Wilsons and the Wainwrights are joined together. Secondly, oppression and intimidation only serve to strengthen the social group. The unity in the social group further leads to a very strong vision of the democratic way of life. The Joads family further develops friendship with the Wilson family.

While crossing the Oklahoma border, Grampa Joad dies in the Wilsons' tent and he gets a good burial with the help of the blankets provided by the Wilsons' family. Moreover, the epitaph, which is buried with Grampa, in Oklahoma soil has been written on a page torn from the Wilson's Bible. In fact, by establishing relationship between the families of the Joads and the Wilsons, Steinbeck has made a microcosm of the migration and the human significance of the process.

The education and conversion of Tom and Casy symbolise the above spirit of unity and tolerance. Tom's first lesson of pragmatism enters his brain when Casy helps him against the onslaughts of the trooper and virtually gives himself up in his place. By the time Casy is killed, Tom is ready for his conversion. Gradually, Tom's conversion is further developed into his spiritual unity with all human beings. In fact, Jim Casy and Tom pass through various changes in their life which many be termed as the Bible-belt, because Jim Casy moves from evangelism to social prophecy. From a profession of preaching, he concentrates on his inner development and finally reaches the highest stage of the revelation of the Oversoul. Hence, Casy's development is symbolic of the Emersonian view of the Oversoul through the process of refinement of intuition.

A little bit of probing into the style and diction of *The Grapes of Wrath* will reveal the fact that there are visible external influences on it, with regard to the syntactical structures and semantic inferences. Whereas the narrative parts of the novel do contain the very basic elements often using dialects in a straightforward manner, the intercalary chapters have been written in a sort of miscellaneous stylistic veins. For example, in chapter third, a symbolic approach has been used, where the focus has been thrown on the turtle. In the intercalary chapter on Highway 66, a staccato style has been used, which, in short, makes the reader feel the weeping of the autos and the speeding of the cars as we stand along the road and watch them rush by. Some intercalary chapters, for example, chapter twenty-seven and twenty-nine, are almost poetic in to as poetic as the style used in the *Bates Bible*. In this connection, Peter Lisca's comments are worth-quoting. "These structural techniques," writes Lisca, "for integrating the two parts of *The Grapes of Wrath* are greatly implemented by a masterful command of prose style. In his novels after *To a God Unknown,* Steinbeck has demonstrated the variety of prose styles that he could wield into the very meaning of a novel — prose styles as different as those of *Tortilla Flat* and in *Dubious Battle.* In *The Grapes of Wrath,* there is such a number of strategically employed prose styles that the novel almost amounts to a *tour de force.* No Steinbeck novel begins so auspiciously."[56]

Intercalary chapter number twenty-three is solely devoted to the presentation of migrant society. The migrants are the type of people who create great folk epics and folk music. There is a sense of something quite mythical and legendary about these folk tales which continue to engage the attention of the readers from one generation to the other. Steinbeck offers one specific tale in this chapter which has a mythical quality and the reader can easily imagine another person taking the same tale and narrating it again and adding his own touch until the tale becomes a part of the culture. The structural unity created by the variety of syntax can eloquently be vouchsafed from such passages like the following, where the stylistic simplicity approximates the *Bates Bible* :

> A harmonica is easy to carry. Take it out of your hip pocket, knock it against your palm to shake out the dirt and pocket fuzz and bits of tobacco. Now it's ready. You can do anything with a harmonica : then reedy single tone, or chords, or melody with rhythm cords. You can mould the music with curved hands, making it wail and cry like bagpipes, making it full and round like an organ, making it as sharp and bitter as the reed pipes

> of the hills. And you can play and put it back in your pocket. It is always with you, always in your pocket. And as you play, you learn new tricks, new ways to mould the tone with your hands, to pinch the tone with your lips, and no one teaches you. You feel around — sometimes alone in the shade at noon, sometimes in the tent door after supper when the women are washing up. Your foot taps gently on the ground. Your eyebrows rise on and fall in rhythm. And if you lose it or break it, why, it's no great loss. You can buy another for a quarter.[57]

Though the whole of the novel is filled with the simplicity and naturalness of structural ease resembling that of the *Old Testament* and the *Bates Bible,* yet one such passage is just the opening passage of the novel, which is often quoted for its variety, vividness, colourfulness and suggestive intonations. The opening passage of the novel may be quoted below even at the expense of being a bit lengthy :

> To the red country and part of the grey country of Oklahoma the last rains came gently, and they did not cut the sacred earth. The ploughs crossed and recrossed the rivulet marks. The last rains lifted the corn quickly and scattered weed colonies and grass along the sides of the roads so that the grey country and the dark red country began to disappear under a green cover. In the last part of May the sky grew pale and the clouds that had hung in high puffs for so long in the spring were dissipated. The sun flared down on the growing corn day after day until a line of brown spread along the edge of each green bayonet. The clouds appeared, and went away, and in a while they did not try any more. The weeds grew darker green to protect themselves, and they did not spread any more. The surface of the earth crusted, a thin hard crust, and as the sky became pale, so the earth became pale, pink in the red country and white in the grey country.[58]

Peter Lisca is of the view that the above paragraph is as carefully worked out as "an overture to an opera." He further suggests, "The themes of red, gray, green, and earth are announced and given parallel developments : red to pink, gray to white, green to brown, and ploughed earth to thin hard crust. The pervading structural rhythm of each sentence is echoed in the paragraph as a whole, a paragraph promising a story of epic sweep and dignity."[59] Lisca also quotes a few stanzas from the

Bates Bible in order to suggest a sort of parallel between the structural resemblance of syntax between the passage just quoted above and the passages going to be quoted below as extracted by Lisca from the *Bates Bible* in his famous book on John Steinbeck :

> The tractors had lights shining,
> For there is no day and night for a tractor,
> And the disks turn the earth in the darkness,
> And they glitter in the daylight.
>
> And when a horse stops work and goes into the barn,
> There is a life and a vitality left,
> There is a breathing and a warmth,
> And the feet shift on the straw,
> And the jaws champ on the hay,
> And the ears and the eyes are alive.
> There is a warmth of life in the barn,
> And the heat and smell of life.
>
> But when the motor of a tractor stops,
> It is as dead as the ore it came from.
> The heat goes out of it,
> Like the living heat that leaves a corpse.[60]

The parallel of grammatical structure and of meanings, the simplicity of diction, the balance, the concrete details, the summary sentences, the reiterations — all are the similar traits common in the *Bates Bible* and in this novel. The four phrases for the tractor, eight for the horse, four again for the tractor — are quite evident for simplicity of diction as the simplicity of *Psalms* and also as the many passages usually strewn through the various intercalary chapters of the novel.

Intercalary chapter seven of *The Grapes of the Wrath,* on the other hand, has the harsh, staccato structural trait. Similarly, in intercalary chapter nine, which presents the loss and despair of people, forced to abandon their household goods, has an encumbersome structural syntax. For example, the following famous paragraph is one such instance, where the style does not resemble with that of the *Bates Bible* :

> The women sat among the doomed things, turning them over and looking past them and back. This book. My father had it.

> He liked a book. *Pilgrim's Progress.* Used to read it. Got his name on it. And his pipe — still smells rank. And this picture — an angel. I looked at that before the first three come — didn't seem to do much good. Think we could get this china dog in ? Aunt Sadie brought it from the St. Louis Fair. See ? Wrote right on it. No, I guess not. Here's a letter my brother wrote the day before he died. Here's an old-time hat. These feathers — never got to use them. No, there isn't from.[61]

Thus, *The Grapes of Wrath* is the Steinbeckian *Bible* of the *Angry Thirties* or the *Great Depression* of the American society. The greatest value of this novel lies in the fact that, whereas it has symbolically presented realism connected with the lives of the Californian migrant tribes through the Joads family, it has also given a new dimension of literary naturalism by using a thematic structure, a style and diction quite unique and ever evolving. In a way, what Darwin talked of evolution in biological terms, Steinbeck talks of the same in literary terms. This is, in fact, a great achievement in the realm of fiction writing, which every novelist always aspires for.[62]

REFERENCES

1. Steinbeck, Johne. *Tortilla Flat.* London : Heinemann, 1935, pp. 11-12.
2. *Ibid.*, p. 11.
3. *Ibid.*, p. 10.
4. *Ibid.*, pp. 10-11.
5. *Ibid.*, pp. 12-14.
6. *Ibid.*, pp. 14-15.
7. *Ibid.*, p. 10.
8. Watt, F.W. *Steinbeck,* Edenburgh and London : Oliver and Boyd, 1962, p. 38.
9. *Tortilla Flat.* p. 11.
10. Watt, F.W. *op. cit.*, p. 39.
11. "My Short Novels," *Wings*, October, 1953, p. 6.
12. Carlos Baker, for example, has said that "to call *Tortilla Flat* a novel insults literary genres... (it) is little more than a sketch-book." "Steinbeck of California," Delphian Quarterly, 23 (Spring, 1940), p. 42.
13. Correspondence between John Steinbeck and McIntosh and Otis (Winter, 1934).
14. Lisca, Peter. *The Wide World of John Steinbeck,* New York : Gordian Press, 1981, p. 77.

15. *Ibid.*, p. 79
16. Correspondence between John Steinbeck and C.V. Wicker.
17. *Tortilla Flat,* p. 153.
18. *Ibid.*, p. 70.
19. Lisca, Peter. *op. cit.*, p. 81.
20. *Ibid.*, p. 71.
21. Hyman, Stanley Edgar. "Some notes on John Steinbeck," *Antioch Review,* 2 (Summer, 1942).
22. Ross, Woodburn. "John Steinbeck : Earth and Stars," *University of Missouri Studies in Honor of A.H.R.* Fairchild, (XXI), ed. by Charles T. Prouty (Columbia, Missouri, 1946).
23. *Tortilla Flat,* p. 75.
24. *Ibid.*
25. *Ibid.*, p. 92.
26. Lisca, Peter. *op. cit.*, p. 86.
27. "The Californians Storm and Steinbeck." *The New Republic,* 103 (December 9, 1949), p. 787.
28. "John Steinbeck, Californian," *Antioch Review,* 7 (Fall, 1947), 355.
29. *Tortilla Flat.* p. 120.
30. *Best Film Plays,* 1945, ed. by John Gassner and Dudley Nichols (New York, 1945), p. 640.
31. *Tortilla Flat,* p. 44.
32. *Ibid.*, p. 60.
33. *Ibid.*, p. 252.
34. *Ibid.*, p. 17.
35. *Ibid.*, p. 276.
36. *Ibid.*, p. 19.
37. John Steinbeck's *Tortilla Flat* was also delivered as an Invited Lecture at the IASE (MPJPR University) on March 24, 2000.
38. "John Steinbeck, A Potrait," Saturday Review of Literature, 16 (September 25, 1937), p. 18.
39. Steinbeck, John. *The Grapes of Wrath.* London : Heinemann, 1939, p. 197.
40. *Ibid.*, p. 415.
41. Miran. *The Truth About John Steinbeck and the Migrants,* New York . Chapel Hill, 1970, p. 272.
42. Hyman, Stanley Edgar. "Some notes on John Steinbeck," *Antioch Review,* 2 (Summer, 1942), p. 195.
43. Steinbeck, John. "The Harvest Gypsies," *San Francisco News,* (October 5, 1936), p. 3.

44. Steinbeck, John. "Dubious Battle in California," *The Nation,* 143 (September 12, 1936), p. 304.
45. Steinbeck, John. "The Harvest Gypsies," *San Francisco News* (October 5, 1936), p. 6.
46. *Ibid.,* p. 8.
47. Eisinger, Chester E. "Jeffersonian agrarianism in *The Grapes of Wrath,*" *University of Kansas City Review*, 14 (Winter, 1947), p. 150.
48. Lisca, Peter. *The Wide World of John Steinbeck.* New York : Gordian Press, 1981, p. 153.
49. *Ibid.,* pp. 154-55.
50. Lubbock, Percy. *The Art of Fiction.* New York : Oliver and Boyd, 1945, p. 33.
51. Lisca, Peter. *op. cit.*, p. 169.
52. (Quoted), Lisca, Peter. *op. cit.*
53. *The Grapes of Wrath.* p. 69.
54. *Ibid.,* p. 102.
55. Lisca, Peter. *The Wide World of John Steinbeck.* New York : Gordian Press, 1958, p. 171.
56. Lisca, Peter. *op. cit.*, p. 260.
57. *The Grapes of Wrath.* p. 300.
58. *Ibid.,* p. 1.
59. Lisca, Peter. *op. cit.*, p. 161.
60. (Quoted), *Ibid.*, pp. 161-62.
61. *The Grapes of Wrath,* p. 78.
62. John Steinbeck's *The Grapes of Wrath* was presented as a Conference Paper at the 43rd AIETC held at Anantapur on January 9-11, 1999.

3

Thomas Love Peacock : *Headlong Hall, Melincourt, Crotchet Castle* and *Gryll Grange*

"PEACOCK'S PLOTS," says George Saintsbury, "are weak and inconsistent."[1] "His novels are not popular and can never be popular," because there is no symmetrical plot in them. Similarly Bill Read finds Peacock's novels "wanting in good structural quality."[2] But on the other hand, there are critics who hold a different view. While for A.C. Ward, Peacock's novels have "enough of story and character to bear the matter along,"[3] Walter Allen regards his plots as "well-orderly" and "delicately-poised," and any attempt "to broaden them," in his opinion, will only lead to their destruction.[4] This critical controversy makes it at once interesting and imperative to make a renewed examination of Peacock's episodes and evaluate his craftsmanship in the light of new experiments and developments that are being made in the field of modern fiction.

Peacock has written in all seven novels which in respect of their general theme and structure can be divided into three distinct groups :

(1) Conversational novels — *Headlong Hall* (1816), *Melincourt* (1817), *Crotchet Castle* (1831), and *Gryll Grange* (1861).

(2) Romantic novels — *Maid Marian* (1822) and *The Misfortunes of Elphin* (1829).

(3) Conversational romance — *Nightmare Abbey* (1818).

Peacock's conversational novels have, as a general rule, "conversation as their essential feature."[5] A number of intellectual faddists, representing different shades of opinion, gather in some solitary country retreat and discuss a large variety of subjects, ranging from "Palestine soup" to "the principles of a Conservative," "the March of Mind," "wisdom and science," and "our higher tone of morality."[6] Representing contradictory views and wishes as they do, their discussion often becomes hot and they take recourse to "physical arguments when abstract logic fails."[7] But after they are delivered of their boisterous heat through words and blows, they develop a reposeful mood and in the "tranquil atmosphere"[8] that dawns upon them they indulge in "wine and whisky", "cakes and ale,"[9] "recite poetry," sing "bacchanalian verses,"[10] "woo and often manage all at once."[11] With the dominance of talk or conversation, there is a natural preponderance of dialogue over narrative in all the novels of this type.

Peacock's romantic novels, on the other hand, offer slightly more story; they are set in the past; they exhibit few spokesmen for intellectual fads; and they involve, proportionately, more narrative than dialogue. Apart from this, the romantic novels are marked with a supernatural tilt and medieval echoes.

Peacock's *Nightmare Abbey* is a conversational romance because it contains features of both. Like that of his conversational novels, its action takes place at a solitary retreat — "One ruined abbey" on the Welsh mountain dales. Again there is a group of intellectual faddists that enter into a heated discussion, but in spite of this, the novel has more narrative than dialogue. It has a "recognizable plot, complete with 'recognitions' and 'reversals',[12] though in the end this plot turns out "to be burlesque," both of romance in general, and of "Goethe's sentimental account of the Sorrows of Young Werther," in particular.[13] The events suggest "romance", but Peacock's treatment of them — his irony, humour, and burlesque — "makes the vehicle satiric."[14]

Headlong Hall, the first of Peacock's conversational novels, centres round one Welsh Squire who is seized with an indomitable passion for books and craves "to be thought a philosopher and a man of taste." Accordingly he sets out on an expedition to Oxford, to inquire for other varieties of "the same genera," namely, men of taste and philosophers, but being assured by a learned philosopher that there are no such things in the university, he proceeds to London, where after, "beating up in several booksellers' shops, theatres, exhibition rooms, and other resorts of literature and taste," he forms an extensive acquaintance "with philosophers and dilettanti." He then wishes to have them all together at Headlong Hall, arguing, over his "old port and Burgandy," various complicated problems which have puzzled "his pericranium." He, therefore, sends them "invitations in due form to pass their Christmas at Headlong Hall." The party that arrives at his house consists of four important guests — Mr. Foster, "the perfectibilian," Mr. Escot, "the deteriorationist," Mr. Jenkinson, "the status-quo-ite," and the Reverend Doctor Gaster, who, though of course "neither a philosopher nor a man of taste," has so won the Squire's fancy, by "a learned dissertation on the art of stuffing a turkey" that the Squire thinks no Christmas party would be complete without him.[15] This is the expository part of the novel.

The four opinionative faddists have diametrically opposite views. Mr. Foster, a thin gentleman, about thirty of age, with "an aquiline nose, white teeth, and black hair," makes the conversation most animated by taking occasion to panegyrize the vehicle in which they have travelled. He talks ecstatically about the distant parts of the kingdom, roads and railways, canals and tunnels, manufactures and machinery. Commenting on a wide range of modern advancements, he concludes that "every thing we look on attests the progress of mankind in all the arts of life, and demonstrates their gradual advancement towards a state of unlimited perfection"[16]

Mr. Escot, who is somewhat younger than Mr. Foster, but rather more "pale and saturine in his aspect," holds a different view. He believes that the human race is "steadily degenerating" and the so-called "improvements" are but only links in the "great chain of corruption, which will soon fetter the whole human race in irreparable slavery and incurable wretchedness." He is very sceptical about the future of mankind. It will be no wonder to him if the succeeding generation is "a helpless compound of perverted inclinations," losing all "independence and singleness of character" and degenerating rapidly from the primitive dignity of its "sylvan origin," into "infinite imbecility and vileness."[17]

Mr. Jenkinson, "a round-faced little gentleman of about forty-five," holds a middle view. He emphatically propounds that "there is no tendency in the human race either to moral perfectibility or to deterioration, but that the quantities of each are so exactly balanced by their reciprocal results, that the species, with respect to the sum of good and evil, knowledge and ignorance, happiness and misery, remains exactly and perpetually in status quo."[18] He is well aware of the progress of different arts and sciences, yet he knows equally well the rapid growth of corruption, luxury and selfishness that it has brought in its wake.

The Reverend Doctor Gaster regards the conversation as "atheistical and sceptical." Like a venerable clergy, "after clearing the husk in his throat with two or three hems", he converses at length on the question of good and evil from a religious rather than a scientific point of view. However, when someone comes and vociferates "Breakfast, gentlemen," the heated discussion suddenly comes to an end and the participants retire gladly for relaxation.[19]

The story reaches its climax when Mr. Escot falls a helpless prey to Cephalis's feminine charms. "The beautiful Cephalis," an independent and witty intellect, offers "a sweet blush"[20] to Mr. Escot who ultimately wins her through her roughish methods. Cranium, Cephalis's father, is crazy after ancient skulls. He regards them as a matchless possession on earth, basing this entire theory of psychology and human history on them. Mr. Escot, whose suit to Cephalis is disapproved of, in the beginning, "in effect buys her father's consent by giving him a large skull dug up by an old Welsh Sexton in the vicinity of Headlong Hall," which he passes of as "the skull of Cadwallader himself."[21] On acquiring this skull in exchange of his daughter,

Cranium replies : "If it were in my possession, I would not part with it for any acquisition on earth, much less for a wife"[22] and this brings about the denouement of the story.

Headlong Hall has a plot "as slight as possible, but it is an extremely efficient machine for providing the necessary minimum action."[23] The real machinery "is the brisk, pithy and incisive dialogue, to which is imparted an ironic twist that barbs the satire.... There is not a word wasted; the sentences seem cut in crystal."[24] Like John Bunyan, Richard Craves and Samuel Johnson, Peacock prefers to let his characters speak for themselves and thus produce "an essentially dramatic sequence."[25] It is through their witty dialogues or intellectual brawls that he exposes the absurdity inherent in popular dogmas and doctrines. In a novel of this type the progress of plot is determined not by action but by ideas, and it is from the portrayal of great ideas that Peacock's unconventional narratives derive their chief charm.

The story of *Melincourt*, though "minimal,"[26] is replete with Peacock's "own serious idealism and natural warmth of heart."[27] The Melincourt Castle with the Rednose Abbey in its vicinity, "wildest valleys in Westmorland"[28] surrounded with beautiful mountain dales, serves as a solitary retreat where, again like *Headlong Hall*, a number of noted intellectual faddists gather to converse on a variety of subjects. The party includes Anthelia, Sir Oran Haut-ton, Mr. Sarcastic, Mr. Paperstamp, Mr. Hippy, Mr. Feathernest, Mr. Fax, Mr. Forester, Mr. Portpine, Lord Anophel, Mrs. Pinmoney and some lesser intellects. As the scene opens we find among many "lovable characters lightly sketched"[29] Anthelia Melincourt, the heroine of the story, who having a "cultivated and independent mind" at the age of twenty-one, is "the mistress of herself and of ten thousand a year."[30] Like Sir Walter Scott or Henry Fielding, Peacock has devoted a plenty of space to the delineation of Anthelia's outward beauty and her intellectual accomplishments that have "sufficient attractions to kindle the flame of disinterested passion"[31] among a host of her admirers. On one Anti-Saccharine festival, Mr. Sarcastic who delivers himself "of a clever and devasting" attack on the selfishness of humanity, is easily set aright by Anthelia's "intelligent and authoritative discussion"[32] on the subject. Anthelia winds up the discussion with him, proclaiming that most acts of selfishness originate from "ignorance rather than cruelty"[33] and that "if the general condition of man is ever to be ameliorated, it can only be through the medium of belief in human virtue."[34] This part of the story may be taken as the exposition of the novel. Now, onwards, with the conversational format, provided by Anthelia and her lovers, the story passes through a series of interesting dialogues towards a crisis.

Mr. Hippy, Anthelia's uncle, a hypochondriac and gloomy fellow, falls in love with her and his passionate love finds an extravagant expression when "he leaps up from his blue devils and his gout on the receipt of a letter from his niece inviting him to Melincourt, Castle."[35] While Anthelia wanders alone and fearlessly among the wild valleys near her home she is "trapped on a rocky island by a rising flood."[36] On this occasion she is saved by one Mr. Sylvan Forester, "an unworldly and philanthropic young gentleman"[37] who lives in "an old abbey", one time known as "Rednose Abbey", but now altered by him to "Rednose Abbey."[38] She feels romantically inclined towards him for there are great affinities of temperament between them. Mr. Forester first comes on proofs of her sympathy and generosity to her tenants; next, when they meet in her library, he finds that they read and enjoy the same books; that she reads Latin and would like to read Greek — "an ambition of which he warmly approves;"[39] and finally — an irresistible touch — the discovery that she, like himself (and like Peacock), refuses to have sugar used in her house because it is the product of slave labour.

Apart from this, Peacock has introduced in the novel an interesting episode of the widow Mrs. Pinmoney, who is generally regarded as one of his "loveliest caricatures."[40] While Anthelia, like a great intellectual, theorizes about love and marriage, though she has no "wish to condemn herself to celibacy,"[41] the widow Mrs. Pinmoney takes a practical view of love and comes to Melincourt to try to persuade Anthelia to take interest in her own nephew, Sir Telegraph Paxarett — "a foolish but well-meaning and very honest young man."[42] Mrs. Pinmoney protests against Anthelia's lonely pattern of living, whereupon her daughter Danaretta remarks that Anthelia's solitude would be all right for a time if there were "a preux chevalier" outside the castle pining for the lady and declaring he had been seven years dying for her favours. At this, Mrs. Pinmoney bursts forth : "Heaven defend me from such hypocritical fops! Seven years indeed! It did not take as many weeks to bring me and poor dear dead Mr. Pinmoney together."[43] Anthelia, however, makes a vigorous defence of intellectual comradeship between husband and wife and talks of "mutual knowledge of each other's tastes, feelings, and character" as "the only sure basis of matrimonial happiness."[44] Mrs. Pinmoney then criticizes such unconventional views of Anthelia, which, however, have an immediate appeal to Mr. Sylvan Forester, who dislikes Mrs. Pinmoney's reprimanding Anthelia for her variegated tastes such a "taste for driving the mail — a taste for the marvellous — a taste for the simple — a taste for the brilliant — a taste for the sombre — a taste for the tender — a taste for the grim — a taste for banditti — a taste for ghosts — a taste for the devil — a taste for French dancers and Italian singers, and German whiskers and tragedies."[45] The dialogue between Mrs. Sylvan Forester and Anthelia becomes a little spacious, embracing a large variety of topics, including the question of "the right of women to be educated" on which both Mr. Sylvan Forester and Anthelia agree, expressing Peacock's own strong opposition to the view that "to think is one of the most unpardonable errors a woman can commit in the eyes of society."[46] Anthelia further goes on to admit that too much reading of poetry unfits a woman for the real world, a view that reminds us of Peacock's low opinion of poetry as expressed in *The Four Ages of Poetry*. Indeed, Anthelia's brilliant discussion attracts everybody, and its shows Peacock's "enthusiasm for intelligent and courageous women," "his hatred of mercenary marriage," and "his contempt for the affectations encouraged by society."[47] Peacock has devoted considerable space to the portrayal of Anthelia's character, because it is through her dialogues and arguments that he reveals the greater part of his own self. Whether Peacock glorifies or condemns the advances of science, whether he joins the side of "the Tories or revolutionaries," whether he looks backward over his shoulder towards the good old days or throws a glance of hope into the future, are some of the questions that have been critically revealed and examined through Anthelia's long discussions with Mr. Sylvan Forester.

The climax is brought about by the introduction of two episodes in the novel — the kidnapping of Anthelia by Lord Anophel Acthar, "a disappointed suitor,"[48] and the election of Sir Oran Haut-ton to the "Borough of Onevote," a theme which Peacock had already attempted in a story entitled *Satyrane* or *Calidore*. About half way through the novel, Anthelia is kidnapped by Lord Anophel Acthar who takes recourse to all wicked means in order to move her to be his wife. He threatens violence and asks her to "go to the church and marry him," but Anthelia, being an independent and fearless lady, does not succumb to the threats and temptations of Lord Anophel Acthar. She boldly says : "Your wickedness would be my disguise, and that false shame would induce me to conceal what both truth and justice would command me to make known."[49] In brief, Lord Anophel Acthar's attempts to seduce Anthelia end in smoke. She is saved by Mr. Forester with whom she is finally united. This is a slightly romantic episode and seems to have been incorporated in the novel by the author because "his publisher wanted a longer book."[50]

Sir Oran Haut-ton's episode which is indicative of Peacock's typical "radical satire"[51] is developed in the Chapter *The Borough of Onevote*. Sir Oran travels with his friends to the constituency of the Borough of Onevote, in order to be elected to Parliament, where, predictably enough, his "natural instincts get the better of civilized restraint."[52] He is described to Mr. Forester's friend Sir Telegraph as of "a contemplative disposition." "You must not be surprised," says Mr. Forester of him, "if he should not speak a word during the whole time you are here. The politeness of his manner makes amends for his habitual taciturnity."[53] Sir Telegraph is rather taken aback by Sir Oran's "ludicrous physiognomy," notwithstanding the "air of high fashion" which is heightened by a "pair of enormous whiskers, and the folds of a vast cravat."[54] The two gentlemen exchange courteous bows; Sir Oran rarely makes a mistake — his good manners and chivalrous feelings are held up as an example; but on one occasion when the impudent Lord Anophel stared at him "through a quizzing glass," Sir Oran "making a polite bow, took his quizzing glass from him, and examined him through it in like manner. Lord Anophel flew into a furious passion; but receiving a gentle hint from Mr. Hippy that the gentleman to whom he was talking had just pulled up a pine, he deemed it prudent to restrain his anger within due bounds."[55] In the course of the story, Sir Oran comes to Anthelia's rescue several times and is finally returned as member for "a rotten Borough." Peacock's real political leanings seem to be reflected in this part of the novel where he humorously attacks the defects of democracy, rusty administration and duality of conduct of the elected representatives. "Sir Oran's strength and faultless courtesy make him an excellent hero; he always behaves like a gentleman, though he never opens his lips."[56] Being "a stalwart champion of the right," a defender of distressed ladies like Anthelia, and an expert in "the retort courteous," he hypnotizes Sir Telegraph, who soon after passing "the evening with the baronet," ventures to question Mr. Forester about him. Mr. Forester calmly remarks : "Sir Oran was caught very young in the woods of Angola."

> *Sir Telegraph* : Caught!
>
> *Mr. Forester* : Very young. He is a specimen of the natural and original man — the wild man of woods.[57]

This gentlemanly Orang-outang and the learned footnotes that accompany him provide an illustration of the way "Peacock's mind rollicked about" among such theories as "those of Rousseau, Buffon and Monboddo an natural man,"[58] finding matter for serious interest as well as for humour and satires. With the conversation between Sir Orang-outang and Mr. Forester, on a medley of social and political theories, the novel comes to a close.

Unlike *Headlong Hall, Melincourt* contains more of dialogue than narrative for the simple reason that Peacock's aim in this novel is to offer "a radical's satire of an obsolete regime."[59] Most of the characters are therefore more or less political figures than ordinary human beings. The heroine Anthelia is, of course, a prototype of Peacock's conception of an ideal lady. The hero Sir Oran is a gentleman who offers a burlesque of the notions, not only of Buffon and Rousseau, but also of Lord Monboddo, a Rousseauistic semi-anthropologist. Though there is little of action, the plot is, on the whole, well-knit, and the general theme of the novel is systematically developed through a series of scintillating dialogues and discussions among the great intellectual faddists.

Crotchet Castle, the best of Peacock's conversational novels, has the same model as *Headlong Hall*, *viz.*, a party of scholars, philosophers, theorists, reformers and faddists that gather at a castle, called Crotchet Castle, and located in the beautiful countryside of Welsh mountain dales. Dr. Folliott, Lady Clarinda, Susannah Touchandgo, Captain Fitzchrome besides Crotchet himself, the host of the party, sit around the breakfast table, and engage themselves in a serious discussion of subjects, ranging from religious and philosophical to social and political riddles. In the initial part of the novel Dr. Folliott occupies the supreme place and his conversation with Mr. Mac Quedy, "the economist," touches a wide range of subjects — "chocolate, coffee, tea, cream, eggs, ham, tongue, and cold fowl," on the one hand, and "the march of mind," "the Steam Intellect Society," "human knowledge," and "the professions of author, lawyer, and politician," on the other.[60] The other participants in the discussion are Mr. Skionar, "the transcendental poet," Mr. Firedamp, "the meteorologist" and Lord Bossnowl, "son of the Earl of Foolincourt, and member for the borough of Rogueingrain."[61] As the story advances, we see that most of the company are occupied with the disinterested pursuit of their eccentric theories. While the intellectual combat is going on, Captain Fitzchrome, "the romantic young gallant," falls in love with Lady Clarinda, "the most vivacious young girl" with high ambitions and aspirations. The company feels distracted by this love affair and by the change they find in the attitude of Captain Fitzchrome and Lady Clarinda towards them. Captain Fitzchrome during dinner is persuaded by Lady Clarinda to believe that Crotchet who was once "a great preserver of game and private morals," has committed a great social crime by enclosing "cottage gardens," taking "the village cricket ground into his own park," convicting "one-third of the peasantry," and passing "nearly the whole of them through a wholesome course of prison discipline, which has finished their education at the expense of the country."[62]

Now, a heated discussion ensues between Dr. Folliott and Crotchet himself. Dr. Folliott talks of "the Alabaster Venus," "the collection of the nude statuettes in his citybred host's drawing room," "the position of a clergyman," and "two full-sized casts of the Uranian and Pandemian Venus, in niches."[63] The discussion between him and Crotchet gathers momentum to the point where the two gentlemen find themselves faced with the supposition of allowing their own wives or daughters to sit as "nude models for a sculptor."[64] The very idea of "poor dear Mrs. Folliott" sitting as a nude model before a stranger leaves the Doctor speechless; and Crotchet's apparent willingness to allow Miss Crotchet to act as such a model finally over-balances him altogether.

The crisis of discussion is converted now into the climax by Captain Fitzchrome's sudden disappearance from the party, who is at the time exploring the rivers of Wales. The various fanatics, of whom the party consists, make their own characteristic comments on the event. Mr. Philpot thinks that Captain Fitzchrome must have been "exploring the river and fallen in" and "got drowned" in the process. Mr. Firedamp has no doubt that while he had been crossing "a mountain bog," he was suddenly deprived of his life by "the exhalations of marsh miasmata." Mr. Henbane deems it probable that he has been tempted in some wood by "the large black brilliant berries of the *Atropa Belladonna*" or "deadly nightshade" and laments that he has not been able "to administer an infallible antidote." Mr. Eavesdrop hopes that the particulars of his fate would be ascertained if anyone present could help him to "any authentic anecdotes of their departed friend." The Reverend Doctor Folliott proposes that an inquiry should be instituted into the fact whether "the march of intellect" has reached that neighbourhood; and if so, the Captain has probably been made a subject for scientific experiment. Mr. Mac Quedy observes it is no such great matter to ascertain the precise mode in which "the surplus population is diminished by one." Mr. Toogood retorts that there is no such thing as "surplus population," and that the existing land, if properly managed, will maintain "twenty times its present inhabitations."[65] Hereupon the contestants fall into a heated disputation, which comes to an end only through Dr. Folliott's mediation. Meanwhile, everybody is startled to come to know of Captain Fitzchrome's being quite safe. "The Captain wandered despondingly up and down hill for several days," passing many hours of each in sitting on rocks; making, almost mechanically, sketches of waterfalls and mountain pools, taking care, nevertheless to be always before nightfall in a "comfortable inn."[66] The party then resumes "wine and whisky", "cake and ale," and with the re-union of Lady Clarinda and Captain Fitzchrome the story comes to a happy close.

Crotchet Castle is undoubtedly "the most concise and finished example of the novel,"[67] containing as it does "more life and much more human nature"[68] than any other conversational novels of Peacock. It has a dominance of dialogue over narrative, comprising for the purpose "a bevy of characters" and exposing "with fluent and pungent wit a good proportion of the world's follies."[69] It is Peacock's greatest skill that without dwelling upon any episodical action, only through a sequence of conversational combats he has been able to give the reader maximum of dramatic pleasure and delight.

Gryll Grange, Peacock's last conversational novel, has almost the same set of characters — "men of letters, philosophers, theorists, reformers, agitators, and faddists"[70] who refute and contradict each other so vehemently that they either pour their vials of wrath against each other or are so completely lost into the labyrinth of their own theories that they find it impossible to drag themselves out of it. The learned party, or "an assortment of crotcheteers" whose "intellectual brawl or crotchet"[71] constitutes the main staple of the narrative, consists of Squire Gryll, "a curiously complicated misnomer," the Reverend Doctor Opimian, who, "is everybody's friend," Mr. Falconer, "the hermit," Miss Niphet and Miss Gryll, "the two vivacious and bouncing heroines," Darby and Joan, "the two noted conversationalists," Mr. Chainmail, "the noted intellectual," and "the fastidious Morgana."[72] The story is set in motion with the discourse of Dr. Opimian with others and his conversation, as a general rule, covers a wide range, showing Peacock's own encyclopaedic range of learning. Taking from "Palestine soups," "Jerusalem artichoke," and "sanitary improvements" to such serious topics as "the dissolution of the monasteries," "several divisions and subdivisions of Ichthyology, Entomology, Herpetology and Conchology," "an Aristophanic Comedy" and "the dramatis personae of the Athenians and Romans,"[73] Dr. Opimian's vast range of discussion surprises every member of the party. Squire Gryll's endeavour for an "intellectual bang,"[74] though clumsy, is finally praise-worthy. His discourse on "political dogmatism, enforced by bludgeons and revolvers," "the wisdom of Parliament," "a glass of old Maderia" and "a series of varieties of music"[75] provides a long sequence to the dialogue between him and Squire Gryll, making up the major part of the novel. Mr. Falconer's discussion with Dr. Opimian gives further movement to the plot. He talks of love — "certainly Peacockian love of seventy-six,"[76] for it was at this age that Peacock wrote this novel — "the pleasure of books"[77] and "ministrations of seven young women" who are as skilful in music as in cookery. Meanwhile, Darby and Joan, "the two gluttonous figures," find greater delight in "good dinners and good wine"[78] than in any kind of intellectual discussion. This reminds us of Peacock's own delight in dinners and good wine in old age. While on the one hand, the conversation continues, on the other, Miss Niphet is seen advancing romantically to Mr. Chainmail, quoting, like Anthelia, Italian verses to impress her culture and scholarship on him. Her discussion with Mr. Chainmail covers "ideal beauty and deep love," "idealisation of worldly affection," "tenderness of worldly wisdom" and "the mode of proceeding of a lover."[79] Squire Gryll's and Dr. Opimian's criticism of the social evils includes, among other things, "the Divorce Court," and "scientific machinery" which they both pronounce, have "substituted rottenness for strength" and "physical degradation" for "comfortable country life."[80] As their discussion reaches a climax, it is reconciled by the very appearance of "an attractive damsel" Miss Gryll, another heroine of the novel, whose love affairs with Mr. Forester cast a spell on every member of the party, who is now led to resume his light mood and enjoy drinking and talking of "youth and age"[81] — the vivacity of youth and the coldness of age. With this happy note the story comes to an end.

Gryll Grange reveals glimpses of Peacock's wide scholarship coupled with a satiric preponderance. Peacock, the political radical, becomes more bitter than ever, denouncing vehemently "stereotyped customs, social disorders and faulty theories."[82] Each discussion on a particular problem serves as an episode in the novel and all the discussions have been adequately and exquisitely co-ordinated. Like an expert "cook" the author has prepared and served "his material with a sauce"[83] of both romance and satire in a manner which is hard to find elsewhere.

Maid Marian, "a kind of boisterous romantic comedy reminiscent of Shakespeare's *Tempest* and *As You Like It*,"[84] is Peacock's first romantic novel. Like the conversational novels, it has its own intellectual party round a dinner table in a solitary retreat but quite unlike them, it has a dominance of narrative over dialogue and a touch of romance, which makes the principal characters more engaged in "love and domestic bliss"[85] than in the intellectual problems of the day. The story starts with the meeting of "the beautiful Matilda Fitzwater," later Marian, the daughter of "the Baron of Arligford," and "the noble Robert Fitz-Oath, Earl of Locksley and Hautingdon" at the altar in the abbey-chapel of Rubygill, which stands in a picturesque valley, at a little distance from "the western boundary of Sherwood Forest."[86] The Baron is planning to marry his daughter with the noble Robert but unluckily she does not like him and feels inclined towards Michael, "the most witty creature."[87] A delicate love-tangle is created by the Baron's insistence on his parental authority on the one hand, and his daughter's disliking the man of her father's choice, on the other. "Why father", says she, "if you coop me up here in this odious castle, I shall pine and die like a lonely swan on a pool."[88] Gradually, the tension subsides with the Baron's sympathizing with his daughter. Really, Matilda is an adorable, fearless and warm-hearted young lady, who can "draw a bow and wield a sword with the best."[89] Her witty dialogues with Friar Tuck impresses Brother Michael and when Brother Michael finds the Friar accusing Marian to be a mad girl, he retorts :

> "Has she not beauty, grace, wit, sense, discretion, dexterity, learning and valour ?" "Learning!" exclaimed the Friar : "What has a woman to do with learning ? Meekness, and mildness, and softness...and obedience to her husband, and faith in her confessor, and domesticity, or as learned doctors call it the faculty of Satay-athomeitiveness, and embroidery, and music, and pickling, and preserving, and the whole complex and multiplex detail of the noble science of dinner...but valour — why who ever heard ?[90]

Through these dialogues, the story advances further and then a pair of ballads is sung at one another by Marian and Friar Tuck, a method of argument in which both are skilled. He is sheltering her and Robin in a lonely hut beside a river and is disturbed by a female voice hallowing to be ferried across. Friar Tuck is greatly embarrassed, and takes refuge in the tale of a ghost who stands by the river edge at midnight and calls out "Over! Over!"[91] To give verisimilitude to his unconvincing narrative he invents a ballad about a drowned young woman. Marian sees through him and caps it with a very different one of her own about a Friar :

> In lonely hut himself shut,
> The Friar of Rubygill,
> Where the ghostly elf absolved himself,
> To follow his own good will.[92]

To this sally the disconcerted Friar Tuck replies with one of Peacock's best-known passages : "You are welcome to laugh if it so please you.... The worst thing is good enough to be laughed at, though it be good for nothing else;..."[93] This is followed by numerous merry songs and the story ends with every body's feeling happy at the reunion of Michael and Marian.

In *Maid Marian*, Peacock has "diverged from his customary formula of assembling a group of eccentrics...and letting each display his particular obsession."[94] He has introduced an "idyllic quality"[95] in the novel, which recalls the Victorian stuffiness of Gilbertin musical comedy. The basic episode seems to have been inspired by Ritson's *Robin Hood* and some other popular ballads which Scott has used in *Ivanhoe*,[96] but Peacock with the aid of "pseudo-medieval breeziness and lustre, mock heroics and mock battles"[97] has transformed the traditional material into an original product.[98]

The Misfortunes of Elphin, "a comic historical romance,"[99] based on "the Arthurian fantasy,"[100] has for its setting the "legendary or pre-historic Wales."[101] Its theme is an admixture of the legend of Seithenyn, the abduction of Gwenyvar, and the romance between the young bard Taliesin and the daughter of his foster-father, ex-king Elphin, having "the Welsh archaeology and bardic writings"[102] as its main sources. Influenced by his Welsh wife Jane Gryffydh, his tour across the Welsh scenery and by his "desultory reading"[103] of the "Welsh myth and folk-lore,"[104] Peacock has offered in this novel a "hilarious yet respectful parody of Arthurian themes,"[105] supplying the missing links in the ancient legends by his own powerful imagination.

Its story is set in the beginning of the sixth century, when "Uther Pendragon held the nominal sovereignty" of Britain and

Gwythno Garanhir was "king of Caredigion."[106] The most valuable part of Gwythno Garanhir's territory was the Great Plain of Gwaelod, which stretched along the counties of "Merioneth and Cardigan," the most populous, highly cultivated and well fortified towns of the Cymry, whose inhabitants resembled the Roman Lords of the world in their language, manners and architecture.[107] It also contained one of the three privileged ports of the isle of Britain, called the Port of Gwythno. King Gwythno Garanhir's Kingdom is well-protected by "an embankment of mossy stone,"[108] whose Lord High Commissioner, Seithenyn ap Seithyn Saidi, is a lusty drunkard and the most comic character.

As the story starts, the King is seen conversing with Prince Teithrin and Elphin telling them how the majestic edifice of his kingdom is fortified against all kinds of dangers. All of a sudden, "a tempest from the west" is heard by Teithrin, with "the intermitting peals of the wind" and "the increasing sound of the rising waves" which swell "progressively into wilder and more menacing tumult."[109] Soon it is noticed that the whole embankment, which had been negligently supervised by Seithenyn, is destroyed by the storm, and gradually "the tremendous crash" touches even the most protected and fortified tower, which has its foot in the sea. In a very short time, it is sapped by the waves, and consequently it "falls into the surf," carrying with it a portion of the wall of the main building. The storm rushes into the hall, "extinguishing the torches," and tossing "the grey locks" and "loose mantle" of the bard, and "the light white drapery and black tresses of Angharad," the daughter of Seithenyn. A great confusion brews up with the crash of the collapsing tower, and "the simultaneous shriek" of the women awakens violently the profound sleepers of the hall, including Seithenyn and "his drunkard band." When a mighty torrent pouring in from the sea upon the plain and rushing immediately beneath the castle walls, terrifies the whole assembly, it is Seithenyn, who is now in a drunken condition, first perceives that there is "an innovation" and remains "at length motionless, leaning against the pillar." Then suddenly he roars out : "Show me the enemy," drawing "his sword furiously and flourishing it over his head." The suspense reaches its climax when he plunges straightway into "the white waves, flourishing his sword more furiously." When Angharad, Elphin, and others start to leave the castle and march into the waves, the tide begins to "recede and the wind to abate somewhat of its violence."[110]

The Prince then reprimands Seithenyn for his negligence in supervising the embankment and for his having spent the money intended for its upkeep on roistering and drinking. Seithenyn gives a very elaborate and eloquent defence of the decayed embankment, which is indeed, highly amusing. For him "decay is one thing and danger is another. Every thing that is old must decay." "Our ancestors," he says further, "were wiser than we : "they built it in their wisdom; and if we should be so rash as to try to mend it, we should only mar it."[111]

After this mock-gallantry of Seithenyn, the story advances through a web of myth and history, including rather colourless romance of Angharad, till after a lapse of many years, Seithenyn turns up again, acting as butler to the blood-thirsty king Melvas, whose warriors having seized the castle of Dinas Vawr, celebrate their victory in a famous war song. The pace and tilt and comical meticulousness of blood-thirsty detail in this "inimitable paen"[112] put it in a class with the Agincourt of Michael Drayton. The poem contains "the quintessence of all the war songs that were ever written, and the sum and substance of all the appetencies, tendencies and consequences of military glory."[113] Meanwhile, Seithenyn relates his adventures to the young bard Taliesin. He has been saved by clinging to some of the many empty barrels which floated out of his cellars on the night of "the inundation of Gwaelod."[114] He tells how, as he floated away, "he kept warm by the good liquor inside him. "I could not help thinking — as I had nothing else to think of just than that touched me so nearly — that if I had left them full, and myself empty, as a sober man would have done, we should all three — that is, I and two barrels, have gone to the bottom together."[115] With this thrilling account of Seithenyn's adventures, the story comes to an end with various passages of Peacock's bitter criticism of the prevailing social ills, which make the novel a kind of mock-romance.

It is interesting to note that the Arthur of *The Misfortunes of Elphin* springs up from the story named *The Dream of Rhonabwy*. Madawe and Iorwerth, sons of Maroddud, the chieftains in Powys, are the two historical personages in this Arthurian tale. Two famous battles, named Camlan and Mount Badon, were fought during King Arthur's reign. In the Battle of Badon, among many fighting heroes was one Elphin, the son of Gwyddno, whose adventures have been related to Taliesin. This Arthurian legend, in short, has been revived by Peacock in *The Misfortunes of Elphin*. But he has done so with certain reservations, partly filling the original gaps by his own creative imagination and partly drawing from *Mabinogion*, another popular book on the Arthurian legend. He has combined the originally separate legends of Seithenyn, Taliesin, and Gwenyvar into one tale, giving his own outfit to the borrowed material. He has re-interpreted the Welsh chronicles in the light of his own mystic ideas and supernatural concepts. The song of Taliesin about his own miraculous birth is a typical Peacockian addition which his contemporaries are supposed to have certainly enjoyed. So far as the legend about "the flooding of Cardigan Bay by the Sea" is concerned, it belongs to a very early time and many of the romantics connected it with an actual catastrophe. Whether the submerged forests of which traces can still be found on some parts of the coast have anything to do with it, is however, a question for the geologists to decide.

Peacock's artistic admixture of fact with fiction in *The Misfortunes of Elphin* reminds us of Sir Walter Scott's *Ivanhoe*, and his Prince Seithenyn of Scott's Wamba, who is the most bibulous, the most Falstaffian of all the characters and more original than Taliesin or Elphin.

Nightmare Abbey hovers somewhere between the novels of talk and the romances, and as it contains features of both, it can rightly be termed as a conversational romance. Scythrop Glowry, the hero, and a "portrait of the young Shelley"[116] lives with his father in damp melancholy in "a partly ruined abbey."[117] He suffers from a disappointment in love, reminding us of Shelley's failure in love with Harriet. He has "determined to devote the rest of his life to writing pamphlets to reform society,"[118] which again reminds us of Shelley's fervent pamphleteering after his amorous frustrations. His cousin, Marionetta, "a gay, coquettish and penniless girl," however deviates from the solemn path of "social reform."[119] Nevertheless, Scythrop falls in love with Marionetta, but his proposal of marriage with her is disapproved by his father, who has "recently arranged with his friend Mr. Toobad, a still more misanthropical and morbid gentleman, that Scythrop should marry Miss Toobad, "a young lady who has beauty, accomplishments, and a fortune into bargain."[120] Glowry, "a portrait of Coleridge"[121] admires Miss Toobad, but Scythrop does not budge an inch from his decision to marry Marionetta, and by "a display of tantrums and mock suicide"[122] he induces his father to agree. Marionetta is a clever girl, who being fully assured of Scythrop's passionate love for her, tantalises him to the maximum. On one occasion she provokes his jealousy by showing love to the Hon. Mr. Listless. But as luck would have it, Stella, "a mysterious, distinguished young lady, very intelligent and independent,"[123] comes to tempt Scythrop. Stella comes to know of Scythrop "as the result of reading one of his pamphlets,"[124] and she demands protection from him against some impending oppression. Scythrop hides her in a dilapidated tower and when the danger is over, he finds himself in love with her. As the story advances, the climax is brought about by the revelation of Stella's real identity. Her disguise drops off and she is found to be no other than Miss Toobad, "who had run away from her father's proposal that she should marry an unknown man of his choice."[125] The old proverb concerning two strings in a bow gives Scythrop some comfort, but that concerning two stools occurs to his head more frequently, and he is badly perplexed. Ultimately Scythrop loses both the ladies and he then vows to commit suicide"[126] at a certain hour, but all the same he compels his valet to declare that the clock in his room is very fast, and allows the fatal moment "to pass harmlessly by."[127]

The plot of *Nightmare Abbey* is more coherent and symmetrical than the plots of other novels. Its general theme reminds us of Sheridan's *Rivals*, in which Captain Absolute resists the advances of Lydia Languish simply because she is his father's choice. Ernest Baker, on the other hand, finds affinities with Congreve's *Incognita*.[128] But unlike both Congreve and Sheridan, Peacock has introduced in his novel real historical characters in guises so thin that one can easily perceive the original behind them — Shelley in Scythrop, Coleridge in Mr. Glowry, and Byron, in Mr. Cypress. Through such a device the novelist mocks at the romanticism of contemporary poets.

The above survey of Peacock's novels reveals it clearly that they do not have episodical plots of Fielding, Dickens and Hardy. Peacock does not tell tales in a conventional sense, nor does he give long descriptive terms, on the basis of which George Saintsbury, among others, chooses to call his productions, not novels but merely "tales or contes," observing that while Peacock wrote them, he only "thought of models of the eighteenth-century French writers of contes."[129] Besides, "if we expect from him the details of daily life and the psychological intricacies of individuals or families, we shall be disappointed."[130] But in spite of this, his novels are not without unity of thought, purpose and action. The episodes are there and they have been wrought out through a graduated chain of exposition, crisis, climax, and denouement, but they have nevertheless no independent value of their own. They are used by the author as pegs to hang his views upon, or as instruments to play "intellectual games, difficult and in some ways inimitable."[131] Unlike enthusiasts for plot as the kernel of a novel,[132] Peacock has given secondary place to story and first importance to "elaborating pictures of idea."[133]

Peacock's plots have often been charged of formlessness, but before we share this charge, let us not fail to bear in our minds that the very term novel at present is no longer "a literary kind but a vague term denoting at most prose medium, some pretence of action, a minimum length, and a minimum of organization."[134] "The literary critic with nothing to point to but the mere volume in his hand, must recognize that his wish to be precise, to be definite, to be clear and exact in his statements, is helplessly vain."[135] Peacock is not different from the great modern novelists like Virginia Woolf, D.H. Lawrence and Aldous Huxley who have sacrificed graces of form and structure to the deeper subtleties of thought. Peacock has created a new kind of fiction in which the interest of narrative is subordinated to character-portrayal through dialogues or intellectual crotchets. "As often as possible" he escapes "from the strait-jacket of narrative into the freedom of unhindered conversation"[136] which makes his novels "witty, teeming with ideas and crotchets, a feast over which the author presides like an Epicurean Socrates, directing the rivers of talk, as a *bon viveur* directs the flow of wine."[137]

As a novelist Peacock has a technique of his own, which many writers have found "inimitable."[138] Barring a few like W.H. Mallock, Evelyn Waugh and Kingsley Amis, all his zealous students, "none has ever dared to follow his brilliant talk and country houses and their format."[139] In fact, Peacock did "write more for our times than for his own"[140] and to-day he is a great fascination for those who look for "fresh woods and pastures new" in the world of mind.[141]

REFERENCES

1. *Thomas Love Peacock*, p. 74.
2. *The Critical Reputation of Thomas Love Peacock*, p. 85.
3. *English Literature*, p. 586.
4. *The English Novel*, p. 133.
5. Dawson, Carl : *Thomas Love Peacock*, p. 20.
6. *Gryll Grange*, pp. 151-52.
7. Baker, Ernest A. : *A History of the English Novel*, Vol. VII, p. 131.
8. Campbell, Olwen W. : *Thomas Love Peacock*, p. 17.
9. Dawson, Carl : *Thomas Love Peacock*, p. 20.
10. Baker, Ernest : *op. cit.*, p. 125.
11. Dawson, Carl : *op. cit.*, p. 20.
12. *Ibid.*, p. 21.

13. Dawson, Carl : *op. cit.*, p. 21.
14. *Ibid.*
13. *Headlong Hall*, p. 4.
16. *Ibid.*, p. 6.
17. *Headlong Hall*, pp. 7-8.
18. *Ibid.*, p. 8.
19. *Headlong Hall*, p. 9.
20. *Ibid.*, p. 25.
21. *Ibid.*, p. 35.
22. *Ibid.*, p. 98.
23. Allen, Walter : *The English Novel*, p. 132.
24. Baker, Ernest : *op. cit.*, p. 127.
25. Dawson, Carl : *op. cit.*, p. 60.
26. *Ibid.*, p. 21.
27. Campbell, Olwen : *op. cit.*, p. 37.
28. *Melincourt*, p. 121.
29. Campbell, Olwen : *op. cit.*, p. 21.
30. *Melincourt*, p. 117.
31. *Ibid.*, p. 153.
32. *Ibid.*
33. *Ibid.*, p. 157.
34. *Ibid.*, p. 160.
35. *Ibid.*, p. 163.
36. *Ibid.*, p. 165.
37. *Ibid.*, p. 174.
38. *Ibid.*, p. 180.
39. *Ibid.*, p. 181.
40. Campbell, Olwen : *op. cit.*, p. 40.
41. *Melincourt*, p. 191.
42. *Ibid.*
43. *Ibid.*
44. *Ibid.*, p. 201.
45. *Ibid.*, p. 197.
46. *Ibid.*, p. 203.
47. Campbell, Olwen : *op. cit.*, p. 43.
48. *Melincourt*, p. 207.
49. *Ibid.*, p. 204.
50. Campbell, Olwen : *op. cit.*, p. 42.
51. Baker, Ernest : *op. cit.*, p. 129.

52. Dawson, Carl : *op. cit.*, p. 97.
53. *Melincourt*, p. 207.
54. *Ibid.,* p. 211.
55. *Ibid.*
56. Baker, Ernest : *op. cit.*, p. 129.
57. *Melincourt,* p. 212.
58. Campbell, Olwen : *op. cit.*, p. 45.
59. Baker, Ernest : *op. cit.*, p. 131.
60. *Crotchet Castle*, p. 14.
61. *Ibid.*
62. *Ibid.*, p. 46.
63. *Ibid.,* p. 71.
64. *Ibid.*
65. *Ibid.,* p. 83.
66. *Ibid.*, p. 87.
67. Baker, Ernest : *op. cit.*, p. 138.
68. *Ibid.*
69. *Ibid.*
70. *Ibid.*, p. 125.
71. Dawson, Carl : *op. cit.*, p. 32.
72. *Gryll Grange,* p. 102.
73. *Ibid.*, p. 159.
74. *Ibid.*, p. 160.
75. *Ibid.*, p. 161.
76. Campbell, Olwen : *op. cit.*, p. 91.
77. *Ibid.*
78. *Ibid.*
79. *Gryll Grange*, p. 180.
80. *Ibid.,* p. 181.
81. *Ibid.*
82. *Ibid.*
83. Saintsbury, George : *The English Novel*, p. 52.
84. Dawson, Carl : *op. cit.*, p. 81.
85. Dawson, Carl : *op. cit.*, p. 84.
86. *Maid Marian*, pp. 7-8.
87. *Ibid.*, p. 24.
88. *Ibid.*, p. 25.
89. *Ibid.,* p. 52.
90. *Ibid.*, p. 57.

91. *Maid Marian*, p. 67.
92. *Ibid.*, p. 73.
93. *Ibid.*, p. 67.
94. Ward, A.C. : *English Literature*, p. 584.
95. Allen, Walter : *The English Novel*, p. 137.
96. Elton, O. : *A Survey of English Literature*, p. 452.
97. Buchanan, Robert : *Thomas Love Peacock*, p. 162.
98. *Ibid.*, p. 163.
99. Dawson, Carl : *op. cit.*, p. 24.
100. Compton-Rickett : *A History of English Literature*, p. 358.
101. Dawson, Carl : *op. cit.*, p. 25.
102. Campbell, Olwen : *op. cit.*, p. 63.
103. *Ibid.*, p. 25.
104. Baker, Ernest : *op. cit.*, p. 136.
105. Ward, A.C. : *op. cit.*, p. 584.
106. *The Misfortunes of Elphin*, p. 3.
107. *Ibid.*, p. 12.
108. *Ibid.*
109. *Ibid.*, p. 25.
110. *Ibid.*, pp. 28-31.
111. *Ibid.*, p. 33.
112. Campbell, Olwen : *op. cit.*, p. 69.
113. *The Misfortunes of Elphin*, p. 65.
114. *Ibid.*, p. 67.
115. *Ibid.*, p. 107.
116. Campbell, Olwen : *op. cit.*, p. 48.
117. *Nightmare Abbey*, p. 19.
118. Campbell, Olwen : *op. cit.*
119. *Nightmare Abbey*, p. 19.
120. *Ibid.*, p. 70.
121. *Ibid.*
122. *Ibid.*, p. 77.
123. *Ibid.*, p. 144.
124. *Ibid.*
125. *Ibid.*, p. 150.
126. *Nightmare Abbey*, p. 146.
127. *Ibid.*, p. 145.
128. Baker, Ernest : *op. cit.*, p. 131.
129. Saintsbury, George : *Thomas Love Peacock*, p. 73. Bill Read likewise remarks that "Peacock's novels are only contes and not novels." (*The

Critical Reputation of Thomas Love Peacock, p. 85.) Similarly Edmund Wilson fails to trace "all the necessary ingredients of a novel in Peacock's novels." (*The Musical Glasses of Thomas Love Peacock*, p. 57.)

130. Dawson, Carl : *op. cit.*, p. 20.
131. *Ibid.*
132. The old Greek philosopher, Aristotle, considered plot more important than character. "Without action there cannot be tragedy," he said, "there may be without character" (*Poetics*, ed. by Butcher, p. 251). Among the moderns, E.M. Forster pronounces that "the fundamental aspect of the novels is its story-telling aspect" (Aspects of the novel, p. 80).
133. Horne, Charles F. : *The Technique of the Novels*, p. 115.
134. Tillyard, E.M.W. : *The Epic Strain in the English Novel*, p. 24.
135. Lubbock, Percy : *The Craft of Fiction*, p. 11.
136. Ward, A.C. : *op. cit.*, p. 586.
137. Church, Richard : *The Growth of the English Novel*, p. 113.
138. Campbell, Olwen : *op. cit.*, p. 97.
139. Dawson, Carl : *op. cit.*, p. 15.
140. *Ibid.*, p. 36.
141. Also published in *TLP*, Delhi, 1986, pp. 35-63, under the head — *Thomas Love Peacock : His Episodes*; *Influences on Thomas Love Peacock*, was also presented at the XIV session of the AIETC, 1974, held at Patiala; TLP'S plot construction was presented at the XVIII session of All India Teachers' Conference, 1968, held at Bangalore, *Thematic Classification of The Misfortunes of Elphin*, published in PJR Vol. 3 (ii), pp. 218-23; also published in *VFSNA*, Delhi, 2002, pp. 1-23.

4

Anita Desai : Feminine Sensibility in *Cry the Peacock*, *Voices in the City*, *Bye-Bye Black Bird*, *Where Shall We Go This Summer* ? And Other Shorter Fiction

ANITA DESAI is certainly a prolific Indian novelist. When we talk of feminine sensibility, we cannot ignore Anita Desai. This chapter has two parts — one dealing with her major novels, and the other with her shorter fiction. Whereas in her novels, the Weltschmerz outlook characterises the whole treatment, in her shorter fiction, her outlook on life is one that resembles *in toto* the Greek view of life, which clearly means that an unflinching faith in the inherent goodness of man has nothing to do with the bestiality hidden in him. Being an incorrigible optimist, Anita sees life as "steady and as a whole." In fact, her final vision of life seems to dictate : "Live Naturally", which certainly means that adaptability to one's environment is the surest way to survive and also to maintain human sensibility.

I

In an interview, Anita Desai admitted, "Of course I do write of the contemporary scene and therefore the characters must contain the modern sensibility."[1] And, in fact, in all her major novels, Anita Desai has dealt with the feminine sensibility more emphatically than the description of the he-man and his exploits. Consequently, Desai's *Cry the Peacock*, *Voices in the City*, *Where Shall We Go This Summer*? *Fire on the Mountain*, *Clear*

Light of Day and *Custody* — all are replete with a powerful description of feminine sensibility. Not only this, even in her short-stories, the central theme is certainly the theme of feminine sensibility.

Cry the Peacock is a tale of Maya's love for Gautam, her husband. Deeply devoted and affectionate in nature, an oversensitised in mental proclivities, Maya requires a love partner with sympathies commensurable with her sensibilities. But the tragedy begins in her life because her husband Gautam does not possess those wide-ranging sympathies.

In *Voices in the City*, Monisha is endowed with higher sensibilities, which is self-evident when she is attuned to music in the conference hall, "I wander in this labyrinth at will and blessedly we never touch, merely remain in mystic communion with each other. I am willing to follow till I die."[2] *In Bye-Bye Black Bird*, there is a powerful encounter of the East and the West. Whereas fascination for England has been presented through Adit and Dev, that for India through Sarah, Emma Moffit and Christine Langford. Disenchantment with England is particularly epitomized through Adit and Dev. However, throughout the novel, it is the feminine sensibility that dominates more than the other thematic strains.

Where Shall We Go This Summer ? is again a very powerful novel delineating feminine sensibility. Despite the fact that this delineation is chiefly expressed through the projection of one single theme, *i.e.,* the crisis of conscience and values, Sita, the female protagonist in the novel, dominates the entire theme of the novel. Anita's *Fire on the Mountain* symbolises feminine sensibility in a heightened way. Nanda Kaul, the protagonist in the novel, symbolises the heightened feminine sensibility.

Anita's *Games at Twilight* — a collection of short stories, is also a skilled record of the likes, dislikes, vanities, prejudices, loyalties, eccentricities and jealousies of feminine nature in particular. It is, of course, refreshing and enlightening to have a peep into the thematic structure of such short stories as 'Private Tuition', 'Studies in the Park', 'Surface texture', 'Sale',

'Pineapple', 'The Accompanist' and 'A Devoted Son' in order to comprehend Desai's feminine sensibility *vis-a-vis* her fictional achievements.

For ages, the human experience has been synonymous only with the masculine experience. Female experience has been rather ignored what Michael Foucault calls 'discontinuity' or 'rupture' in history. Alex Comfort is also of the view that in order to have "the ideology of the whole human being",[3] the female experience must also be given an equal importance. Carl Jung considers a woman the prime mover of the psychic activity which transcends the limit of consciousness. But it is a sad commentary on the existing affairs of events that female experiences have been either dubbed as inconsequential or ignored absolutely, which is certainly a prejudiced view. Latest advances in psycholinguistics and sociolinguistics have revealed many startling facts. Female sex is as powerful, to be precise, as the male sex in the domain of semantics and syntax. As such, female semantics and syntax have a distinct category of its own and the feminine sensibility is also a distinct category of its own having very distinct differences with those of male sensibilities.

Anita Desai's novels offer us a rewarding study not only in the domain of socio-psycho activities but also in semantics and syntax. Her novels, synoptically speaking, offer a view of the long-smothered wail of a lacerated psyche of a female. They, of course, tell us the harrowing tale of blunted human relationships. The fate of Maya, Monisha, Sita and Nanda Kaul remind us of Mr. and Mrs. Ramsay in Virginia Woolf's *To the Lighthouse.* Maya in *Cry the Peacock* is married to an older man, a detached, sober, industrious lawyer, who is unable to recognize and understand the female sensibility. The following passage in the novel is a telling predicament of the likes of Maya and the total disregard for their existence :

> How little he knew my suffering, or of how to comfort me.... Telling me to go to sleep while he worked at his papers, he did not give another thought to me, to either the soft willing body, or the lonely wanting mind that waited near his bed.

Monisha in *Voices in the City* is a psychic case. Her relationship with her husband is characterized only by loneliness and lack of proper understanding. Whereas her husband is a pseudo-moralist, a rotund, minute-minded and 'limited' official, always given to the habit of quoting from Burke, Wordsworth, Gandhi and Tagore, she herself gets bored of him. Ultimately she develops an incurable claustrophobia and commits suicide.

Anita Desai's novels have been interpreted in a number of ways. Some have interpreted them from the standpoint of social criticism, whereas others from that of economic and cultural crisis. Some have traced linguistic inventiveness in them, whereas others find psycho-moral delineations. A perfect artist as Anita is, her novels naturally offer a wide variety of social, cultural and psychological interpretations. However, here our main concern is to show feminine sensibilities and other related issues connected to them and to digress from this main theme will certainly prove preposterous.

Hence, in main, in this domain the following issues have largely been treated in Anita's novels :

(a) love, marriage, divorce;
(b) social taboos and inhibitions;
(c) cruelty and violence to the female sex;
(d) problem of rehabilitation after divorce;
(e) extent of liberty and freedom to the female sex;
(f) recognition to the female sex; and,
(g) crisis of conscience and values.

If a deeper analysis of Anita's novels is made from the standpoint of feminine sensibility, completely ignoring the he-man approach and the connected conccpts attached thereto, then we shall arrive at a stage where all the issues listed above may appear to be related directly or indirectly to the last one, *i.e.*, crisis of conscience and values. In a mathematical way, the semiotics of the entire problem may be summarized in the following way :

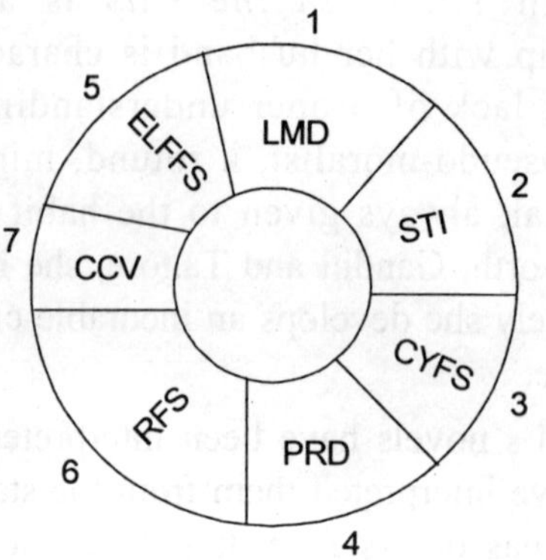

Wherein

1. LMD stands for love, marriage and divorce;
2. STI for social taboos and inhibition;
3. CVFS for cruelty and violence for the female sex;
4. PRD for problem of rehabilitation after divorce;
5. ELFFS for extent of liberty and freedom to the female sex;
6. RFS for recognition to the female sex; and
7. CCV crisis of conscience and values.

Out of the above semiotic circles, the pivotal is the CCV. Of all the six possible semiotic circles, which almost complete Anita's novels from the point of view of feminine sensibility, the circle of CCV is the only one to which all other circles get connected. So what is prudent on the part of a wise reader is to have the key of CCV and then try to understand other circles, which are automatically revealed one after another.

But for this, first of all, *Where Shall We Go This Summer* ? has to analysed in detail; for, the CCV semiotic circle is absolutely complete in this novel. And once Anita's novels are analysed from this angle, it is also worthwhile to understand her shorter fiction by applying the principle of the CCV semiotic principle.

As a matter of fact, Anita Desai has raised a question of crisis of conscience and values (CCV) of universal import in her novel named *Where Shall We Go This Summer* ? If we delete *This Summer* from the title, the perennial question remains — where shall we do ? The confusion, as is obtaining today, is still worse confounded; for, the citadel of conscience and values has almost crumbled or is likely to crumble. The brute forces of money, corruption, machines, automatons, skepticism and violence have resulted in despair, maladjustment, divorce, rape, illicit sex, melancholy and frequent emotional and psychological breakdowns. Nobody feels secure : even mothers feel scared of giving birth to their children, not to talk of providing security to the children already wanting in nutrition and prosperity. "Skepticism surreptitiously increased due to extreme paucity of faith;"[4] for, "man ceases to have faith even in his own self."[5] Luxurious life purchased through the power of money renders every one fragile in matters of righteous conduct. Sita, Anita's protagonist, is greatly confused not finding a fit society where she can breathe calmly and where she can give birth to her child. In a fit of anger and despondency she utters with a baffled conscience :

> Beginning to pace up and down, up and down, she would strain to catch the precise language of this invisible unquiet. "Where shall we go this summer ?" the words, appearing out of nowhere, worried her and plagued her. "Nowhere, nowhere," she made an effort to control herself and quietly replies. "I'll keep you safe inside. We'll go nowhere." Soothing herself, reassuring herself, she silenced the doubts and walked more slowly till there entered into her mind again those wavering, disconnected lines she could not place or capture :
>
> Even the slumberous egg, as it labours under the shell. Patienty to divide and sub-divide.[6]

Crisis of conscience and values (CCV) leads to a gradual decline in loss of faith, which obviously means a total "collapse of culture and civilization."[7] A civilization based on magnificent multi-storeyed buildings, perverted vision, sychopancy and cajolery with murder, infanticide, incest, theft and robbery galore practised by frauds, mountebanks, rough, raucous, rasping tatterdemalions is meaningless, is no better than a prison. Sita hates such a civilization of the metros, such a culture of the haves, "where there is no mental peace, no emotional richness."[8] Raman, Menaka and Karan love a city of flats and alleys, but Sita is extremely bored of it. Like Moses and Miriam, she prefers

Manori to a metro; a birdsong to a pop and zaz music. In fact, she has inherited from her father a genuine love for natural objects; for nature is a magic for her. A few incidents have been incorporated by Anita Desai to demonstrate how a sensitive soul like Sita may fell ill at ease in a city culture of Bombay. One very strange incident is "an exceptionally cruel drama that had aroused the crow world outside and made them churn the air, joyously screeching, then abash with rapacious claws and breaks at something that lay struggling in a mound of rust on the ledge that jutted out below their balcony."[9] It is, indeed, a black drama, a cruel drama as that of human beings voracious for power and pelf quite unmindful of their true self. In such a cruel city culture, Sita does not find any qualms of conscience left even in her husband, Raman, not to talk of her other neighbours. Even her own children — Menaka and Karan, appear to her as two machine procreations wholly bereft of conscience and finer feelings.

A very significant question closely related to the crisis of conscience and values (CCV) as raised in the novel, is the question of human survival, of noble existence and of dignified adjustment in the society, in the married life. Whether one should try to face the odds and buffets of life "with total submission and surrender to what exists,"[10] to what one's fate dictates one to endure or whether one should architect one's own future. Sita's survival, her existence, her adjustment are symbolical of the entire humanity. Her rebellious mood is indicative of thousands of sensitive souls who do not find peace in environs of distrust and corruption spawned by material advancements of all sorts. Her problem of maladjustment is symptomatic of hundreds of thousands of Sitas and Ramans, Deedars, Rekhas, Jivans, Moses, Miriams, Menakas and Karans do adjust but not Sitas. Is it a difference of temperaments ? Is it a problem of ego or sublimation to higher issues in life ? To a great extent, it is certainly the vision, the outlook that presents before us conscience, values, spectacles whereby to live, to exist, to survive, Sita clearly specifies for herself that life is a constant struggle, and the fiercer the struggle, the clearer, the more lasting will be the existence, the survival. Self-improvement, self-preservation is most human, but this will occur with our faith in our Creator. This is precisely the evolution of man taking place under the kind and benevolent superintendence of God. This is the kind of evolution of man, the golden mean hitherto preached by the seers and saints of all mankind for a noble survival. The instinct to endure challenges of life with a spirit of self-abnegation and commiseration is exactly the stoic instinct which asks Sita to synthesise between what is and what ought to be. Her assertion is quite conspicuous :

> Life is a challenge to one's instinct for self-improvement. As soon as you have grasped one rung, reach for the next... followed often, by a murmur of approval if not a roar of assent.[11]

But endurance without faith will not bear fruit :

> "No," came the soft, bubbling reply, made effervescent with something like laughter. "No student of chemistry can believe that.... But what have these islanders see ? Nothing. Where they have been ? Nowhere ? Their faith has never been shaken. And do you deny the therapeutic value of faith ? They believe gold is the best thing on earth — best because most valuable. So why not add a little to these powers with which I treat their boils and tumours ? They believe it does them good and then it really does.[12]

Emotional maturity is very necessary for leading a life of conscience and values (CCV). It is also equally essential for proper adjustment in the society. Wherever Sita commiserates with Raman for his problems in the factory, she feels fully adjusted; her emotional maturity guides her to be a co-sharer of her husband's misfortunes and discomfitures. In a mood of self-introspection, she ruminates, "His (Raman's) boys at home must have worried him, while he was at work in the factory which was not without its problems either.... He looked worn, much older than his years. Nor could he stay here, resting, as she was doing."[13] But in moments of frequent emotional breakdowns, Sita fails to respond to love and affection of her husband. She treats, in such moods of despondency and melancholy, emotional and affectionate reassurances, so frequently needed to sweeten life, as false promises and displays of weak brains : "It simply does not exist for her and should not make to exist. So she did not speak any words of love or reassurance to him. She looked away."[14]

The existing gulf between the old and the young : the looming hiatus between the experienced and the inexperienced, apparently looking like a generation gap, is partly because of psychological differences between the two ages and largely because of a crisis of values and conscience (CCV). Deedar is an incarnate of all those values which make life truly sublime. In his self-abnegating national devotion : in his commiseration with the downtrodden, he certainly stands apart from Menaka and Karan, who represent younger generation brought up in a metro culture with their well-beleaguered fads and caprices. Here arises the question of a crisis of conscience and values. Sita inherits from her father all that which enriches a life with higher values : Menaka inherits from her father (Raman) all that which makes life rational but bereft of all noble values. For the one, art is much preferable to science, for the other, science is more valuable than art.

Crisis of conscience is deepened all the more with frequent emotional and psychological breakdowns. Mistrust is spawned in an atmosphere surcharged with lust for power and material comforts. Where shall we go in such a state of confusion ? What shall we achieve by becoming rich with broken, maladjusted hearts ? How long shall we survive with bombs and nuclear weapons in our hands ? How shall the coming posterity remain alive with the Sword of Damocles of total devastation hanging on its head ? We have no compunction of conscience, no qualms of it left within us to ponder over a bit on this very vital issue. We are busy in spreading the vicious dragnets of material civilization founded on very weak basis of mistrust, maladjustment, greed and just. Sita feels utterly confused at the very prospect of such a degenerating civilization almost coming to naught :

> She folded her hands over it, frightened, certain now that civilization had been created by the god-like efforts of the few,

> in the face of a constant, timeless war of destruction that had begun with time and was now roaring around her, battering her and her fish-foetus so that survival seemed hopeless. How could civilization survive, how could the child ? How could she hold them whole and pure and unimpeached in the midst of this bloodshed. They would surely be wounded, fall and die.[15]

The theme of crisis of conscience and values (CCV) is not a sporadic, a passing reference but a recurrent, a pervading strain in all Anita Desai's monumental works. *Voices In The City* is a tale of struggle by men and women of Calcutta for higher life of conscience and values. Nirode, the protagonist, aspires for a life full of values. In fact, he solicits Dharma's friendship for "something unique, astonishing, valuable."[16] Monisha, another major character in the same novel, is enthralled by music and aesthetics. The recital of sitar transports her to a higher region of ecstasy and placid happiness. "I wander in this labyrinth at will and, blessedly, we never touch, merely remain in mystic communion with each other. I am willing to follow till I die."[17] Maya, the heroine of *Cry, The Peacock* is a love-sick and love-impoverished heart, who demands her rightful love from Gautama "I live my life for you…you are untouched…you shall never help me. It is all true one of us will win, the other must lose."[18]

Adit and Dev, Sarah, Emma Moffit and Christine Longford are the chief exponents of the East-West concord and discord in *Bye-Bye, Black Bird*. In Emma's opinion wise and wonderful people like Swami Binodananda of Hampstead should come and lecture to "us lesser beings, us little ones, and help us to expand, to set our sights on farther, on Eastern horizons."[19] Emma and Sarah together are in love with everything Indian — the Himalayan flowers, the bandits of Rajasthan, the henna pattern on the palms of ladies, the perfumes of attars, monsoons and famines, items of food and music of Bismillah Khan and Ravi Shankar. It is so because they have an urge to move towards the higher side of life.

Ila Das in *Fire On The Mountains* tries to rise to the higher planes of life notwithstanding her glaring pitfalls; for, "her screeching, horrid, anti-social sound was such as no human being should have possessed as it sent shivers down the spines...."[20] In *Clear Light of Day*, Bim has many qualms of conscience and a woman who cherishes values as dearer than anything else. Even the slightest occurrences hurt her deeply. Raja's departure for Hyderabad to lead a life of his own is less pricking to her sensitive soul than his (Raja's) letter directing her (Bim) to retain Hyder Ali's house after his demise : "You may continue to have it at the same rent, I shall never think of raising it or of selling the house as long as you and Baba need it."[21] In *The Village By The Sea*, Hari and Lila's struggle for survival is a moral, righteous struggle, which "seemed to tell Lila to be calm and happy and all would be well."[22]

Devan in, *In Custody*, loves poetry and art. He is enamoured of Nur and wants to be transported to a world of ecstasy and placid happiness through the paths of values. Good men are really inspiring to him and he, therefore, aspires for a contact with Nur : "Another realm it would surely be if his god dwelt there, the domain of poetry, beauty and illumination. He mounted... casting away the meanness and dross of his past experience."[23]

Weltschmerz is just "the opposite of crisis of conscience and values :"[24] it connotes "a universal sympathy for those who are suffering,"[25] who are wanting in money and means. Anita Desai's life-breath of her inner being appears to be Weltschmerz : for, the spectacle of suffering among human beings, animals, moths, insects and lower animated world magnificently and magnetically draws her mind and heart. A sensitive soul, as Desai is; a woman of conscience and values as she is, the very sight of human sorrow lacerates her heart as deeply as that of the insects snapping under the pull of the beak of a sparrow or any small bird. Though often, Weltschmerz provides her cosmic vision a tinge of deterministic pessimism as in most of her earlier novels such as *Cry, The Peacock* and *Voices In The City*, yet her sombre vision does remain unimpaired by a deep sense of helplessness as in Hardy's case. Her moral and psychological propinquities are more with George Eliot's than with Jane Austen's, Emile

Bronte's and Maria Edgeworth's. In fact, she endeavours to view life with the spectacles of "a True Greek,"[26] that is, steady and as a whole, not fragmented and punctured. After all, she delights to see human conscience intact and his life whole and untainted, despite all odds and discomfitures."[27]

Anita's shorter fiction is rich in the semiotic CCV circle : for, it offers more than her novels to the readers so far as the domain of feminine sensibilities is concerned, chiefly grounded on the CCV. Nanda Kaul in *Fire On The Mountain* conducts herself in a way that reminds one of the possibility of spiritual evolution of man; of the likely extinction of bestiality in man; and, of course, of the emerging potential that may deter him from indulging in whatever is subversive of the divine scheme of things. Anita Desai quotes a few lines from Gerard Manley Hookins in reference to what Nanda intuitively and instinctively feels to attain or, at the best, what she genuinely struggles to be on a moral plane :

> I have desired to go
> Where springs not fail,
> To fields where flies no sharp and sided hail,
> And a few lilies below.
> And I have asked to be
> Where no storms come,
> Where the green swell is in the havens dumb,
> And out of the swing of the sea.[28]

The same strain of moral questioning; of spiritual struggle; of righteous conduct or the semiotic CCV circle is copiously woven into the basic texture of her short stories, notwithstanding the fact that the approach adopted by Anita Desai here is that of a psychologist, of a writer who is keen to draw a psychograph_of her characters by exploring their true psyche rather doggedly. The life situations offered in her short stories are doubtless less significant; the thematic strain; too, rather scanty; the action not episodical either, nevertheless the type of exploration of mind and heart rendered possible is, of course, a remarkable artistic feat.

Before attempting at a detailed thematic classification of her short stories, let us know it clearly that she is an adept in creating an atmosphere through the use of words and of the mechanism of setting, that even apparently ordinary looking events become live with the feelings the writer really wants to create. In this respect, she deserves a befitting comparison she really deserves with Thomas Love Peacock, George Eliot, Thomas Hardy and George Meredith. On her diction, there is a palpable impact of scientific spirit with which she uses terse and technical words and expressions so that the effect of the created atmosphere is a finished one. Wherever she delineates a situation with external aides, she appears to adopt a scientific and technical style, which is thoroughly permeated with brevity, clarity, simplicity, technical presentation and utility. Her diction changes from one passage to another in accordance with the changing moods and caprices of her characters. This method of psychological delineation is not entirely a new device employed by Anita, but the fact remains that the finale with which she does it is certainly her preserve. If her novels are psychological studies on a macro level, her short stories are certainly on a micro one. If Sita, the protagonist in *Where Shall We Go This Summer* ? is a psychological study on a big scale, Pat in *Scholar and Gypsy*, (a famous short story) is a psychograph on a micro plane. Raman versus David, Karan versus Ravi, Monisha versus Mrs. Amul Bose are very many psychosomatic character portrayals on macro versus micro levels.

II

Though it is always hazardous to embark upon any scheme of thematic classification of Anita Desai's short stories : for, it is just limiting the sphere of her imaginative world, yet for an easier comprehension and better artistic appraisal, this sort of attempt is worth doing. As a matter of fact, some of her short-stories spell out the theme of temperamental differences, some wordily outlooks, some psychological insights, some miserable social plights, some pessimistic philosophies and some just sentimental outbursts. Nonetheless, all revolve round the semiotic circle of CCV. Whereas *Scholar and Gypsy* is a micro study of temperamental differences between David, the husband, and Pat, the wife : *Sala* is the study of the miserable plight of a talented artist, whose paintings never sell. If *The Accompanist* is the micro study of devotion of Mr. Misra, the Tanpura Player to master Ustad Rahim Khan, the famous musician, then *Pigeons at Daybreak* tells the tale of Mr. Amul Bose as a valetudinarian, an asthma patient, who feigns to feel ill even at ease. *Games at Twilight* is the study of a child psychology : for, Ravi does something childlike but also some which is certainly the domain of adults. His philosophical attitude resembles Harish's. Likewise *Surface Textures* studies the psychology of a man who suffers from low spirits of evasiveness and pusillanimity; who is an escapist and a shirker of responsibility. Another short story named *Pineapple Cake* is the portrayal of the pessimistic mood of Victor, on the one side, and the ironic and worldly behaviour of Mrs. Fernandez, on the other. *Private Tuition* gives an insight into the teacher psychology of Mr. Bose, who does some ridiculous acts in the presence of his pupils. *A Devoted Son* studies the attitudinal contrast between the father and his son. Dr. Rakesh, the son, thinks quite differently of old age from what his father does. *The Farewell Party* is a study of the sentimentality of the Ramans. Synoptically, the semiotic circle of CCV dominates the basic texture of Anita's lesser fiction.

The plot of her short stories is rather sleek, but it does not lack in coherence, symmetry and organic quality, though there are deviations here and there because of the CCV. *Games at Twilight* centres itself round Raghu and Ravi and other children, who usually play the game of hide and seek at twilight. One day, the children are busy playing the game. Raghu seeks others who are hiding themselves in secret places. Ravi hides himself in a corner of a garage, wherefrom through a crack he slides into shed. There Ravi is frightened to see very strange things — crawling moths and uncanny insects which are trying to eat one another. Raghu vaingloriously tries to find Ravi, who is still watching the drama of struggle among the lesser species. Ravi is thrilled at bit, but, at the same time, he is frightened also. Nevertheless, he feels he is securely placed and positioned. Ravi whistles and whacks his stick in despair. Raghu now touches the den so that he may emerge to be the football champion, which Raghu actually is at present. He does so with a sense of triumph. But while Ravi is doing all this, that is, struggling to touch the den and cherishing the hope to replace Raghu as football champion, other children cease to take any interest in the game of hide and seek. Moreover, it is now the twilight time and the pall of darkness deepens all around. The children are now playing a different game, not taking any notice of what Ravi has just done. His hope of the football championship is dashed to the ground. He then ruminates over the petty and puny actions of his own race — the children. He also develops a sense of helplessness over the insignificant position of his, he has now been destined to hold. He also treats his victory as inconsequential : for, nobody is now interested in him. The child psychology of Ravi has, thus, deftly been drawn alongwith that of Raghu and other children. The plot is, therefore, trivial, yet the presentation is wholly surcharged with a psychological delineation of the children, particularly of Ravi and Raghu. Seeing moths and insects, Ravi, develops a conspicuous strain of philosophy, and a "terrible sense of his insignificance,"[29] which is both appealing and also in tune with Anita Desai's general outlook on life and world.

Scholar and Gypsy is a short story of temperamental contrasts. It centres round an American couple named David and Pat, who have come to India to explore her mystery. David is certainly a scholar, whose interest in sociology entitles him to fame. Pat has entirely a different temperament and attitude from David's : for, she is interested only in visiting other countries. In a way, she is a globe trotter. She, in fact, comes of an American farmer family and loves to be free, unfettered and unchained by bonds of any sort. The environs of Delhi and Bombay appear to her as suffocating, teasing and nauseating. On their arrival in India, David finds Bombay an enchanting city, which Pat disapproves. On the contrary, she feels bored of "the wild jungles of the city of Bombay."[30] Even the climate of Delhi is suffocating to her, though she assures David that she will somehow tolerate it. "I must" she confides in David, "pull myself together,"[31] which she betrays later. Finding both Bombay and Delhi boring and nauseatic, she naturally recollects "the lost home, for apple trees and cows, for red barns and swallows — all that was innocent and sweet and lost, lost, lost."[32] Tired of life in India, she joins the hippies being sermonized by an Indian preacher who masquerades to cure "these seekers of *nirvan* and bliss"[33] by administering *bhang*[34] and who often ridicules them more than "meditating or discoursing on theology."[35]

In Delhi, Pat meets a number of people. She develops a sense of antipathy towards the people living in Delhi. Though educated only upto high school, she considers herself to be far superior to the well-educated Indians. For sometime, she associates herself with the social activities of Mrs. Sharma, who is a social worker herself of longstanding. Pat does not find social work congenial to her temperament and, as such, she gives it up in despair. Fat Indian ladies appear to her as terrifying and provocating as a red rag to a bull. Earlier, when she was in Bombay, she was given a party by the Gidwanis. Mrs. Gidwani is very courteous to Pat at the party, but her obesity drives Pat almost nauseatic. For her physical charm is more tempting than the simplicity of her heart. Pat fails to reciprocate the generous feelings of Mr. Gidwani, because of her wrong notions of virtue and vice, of moral and immoral.

In disgust, she goes to Manali in Kullu Valley (Himachal Pradesh) in order to feel happy. The natural beauty, the flora and fauna of this place provide happiness to her. She does a lot of shopping in the Tibetan quarters of Manali Bazaar, where she encounters many hippies roaming to and fro. She likes them, their way of life, which she likes. David regards his wife as a woman of blurred outlook. They enter into heated discussion on religion, hippies, Buddhists *et cetera* at this juncture. David ultimately fails to prevail upon his wife Pat and there ensues an exchange of heated arguments. Pat and David are now separated from each other.

Disgusted and broken-hearted, David returns to his country all alone. Pat joins hippies in search of spiritual solace and finally plans to be a Buddhist monk. With high hopes to get *nirvan*, she joins the Nasogi commune of hippies and tries to justify her stand to become a Buddhist monk. She also finds fault with her husband for unnecessarily impeding her religious and spiritual quest. Precisely, this short-story deals with the problem of adjustment where there is a lot of difference between the temperaments of husband and wife; where the husband is a scholar with a broader vision of life and the wife an incorrigible wanderer with a blurred vision of life, of good and bad, of virtue and vice.

The semiotic CCV circle comes to the fore in *Pigeons at Daybreak, Pineapple Cake, A Devoted Son* and in *The Farewell Party*. *Pigeons at Daybreak* is a story of the valetudinarian psychology of Amul Bose. A valetudinarian is one who walks even while sleeping. Amul Bose has been suffering from the ailment of asthma for long. His wife, Otima Bosu, is a highly devoted and sincere lady. Amul Bose is a type of asthma patient who has many real but so many imagined problems. Otima has to attend to all real and imagined problems of her husband in addition to all her tiring daily domestic choirs. A very committed and obedient lady as Otima is, she never harbours any grudge against any complaint of her husband whether real or imagined. On the receipt of information that there will be an electric break-down the whole night, Amul Bose's problems naturally multiply. Otima does not grudge. She tends him well and when her husband's breathing problem increases, she carries him to the roof-top, where Amul Bose is scared of his quarrelsome neighbour. Throughout the night, Otima massages Amul's body and there are some cool breezes also. This brings Amul some respite. Pigeons fly at the daybreak, and the flight of the pigeons also brings a temporary respite for Amul :

> Then, with a swirl and flutter of feathers, a flock of pigeons hurled upwards and spread out against the dome of the sky — opalescent, sunlit, like small pearls.... Then they disappeared into the soft, deep blue of the morning.[36]

In fact, Otima knows the psychology of her husband well. Even the slightest occasion enhances her husband's problems to the extent that Otima finds it extremely difficult to deal with these weak moments of her husband : "She knew how rapidly he would advance from imagined breathlessness into the first frightening stage of a full-blown attack of asthma."[37] Precisely, this short-story is a psychological story dealing with the imagined problems of an asthmatic patient like Amul Bose. This story also tells how a patient's wife like Otima tended her husband well. Pigeons figure in the story as emblems of peace and liberation. At the time of daybreak, the pigeons like other birds flutter in the air feeling free, liberated and happy. Amul usually sleeps at the daybreak getting a temporary respite from the night's suffocating air and physical groaning. Dwelling upon a very common-place life situation, Anita has raised a very serious question of an honourable existence being buffeted by such a predicament as that of Otima's.

Pineapple Cake, another memorable short-story by Anita Desai, is replete with a pathetic touch in the end. What one really does and what one indeed is, that is, the chasm between words and actions, is precisely the key-stone of this story. It is based on the child psychology, which is usually highly sensitive and delicate. Victor is the child who is given assurances a number of times to get a pineapple cake by his mother named Mrs. Fernandez, who is worldly-wise lady having an ostrich-like appetite and whose deeds don't tally with her promises. Victor does not feel assured of her mother ever providing him the pineapple cake. Carmen Maria, who hails from Goa and de Millo, who hails from Bombay are to marry and their wedding ceremony is to be performed in the Church, where Mrs. Fernandez will also join the marriage. Victor insists on accompanying her mother to the Church. Mrs. Fernandez agrees to carry Victor to the Church and provide him the pineapple cake on the condition if Victor behaves properly there. But at the time of wedding, a gentleman dies, which sends shocks to Victor, who is a child of very sensitive temperament. Instead of enjoying the pineapple cake, which is served at the time of wedding, Victor ruminates over the death of the gentleman. To him, the pineapple cake appears as if it were a corpse. He does not eat the pineapple cake, but his mother eats a lot. She is not at all sorry for the death of a man. Victor finds his mother's conduct at the party quite inconsistent with her utterances.

A Devoted Son is the short story of attitudinal clashes between a doctor son and his retired, aged father. Rakesh is a doctor who by dint of hard work gets a brilliant success in his medical profession. He rises to the rank of Director and now runs his own clinic in his father's house. His father is a retired assistant to a kerosene dealer. Rakesh is a very devoted son and obeys his parents more than ordinary sons and daughters. He takes utmost care of his father after the death of his mother. He is keen to see his father healthy and wishes him a long life. With this end in view, he prescribes many medicines, pills and powders to be used regularly by his father. Fried and spicy foods, sweets and irregular diets are completely restricted so that his father may keep fit. But the father is impatient to continue his old food habits. He prefers tasty dishes to simple ones. And when this is checked, he complains of his son's callous behaviour to his neighbour Bhatia. He also complains of his being starved. He prefers death to such restricted diet. In a word, here arises the clash of attitudes. Rakesh is guided by a very rational approach of a doctor whereas his father by a sentimental one of an aged, a retired man, for whom the great pleasure on the earth seems to be that of eating. Even a young devoted son and a very competent doctor like Rakesh is suspected of his aged father of tyranny and maltreatment.

The Farewell Party is a story of emotions, sentiments and human relations. Though artistically a powerful portrayal of human emotions, yet its plot is extremely weak. Third person universal observer pattern of narration which we find in this short story, does not, in fact, make it a story complete and perfect in all respects. The slender theme is gradually threaded around human passions and emotions. The Raman family is the centre of discussion by the neighbours. The guests who arrive profusely congratulate Mr. Raman on his getting promotion in the Indian Mercantile Company, which deals in the manufacture of cigarettes. The Raman family is known for their altruistic activities and their commiseration with the suffering people in the neighbourhood has become fairly proverbial. The farewell party is, therefore, arranged by the Ramans, and the guests and the neighbours are sumptuously entertained. All praise the Ramans. One after the other, the whole gathering becomes emotional : few of them highly sentimental and maudlin. Some start even weeping for the Ramans will not be seen by them in their neighbourhood on their transfer. Moreover, Mrs. Raman is a lady of some extrovert temperament. Her associations with any of her neighbours are quite deep and long-lasting. All this leads to an atmosphere in the farewell party surcharged with emotions and sentimentality. There was about it exactly that kind of sentimental euphoria that is generated at a ship-board party, the one given on the last night before the end of the voyage."[38]

Thus the above shorter fiction of Anita Desai has a predominant delineation of the feminine sensibility and that, too, firmly grounded on the semiotic circle of CCV. *The Accompanist, In Custody, Surface Textures, Private Tuition, Sale* and *Studies in The Park* may further be analysed under the overall impact of CCV.

The Accompanist deals with the life of those characters who feel happy to pursue the path of virtue and commitment. Devotion appears to be the key-note of this story and aspiration to be an elevated soul seems to be the underlying idea. Mr. Misra and Ustad Rahim Khan are two major characters round whom the whole story revolves. Mr. Misra is a devoted fellow. He is a Tanpura player to his master Ustad Rahim Khan, a noted musician. Mr. Misra is now thirty years of age. He comes to his master just as a boy of fifteen years. As a boy, Mr. Misra gets a lot of elementary knowledge of music as well as training from his own father, who himself is a musical instrument maker. Mr. Misra remains a life-long accompanist to his master. He admires his master very profoundly. He has unbounded love for his master and does not see any blemish in him (master) as a true and obedient pupil strictly in the traditional sense of the teacher-taught relationship.

In her monumental novel named *In Custody*, Anita Desai has dwelt upon the similar theme of relationship between a poet and his admirer. Devan is the idolater and Nur is the idol, as Mr. Misra is the idolater and his master is the idol. Deven has high aspirations for being transported and elevated with his contact with Nur : "Another realm it would surely be if his god dwelt there, the domain of poetry, beauty and illumination. He mounted...casting away the meanness and dross of his past existence...."[39] Devan, though a University Professor, finds his life monotonous because as an intellectual, he peels off a creative work like that of Nur's of its real substance. Imtiaz Begum's observation about the intellectuals of the Devan tribe is certainly far-reaching and raises a separate issue as to the exact relationship between a critic and an artist : "I know your kind jackals from the so-called universities that are really asylums for failures, trained to feed upon our carcasses."[40] Mr. Misra does not doubt at all the aesthetic excellence in his master's music, so Devan is perfectly enamoured of Nur's poetry and creativity. Ustad Rahim Khan thinks that creativity is the key-stone of music, so does Nur consider poetic inspiration just to be a component of creative process. The view both the Ustad Rahim Khan and of Nur perfectly tally with P.B. Shelley's on this count :

Like a poet hidden
    In the light of thought,
Singing hymns unbidden,
    Till the world is wrought
To sympathy with hopes and fears it needed not.[41]

But the bitter note on university teachers by Nur, the creative artist, is conspicuously missing in *The Accompanist* : for, Mr. Misra never finds his master Ustad Rahim Khan wanting in any respect. Nur's denunciation of a critic *vis-a-vis* a creative artist is noteworthy : "Do you think a poet can be grounded between stones, and bled, in order to produce poetry for you ?

You think you can switch on that mincing machine, and I will instantly produce for you a length of raw, minced meat that you can carry off to your professors to eat."[42] However, *The Accompanist* gives the germinal idea of the theme which Anita Desai has developed in her novel *In Custory* later. One of the salient features of this short story is the use of first person narrative.

Another important short story by Anita Desai is *Surface Textures*, which is the study of a person who shirks responsibility, behaves non-seriously and is unable to carry on his duties. Harish is the chief character in this story. He is a clerk in a supply office, earning a meagre salary not perhaps sufficient for his wife and children. He neglects his work; even in his office, he tries to do as little as possible. He is derelict of his duties and his superiors have no confidence in his efficiency and calibre. He deliberately invites action against him so that he may be sacked from his job. He finds himself incapable of enduring the burden of his family any longer. He wants to relinquish this world to become a *sadhu*. He considers the life of a *sanyasi* much far better than that of a clerk in an office, earning a meagre salary and surrounded by a number of worries and anxieties. He also thinks that once he becomes a *sadhu*, probably he will profoundly be respected by the people. He is an escapist and hence even his becoming a saint does not bring happiness to him. Being a lazy and idiot fellow by temperament, he brings discredit to the life of a saint and puts a blot on sainthood by his various acts of omission and commission. His *surface texture* of incompetence and indolence, of indifference and antipathy, boredom and tedium to him in office, are now equally impeding his new life of a *sadhu*.

In fact, this short story is an attack on evasiveness and pusillanimity, cowardice and irresponsibility of a person. Harish's sainthood prospers, if at all, on utter neglect of his family and relatives. The satiric vein runs throughout the story. Its tone is slightly bitter and more biting than that of other short-stories.

Private Tuition is a psychological short story, which deals with the psychology of a school teacher while engaged in private tuitions. Mr. Bose undertakes tuitions to free his family from pecuniary strains.[43] Students usually behave in a strange manner when their teacher teaches them. But with Mr. Bose, there are many other problems. The place where he imparts instruction is open to the view of all. Pupils know it well as to what Mrs. Bose is doing at present in the kitchen. Radio is also on, which distracts the attention of his students. Moreover, Mr. Bose's children are very naughty. They do such activities as also divert concentration of students. There is a lot of clatter of utensils, rolling of other domestic items and the students laugh in their sleeves. Mr. Bose is upset; his pupils enjoy the situation. Added to all these, is the problem of certain students who need special care. Mr. Bose feels that teaching a brahmin priest's son is easier, but to teach Bengali to Upneet (the girl in flamboyant garments, always giggling with irresponsible laughter) makes Mr. Bose very much self-conscious.

Sale is a study of an artist whose paintings never sell. He is a painter gifted with unusual talents and calibre, but his misfortune is that nobody has the capacity to appreciate his creation in an unbiased manner. He complains of the degenerating aesthetic taste of the persons. Once it so happens that three visitors come and make a long perusal of his paintings. They ask a number of questions from the artist ranging from professional to private affairs. However, the painter answers them well and he is quite hopeful that the visitors may purchase his paintings. Being encouraged a little by the interest shown by the visitors in his paintings, he tells them various specifications of his paintings in detail : "One cannot pinpoint any school, any style — one can only admit oneself in the presence of a continuous and inspired act of creation."[43] But despite all his pleadings and persuasions, the painter fails to prevail upon the visitors : for, they do not find anything substantial in his paintings. As a matter of fact, Anita Desai has projected an idea of neglect of artists in the society through this short story. She considers the declining aesthetic taste of the people wholly responsible for the plight of the artists. Vulgar tastes demand vulgar arts and Anita Desai does not ditto the idea that an artist should ever make any compromise with the standard of his art just for the sake of money.

Studies in the Park deals with the genuine problems of a student named Suno who is preparing for his I.A.S. examinations. He does not find a conducive atmosphere for studies at his home : for, there is disturbances of all sorts. When he concentrates on his studies, his father listens to the news in six languages. His mother clutters in the kitchen, constantly pressing her glass of sugared milk on Suno. Not only this, other children make an intolerable noise rendering the whole atmosphere rent up with chattering and loud talking. He is completely enervated, but there is none to commiserate with him. To add to his plight, the water tap remains constantly splashing. His concentration on his studies is certainly impossible in such a disturbed atmosphere. He prefers a corner of a restaurant to his home, where too, the proprietor and the waiter, are both garrulous, talkative and glib liars. He then selects a park for his studies, but there too he finds a number of students already positioned with grimaced faces — some mentally dying, some physically constipated, some demented whereas some with wide lines of worries and anxieties writ large on their pale faces.

Suno feels disappointed, but his disappointment is transformed into hope and optimism, when he sees a pale, white, suffering Muslim lady in the lap of an elderly gentleman, who is looking like a benevolent scholar with a long beard and affectionate face. The lady is being tenderly caressed by the gentleman and there is an aura of immortal solace and succour around them. Suno feels that the burden of studies is decidedly useless in the face of love and kindness. Suno treats himself as a completely liberated soul at this juncture at the sight of the lady and the old man.

Almost a similar scene is there in *Where Shall We Go This Summer* ? where Sita feels liberated at the sight of a pale, weak Muslim lady being loved intensely by her anxious husband. The lady is about to collapse, but the husband embraces his hands around her in order to provide her strong protection. Sita regards these moments of love and sympathy as truly divine attributes and life spent during these fractions of time as an immortal bliss. For sometime, she forgets all her anxieties and cares about Menaka and Karan : for, she treats life as not a lengthy span of right and wrong actions, but as a little but beautiful, resplendent but satisfying experience. Raman, her husband, appears to her not as something to be hated and despised, but as a life-partner of very low and dull sensibilities. Her father, Deedar, appears to her truly an incarnate of virtue and her overall view of life is that of a one who wants to fight the challenges with high spirits.

On Raman's insistence to reveal that event when Sita felt extremely happy in her life, Sita utters : "It was in the Hanging Gardens," she recalled, slowly pacing beside him. "One evening I took the children there. We were walking about. Near a tall hedge, on a bench, I saw a woman stretched out. A Muslim woman — she was wrapped up in her black *burqa*. Then she raised her veil and I saw her face. I saw her face lying in those black folds like a flower — a dead-white flower. Like a Persian lily, or a tobacco flower at night...fatally anemic — or fatally tubercular. Her head...lay in the lap of an old man.... He had spectacles and a long grey beard. He looked down at her and caressed her face — so tenderly, so tenderly.... But the man and the woman never looked at anyone else, they looked at each other with such, such a strange, strange expression — I can't forget it. I can't explain it. Tender, loving eyes, ...quite divine...."[44]

Sita is the protagonist in *Where Shall We Go This Summer* ? Suno is the main character in *Studies in the Park*. The former is Anita Desai's novel, whereas the latter is her short-story. Suno is just a micro, a short sketch of Sita : for, Anita Desai postulates her vision or outlook of life through Suno on a micro plane, whereas through Sita's on a macro level. However, Suno is the prototype of Sita in espousing a particular view for which Anita Desai is generally known. This view resembles Weltschmerz's, which means that notwithstanding a gloomy position of man in the scheme of things in this world, it is always worthwhile to struggle. This view is often mistaken as a pessimistic view, but Anita Desai's over all vision of life is not merely to feel helpless in the face of realities of life, but to face them boldly. Harish in *Surface Textures* is an escapist and his entire being just a psychograph of evasive personality — a personality of pusillanimity. He invites disciplinary action so that he can get rid of his family burdens and also to become a *sadhu* in order to lead a life where he has to do nothing but to prosper on other's earnings. This is a negative side of life, which Anita decidedly hates.

So far as the characterisation of Desai's stories is concerned, it has both plus and minus points of its own. But it has the dominant impact of the CCV. For example, the character-sketches of Dr. Rakesh in *A Devoted Son*; of Mr. Misra in *The Accompanist*; of David in *Scholar and Gypsy*; of Ravi in *Games at Twilight*; of Suno in *Studies in the Park*; and of Mr. Raman in *The Farewell Party* have many traits in common. More or less, these human sketches weigh more towards good than to bad. They are often obsessed with very probing questions of how to exist; how to survive in a society inhabited by frauds and mountebanks. David is a good tempered scholar of sociology but he is constantly tormented by Pat. Dr. Rakesh wishes his father well, but his aged, diabetic father has a very peevish temperament and does not want to remain physically fit despite Rakesh's best prescriptions. Mr. Misra wants to adore his mentor does not matter it costs him his life-long devotion and commitment. Ravi wants to see deeper meaning in life : for, he looks upon his childish play just a very trite source of happiness. In his philosophical introspection, the child broods over the big problems of life and finds happiness, in a true Hardyian vein, just an occasional episode in the general drama of pain. Mr. Raman has an altruistic motto : for, he finds great pleasure to feeding and entertaining others. In his altruistic pursuit, his wife Mrs. Raman fully cooperates and on their promotion during the course of a party, everybody present feels unhappy to be separated from a couple really lovable and sociable.

Raghu, Ravi, Victor and Suno are all children depicted as heroes in *Games at Twilight, Pineapple Cake* and *Studies in the Park* respectively. Their character-portrayal constitutes a very convincing child psychology. Ravi, Victor and Suno — all have many common personality traits : for, all of them have an introvert type of personality : all possess a pessimistic view of life : all do want to live by idealism; and, moreover, all of them doggedly want to know the real meaning of life. Suno finds complete happiness not in studies of dry subjects of science and dead details of history, but in sights full of commiseration and love. Tired of his home atmosphere which is full of din and clatter; getting bored of talkative restaurant proprietor and greedy waiter, he goes to the park fully crammed with all sorts of people, where the sight of a Muslim lady suffering from a terminal disease resting in the lap of an old, commiserate scholar gentleman is highly soothing to Suno. In portraying child psychology, Anita Desai seeks to have closer affinity with Charles Dickens whose child heroes such as David and Pip are immortal creations from the point of view of child psychology.

Anita Desai's female characters have their own specific identity in her short-stories. They fully exhibit their female sensibilities. Mrs. Fernandez in *Pineapple Cake* is less educated but more worldly wise lady. She is used to the realities of life. At the time of wedding of Carmen Maria and de Millo, she eats a lot of pineapple cake, though a gentleman has just died and his dead body appears as if it were a corpse to her son Victor. But she satisfied her lust for eating and does not philosophise like her son. She is, therefore, practical out and out and has nothing to do with the contemplative side of life. Mrs. Bose in *Private Tuition* is ill-cultured and does not possess sophisticated manners. Mr. Bose is scared of her ill-manners as much as he is bored of his students. She makes a lot of noise in the kitchen, when her husband is busy teaching his pupils. She is also incapable of controlling her children who start fighting the moment Mr. Bose undertakes private tuitions. She brings disgrace to her husband in the presence of his students and makes his situation very precarious. Mrs. Raman in *The Farewell Party* is a lady of good taste and good manners. She is always ready to help others. She considers others' help as more significant than glorification of the self. That is why others feels unhappy when the Ramans go elsewhere on their promotion. Everyone in the neighbourhood appreciates her for her good deeds and cooperative nature. Pat in *Scholar and Gipsy* is a lady of very independent nature. She does not like Bombay and Delhi. She goes to Manali, where she prefers the hippie cult to the accompaniment of her husband to America. She believes in the seamy side of life more than its realities. But Otima Bosu in *Pigeons at Daybreak* is a very devoted lady.

Rakesh in *A Devoted Son*, Mr. Misra in *The Accompanist*, and David in *Scholar and Gispy* are fully grown characters and they are, in a word, embodiments of virtue and good; for, Rakesh does everything possible to keep his father happy : David, likewise proves to be a devoted husband : and Mr. Misra regards his master Ustad Rahim Khan as his God. Each one of them tries to search a meaning — a gainful meaning, indeed, in life. Amul Bose in *Pigeons at Daybreak* is a valetudinarian and he constitutes a class apart of his own.

Thus Anita has drawn the character-sketches of children, men, women, valctudinarians, mothers and wives in her short-stories under the impact of CCV. Her child characters are very much convincing particularly from the point of view of psychosomatic delineations. Her sketches of full grown men and women too are quiet convincing; but her treatment of good through these characters is more appealing than that for vicc. Her sketches of wives is certainly her forte : for, they are paragons of virtue not because that they have been made so intentionally but because their quest for higher values is extra-ordinarily convincing and of a universal appeal.

Her stores may have a thin substance, but even the thin substance that is there is certainly the substance, the elixir of life

(CCV) that sustains us. In fact, her characters have a unique capacity to move upward towards the higher side of life, notwithstanding the fact that they miserably fail many a time while doing so. This tendency tilts more towards the good, the virtuous, which is an underlying strain even in her novels. For example, Gautam in *Cry, The Peacock* constantly endeavours to follow the path of detached actions, as his wife Maya truly explains : "He is fit to attain immortality who is serene and not affected by these sensations, but is the same in pleasure and pain.... When he completely withdraws his senses from sense objects as the tortoise withdraws its limbs, then wisdom becomes well established."[45]

In *By-By Black Bird*, Adit and Dev, Sarah and Christine Langford — all struggle to seek a meaning in life in their own ways. There are moments of transformation and transmogrification in their life : there are moments of moral bliss which they find more valuable than anything else. On his departure to India, having a changed outlook, Adit feels, "as though he saw the Union Jack being lowered in sadness at his departure and saw the Indian tricolour rising upon the opposite horizon."[46] In *Where Shall We Go This Summer* ? Sita and Deedar ruminate over the intricate issues of life rather doggedly and try to find a moral answer to them. Sita like Otima Bosu feels cast down very frequently because she fails to find an appropriate answer to serious puzzles of life. Sita's postulate about life is worth consideration : "Life is a challenge to one's instinct for self-improvement. As soon as you have grasped one rung, reach for the next...followed, often, by a murmur of approval if not a roar of assent."[47]

The same questioning strain to find a real meaning in life is copiously traceable in *Fire On The Mountain, Clear Light Of Day, In Custody* and in *The Village By The Sea*. Had Nanda Kaul had the gift of religious grace, spiritual faith, had the rains come in time, there would have been no fire on the mountains. Raja, Bim and Tara see clear light of the day because they feel themselves spiritually and morally more evolved than other characters. *The Village By The Sea* is concerned with the problem of survival and change keeping moral proclivity alive and untainted. Despite the fact that Hari and Lila lead a life of want, their spirits have not been drooped from the point of morality : "Their belongings, in tin and cardboard boxes, were perched on top of bricks and stones along the edge. Some bundles hung from the bamboo poles that acted as rafters."[48] Yet they remain undaunted by their life of want and misery and try hard to exist, to survive. *In Custody* deals with Devan's higher aspirations to become a great creative artist and poet. His adoration of Nur is exactly the same as that of Mr. Misra for his master Ustad Rahim Khan in *The Accompanist.*

The above appraisal of Anita Desai's short stories reveals the fact that she is a very conscious craftsman and assiduously works to produce the desired effect grounding her plots on the CCV. One very significant point about her excellence as a short-story writer is that her art is certainly a process of growth. Only time will tell as to what will be the final stock of variety and diversity. As in her novels, one encounters a variety of themes changing from one novel to another, likewise in her short stories (only eleven studied in the only volume of her short stories named *Games at Twilight and Other Stories* hitherto extant) form a good variety. If *Games at Twilight, Pineapple Cake*, and *Studies in the Park* form one group dealing with child psychology, then *A Devoted Son, The Accompanist, Sale*, and *Scholar and Gypsy* form another category which deals with the problem of finding a meaningful existence in life. *Surface Textures* stands apart from other short stories forming an independent group : for, it deals with the problem of wilful negligence of duty and of escapism. *Private Tuition* deals with the child psychology *vis-a-vis* a teacher and this story may also be listed as forming its own separate category. Likewise, *The Farewell Party* cannot be bracketed with any other short story on the basis of its theme. *Pigeons at Daybreak* deals with the psychology of a valetudinarian, and hence, this story, too, forms its own separate category on the basis of its plot and the foregoing thematic treatment is based more on the similarity of underlying idea than on anything else.

The people inhabiting the world of her short-stories are children, fully experienced men and worldly-wise women, old fathers and mothers, artists devoted sons and daughters, foreign ladies proselytizing into hippies *et cetera*. But the children such as Raghu, Victor, and Suno appear to be more convincing than Harish, Pat, and David. Rakesh is a devoted doctor and an obedient son, but his father is an old man of very peevish temperament. Mrs. Fernandez and Pat have not convincingly been drawn : for, they certainly lack an organic quality ennobling them to grow in accordance with the development in the story.

Desai has a marvellous mastery over language and style, fit to delineate a feminine sensibility. Her diction is highly sensitive, responsive, sensuous, but nervous. Her style is fit for all modes of thought and tension. Whether she describes the morose Raghu or pessimistic Victor, or the derelict Harish, her language always catches the right words. As in her novels, the subtle nuances and shades have nicely been presented, so in her short stories, the thoughts, the modes and the tensions have excellently been narrated with the force and deftness of a big creative writer.

Her range of vision is certainly limited : for, most of her plots are sleek and airy dealing with the life of cities. The Hardyian touch of external details, the Meredithian effect of psychological growth, the Dickensian force of external specifications are commonly and often even conspicuously absent in her short stories and novels.

Despite all these limitations, Anita Desai has immense potential, as a short story writer. As in her novels the Weltschmerz outlook characterises the whole treatment, likewise, in her short stories, her outlook on life is one that resembles *in toto* the Greek view of life, which clearly means that she has an unflinching faith in the inherent goodness of man and has nothing to do with the bestiality hidden in him. She is an incorrigible optimist : for, she is used to see life "steady and as a whole" which the Greeks were usually wont to. Her final vision of life seems to dictate : "*Live Naturally*", which means that we should try to develop our adaptability as much as possible so that in the struggle for existence, we may survive for long. Sita's character precisely synthesises what Anita wants to convey by natural living. Sita compromises between *What is* and *What ought to be* :[49] the struggle before us and the efforts which we should harness to surmount the struggle : "Life had no periods, no stretches. It simply swirled around, muddling and confusing, leading nowhere."[50] This is, in fact, the sum total of the semiotic circle of CCV. And, indeed, this approach to her novels and shorter fiction may truly point out Anita Desai's place as a forerunner to fight for the cause of Women's Liberation Movement (WLM) in India and abroad.[51]

REFERENCES

1. Ram, Atma. Interviews *with Indian English Writers* (Calcutta : Writers Workshop, 1983), pp. 24-25.
2. Desai, Anita. *Voices in the City* (Delhi : Orient Paperback, 1965), p. 123.
3. "The Ideology of Romanticism," in R.F. Gleckner and G.E. Enscoe, eds., *Romanticism : Points of View* (New Jersey : Prentice-Hall, 1970), p. 170.
4. *Cry the Peacock*, p. 9.
5. Sharma, S.D. *Thomas Love Peacock As a Novelist*, SPH, Delhi, Vol. I, Edn. I, 1986, p. 73.
6. Sharma, S.D., *Thematic Dichotomy of Writings in Indian English, Indology and Culture,* PBD Publication, Delhi, Vol. I, 1985, p. 30.
7. Desai, Anita, *Where Shall We Go This Summer* ? Vikas Publishing House Pvt., Ltd., Delhi, 1975; p. 93 therein after referred to as VPH). The protagonist (Sita) echoes the same views elsewhere too. "Sita felt a spasm of fear at her bravado, her wild words, her impulsive actions that had flung them allonge onto this island surrounded by wild seas. It was no place in which to give birth.... The more physical details of the matter crowded her mind. Usually she repressed them with an agonized determination but the rain drumming, thrumming, pouring all about her locked her in, locked her up, forced her to turn on herself" (VPH, p. 82).
8. Sharma, S.D. *Perspectives on Creativity* (ed.), Proceedings of the National Symposium, Faculty of New Education, G.B. Pant University, Pantnagar-263145, Vol. I, Edn. I, 1989, p. 152.
9. Sharma, S.D. *Longinus on the Sublime*. PBP Publication, Delhi, Vol. I, Edn. III, 1990, p. 190.

10. *Ibid.*, p. 25. (Sita makes similar socking cries seeping big buildings inhabited by murderers and frauds : "Crows formed the shadow civilization in that city of flats and alleys. She watched them from the balcony, hopping clannishly about the rocks on which the sea broke, scrambling to catch a rotten fish or scraps of edible flotsam left by the waves to stink in the sun. They even sat on the ledges and balcony rails of the flats, waiting for lazy cooks to throw out a bucketful of kitchen garbage into the alley — scraps were caught by them in mid-air, expert for all their clownishness, tattered wings holding them aloft as they twisted and flapped to get the largest bigs.") p. 25.
11. Sharma, S.D. *Semantics and Syntax,* PBD Publication, Delhi, Vol. I, Edn. I, 1990, p. 19.
12. *Ibid.*, p. 65 (Sita elsewhere feels : "She felt the long, straight monotonous track of her life whip itself round her in swift circles, perhaps a spiral, whirling around and around till its very lines dissolved and turned to a blur of silver, the blurred silver of mirror-like windowpanes. All was bright, all was blurred, all was in a whirl. Life has no periods, no stretches. It simply swirled around muddling and confusion, leading, nowhere.") p. 112.
13. *Ibid.*, p. 59 (Sita's faith in the supernatural powers of Manjori may appear to be most unscientific, but it often works wonders. Note her faith in the magical world of the island : "If reality were to be borne, then illusion was the only alternative. She saw that island illusion as a refuge, a protection. It would hold her baby safely unborn, by magic. Then there would be see — it would wash the frenzy out of her, drown it. Perhaps the tides would lull the children, too, into smoother, softer beings. The grooves of the trees would shade them and protect them.") p. 72.
14. *Ibid.*, p. 133 (OPB edition).
15. *Ibid.*, p. 41.
16. *Ibid.*, p. 37 (VPH edition).
17. *Voices In The City*, p. 44 (OPB edition).
18. *Ibid.*, p. 123.
19. *Cry, The Peacock,* p. 114.
20. *Bye-Bye, Black Bird,* p. 48.
21. *Fire On The Mountain,* p. 118.
22. *Clear Light of Day,* p. 27 (Penguin Books, 1980).
23. *The Village By The Sea,* p. 9 (William Heinemann, London, 1982).
24. *In Custory,* p. 40.
25. Sharma, S.D. *Dr. Johnson's Preface to the Plays of Shakespeare*, PBD Publication, Delhi, Vol. I, Edn. III, 1986, p. 83.
26. Sharma, S.D. *Makers of Criticism*, PBD Publication, Delhi, Vol. I, Edn. I, 1985, p. 201.

27. Sharma, S.D. Aristotle's Poetics, SS Publication, Delhi, Vol. I, Edn. II, 1984, p. 170.
28. This paper was initially accepted for presentation at the thirty seventh session of AIETC held at Kohlapur (India) on November 24-26, 1988.
29. Desai, Anita. *Fire On The Mountain* (Penguin Books, 1982), p. 58.
30. *Games at Twilight and Other Stories*, first published by W. Heinemann, London, 1978, Penguin Books, 1982, p. 8.
31. *Scholar and Gipsy,* p. 112.
32. *Ibid.,* p. 112.
33. *Ibid.,* pp. 112-13.
34. *Ibid.,* p. 132.
35. *Ibid.,* p. 131.
36. *Ibid.,* p. 132.
37. *Pigeons at Daybreak,* p. 109.
38. *The Farewell Party,* p. 94.
39. *In Custody,* p. 40 (London : W. Heinemann, 1984).
40. *Ibid.*
41. Palgrave, F.T. *The Golden Treasury*, Macmillan, 1969, p. 275.
42. *In Custody*, p. 156.
43. *Private Tuition,* p. 9.
44. *Sale*, p. 43.
45. *Where Shall We Go This Summer* ? (VPH edition, 1975), pp. 105-6.
46. *Cry, The Peacock*, Orient Paperbacks, Delhi, 1980, pp. 108-9. (Maya also struggles to find a meaning in life. Her dialogue with Gautam is worth quoting : "I live my life for you.... You are untouched.... You shall never help me. It is all true one of us will win, the other must lose.") *Ibid.*, p. 114.

    In Voices In The City, Nirode and Dharma struggle for higher values of life. Nirode finds life in city boring with "muddy river air" superadded by "exhilaration, determination and pride." p. 11.
47. *Bye-Bye Black Bird*, p. 257.
48. *Where Shall, We Go This Summer* ? p. 65 (Elsewhere, too, Sita utters similar words which reflect upon his delving deep into a quest for higher issues : "Everyone around her winced — she saw them wincing at her harshness, her wildness that they so dreaded. But she could not stop herself now, not even Karan's sake. Their betrayal had torn her open with such violence, now violence poured from her like blood. In it was also the shame, the disappointment : he had not come to see her, to fetch her, as she had supposed : he had come because Menaka had called him. He had betrayed her too. They had all betrayed her. Why ?") *Ibid.*, p. 97.

49. *The Village by The Sea*, p. 116.
50. *Where Shall We Go This Summer*, p. 112.
51. Anita Desai's Shorter Fiction also appeared in *SICIESS*, Delhi, 1991, pp. 25-44; '*Where Shall We Go This Summer* ? A Crisis of Conscience and Values' published in *Quest*, Vol. V, No. 3, December, 1991, pp. 1-9.

5

Jerome David Salinger : *The Catcher in the Rye* and *Franny and Jooey*

THIS CHAPTER deals with Jerome David Salinger's *The Catcher in the Rye* and *Franny and Jooey* in two parts. The first part is based on the *Catcher in the Rye* and the second one on *Franny and Jooey.* Salinger is regarded as the harbinger of the New Yorker School of Fiction. It is true that eminent American novelists such as John Cheever, Irwin Shaw and Edward Newhouse also were the great practitioners of the New Yorker School of Fiction, yet Stalinger, by virtue of his contribution, deserves a much higher place in the niche of fame than these novelists.

Being a spokesman of the mid-fifties in America, Salinger's works truly and faithfully represent the aftermath of the World War II, manifested in social disintegration, loss of moral and ethical values. *The Catcher in the Rye* and *Franny and Jooey* must be studied in this height.

I

James E. Miller treats *The Catcher in the Rye* as "a deceptively simple, enormously rich book whose sources of appeal run in deep and complexly varied veins. The very young are likely to identify with Holden and to see the adult world in which he sojourns as completely phony and worthless — the book thus becomes a handbook for rebels and a guide to identification of squares."[1] In fact, *The Catcher in the Rye* is Salinger's *magnum opus,* which has been interpreted by the critics in a number of ways. To Arthur Mizener, this novel is a failure, whereas George Steiner considers it a great "literary masterpiece — a classic novel of adolescence."[2] If *The Catcher in the Rye* is "an adolescent revolt against the adult world,"[3] it is also looked upon as "a modern version of the Orestes — Iphigenia myth."[4] In one sense, it is a quest not only for the preservation of innocence and for ideal love, but also an incessant struggle for maintaining identity. The central character of the novel — Holden Caulfield — is essentially an American adolescent, who encounters all odds of life, finally resulting in a deep psychological crisis and, subsequently, a desperate search for personal relationships and identity in the society.

Synoptically, the thematic strands in *The Catcher in the Rye* are apparently not episodical. The entire action of the novel takes just forty-eight hours in the life of Holden Caulfield, "who flungs out of Pency Prep in Pennsylvania and starts out on the terrible journey to his home in New York."[5] The journey turns out to be a very sad experience for Holden, because he had to face not only the inclemency of weather but also unbearable indignation at the hands of his school teacher and seniors. In Holden's own words :

> ...This teacher that taught biology, Mr. Zambesi struck his head out of this window in the academic building and told us to go back to the dorm and get ready for dinner. If I get a chance to remember that kind of stuff, I can get a good-buy when I needed one — at least, most of the time I can...any way as soon as I got my breath back I ran across Route 204. It was icy as hell and I damn near fell down....
>
> "Holden!" Mrs Spencer said. "How lovely to see you! Come in, dear! Are you frozen to death?"[6]

Holden's roommate at Pency is a youth named Stradlater and his next door boy is another youth named Ackley. Holden continues his journey to New York, where he meets the mother of one of his classmates and gives her an erroneous impression about her son. Assuming a *non de plume* in a big city, Holden then comes in contact with three female tourists, all naive greenhorns in a night club. Next night, at another night club he comes in contact with a friend of his brother named D.B. Back at his hotel, the brutish elevator boy named Maurice arranges a meeting between him and Sunny, a girl without strong moral qualms of conscience. The girl demands for ten dollars instead of five and there ensues an acrimonious skirmish between Holden and Maurice.

Tired of his journey, full of odds and oddities, Holden ends his odyssey of the first day. The next day, Holden meets two nuns, whom he gives the remaining part of ten dollars of his money. He then passes a poor, sunday-dressed family whose little boy is singing — "If a body catch a body coming through the rye." He then goes to the Museum of Natural History. In the afternoon, he takes his old girl friend Sally Hayes to see a play, quarrels with her over his proposal to run away and is left alone. Then he goes to Rodio City Music Hall and sees a phony movie after which he meets Carl Luce, an old schoolmate. Carl Luce does not give company to him for long and Holden is again left all alone in a very meloncholic mood. Broken hearted and despondent, as he is now, Holden is sozzled with wine and finally invites Sally, who rebukes him for his childish actions. Holden now meets his sister named Phoebe. He stays with her sister for some hours and then finally decides to leave for New York.

He stays with his former English teacher named Mr. Antolini, who is fairly handsome and young. He is a believer in strict discipline and readily faces challenges in life. Holden admires some of Antolini's qualities with full-throated ease :

> Mr. Antolini was a pretty young gug, not much older than my brother D.B., and you could kid around with him without losing your respect for him. He was the one that finally picked up that boy that jumped out of window I told you about, James Castle. Old Mr. Antolini felt his pulse and all, and then he took off his coat and put it over James Castle and carried him all the way over to the infirmary....[7]

Holden discusses with Antolini a variety of topics including his own capacity to appreciate literature while he was a student. He reminiscences with a nostalgic strain :

> "Oh, I passed English all right. It was mostly literature, though. I only wrote about two compositions the whole termy," I said.

> "I flunked Oral Expression, though. They had this course you had to take, Oral Expression. That I flunked."
> "Why ?"
> "Oh, I don't know," I didn't feel much like going into it. I was still feeling sort of dizzy or something, and I had a helluva headache all of a sudden. I really did.... It's this course where each boy in class has to get up in class and make a speech.... Spontaneous and all. And if the boy digresses at all, you're supposed to yell 'Digression' at him as far as you can. It just about drove me crazy. I got an *F* in it."[8]

In fact, Holden cherishes a nauseating feeling for that type of teacher whose actions sound hollow and whose preachings prove to be a big sham. In his free, frank and candid discussion with Antolini, Holden does not agree to his views on the contemporary American life and society. He knows it very well that his teacher, though a well-intentioned gentleman, is an inveterate drunkard and that he himself does not confirm to the high ideals of discipline and decorum in his own personal life. Despite his being a revellious against rigid educational trammels imposed on the teenagers and the adolescents in schools and colleges, Holden patiently listens to Antolini's quoting from a famous psychoanalyst named Wilhelm Stekel, "The mark of the immature man is that he wants to die nobly for a cause, while the mark of a mature man is that he wants to live humbly for one."[9] In the same vein, Mr. Antolini makes Holden understand, "Many, many men have been just as troubled morally and spiritually as you are right now."[10]

Emphasizing on the paramountcy of perseverence, Antolini makes him understand further — "that only educated and scholarly men are able to contribute something valuable to the world. It's not so. But I do say that educated and scholarly men, if they're brilliant and creative to begin with — which, unfortunately, is rarely the case — tend to leave infinitely more valuable records behind them then men do when they are merely brilliant and creative. They tend to express themselves more clearly, and they usually have a passion for following their thoughts through to the end. And — most important — nine times out of ten they have more humility than the unscholarly thinker.

Mr. Antolini refers to Sally Hayes and Jane Gallagher, whom Holden is well acquainted with. During the course of conversation, Holden talks to Mrs. Antolini too. In brief, Holden is now fully exhausted and wants to sleep. His teacher showers fatherly affection on him, which is misunderstood by Holden. Engulfed in ignorance and lacking in worldly experience, as Holden himself is by now, he decides to leave Antolini's apartment on a flimsy pretext. The dialogue which ensues is really the one in *The Catcher in the Rye* that points to a direction leading to light from darkness in the life of Holden :

> "What the hellya *doing* ?" I said. "Nothing!
>
> I'm simply sitting here, admiring —"
>
> "What're ya doing anyway ?" I said over again.
>
> I didn't know what the hell to say — I mean
>
> I was embarrassed as hell.
>
> I know more damn perverts, at schools and all, than anybody you ever meet....
>
> "I left my bags and all at the station...."
>
> I was shaking like a mad man. I was sweating, too. When something perverty like that happens, I start sweating like a bastard. That kind of stuff's happened to me about twenty times since I was a kid. I cannot stand it.[11]

It is now Monday and Holden, after leaving Antolini's apartment, is again uncertain as to where he should go. However he walks over to Lexington and takes the subway down to Grand Central. He sleeps till around nine O'clock and at the dawn of the day, he decides to write a note to Phoebe and hands over that note at her school. He informs Phoebe that he will wait for her at noon near the Metropolitan Museum. While waiting for Phoebe, he visits the depth of Egyptian tomb. Looking at various old and dilapidated buildings, he is filled with an apprehensive nature and inquisitive temperament. He reflects upon various conundrums of life. The more he thinks about them, the more he feels confused and helpless. Waiting tirelessly of Phoebe, he feels fatigued. In his own words :

> Then I sat down on this bench. I could hardly get my breath and was still sweating like a bastard. I sat there, I guess for about an hour. Finally, what I decided I'd do, I decided I'd go away....[12]

The note Holden writes to Phoebe is a note reflecting his deep rooted love for her. Somehow, he manages it that the note reaches Phoebe in school. In the meantime, Holden looks at a number of foul and dirty writings on the walls reflecting upon the loose morals of the American society. In a fit of rage, he ruminates over the possibility of killing those who have written such ugly and damnable writings at public places :

> I kept wanting to kill whoever'd written it. I figured it was some perverty beem that'd sneaked in the school late at night to take a leak or something and then wrote in on the wall. I kept picturing myself catching him at it and how'd smash his head on the stone steps till he was good and goddam dead and bloody.[13]

Phoebe now comes to run away with him but Holden tells her that she must stay at home and that he is not going anywhere. Knowledge dawns on Holden and both Phoebe and Holden now visit the zoo, watch the bears and go to the carrousel. Phoebe rides round and round on the carrousel and Holden decides to quit running again and again. He is extremely happy realizing that the God's bounty lies in sharing others' happiness, in loving them and in caring for their worries, "I was damn near bawling, I felt so damn happy, if you want to know the truth. I don't know why. It was just that she looked so damn nice, the way she kept going around and around, in her blue coat and all. God, I wish you could've been there."[14]

In a way, the thematic strands in *The Catcher in the Rye* chiefly hinge on the incidental details which James E. Miller terms as "plot irrelevancies."[15] Nevertheless, the very texture of the novel achieves an organic whole by dint of "ingenious exploitation of chosen point of view"[16] of the novelist. Salinger has his unique way of telling of tale which is more or less the method resembling Mark Twain's. In this method, the details are not necessarily long, spun out of external revelations, but a coherent movement springing from within. "Like Mark Twain in *Huckleberry Finn,* Salinger appears to have hit upon the perfect way of telling a tale or of letting the tale-tell itself."[17]

J.D. Salinger worked on *The Catcher in the Rye* for about ten years and when it finally appeared in 1951, it evoked both critical and popular acclaim. Clifton Fadiman treats this novel as "uncannily true, perceptive and compassionate."[18] Charles Poore regards this novel as "probably the most distinguished first novel of the year."[19] In fact, *The Catcher in the Rye* became almost a success because its very texture is the very "time spirit"[20] or to the time movement, which J.D. Salinger artistically catches in order to highlight some of the ills the contemporary society was suffering from.

As such, Salinger creates Holden who actually holds on the time spirit of the day. Like any contemporary adolescent, Holden Caulfield passes through various trials and tribulations which an adolescent of the age was very likely to suffer from. Holden has been expelled from Pency Prep as the climax of a long adolescent protest. The history teacher who tries to get at the causes of Holden Caulfield's discontent emerges as a moralistic pedagogue. Holden is scornful of all the established conventions treating them as big shams. Encountered with such scoundrels as the athletic Stradlater, he gets not only humiliation but deceit. Seeking companionship with old Ackley, he gets repulsion due to dirt and squalor in his room. In fact, there are many eminently readable and quotable prose passages in *The Catcher in the Rye* in their tragic comic narrative of preadolescent revolt. "Compact, taught, and colourful, the first half of the novel presents in brief compass all the petty horrors, the banalities, the final mediocrity of the typical American prep school. For the later sections of the narrative are simply an episodic account of Holden Caulfield's "lost weekend" in New York City which manages to sustain our interest...."[21]

However, Salinger carefully places Holden on psychiatrist's couch in California, apparently on the way to some kind of recovery from his spiritual collapse. This, in summation, allows

Holden a free play of mind around the events he recounts. This cycle of events enables Holden to recount rather in an objective way to conjure up ups and downs in his life far beyond those critical days into his past "in recollection of more distant excursions, encounters, and collisions that seem somehow to have a bearing on his predicament. This point of view results in the novel's marvellous richness of texture."[22]

The theme of alienation in *The Catcher in the Rye* is one of the recurrent themes. Holden is alienated at Pencey Prep and is compelled to start out on the terrible journey to his home in New York. The journey becomes a nightmare : for, Holden meets a motley of people who turn out to be wicked to him. On the second day he meets Sally Hayes, who too quarrels with him; Carl Luce, who too turns out to be a bad fellow; Antolini, a school teacher, whom Holden misunderstands. On the third day, he meets Phoebe, with whom he finally decides to stay. Holden's alienation is connected with the deep rooted ills in the society which every adolescent faces like Holden. One is reminded of *Huckleberry Finn's* despair and helplessness as a young boy while facing a number of incorrigibly incurable ailments eating into the very vitals of the society. One is also reminded of Chandran's alienation in R.K. Narayan's *The Bachelor of Arts.* Chandran, as an adolescent is unable to bear with the horrible corruption, religious hypocrisy, problem of unemployment, problem of readjustment and the likes of such other deep-rooted and incurable problems in the contemporary Indian society. As such, the problem of alienation may, therefore, be seen in Salinger's effort to interpret it in different artistic modes.

First of all, *The Catcher in the Rye* is for James E. Miller, "a movement from innocence to knowledge, from self-ignorance to self-awareness, from isolation to involvement."[23] In order to elaborate the above point, the Sally Hayes' episode in which Holden urges her to run off with him is a subtle illustration. Sally Hayes terms Holden's urges as immature. Holden ruminates over his innocence, over his own phoniness again and again, after the episode is over.

Holden's quest is remarkably a quest for purity and idealism in life which Salinger creates with memorable artistic touches. In one sense, Holden's quest is quest "to preserve an innocence that is in peril of vanishing — the innocence of childhood, the spotless innocence of a self-horrified at contamination in the ordinary and inevitable involvements of life."[24] In another sense, the quest is for a kind of durable love, the bonds of which will reunite even the depressed, the alienated and the vanquished. In yet another sense, Holden's quest is a quest for identify too, which James E. Miller terms as "a search for the self."[25] In order to maintain his quest or identity, Holden does what he does, not like to do. He also assumes a number of *non de plumes* and guises such as Rudolf Schmidt when he talks with his classmate's mother. He also calls himself Jim Steele when Sunny, the bad fellow, visits him. However, Holden remains essentially and preeminently Holden Caulfield, a true pursuer of his own identity, the identity of a human self, which Hawthorne popularly calls a 'magnetic chain of humanity.' Holden's involvement and revulsion of involvement act as a magnet which attracts as well as repels. As first, he is attracted towards things but later on gets revulsion or disinvolvement finding things not what they appear to be. In all situations, in all connections and in all involvements, Holden finds a casual relationship. In his journey, he finds that people are not what they appear to be. His classmates, his teachers, his girl friends — all appear to be attractive in the very beginning to him, but later on, they prove to be repulsive. Holden's responsive relationship is fraught with disastrous consequences. Holden's wish for death, for suicide and for being betrayed, is deeply rooted in his frustration for not getting responsive relationship. It is Phoebe in the end, with whom Holden seeks his readjustment.

The theme of death and rebirth is also one of recurrent themes in *The Catcher in the Rye*. The deep winter suggests rather symbolically of the arrival of death. The time of Christmas suggests the experiences of rebirth. The same theme of death and rebirth becomes alive in Salinger's famous story *Teddy*. At one place, Teddy speaks fairly eloquently of his mystical experience while he was just six years old :

> "I was six when I saw that everything was God, and my hair stood up and all that," Teddy said. "It was on a Sunday, I remember. My sister was only a very tiny child then, and she was drinking her milk and all of a sudden I saw that she was God and the milk was God. I mean, all she was doing was pouring God into God, if you know what I mean."[26]

But Holden is neither a Vedantic nor a Christian mystic. Nor is he a master of what the analyst in *Raise High the Roof Beam, Carpenters* calls the 'virtues of living the imperfect life,' the grand art of compromise. What particularly maddens Holden is the horror of the orderliness of life. He tells Sally Hayes :

> But it isn't just that. It's everything. I hate living in New York and all. Taxicabs and Madison Avenue buses, with the drivers and all always yelling at you to get out at the rear door, and being introduced to phoney guys that call the Lunts angels, and going up and down in elevators when you want to go outside, and guys fitting your pants all the time at Brooks....[27]

The symbols in *The Catcher in the Rye* represent, *inter alia,* triumphant assertions of saintly innocence to a shocking spiritual bankruptcy. Nevertheless, *The Catcher in the Rye* is not a symbolic novel in which *Moby Dick* or *The Old Man and the Sea* are. However, symbols in this novel have two important functions to perform : first, the creation of an inner world; and secondly, meditation between the inner and the external world. According to William York Tindall, "As symbol can serve structure so structure can serve as symbol."[28] A series of concrete and symbolic images in *The Catcher in the Rye* range from the purely romantic and private symbols like the red-hunting that to traditional and archetypal water symbols like the rain and the lake. In fact, the red hunting hat is one of the most striking of Salinger's private symbols. Holden explains to Ackley, "This is a people shooting that : I shoot people in that hat. The hat has ear lapse and Holden often uses it as a protection against cold. Whenever Holden seeks refuge from stresses and shocks of social life, Salinger uses the symbol as a withdrawal into a psychic or neurotic world. Maxwell Geismar describes it as "a talisman of true rebellion and creativity."[29] On another occasion, Holden humbly presents his hat to Phoebe which symbolises readjustment. In the carrousel scene, Phoebe returns that hat to Holden, which represents compromise and solace.

Allice's baseball milt and Holden's attachment to his dead brother symbolically represent jealousy and death wish respectively; Jane Gallagher's Kings in the back row, Phoebe's notebook represents Holden's view of pure and highly satisfactory personal relationship. The young drummer symbolically represents Holden's heroic approach to the problem of finding fulfilment in a world of paucity and misery. The half frozen lake, the ducks of the Central Park Lagoon, the rain that comes as Holden watches the carrousel and the carrousel itself — are the literary symbols which go a long way in keeping up the symmetrical and coherent development of the structure of the novel, which William York Tindall considers an essential precondition of a telling affect. The ducks in the half frozen lake symbolically represent Holden's own situation in his own half frozen environment. The flight of the ducks of the Central Park lagoon symbolically represents Holden's own contemplation of flying away from his mindless social atmosphere. The rain represents for Holden the rain of baptism which instils in him the desire to live and the strength to survive in the world. The carrousel symbolises for Holden the ushering in of an era of peace and contentment. Synoptically, Salinger's symbols are aritistic devices helpful in maintaining a firm controlling intention.

The Catcher in the Rye may be well appreciated, despite Arthur Mizener's views to the contrary, by arithmetically counting four *Rs* which in their order of significance and paramountcy may be enumerated as under :

(1) R = Revival
(2) R = Redemption
(3) R = Recollection
(4) R = Resurrection

If the big L is taken to be Life, the primary instinct of survival in a Darwinian sense of the term, then the above scheme of things may further be understood by taking help of the following diagram :

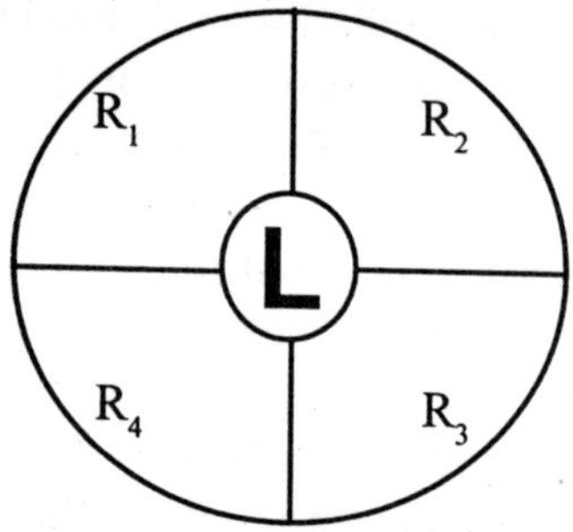

In fact, the above cycle of four Rs may sum up Salinger's entire literary output — novels, short stories and other writings. A little bit of deep probing into *The Catcher in the Rye* reveals the fact that Holden's full personality may be understood by knowing four stages of revival, which Warren French terms as "pilgrimage,"[30] of redemption, of recollection, and finally of resurrection. The first stage of *revival* presents oddities of life *vis-a-vis* realities, too, resulting in revival of faith, too. The stage of redemption liberates Holden from all neurotic strains, enabling him to face the ugliness of life. The third stage of recollection is the stage where Holden identifies his past with the present and puts exclusive emphasis on his own identity. The fourth stage of resurrection is the final stage where Holden appears as an incarnation of faith and humility. If all these stages of liberation and redemption in Holden's life are properly understood, *The Catcher in the Rye* may then well be understood. However, whatever imperfections may exist in the novel, it cannot be taken as "a sweeping indictment on the American society,"[31] as Marc Rosenberg treats it to be.

So far as the language of *The Catcher in the Rye* is concerned, it will be remembered as "an example of teenage vernacular in the 1950's. As such, the book will be a significant linguistic record of a type of speech rarely made available in a permanent form."[32] This opinion of Donald P. Costello is based on linguistic facts. Holden's speech is typically teenage speech, overlaid with strong personal idiosyncrasies. It is certainly common for teenagers to end thoughts with a loosely dangling "and all," just as it is common for them to add an insistent "I really did," "It really was." Holden uses "these phrases to such an overpowering degree that they become a clear part of the flavour of the book : they become, a part of Holden himself and actually help to characterize him."[33] Holden's "and all" and its twins, "or something," "or anything," serve no real linguistic function. They simply represent Holden's confused state of mind. For example, alone in chapter 18, "and all" has been repeated in as many as ten different contexts. Some of them make some sense whereas others do not at all. At page 179, the following sentences are worth-quoting in order to show the repeated use of "and all" :

(i) He's both their favourite author and all. (for Charles Dickens).
(ii) Any way, they fall in love right away...about Charles Dickens and all.
(iii) ...so he boozes all the time, but he's pretty witty and all.[34]

Likewise in chapter 19, just notc the use of "and all" :

(i) If you set around...all the phonies applauding and all.
(ii) I stood up...I was and all.
(iii) The only thing he ever did...talks and all.
(iv) He quite knew...perverts and all.[35]

Likewise the use of "hell" occurs many a time in the novel. Perhaps this word is the most versatile word in Holden's entire vocabulary. It serves most of the meanings and constructions which Mencken lists in his American Speech article on American Profanity. The most common function of "hell" is to magnify the effect. Such expressions like the following add to the magnitude and efficacy of the given meaning :

(i) "hot as hell"
(ii) "cold as hell"

(iii) "sad as hell"
(iv) "playful as hell"
(v) "old as hell"
(vi) "pretty as hell"

"Bastard" and "sonuvabitch" occur many a time in the novel. Whenever Holden dislikes things and people, he uses the word "bastard". Whenever Holden is extremely angry, he uses the word "sonuvabitch." For example, when Holden is furious with Stradlater over his treatment of Jane Gallagher, Holden repeats again and again the word "sonuvabitch." Holden's slang terms, numbering over a hundred, often colourful and rich, also sometimes lack precise communication. For example, Holden uses "crap" in several different ways. It can mean foolishness as in the expression — "David Copperfield kind of crap," or as messy matter as in "I spilled some crap all over my grey flannel."

Holden's views of "crazy" indicates violent dislike for something. His use of "to be killed" shows emotional effect. Whenever Holden expresses hatred or dislike, he uses such slangs as "old Maurice", "old Phoebe" or "old Jesus." The repeated use of such words as "lousy," "pretty," "crumby," "terrific", "quite," "stupid," represents teenagers' choice to repeat their favourite words. Salinger's use of trite figures of speech is an object of criticism. Holden uses most common similes such as "like a mad man," "like a bastard," "hot as a fire cracker," "laugh like a hyena," "drove off like a boat out of hell," "blind as a bat," etc., which reflect on Salinger's use of a "lousy vocabulary."

"The language of *The Catcher in the Rye*," remarks Donald P. Costello, "is an authentic artistic rendering of a type of informal, colloquial, teenage American spoken speech. It is strongly typical and trite, yet often somewhat individual, it is crude and slangy and imprecise, imitative yet occasionally imaginative, and affected towards standardization by the strong effects of school...."[36]

Together with language, diction used and local atmosphere created in *The Catcher in the Rye,* too, are remarkable for producing the desired artistic effect. For example, in Chapter 18, the Salinger protagonist has condemned war in plain and strong words. Alec, the English soldier, who participated in the war, loses his memory in the hospital. He meets Allie and the dialogue that takes place between them is suggestive of their deep-rooted hatred for war. Alec and Marcia do not meet each other because Alec is forced to participate in war. Holden, while walking down to the Wicker Bar in order to meet Carl Luce, comes across a number of old, dilapidated buildings which still testify to the horrors of war. His own elder brother D.B. was in the army and he was painfully wounded in the war. The passage that follows gives rather a nauseating picture of the horrors of war :

> My brother D.B. was in the Army for four Goddam years. He was in the war, too — ...he hated the Army worse than the war. I was practically a child at the time, but I remember when he used to come home on furlough and all, all he did was lie on his bed, practically.... All he had to do was drive some cowboy general around all day in command war. He once told Allie and I that if he'd to shoot anybody he wouldn't have known which direction to shoot in. He said the Army was practically as full of *bastards* as the *Nazis* were.[37]

Holden is inspired by his brother to read books which extolled war, bravery and heroism when he was just a child. His elder brother D.B., gave him *A Farewell to Arms* for a thorough study. He was also taught to appreciate heroic deeds in war as something worth worship. But Holden is temperamently incapable of admiring the great heroes of war, because he treats war as an outcome of evil designs generally perpetuated by dictators to destroy humanity at large. For him the notion of bravery is absolutely false. He considers chivalry as a conceited, feigned mental perversion and heroism simply arising out of senseless display of cruelty as most inhuman. Holden regards dialogue, communication and negotiation as much preferable to war. He satirizes war of any form — whether atomic or nuclear war : for, war is essentially ingrained in bestiality of human nature. "Any way, I'm sort of glad," Holden cries rather sardonically, "They've got the *atomic bomb* invented. If there's ever another war, I'm going to sit right in the hell on top of it. I'll volunteer for it. I swear to God *I will*."[38]

Salinger uses all his artistic devices as a novelist in *The Catcher in the Rye* to epitomise the weaknesses as well as merits of the contemporary American society. As such, diction, images, symbols, figures of speech — all go a long way cumulatively to reflect the spirit of the age. Salinger is basically preoccupied with the collapse of nerve, with the cracking laugh of the outraged and with terrifying feelings of loneliness and alienation. He seems to correspond peculiarly to psychological aura of the contemporary moment of history. As such, his protagonists are the tormented souls with insulted psyche. So, Holden Caulfield's language, diction, images and figures of speech are mixed parodies with a desired effect of pathos. Donald Bar rightly eulogises keeping in view the overall impression of Salinger's Holden as a great human being despite his suffering from many betrayals and humiliations in life. "*This* is a human being," remarks Donald Bar, "he's troubled (Holden), lost but not in image of God."[39] Moreover, Salinger has an ear not only for idiosyncrasies of diction and syntax, but also for mental processes. Holden's proverbial phrase is — "and all" — "she looked so damn nice, the way she kept going around and around in her blue coat and all, which not only indicates idiosyncrasies of diction and syntax but also a process of mental working. Holden's proverbial closing words are — "It's funny. Don't ever tell anybody anything. If you do, you start missing anybody." Each word is a unique experience in itself and it fills "the whole universe for a moment."[40] Holden's terrible word of condemnation "phony", which generalises adolescent psychology at large.

Salinger's characters in *The Catcher in the Rye* evince hope not despair. Holden is an incorrigible optimist : he loves the whole world. Likewise, his concept of hell does not infer a place where the soul suffers. Holden's hell is different from the hell of *Purgatorio* or the *Inferno* or the *Paradiso.* It is hell for the good, who can feel pain, who really loves or hopes to love. To a Christian, hell is in the afterlife; to an atheist it is in this life; but to both hell is eternal, because it co-exists as long as the soul exists. To a Mahayana Buddhist, hell is not eternal. Salinger's hell is not a place for suffering but a challenge for struggle and his God is a God offering a number of bounties on his devotees. Salinger's mystic experience is the experience of a spiritual perfectionist. The Glass family created by him in his short stories constantly strives for spiritual perfection. Holden's hell is not a condemnable place but a place for apprenticeship to learn more to struggle in life. Some of the illustrations in which hell has been used will make the idea sufficiently clear :

(i) "I was shivering like a bastard. It's a funny thing. I always shiver like *hell* when I'm drunk."[41]

(ii) "Then, when she was all done whispering and being cute as *hell*, she'd sing some dopey song, half in English and half in French, and drive all the phonies in the place mad with joy."[42]

(iii) "She had this little kid with her that was bored as *hell*...."[43]

(iv) "It's supposed to be religious as *hell*, I know, and very pretty and all...."[44]

A discussion on *The Catcher in the Rye* will be incomplete without attempting its close comparison and contrast with Mark Twain's *Adventures of Huckleberry Finn.* In fact, *The Catcher in the Rye* was published in 1951 whereas *Adventures of Huckleberry Finn* in 1884. Their narratives are, therefore, separated in time by almost 70 years, but the psychic connections between them eliminates mere temporal distance, because Huck Finn and Holden Caulfield are true-blood brothers. In fact, each novel is a masterpiece, rich in incident, varied in characterization and meaningful in its entirety. The central figure in each novel is an adolescent whose remarkable language as well as presentation is a wholesale commentary on his education, environment and milieu. Each is fundamentally a story of a quest — a quest from ignorance to knowledge, from self-innocence to self-realization. An outcast, to all intents, without familiar friends, the protagonist flees the restraint of the civilization which would make him its victim, and journeys through the world in search of what he thinks is liberation. Society looks down upon him no better than as a rogue. The protagonist is a believer in the cult of realism. In a way he does not understand the world. The slangy, idiomatic, frequently vulgar language of the protagonist highlights his own identity.

Holden and Huck are refugees in the sense that both suffer from the pangs of alienation. But their alienation is in the end turns out a rich store of experience. Both Huck and Holden are aware of sham and hypocrisy of the contemporary society. Huck's world is based on the established codes imbued with hypocrisy and superficiality. Huck finds peace and reassurance away from the haunts of man, out on the river. Holden's world is a post-war New York City from the Metropolitan Museum to Greenwich Village, during Christmas week, where, in successive incidents he encounters pompous hypocrisy, enormous ignorance, horrifying perverty and shocking moral corruption. Holden's older brother, once a promising writer, now a Hollywood scenarist, and the decay of his talent are all symptomatic of the all pervading corruption. Like Huck, who has to retreat regularly to the river in order to get inspiration to sustain his moral fabric, Holden visits natural objects like lake, river etc., several times to get reassured of his creative and survival instincts.

Despite the above similarities in both the novels, there are some obvious dissimilarities too. Mark Twain and J.D. Salinger use dissimilar means for solving the same technical problem. Mark Twain solves the problem largely by exploiting the assumed *naivete* of the child. His chief artistic devices including naive comments are innocently utterred but ticked with truth. Huck, an underbred country boy living on the periphery of civilization and ostensibly differential towards the attitudes and opinions of the adults who compose that civilization, yet ultimately guided by his own instinctive reactions, may be expected to misinterpret a great deal of what he actually experiences and feels.

Likewise, Salinger, despite the fact that he draws a considerable fund of humour from the device of naive comment, his primary means of solving the problem of inarticulateness are symbolism or verbal gesture. Holden is less capable of articulating his own predicament than Huck. His confession that, his is lousy vocabulary, testifies to his problem. He essentially lacks the capacity to conceptualise either his aesthetic experiences or inner conflicts. But Holden's apparent indifference or incapacity is itself a guise or a kind of mask.

By way of contrast, *The Catcher in the Rye,* not too far removed from the picaresque structure of *Huckleberry Finn,* gives the final impression of being closely controlled throughout by a unifying intention. Salinger has effaced himself from the novel, because he never undermines the integrity of his narrator protagonist. On the other hand, Mark Twain is Henry James's contemporary and belongs to an older and different tradition — the tradition of raconteur and the public entertainer. This major difference obviously puts *Huckleberry Finn* and *The Catcher in the Rye* on two different artistic pedestals. Moreover, the events in the *Huckleberry Finn* are disposed and bound together primarily by their relationship to the river. But the events in *The Catcher in the Rye* are selected and arranged by their relevance to Holden's inner conflict. Huck's inner conflict arises out of the opposition between his instinctive moral decency and dictates of moral society but Holden's inner conflict is the outcome of adolescent maladjustment. The difference in the nature of the central conflict in both these novels also divides a demarcating line. The central conflict in *Huckleberry Finn* is the outcome of the generous fund of common sense of Huck and the single minded efforts of Holden in *The Catcher in the Rye,* which gives an obvious cleavage of difference between both the novels.

One more difference is also to be noted : Holden Caulfield is neurotic but Huck Finn is not. Holden's neuroticism is not self-generated; it is a by-product of the discrepency between what Holden implicitly demands of society and what society actually affords. Holden's moral instinct and his society producing its neurotic types such as Pap, Mrs. Whatson and Emmeline Grangerford are similar to Huck's in many respects but Huck's world is much larger and more varied in which there is more generosity than cynicism. That is why perhaps A.R. Wells treats *Huckleberry Finn* as "an optimistic book expressing an optimistic age"[45] with all its undertones of cynicism and imperfection.

The Catcher in the Rye has undoubtedly an American idiom and setting, yet it has by no means been confined to an American audience. In an age of nuclear terror, adolescents everywhere — despite cultural differences — are perplexed by the same problems. Within a period of one month of its publication in America, *The Catcher in the Rye* was published in England also. It was an instant success. It was included in the paper bound Penguin series and as David Leitch reported that 180,000 copies of the latter edition were sold in two years.[46]

The Times Literary Supplement found in *The Catcher in the Rye* "the endless stream of blesphemy and obscenity...."[47] R.D. Charques wrote about the novel in the *Spectator* that "the tail is rather too formless to do quite the sort of things it was evidently intended to do."[48] One of the most perceptive criticisms to appear on either side of Atlantic, however, was contributed to *Punch* by R.G.G. Price :

> The weakness of the novel is its sentimentality. The boys looking for something and the reader is rightly left as doubtful as the boy what it is. It may be a cause, an attitude, a security. The search, while the basis for some of the greatest of allegories, is also too often an occasion for self-pity and a sensuous enjoyment of failure.... I suspect that this sentimentality is in character that the author has not invented it but approves of it. This may be merely the reaction of a corrupt European, who prefers a soft surface to a hard core.[49]

But despite the above criticism, the novel rose in demand day by day. The formidable task of translating *The Catcher in the Rye's* dinstinctive idiom was also undertaken in a dozen countries mostly in northern Europe. According to the United Nations Economic and Social Council's annual *Index Translationum, Catcher* appeared in three foreign language editions in 1952. In

Italy, it was translated by Jacopo Darca under the title called *Vita da Uomo* (A Man's Life). Its Japanese translation was made by Fuoko Hashimoto titled as *Kikenna Nenrei* (Dangerous Time of Life). Its translations were also made in Norway, Scandinavia, Sweden and Denmark. Its French edition also appeared in 1953 prepared by Jean Baptiste Rossi. Even in a non-English speaking country — West Germany, this novel attracted critical attention. The most distinguished novelist Hermann Hasse himself reviewed *The Catcher* and commented, "Whether one reads this novel as an individual history of a temperamental adolescent boy or as a symbol for a whole nation and people, one is led by the author down the beautiful path from unfamiliarity to understanding, from distaste to love. In a problematical world and time, literary art can achieve nothing higher."[50]

But Salinger's *The Catcher in the Rye* is not the only work which gave him fame. His stories, too, made him equally famous. Let us then deal with his stories in this Chapter in second part and see how the novelist is similar to or different from the story-writer.

II

Franny and Jooey, let us know it at the very outset, is highly philosophical in the sense that it teaches us the sterling values of life. Almost every philosophy and religion finds mention in it. Be it oriental or occidental, Christian or Indian, Chinese or Buddhist, Salinger talks of the very spirit of all religions. From the *Vedas*, Salinger quotes too often to give proper effect to his belief in the immortality of human soul. From the *Bible*, he imbibes the spirit of benevolence and humility. He also talks of the *Atman* and tries to be very familiar with the Hindus. Even detachment which the *Bhagavad Gita* preaches to its followers, is heard through Franny at least two times. Even Zobey is very much impressed by looking at the quotations from the *Bhagavad Gita* in the old room of Seymour.

Salinger, the philosopher, comes the fore in *Franny and Jooey* in a much clearer form than in *The Catcher in the Rye*. It is because of the very fact that the former work has a stronger base of philosophy and wisdom than the latter one. However, *The Catcher in the Rye*, as a work of fiction, may be counted as one of the best novels ever written by an American author.

J.D. Salinger's "Franny" was published in *New Yorker* in 1955 in its January issue. His "Zooey", too, was published in 1957 in *New Yorker* in its May issue. Both these stories were published together in 1961 as *Franny and Zooey* by Little, Brown and Company, Boston. James E. Miller regards their joint publication under the head *Franny and Brown* as "a remarkable unified novel."[51] In fact, the Glass family forms the central theme in both these stories. Despite the fact that Seymour commits suicide in *Nine Stories*, a reference to which has already been made, Seymour appears to play a key-role again in both these stories.

Synoptically, Franny is the youngest of the Glasses' seven children. She goes to visit her college boy-friend named Lane Coutell at his Ivy League School. Hardly did she step out of train, when Lane immediately recognized her. Franny is so well dressed and so charmingly groomed that Lane does not resist himself from kissing her many a time with the force of almost an infatuation. "Wearing a sheared raccoon coat,"[52] Franny looked extremely beautiful on the platform and her person involuntarily arrested the attention of the passers by :

> Franny was among the first of the girls to get off the train, from a car at the far, northern end of the platform. Lane spotted her immediately, and despite whatever it was he was trying to do with his face, his arm that shot up into the air was the whole truth. Franny saw it, and him, and waved extravagantly back. She was wearing a sheared raccoon coat, and Lane, walking toward her quickly but with a slow face, reasoned to himself, with suppressed excitement, that he was the only one on the platform who really *knew* Franny's coat. He remembered that once, in a borrowed car, after kissing Franny for a half hour or so, he had kissed her coat lapel, as though it were a perfectly desirable, organic extension of the person himself.[53]

But before this happening, Franny writes a detailed letter to Coutell Lane informing him of her arrival for the weekend of the

Yale game. In the letter, Franny confesses to Lane that she loves him rather intensely. She also informs him that her father has been back from the hospital. After many tests on her father, doctors diagnose the growth of tumour, not yet malignant and she afterwards feels relaxed. Franny also admires Lane's style, language and excellent way of presentation. She also likes only the celebrated poets :

> I absolutely adore your letter, especially the past about Eliot. I think I'm beginning to look down on all poets except Sappho. I've been reading her like mad, and no vulgar remarks, please. I may even do my term thing on her if I decide to go out for honours and if I can get the moron they assigned me as an advisor to let me. "Delicate Adonais is dying, Cytherea, what shall we do ? Beat your breasts, maiden, and rend your tunics." Isn't that marvellous ? ...Anyway I love you and want to get this off special delivery so you can get it in plenty of time if I can find a stamp in this madhouse. *I Love You I love you I love you.* Do you actually know I've only danced with you twice in eleven months ?[54]

Franny and Lane, after meeting each other, start talking on a variety of topics. Franny tells Lane that the three girls on the train — Martha Farrar, Tippie Tibbett and Eleanor — were talking about Exeter. Both now hire a taxi and reach a comparatively isolated table in a restaurant called Sicker's. They order for Martinis. When the drink is over, Lane speaks to Franny about the success of one of his papers on Flaubert's testicularity, a Freudian analysis which he might try to publish. Franny shows her indifference about the subject. She doubts pedants and professors, "I'm just so sick", says she, "of pedants and conceited little tearer — downers I could scream...."[55] To this, Lane retorts, "there are incompetent people in all walks of life. I mean that is basic. Let's drop the goddam section men for a minute."[56]

Lane then argues that Manlius and Esposito were the celebrated poets in the English Department. To this Franny retorts, "They're not that's partly what's so awful. I mean they are not real poets. They're just people that write poems that get published and anthologized all over the place, but they're not poets."[57] Franny continues to smoke her cigarette and squashes its stub in the ashtray. In the meantime, the waiter brings a second Martini. Both Franny and Lane enjoy Martini and discussion simultaneously. Franny now goes to the ladies' room and gives way to a violent fit of trembling and tears :

> Abruptly, then, and very quickly, she went into the farthest and most anonymous — looking of the seven or eight enclosures — which, by luck, didn't require a coin for entrance — closed the door behind her, and, with some little difficulty, manipulated the bolt to a locked position.... Her extended fingers, though trembling, or because they were trembling looked oddly graceful and pretty. She held that tense, almost fetal position for a suspensory moment — then broke down. She cried for full five minutes. She cried without trying to suppress any of the noisier manifestations of grief and confusion, with all the convulsive throat sounds that a hysterical child makes when the breath is trying to get up through a partly closed epiglottis....[58]

When the violent fit is over, Franny returns and Lane notices a little pea-green book in her purse. "She put it on her lap, on her knees, and looked down at it."[59] Franny now eats a chicken sandwich and drinks a glass of milk. Lane also enjoys frogs' legs. The book she carries in her purse is *The Way of a Pilgrim*, written by a Russian peasant, whose actual name remains ambiguous. The peasant is reported to be thirty-three years old. Prior to it, Franny suffers from another violent fit. When she recovers, she shows her hatred for bad plays. She says rather remorsefully, "All I know is I'm losing my mind. I'm just sick of *ego, ego, ego*. My own and everybody else's. I'm sick of everybody that wants to get somewhere, do something distinguished and all."[60] She is so overpowered by the feeling of depression that she sees darkness and degeneration all around. "Just because," she says, "I'm so horribly conditioned to accept everybody else's values, to rave about me, doesn't make it right. I'm ashamed of it. "I'm *sick* of it. I'm *sick* of not having the courage to be an absolute body. I'm sick of myself and everybody else that wants to make some kind of a splash."[61]

Franny now tells, in detail, about *The Way of a Pilgrim*. She treats the book as "primarily religious."[62] The peasant-writer of

Russia tells rather elaborately the complex way of prayer. The writer of the book undertakes a journey and meets a number of persons and faces a number of odd situations. The writer as a pilgrim also undertakes the pilgrimage so that he may learn from the book of life itself. The pilgrim learns from the *Bible* the valuable virtue to bestow mercy on others. Lord Jesus Christ himself taught his followers to love others. In the Jesus Prayer, it is preached, first of all, that one should have mercy on others, because "the word mercy is a really enormous word and can mean so many things."[63] Incessant prayer brings about permanent bliss. It also changes mental outlook and also ushers in an era of tranquillity and peace. So much is Franny's praise for this book that she admits :

> I don't know what, but something happens, and the words get synchronized with the person's heartbeats, and then you're actually praying without easing, which has a really tremendous, mystical effect on your whole outlook. I mean that's the whole point of it, more or less. I mean you do it to purify your whole outlook and get an absolutely new conception of what everything's about.[64]

Franny tells Lane rather emphatically that she is a strong believer in the magical impact of incessantly offering prayer. She also believes that everything inherent and vitally magical in the power of art cannot be explained in terms of reason or logic. Mind has its own limitations. Psychological analysis is an interrelated phenomenon. The mystic aspect of soul is another name of God which can become visible to us only through the link of offering constant prayer. "All you have," Franny explains to Lane in the tone of an expert mystic, "to have in the beginning is quantity. Then, later on, it becomes by quality itself. On its own power or something. He says that any name of God — any name at all — has this peculiar, self-active power of its own, and it starts working after you've sort of startled it up."[65] Franny further explains this magical force and quotes from other religions also. Alluding to the Buddhism and the importance of offering praises to Lord Buddha, she asserts again, "As a matter of fact, that makes absolute sense, because in the Nembutsu sects of Buddhism, people keep saying '*Namu Amida Butsu*' over and over again — which means 'Praises to the Buddha' or something like that — and the *same thing* happens...the same thing happens in '*The Cloud of Unknowing*,' to. Just with the word *God*. I mean just you keep saying the word God."[66]

Lane does not believe Franny's unusual faith in the magnetic power of prayer and connects mental makeup of offering prayers as deeply anchored in psychological moorings. In the mean time, another epiphany dawns on Franny. She is swept up again in a wave of nausea and she comes to the manager's office. She talks of *Atman, Om* and *God*. Talking of Indian religion, she also talks of the significance of meditation. She also mentions *Om* as the centre of the Hindu religion. She frankly admits the "all the really advanced and absolutely unbogus religious persons keep telling you, if you repeat the name of God incessantly, something *happens*, even in India. In India, they tell you to meditate on the *Om*, which means the same thing, really, and the exact same result is supposed to happen.

Franny, while standing at the threshold of her second epiphany, visibly sees that the non-physical part of the heart is closely connected with *Atman*. To her, *Atman* is just a fraction of God. "Something happens," Franny prophetically announces, "in some absolutely nonphysical part of the heart — where the Hindus say that *Atman* resides, if you ever took any Religion — and you see God, that's all."[67]

Nevertheless, Franny recovers from the violent attack of the second epiphany. She concurs in Lane's plans for a quiet afternoon of rest. She is left alone and her lips are moving with a repetition of the Jesus prayer. She just demands a glass of water and really feels spiritually much better than before. In the night, she gently says, "I'll get the head waiter and call off the spirits of ammonia — and, incidentally, pays the cheque... O.K., I will be right back."[68]

In fact, Franny resembles Holden in many respects. Like Holden, Franny undergoes epiphany twice. From a vivacious child, she becomes a mature adult. Like Holden, she gets knowledge and experience after the second epiphany. She looks at life from various viewpoints, but her vision after the second revelation or epiphany is decidedly much brighter than the first one. It appears that Salinger, by the time of the publication of this short-story, was very much influenced by the Hindu thought. That is why Franny talks more of *Atman*, God, meditation and Om than Holden. It is almost trite now that a wholesome view of life is the only enlightened vision which approximates to the Greek view of life and which is decidedly "steady and whole." Franny, who earlier appears to us an imperfect child, now appears as endowed with a wholesome vision of life.

Salinger's use of language in this short story is markedly different from that of *Nine Stories*. Whereas the language used in earlier short stories is terse with smaller clauses, few connectives, simpler sentences and grammatically unviable sentences, the language in this story is, in a sense, conventional or traditional one. For example, if a small passage is taken from "A Perfect Day for Bananafish" and another one from "Franny", we can notice the real difference. The passage that follows is first from "A Perfect Day for Bananafish :"

> "All right," said the girl.
> "Did he keep calling you that awful —"
> "No. He has something knew now."
> "What"
> "Oh, what's the difference, Mother —?"
> "Muriel, I want to know. Your father."[69]

Now take, another example, from "Franny":

> "I don't *know* what a real poet is. I wish you'd *stop* it, Lane. I'm serious. I'm feeling very peculiar and funny, and I can't —."
> "All right, all right — O.K. Relax," Lane said.
> "I was only trying—."
> "I know this much, is all," Franny said. "If you a poet, you do something beautiful. I mean you're supposed to *leave* something beautiful after you get off the page and everything."[70]

Salinger uses words from other languages in "Franny". For example, "cashmere"[71], a borrowed word from Indian languages has been used twice — one, at page 4 and another at page 11 in the following contexts :

1. "He was wearing a maroon *cashmere* muffler...."[72]
2. "...a girl who was not only extraordinarily pretty but, so much the better, not too categorically *cashmere* sweater...."[73]

Salinger uses the words "hell" and "goddam" a number of times in "Franny". Alone "hell" has been used ninė times in different contexts, whereas "goddam" has been used seven times. "Bastard" has also been used thrice. "Frog's legs" and "sheared-raccoon coat" have been used symbolically. Salinger's method of presentation with minute details achieves the *ne plus ultra* in "Franny". For example, the following passage is often quoted as a perfect specimen of Salinger's style of putting even minute details with a touch of perfection :

> Without any apparent regard to the suchness of her environment, she sat down. She brought her knees together very firmly, as if to make herself a smaller, more compact unit. Then she placed her hands, vertically, over her eyes and pressed the heels hard, as though to paralyse the optic nerve and drown all images into a void like black. He extended fingers, though trembling, or because they were trembling, looked oddly graceful and pretty. She held that tense, almost fetal position for a suspensory moment — then broke down.[74]

"Franny" covers only forty-three pages whereas "zooey" approximately hundred fifty-seven pages out of the unified volume of two hundred pages of *Franny and Zooey*. The fact to be proved is that "Franny" is just one-fourth of the total volume of two hundred pages, nevertheless, it appears as if it were Salinger's manifesto of his religious views and convictions. By the time *Franny and Zooey* appeared in 1961, Salinger was about fifty-two years of age. After the publication of *Franny and Zooey*, Salinger published his last significant book titled *Raise High the Roof Beam, Carpenters;* and *Seymour : An Introduction* in 1963. It naturally infers that Salinger during 1962-63 was about to close writing short stories. The year 1962-63 was, therefore, the most decisive year in Salinger's life. As such, Salinger developed a very compassionate outlook towards life and "Franny" represents, in real sense, the Salinger at fifty-two during 1962-63. Salinger's compassion for the downtrodden is Franny's love for the outcast and the socially boycotted. His love for spiritual advancement, meditation, Buddhism, *Atman* and the Hindu religion is Franny's love for all these spiritual phenomena. Even *detachment* which the *Bhagavad Gita* preaches to its followers, is heard through Franny at least two times in the short story.

Having discussed various aspects of "Franny" let us now deal with "Zooey", without which a comprehensive treatment of *Franny and Zooey* will be incomplete. "Zooey" was published in *New Yorker* in 1957 but with "Franny", as a unified novel, it appeared in 1961. In fact, this story is a sequel to "Franny". The narrator appears in the beginning in the first person but the first person becomes the third person. Buddy Glass is the narrator, who begins the story as a prologue to the coming events :

> The facts at hand presumably speak for themselves but a trifle more vulgarly, I suspect, than facts even usually do.... The one I have in mind not only is wordy and earnest beyond my wildest dreams but is, to boot, rather excruciatingly personal....[75]

The narrator — Buddy Glass, narrates his ancestors in a very dramatic manner just after three pages of the story. "Our family's surname", Buddy Glass narrates, "is *Glass*. In just a moment, the youngest Glass boy will be seen reading an exceedingly lengthy letter (which will be reprinted here in full, I can safely promise) send to him by his eldest living brother, Buddy Glass...we will, however, leave this Buddy Glass in the third person from here on in. At least, I see no good reason to take him out of it."[76] Now, the scene shifts to the Glass family apartment in New York. The mother Bessie has been shown as a very mature lady, who is looking after the needs of Franny. In this task, Bessie takes help of Zooey, who is the sixth of the seven Glass children. "By profession, Zooey is an actor, a leading man in television, and had been for a little more than three years.... Zooey has made a formal and serious debut as a public performer at the age of seven"[77] About his parentage, some details are readily available. In fact, "He was the second youngest of what had originally been seven brothers and sisters — five boys and two girls — all of whom, at rather conveniently spaced intervals during childhood, had been heard regularly on a network radio programme, a children's quiz show called "It's a wise child." An age difference of almost eighteen years between the eldest of the Glass children, Seymour, and the youngest, Franny, had helped very considerably to allow the family to reserve a kind of dynastic seating arrangement at the "Wise Child" microphones — which lasted just over sixteen years — from 1927 well into 1943, a span of years connecting the Charleston and B-17 Eras…."[78]

In the story, there are three major scenes, all domestic. The first takes place in the family bathroom where Zooey is first discovered in the tub re-reading a four-year old letter from his older brother Buddy. The letter roughly runs into fourteen pages, probably the longest letter ever written in English literature. "I have just finished," thus the letter begins, "decoding a long letter that came from Mother this morning, all about you and General Eisenhower's smile and small boys in the *Daily News* who fell down elevator shafts and when I'm going to have my phone in *New York* taken out and get one installed up there in the country, where I shall need it…."[79] To cut the letter short, Mother Bessie enters the room and she instructs Zooey to help his ailing sister Franny. Bessie, being too much indulgent in her children, generally overlooks the fact that her children are suffering from the soul sickness.

In the next scene, Zooey goes to the living room where he gradually and gently lures Franny out of her shell and then tries to shook her out of her sickness by describing to her "little instinct of piousness" and the "little snotty crusade" she is "leading against everybody." This shock merely intensifies Franny's anguish, and Zooey retreats, this time to the sacrosanct room once occupied by Seymour and Buddy Glass and which still has the phone listed in Seymour's name.

Zooey talks to Seymour's spirit. Zooey puts a handkerchief over his mouth to disguise his own voice. Zooey calls Franny over the phone and thinking that it was Buddy Glass's call, she continues to listen on the phone. The fact of the matter is that it is not Buddy who is speaking on the phone but Zooey himself. Subsequently, she comes to know of it. She feels happy and takes part in human activities rather than avoiding them. Franny enjoys inexplicable joy which makes her smile just before falling into "deep dreamless sleep."

An important feature of "Zooey" is that the cycle of resurrection is fructified through Franny and not through Zooey. In *The Catcher in the Rye*, Holden is the central character through whom the cycle of resurrection is materialised. In another story, it is Sergeant X, through whom the cycle of resurrection is completed. But it is for the first time that Salinger shows his predilection for a female character in order to present her as an embodiment of enlightenment, compassion and love. Accordingly, Franny passes from nausea to joy, from withdrawal to return, from detachment to involvement. As it has been noted in "Franny", it is Franny, the central character of the story, who suffers from spiritual crisis, dehumanising effect of the moral collapse and even detachment arising out of her deep rooted whim-whams and crotchets. Tormented by a nauseatic conflict in herself, she cries out rather abominably that she is sick of *ego, ego, ego* even of her own and of anybody else's. In a sense, she feels entirely cut off from all human beings which Hawthorn terms as the magnetic chain of humanity. But the Franny resurrected in "Zooey" is the Franny wholesomely enlightened, spiritually invigorating Glass child. It is also a fact that despite two paralytic attacks of epiphany, the cycle of revelation and resurrection could not become complete without Zooey's making her understand the proper use of the Zesus prayer. It is Zooey again who unravels before her "the God's universe." Zooey asks Franny to understand the fact that it is Jesus who himself knew the ways of God. The kingdom of heaven, which is with us, inside us, is not understood by us till we develop "Christ-consciousness." After correcting Franny's distorted notion, Zooey tells Franny that God needs virtuous path and not merely hollow utterances.

Shocked out of her alienating, self-righteous pity, Franny is now prepared for accepting Zooey's practical wisdom. In a radio programme entitled "It's a Wise Child", it is Seymour who tells Zooey despite his indifference, he should shine his shoes for "the fat lady." The image of "fat lady", sitting on a poach, swatting flies, suffering from cancer, grows in Zooey's mind as an image of suffering humanity and also as an embodiment of Lord Christ. Franny understands now through this radio programme that through Christ Himself, there is nothing permanent that actually exists. The "fat lady" is just a symbol, an image of human suffering. Hence, it is the inborn intuitive knowledge that dawns upon Franny and her revulsion gives place to joy. This episode also brings about a transparent smile on her lips — the smile of return, of involvement and of struggle. James E. Miller considers "Zooey" to be "the story of Franny's comeback."[80] However, it is, in a way, the story of Zooey's experimentation in wordly wisdom in himself. Seymour and Buddy groom Zooey in such a way that their mental make-up becomes almost static. In a freak of madness, Zooey exclaims that he will either turn into a seer or a human hatpin. He even sees the *phoniness* of his television associates. He frankly admits to Franny that he is sick to death of being the heavy or obstructive in everybody's life. Along with Franny's spiritual resurrection, for which the absolute credit certainly goes to him, he himself undertakes a lot of techniques to perfect his spiritual journey. For acquiring intuitive wisdom, he himself has to undergo various trials, odds and tribulations.

The atmosphere in "Zooey" is such that foretells of something which may ultimately lead to a spiritual resonance. It is Salinger's specific technique or pattern which he takes help of in his earlier short stories also. When Zooey goes to Seymour's old room, he finds there quotations culled from the *Bhagavad Gita*, Marcus Aurelius, Issa, Epictetus, Ringlardner, De Caussade, Anna Karenina, Shri Ramkrishna, and Mu-Mon-Kwan. Out of all the quotations, which left an indelible impact on Zooey, these were the quotations from the *Bhagavad Gita*, Epictetus and De Caussade, which he took help of again and again to instruct Franny. From the *Bhagavad Gita*, the following quotations decorated Seymour's wall :

(i) "You have the right to work but for the work sake only. You have no right to the fruits of work. Desire for the fruits of work must never be your motive in working. Never give way to laziness either."

(ii) "Perform every action with your heart fixed on the Supreme Lord. Renounce attachments to the fruits. Be even tempered in success and failure : for it is this evenness of temper which is learnt by yoga."

(iii) "Work done with anxiety about results is far inferior to work done without such anxiety, in the calm of self-surrender. Seek refuge in the knowledge of Brahman. They who work selfishly for results are miserable."[81]

Here it is thought prudent as well as in proper fitness of things to reproduce the original quotations from the *Bhagavad Gita* in Sanskrit language, too :

(i) कर्मण्येवाधिकारस्ते मा फलेषु कदाचन।
मा कर्मफलहेतुर्भूर्मा ते सङ्गोऽस्त्वकर्मणि। (II : 47)

(ii) योगस्थः कुरु कर्माणि सङ्गं त्यक्स्वा धनंजय।
सिद्धयसिद्धयौः समो भूत्वा समस्वं योग उच्यते।। (II : 48)

(iii) दूरेण ह्मवरं कर्म वुद्धियोगाद्धसंजय।
बुद्धौ शरणमन्विच्छ कृपणाः फलहेतवः ।। (II : 49)

The above quotations taken from the *Gita* indicate that Salinger had immense love for the spiritual wisdom contained in them. Seymour's love for the above quotations of the *Bhagavad Gita* is Salinger's own. It is hard to established whether in his own personal life Salinger was as religious minded as his immortal creation Zooey is. It is also not clear whether Zooey's religious and spiritual efforts have, in any way, any connection or relationship with Salinger's own efforts for spiritual elevation in his own personal life. Nevertheless, one fact comes to the fore that by the time Salinger wrote "Zooey", his predilection for religious and spiritual matters grew stronger than before.

The quotation from Shri Ramkrishna suggests a different reference and context, which in brief suggests that the approach of a iconoclast is not a right one and is fraught with many disastrous consequences :

> "Sir we ought to teach the people that they are doing wrong in worshipping images and pictures in the temple."
>
> "That's the way with you Calcutta people : you want to teach and preach. You want to give millions when you are beggars yourselves.... Do you think God does not know that he is being worshipped in images and pictures? If a worshipper should make a mistake, do you not think God will know his intent?"[82]

The concluding part of the quotation taken from Epictetus is, "I move not without Thy knowledge!"[83] From De Caussade, Salinger quotes the following brief but relevant line :

> "God instructs the heart, not by ideas, but by pains and contradictions."[84]

The techniques introduced in *Franny and Zooey* are characteristic of Salinger's later work. As has been pointed earlier, Salinger used black humour in *The Catcher in the Rye.* But in *Franny and Zooey*, in place of black humour, there is kind of persuasive humour. The narrative pattern is also static, sedate type, which moves from one long conversation to another, interspersed with occasional monologues or individual readings of letters, diaries, or journals. In his earlier works, Salinger uses a fast-moving and richly varied narrative sequence. For example, the very opening of "Zooey" is suggestive of long, conventional settings :

> Ten-thirty on a Monday morning in November of 1955 Zooey Glass, a young man of twenty-five, was seated in a very full bath, reading a four-year-old letter. It was in almost endless-looking letter, typewritten on several pages of second-sheet yellow paper, and he was having some little trouble keeping it propped up against dry islands on his knees. At his right, a dampish looking cigarette was balanced on the edge of the built

> in enamel soap-catch, and evidently it was burning well enough, for every now and then he picked it off and took a drag or two without quite having to look up from his letter...."[85]

The accretion of physical details in "Zooey" hints at Salinger's perfection of art. For example, Zooey's cigar serves as material and substantial ballast both to his slight build and mystic tendencies of thought. Though Franny also smokes, yet, the way Salinger presents Zooey with his cigarette is perhaps immortalised by the way Zooey's thoughts are connected with it. In the very beginning of the story, Zooey's cigarette "burns well" as he gradually goes through the letter. Even "his ashes invariably fell into the tub water, either straightway or down one of the letter page."[86] In this respect, Zooey resembles Lane, who too is very much addicted to smoking cigarettes. When the reader is introduced, in "Zooey", to the contents of the Glass medicine cabinet, the minute details presented by Salinger are indicative of his mastery in giving desired effects. Perhaps his technique of introducing minute details of particular places duly compensates the absence of black humour in this story. Minor details presented with a touch of finality, further reflects on Salinger's profundity not only of knowledge but also of his own craftsmanship. The psycho-analysis presented in "Zooey" is, therefore, much better than in *The Catcher in the Rye*. As such, the psychological presentation of Holden is less convincing than that of *Franny and Zooey*.

Franny and Zooey often appears less as a unified book of fiction and more as an index of comparative religion or of religious encyclopaedia. The narrator Buddy is a college teacher who lectures to the faculty once a week on Zen and Mahayan Buddhism. Buddy wishes that Franny and Zooey would know "who and what Jesus and Gautam and Lao-tse and Shankaracharya and Hii-neng and Shri Ramkrishna" were before and after attaining perfection in life. Buddy also wishes that both Franny and Zooey should know something about these great spiritual souls before they know a lot about Homer, Shakespeare, Blake and Whitman.

While speaking on education, on Jesus prayer, on detachment and on moral values, the protagonist speaks like a pilgrim, a saint, or a seer. "You can say," advises the protagonist in "Zooey", "the Jesus prayer from now till domsday, but if you do not realize, that the only thing that counts in the religious life is *detachment*, I do not see how you'll ever see even move an *inch*. Detachment, Buddy and only detachment. Desirelessness, 'Cessation from all hankerings'. It's this business of desiring... that brings cause and effect...the only thing you can do now, the only *religious* thing you can do, is act. Act for God."[87]

The reference to the fat lady is really on obvious reference to Christ Himself. Throughout the story, the final impression which a dispassionate reader gathers is that of a pilgrim set out in search of God. Warren French has termed the spiritual experimentation, both by Franny and Zooey, as a "unique pilgrimage."[88] The book entitled *The Way of a Pilgrim*, found in Franny's purse by Coutell Lane is symbolic of Franny's final destination in life. Her two violent epiphanies are nothing but two distinct divine revelations. The quotation, in Seymour's room, which Zooey goes through a number of times, is a quotation from Epictetus. In this quotation, the message to the reader is that without the knowledge of God, one cannot know anything which in other words means that those who perceive this universe as Godless are inhuman themselves :

> Concerning the Gods, there are those who deny the very existence of Godhead; others say that it exists, but neither bisters nor concerns itself nor has forethought for anything. A third party attributes to it existence and forethought, but only for great and heavenly matters, not for anything that is on earth, but the only in general and not with respect to each individual, a fifth, of whom were Ulysses and Socrates, are those that cry, "I move not without Thy knowledge!"[89]

Both "Franny" and "Zooey" are stories which teach involvement and not indifference to human activities. Detachment, of which Zooey talks again and again, is the detachment as preached by *The Bhagavad Gita*. The keynote of detachment as enunciated in *The Bhagavad Gita* is that work is our duty and that result is not our concern. In other words, it is selfless devotion to duty which is, in summation, the end-result of a life-long pursuit of the real worship of God. A divinely, blessed soul is really the one who never says "NO" to his Master's orders. The quotation in Seymour's room culled from Mu-Mon-Kwan epitomises the whole idea as has been projected in "Zooey" :

> St. Francis de Sales' prayer : "Yes, Father!
> Yes, and always, Yes."
> Zui-Gan called out to himself everyday, "Master."
> Then he answered himself, "Yes, sir."
> And then he added, "Become sober."
> Again he answered, "Yes, sir."
> "And after that," he continued, "do not be deceived by others."
> "Yes, sir; yes, sir," he replied.[90]

However, despite the fact that "Franny" and "Zooey" appear to be religious tracts, there seems a grain of truth in Buddy's declaration in prologue to Zooey, "I say that my current offering isn't a mystical story, or a religiously mystifying story, at all."[91] I say it's a compound, or multiple, love-story, pure and complicated. Buddy further convinces us by explaining that they "are, all four of them, blood relatives and speak a kind of esoteric, family language, a sort of semantic geometry in which the shortest distance between any two points is a fullish circle."[92] Salinger's assertion that both "Franny" and "Zooey" are based on the warm human acts and not on the cold printed words of the sages, carries a lot of conviction in it.

Critics like Warren French and Perry Frank have appreciated Salinger for not leaving Franny "incomplete without Zooey."[93] In fact, Salinger left Franny incomplete with Franny's being bed-ridden. Her resurrection has been, therefore, made possible by creating the Glass family and particularly Zooey. In contrast, to Miss McCarthy's or Jarrell's novels or even Vladimir Nabokov's delightful *Pnin*, Salinger's story does seem to have been motivated by the principle rather than personal spite : and despite varying views of the critics, Salinger's stories are "still tales of people who teach in colleges because they attempt to maintain principles.[94]

In one way, *Franny and Zooey* may be taken to be a satire on an academic world which is full of snobbish pedants, eager to display their shallow knowledge rather than behaving themselves as pilgrims to seek more and more learning. But Salinger is not essentially a satirist, whatever mild satire, we do find in "Zooey", it is his hatred for conceited behaviour of human beings at large. One of his minor characters in "Zooey" propounds the biggest philosophy of the world, the quintessence of which is that actions speak louder than words. Hence, Salinger hates people with hypocritical postures. At best, "Zooey" appears to have been written by Salinger "to make people see that what matters is not the negative burlesque of the inflated ego, but the positive conquest of it."[95] Likewise, Salinger's "Franny" is "simply a prologue to an account of the search for individual salvation."[96]

With this detailed treatment of Salinger's *Franny and Zooey*, let us also know his *Raise High the Roof Beam, Carpenters* and *Seymour : An Introduction* — another famous collection of short-stories, which, too, forms a unified novel, if taken together as a whole book for the purpose of deeper analysis.[97]

REFERENCES

1. Miller, James E. *J.D. Salinger,* Minneapolis : University of Minnesota Press, 1965, p. 8.
2. *Studies in J.D. Salinger,* New York : Odyssey Press, 1963, p. 239.
3. *Ibid.*
4. *Ibid.*
5. *Studies,* p. 9.
6. *The Catcher in the Rye,* Boston : Little, Brown and Company, 1951, pp. 8-9.
7. *Ibid.,* p. 226.
8. *Ibid.,* pp. 237-38.
9. *Ibid.,* p. 244.
10. *Ibid.,* p. 246.
11. *Ibid.,* pp. 249-50.
12. *Ibid.,* p. 257.
13. *Ibid.,* p. 261.
14. *Ibid.,* p. 275.
15. *J.D. Salinger,* p. 11.

16. *Ibid.*, p. 11.
17. *Ibid.*, p. 11.
18. Geismar, Maxwell. *American Moderns,* New York : Hill and Wang, 1958, p. 195.
19. *Ibid.*, p. 195.
20. *Ibid.*, p. 195.
21. *Ibid.*, p. 197.
22. Miller, James E. *op. cit.*, p. 11.
23. *Op. cit.*, p. 12.
24. *Ibid.*, pp. 12-13.
25. *Ibid.*, p. 13.
26. *Teddy,* p. 288.
27. *The Catcher in the Rye,* p. 136.
28. *The Literary Symbol,* p. 229.
29. *Studies,* p. 73.
30. *J.D. Salinger,* New York : Twayne Publishers, 1963, p. 139.
31. *Ibid.*, p. 163.
32. *Grunwald, Henry Anatole, Salinger*, New York : Harper and Brothers, 1962, p. 266.
33. *Ibid.*, p. 267.
34. *The Catcher in the Rye,* p. 179.
35. *Ibid.*, pp. 184-85.
36. *Op. cit.*, p. 276.
37. *Ibid.*, pp. 181-82.
38. *Ibid.*, p. 183.
39. *Op. cit.*, p. 172.
40. *Ibid.*, p. 172.
41. *Ibid.*, p. 197.
42. *Ibid.*, p. 184.
43. *Ibid.*, p. 181.
44. *Ibid.*, p. 178.
45. *If You Really Want to Know a Catcher Case Book,* p. 42.
46. "The Salinger Myth," *Twentieth Century,* No. 168 (Nov. 1960), p. 431.
47. *The Times Literary Supplement,* Sept. 7, 1951, p. 561.
48. *Spectator,* Aug. 8, 1951, p. 224.
49. *Punch,* CCXXI, 192, Aug. 15, 1951.
50. Quoted in W.S. Field, "Hermann Hesse As Critic of English and American Literature, Monatchefte, LIII (April-May 1961), p. 156.
51. Miller, James E. *op. cit.*, p. 30.
52. *Franny and Zooey* (Boston : Little, Brown and Company, 1961), p. 7.

53. *Ibid.*, p. 7.
54. *Ibid.*, p. 5.
55. *Ibid.*, p. 17.
56. *Ibid.*, pp. 17-18.
57. *Ibid.*, p. 18.
58. *Ibid.*, p. 22.
59. *Ibid.*, p. 22.
60. *Ibid.*, p. 29.
61. *Ibid.*, p. 30.
62. *Ibid.*, p. 33.
63. *Ibid.*, p. 36.
64. *Ibid.*, p. 37.
65. *Ibid.*
66. *Ibid.*, p. 38.
67. *Ibid.*, p. 39.
68. *Ibid.*, p. 43.
69. "A Perfect Day for Bananafish", p. 67.
70. "Franny", p. 19.
71. *Ibid.*, p. 4.
72. *Ibid.*, p. 4.
73. *Ibid.*, p. 11.
74. *Ibid.*, p. 22.
75. "Zooey", p. 47.
76. *Ibid.*, p. 50.
77. *Ibid.*, p. 52.
78. *Ibid.*, p. 53.
79. *Ibid.*, p. 56.
80. *Op. cit.*, p. 33.
81. "Zooey", p. 176
82. *Ibid.*, p. 177.
83. *Ibid.*, p. 176.
84. *Ibid.*, p. 172.
85. *Ibid.*, p. 150.
86. *Ibid.*, p. 50.
87. *Ibid.*, pp. 196-97.
88. *J.D. Salinger,* p. 139.
89. "Zooey", p. 176.
90. *Ibid.*, p. 178.
91. *Ibid.*, p. 49.

92. *Ibid.*, p. 49.
93. *J.D. Salinger,* p. 142.
94. *Ibid.*, p. 142.
95. *Ibid.*, p. 143.
96. *Ibid.*, p. 142.
97. Presented at the XXXVII Session of the AIETC held at Kohlapur on Nov. 24-26, 1988.

6

Thomas Hardy : *Far From the Madding Crowd*, Cosmic Consciousness and Immanent Will

I

THOMAS HARDY'S *Far From the Madding Crowd* is certainly a fictional feat in story telling; and is decidedly better than his other famous novels even than *Tess of the D'urverbilles*. Hardy has taken every care to weave all the threads of the story of this novel in such a way that there is apparently a touch of compactness and wholesomeness. There is a beginning, a middle, and an end in the Aristotelian sense of the term. The whole plot is characterized by a unique touch of architechtonic quality. Unlike Charles Dickens, he tells a story so compactly and tersely that there does not remain any loose strand standing independently to mar the basic structure of the story.

In fact, unity of structure makes a story of a novel superb. "Self-contained and satisfying plot is the prime necessity of a novel."[1] Dittoing the same idea, Lionel Stevenson says, "Considered as a work of art, a piece of fiction cannot be regarded as a novel unless it has a unity of structure."[2] Thomas Hardy lays utmost emphasis on the unity of structure and that is why his novels have perfect organic quality in general. This organic quality in *Far From the Madding Crowd* is all the more sharpened because of too much constructive technique which Katherine Lever considers to be "the kernel of good story telling."[3]

With these opening comments, let us see how the story of the novel under discussion moves on and how proportionately the organic whole has been achieved. For this, we have to recapitulate the story of the whole novel and to devote space for discussion in accordance with the importance of a particular episode. Hardy has maintained this balance by giving more emphasis on major strands and less space to minor strands. As a rule, the main plot should not be made subservient to sub-plots and Hardy has maintained this distinction very clearly. Another important thing in advancing the story by Hardy is an underlying connection among all major and minor strands which are lighted in accordance with their relevance.

In fact, this novel is based on a love story chiefly centring round Gabriel Oak and Bathsheba Everdene on the one hand, and Farmer Boldwood and Bathsheba on the other. This constitutes one strand of the love story. The another strand of love runs between Sergeant Troy and Bathsheba, on the one hand, and between Sergeant Troy and Fanny Robin, on the other. This love conflict may further be explained in its conclusive dimensions. Sergeant Troy is killed by Boldwood in a fit of anger in the end. Bathsheba who till now does not respond to the love of Gabriel Oak starts loving him after the death of Troy. Before that Troy ill-treats Fanny Robin and somehow wins over Bathsheba, who then rejects Oak. This is very briefly the basic fabric of this novel.

In order to have a full view of the story, we should go into its details a little further. The novel opens with the description of Farmer Oak. He has been shown as a man of resolute will and strong physique. His Christian name is Gabriel and on working days, he is a young man of sound judgment, proper dress and general good character. But on Sundays, he is a man of misty views and postpones his important works to some other days. He enjoys a good public reputation like any ordinary being. He wears a low-crowned felt hat, spread out at the base by tight jamming upon the head for security in high winds, and a coat like

Dr. Johnson's. He also carries with him a small silver clock, which he inherited from his grandfather.

In the very first chapter also, we find how the heroine of the novel, *i.e.*, Bathsheba Everdene has been introduced. She has been shown as a very beautiful girl. Her temperament is thoroughly romantic. She lives in a world of dreams. She spends a lot of time in her dressing and make-up. She also thinks that she is the most beautiful creature of nature and God.

Once it so happens that Bathsheba travels in a waggon. In the way, her waggon or cart stopped to pay the toll-tax. The man at the toll-bar enters into controversy with Bathsheba over paying two pence more, which she refuses. At this stage, Oak sees Bathsheba from a very close distance and he immediately pays two pence to the turnpike keeper. He now requests the gate-man of the toll-post to let the young woman's waggon pass. Somehow, Oak feels inclined to talk to the young lady (Bathsheba). But, proud as Bathsheba is of her young and beautiful person, she asks her coach man to drive the waggon at once, without returning even words of thanks to Oak. He now tries to understand the strange behaviour of Bathsheba.

Oak is a shepherd and he has acquired sufficient mastery in tending lambs and ewes. He is very hard working and spends most of his time in looking after his sheep. He resides near Toller-Down, which is near the famous Norcombe Hill. To move between Toller-Down and Norcombe Hill is extremely exciting. Whenever he moves between these two localities, he feels very much pleased and, he therefore, plays on his flute. His playing on flute makes him endeared to the whole neighbourhood. Near the same locality, Bathsheba also lives with her beautiful aunt. One day, while Oak was coming down the mountains, he meets Bathsheba, the second time, and this time, he observes the beauty of Bathsheba in minute details.

In the third chapter named 'A Girl On Horseback-Conversation', we find that when one day Bathsheba was riding on her horseback, she meets Oak. Actually, Oak had come to return her hat, which he catches hold the other day, while going down the hill. Bathsheba then asks a number of questions from Oak regarding his whereabouts, which Oak response rather politely. Oak tells her that he has come to that locality only lately and that he has about one hundred acres of land in addition to many sheep and lambs. He also tells her that between Tewnell Mill and Toller-Down, he has often seen her going up and down the mountains. Now, five mornings and five evenings passed, and Bathsheba regularly came to milk the healthy cow or to attend to the sick one, but she never allowed her face to stray in the direction of Oak's person. She now thinks that Oak knows more about her life and that is why she wants to keep herself slightly reserved. But one evening, she goes to his hut, where he all alone was meditating on some graver issues of life. Both of them talk to each other for sometime. During the course of their talk, Oak takes Bathsheba's hand into his hand and holds it for sometime. She blushes to see her hand in his, but Oak is still not very much forthright in prevailing on her.

Now one day Oak visits Bathsheba's place. Instead of meeting Bathsheba, he meets Mrs. Hurst, her aunt. Bathsheba is out at that moment, but her aunt tells Oak that she has frought a lamb for Bathsheba which she would rear up. Oak talks a lot to Mrs. Hurst about Bathsheba in her absence. He also makes it clear during his talk to Mrs. Hurst that he loves Bathsheba. When Oak goes away some two hundred yards, he sees a young girl racing behind him waving a white handkerchief. Oak stands still and the girl came nearer and nearer. It was Bathsheba Everdene. She now begs pardon of him for not being present at his visit to her place. Both of them talk to each other lovingly. Bathsheba offers her hand to Oak, which he holds for long. She then tells him that whatever her aunt has informed him of the aspirants of marriage with her is not correct. She has no lover so far and Oak is the only man who has come in her life for the first time. Oak now proposes to marry her, which she postpones for the time being very cunningly and cleverly. Her temperament is of a romantic stuff and she does not care much for the earnest request of Oak. On Oak's assuring her of a decent living after marriage, she merely says, "Wait, wait, and don't be improper".[4] When Oak requests further and presses the issue of marriage more consistently, Bathsheba says, "I cannot marry you, because I don't love you."[5] With a broken heart, Oak re-assures her of his love and says, "I shall do one thing in this life — one thing certain — that is, love you, and long for you, and keep wanting you till I die."[6] *His* voice has a genuine pathos now and his large brown hands perceptibly trembled. Bathsheba admits her too independent nature at this heart-rending scene by uttering, "It wouldn't do, Mr. Oak. I want somebody to tame me; I am too independent; and you would never be able to, I know."[7]

After sometime, Bathsheba leaves the neighbourhood of Oak, which leaves a great impact on Oak. He is rather surprised at this news. He now realises the great fact that "There is no regular path for getting out of love as there is for getting in."[8] But Oak "belongs to the even-tempered order of humanity, and feels the secret fusion of himself in Bathsheba to be burning with a finer flame now that she was gone — that was all."[9]

Gabriel has two dogs — George, the elder, and another George's son. Now Oak passes most of his time with his pets, particularly the dogs. One night, when Farmer Oak returns to his house, he finds one of the dogs dead. Because of suffocating air in his hut, which he leaves closed on all sides, his dog also dies. Oak is greatly unhappy now.

After two months, one day in February, Oak goes to a country-town of Casterbridge to attend to a fair. He sees there that from two to three hundred blithe and hearty labourers were waiting up *Chance*, among these mostly carters and waggoners. Oak purchases somethings from there. He also comes to know that there will be another fair at Shootsford the next day, which was about 10 miles away from Weatherbury, where Bathsheba had gone two months before. Oak now decides to go to Weatherbury at once; because he wants to see Bathsheba. He comes down the Yalbury Hill while moving towards Weatherbury and comes across a waggon in the way. On coming close to the waggon, he found that it was empty. He takes his slices of bread and ham, drinks from the bottle of cider and gets into the lonely waggon to spend some hours of the night. When he sleeps, the waggon moves on all of a sudden. While in the back part of the waggon, he listens to the conversation in coach between Billy Smallbury and Master Poorgrass, who talk about Bathsheba. Oak sees further that there was a big fire near there. He leaps over the hedge and helps Mark, Clark, Maryann, Coggan and others who were trying to extinguish fire. Actually, a ladder is brought to reach the top of a place from where the fire could be controlled. Oak himself climbs the ladder and helps extinguish the blazing fire. He is now almost taken aback to see Bathsheba standing before him, as the fire is being put under control in her fields.

Bathsheba recognizes Oak, but withdraws to a side and starts thinking about this coincidence of their meeting again. She is also thinking about her superior position and that of the poor condition of Oak quietly. She is not altogether forgetful of Oak's offer of marriage to her at Norcombe. In the meantime, other of her servants and villagers say that Oak may be employed as a shepherd by her. Ultimately, she asks them all to talk to the bailiff on this point, who in turn, allows him to work as shepherd under him. He also asks Bathsheba to make arrangements for his stay. Now Oak and Bathsheba talk to each other. The other day Oak comes to the Warren's Malthouse, where he drinks alongwith Henry Fray and Jan Coggan.

Liddy and Bathsheba live in a grand house, Oak is slightly happy in his new employment. Liddy describes to Bathsheba some of the qualities of Oak. Apparently, Bathsheba does not betray her love for Oak. In the heart of her hearts, she has some love feelings for Oak. She is happy that Oak has come to the employment of her, and that she has many occasions to meet him and to cherish her love for him. After sometime, she dismisses the bailiff from her employment on the charges of theft and misuse of power. She also makes her resolution known to other labourers that she will now have no more bailiff.

In the meantime, Fanny has run away with a soldier; and Bathsheba sends Henery and Billy Smallbury to collect some more news regarding Fanny. Now William tells the whole story of how Fanny eloped with a soldier named Troy. Everybody talks ill about the loose morals of the girl and Bathsheba too criticises this action of Fanny. Oak stands still and calm without commenting anything on this issue.

Sergeant Troy entices Fanny, but he is not sincere in his love to her. One day, when she comes to him to get money, he shows clear signs of getting riddance of him. When a conversation was going on between them, Oak overhears their talk. He feels sympathised for the poor girl, who is being deceived by Troy. Fanny requests him to marry her, but the clever soldier postpones it to some other appropriate time by taking recourse to one or the other tactics.

Bathsheba declares publicly that she has now almostly decided to be a farmer. She also makes up her mind personally to attend a cornmarket at Casterbridge. Initially, she hesitates to visit such places which are mainly dominated by men. But she now grows in expertise and experience. When the marketing is over, Bathsheba rushes off to Liddy who was waiting for her beside the yellow gig in which both have driven to town. The horse is put in and they drove towards their home. In the way, Bathsheba mentions to Liddy that while all men were gazing at her, there was a man about forty, who did not waste his time on gazing at her. His name was Farmer Boldwood. In the meantime, Boldwood's carriage overtakes theirs and passes them. Boldwood pays no attention to her person even now and goes on unconcerned. Bathsheba then comments upon him, "I wonder why he is so wrapt up and indifferent, and seemingly so far away from all he sees around him."[10] To which, Liddy says that uncommon behaviour in him is due to the fact that he has already got disappointment in his love two times.

On the thirteenth of February, dinner being over, Bathsheba for want of a better companion asks Liddy to come and sit with her. The mouldy pile was dreary in winter-time before the candles were lighted and the shutters closed. The atmosphere of the place seems as old as the walls; every nook behind the furniture has a temperature of its own. Liddy nows asks Bathsheba if she could see the doings of Boldwood in the church that morning, to which Bathsheba replies in negative. Liddy then tells her that while everybody was looking to her beautiful person in the church it was Boldwood who was paying no attention at all. Therefore, Bathsheba feels infuriated. They chalk out a plan and accordingly write the following on a nicely designed piece of paper, which they purchased the other day, and drop it to Boldwood in order to be fool him :

> "The rose is red,
> The violet blue,
> Carnation's sweet
> And so are you."[11]

The effect of this letter on Boldwood is really magical. At dusk, on the evening of St. Valentine's Day, Boldwood sits down to supper as usual by a beaming fire of aged logs. Upon the mantel self before him is a time piece, surmounted by a spread eagle, and upon the eagle's wings is the letter Bathsheba has sent. Here the bachelor's gaze is continuously fastening itself, till the large red seal becomes a blot of blood on the retina of his eye. As he sits and drinks, he still reads in fancy the words thereon, although they are too remote for his sight —

> "MARRY ME."[12]

The impact of this letter continues to intensify. When Boldwood goes to bed he places the Valentine in the corner of the looking glass. It is the first time in his life that such an event has occurred. He is still not sure of the hand who has written it. But it becomes quite clear to him that is the handwriting of a lady.

On Saturday, Boldwood is seen in Cambride market-house as usual, when Bathsheba, the disturber of his dreams, enters and becomes visible to him. On common points of business, they talk to each other. Bathsheba, a very clever lady, as she is, talks to Boldwood very indifferently. Boldwood feels greatly attracted to her person, but Bathsheba does not love her. She is a beautiful girl, no doubt, but does not seem to be sincere in her love. This reflects upon her romantic temperament. She does not find the fittest person of her ideal lover in Boldwood. She, therefore, does not feel greatly encouraged in her love to Boldwood.

Bathsheba is an impulsive nature under a deliberative aspect. An Elizabethan in brain and Mary Stuart in spirit, she often performs actions of the greatest temerity with a manner of extreme discretion. Many of her thoughts were perfect syllogisms, and unluckily they always remained thoughts. Only a few have been irrational assumptions, but what she cares for are these irrational ideas to put into practice.

Next day, she finds Oak at the bottom of her garden, grinding his shears for the sheep-shearing. She sees Oak's expertise in tending the sheep. She then orders Cain to go to the other end so that she can talk to Oak in privacy. She helps Oak in his work. She asks him if there was any talk about her going behind the sedge with Boldwood the previous day. Oak then tells her that there has been a talk of her marriage with him. To this, Bathsheba says that she will contradict this, as she does not like to marry Boldwood. Then she asks Oak about her conduct the previous day, to which he replies, "That it is unworthy of any thoughtful, and meek, and comely woman".[13] In an instant, Bathsheba's face is coloured with the angry crimson of a Danby sunset, and subsiding her angry mood somehow she retorts to Oak, "I may ask, I suppose where in particular my unworthiness lies? In my not marrying you, perhaps!"[14] Further controversy ensues between Bathsheba and Oak. Oak tells Bathsheba, "My opinion is (since you ask it) that you are greatly to blame for playing pranks upon a man like Mr. Boldwood, merely as a pastime. Leading on a man you don't care for is not a praiseworthy action. And even, Miss Everdene, if you are seriously inclined towards him, you might have let find it out in some way of true loving kindness, and not by sending him a Valentine's letter".[15] Bathsheba lays down the shears and angrily says, "I cannot allow any man to — to criticize my private conduct! Nor will I for a minute. So you'll please leave the farm at the end of the week!"[16] She further orders him in anger, "Go at once then, in Heaven's name!", "Don't let me see your face any more."[17] Then Gabriel Oak leaves the employment of Bathsheba Everdene as calmly and with placid dignity, as Moses left the presence of Pharaoh.

Just after three days of Oak's departure from the Weatherbury farm, on Sunday afternoon, it was reported by Joseph Poorgrass, Mathew Moon and Fray to Bathsheba at her house at the Upper Farm that a formidable disease had spread amongst the sheep and lambs. They also report that already many lambs and ewes have died. Poorgrass reports that sixty have suffered from disease whereas Moon says that some seventy have been in a precarious condition and that all will soon die. This puts Bathsheba Everdene in a very bad situation. She does not know how she should request Oak to come again and to tend and protect the block of sheep. Only Oak had the requisite expertise to save the innocent lives of the lambs. Many of them start dying before her own eyes. He feels utterly helpless and does not want to bear such an ugly and cruel spectacle of death. Bathsheba does not brook or tolerate this sight of death any longer. Her pride is dashed to ground. Finding no other alternative immediately in sight, she sits down and writes a small letter or note to Oak with the following words at the bottom with emphasis :

"Do Not Desert Me, Gabriel !"[18]

Within a quarter of an hour, Gabriel comes back not as much out of Bathsheba's love for him, but for the lambs' sake. He is a true Christian in action, and like a true Christian, he immediately rushes to help the dying animals. Here Hardy puts his own ideas about service to others through the mouth of Oak, who may be regarded, though to some extent, as the spokesman or the mouthpiece, of the novelist. Gabriel immediately springs to action, employs his best expertise, and within no time, many lambs struggling for life, become quite perfect. Bathsheba looks at Oak working patiently on the sheep. Like a veterinary surgeon, he punctures the affected part of the animals and administers the medicine with much deftness and alacrity. 49 operations were made by Oak. Only 4 died, 3 recovered without an operation. 57 sheep were saved in all. Bathsheba then requests Oak to stay on in her employment and not to desert her, to which Oak agrees, in the end.

One day when Bathsheba and Oak are talking to each other in the field, Boldwood again comes to meet her. Bathsheba comes to Boldwood and both continue to talk. She asks again Oak not to intervene in their conversation. Boldwood renews his proposal of marriage to her, but again she tactfully avoids any definite answer to his proposal of marriage. This shows how Bathsheba is faithless both to Oak and Boldwood. This infidelity of Bathsheba leads Oak to utter, "I find more bitter than death the woman whose heart is snares and nets."[19]

The next day Bathsheba feels very much perturbed. She does attend to her normal routine work. While she was still meditating and feeling disturbed, Boldwood again comes. Both again talk to each other. Boldwood pleads to be loved by her, to which she says, "I will try to love you…. I don't want to give a solemn promise tonight. I would rather ask you to wait a few weeks till I can see my situation better."[20] In fact, Bathsheba is not sincere in her love. Here we are reminded of Hardy's oft-quoted lines through the mouth of Gabriel that, "Women are never tired of bewailing man's fickleness in love, but they only seem to snub his constancy."[21]

On another night, while Bathsheba is returning home, she meets Sergeant Troy. Troy is as romantic minded as Bathsheba is. Troy is brilliantly dressed in brass and scarlet. He is a perfect soldier. His spur had become entangled in the gimp which decorated the skirt of her dress. While trying to unfasten her skirt, Troy takes his full time to come nearer to Bathsheba. He looks hard into her eyes, and Bathsheba looks down, for his gaze is too strong to be received point-blank with her own. Somehow, Bathsheba notices rather obliquely that Troy is young and slim, and that he wore three chevrons upon his sleeve. Bathsheba pulls again, but Troy cunningly says, "You are a prisoner, miss; it is no use blinking the matter. I must cut your dress if you are in such a hurry."[22] Bathsheba looks on helplessly what Troy was doing. When Bathsheba is freed of her dress from Troy, he says to her, "Thank you for the sight of such a beautiful face."[23] He treats her in such a romantic manner that Bathsheba feels inclined towards him. Troy again and again reminds Bathsheba of her beauty — a weakness in every woman. Bathsheba feels agreeable to Troy now and wants to know his whereabouts. Troy tells everything about him and his present posting in the military. Bathsheba now compares Oak and Boldwood with Troy and finds him definitely better than these lovers.

Sergeant Troy is as ficklemined as Bathsheba is. He has determined to come nearer to her and for that he wants to play all sorts of tricks. While Bathsheba is in her fields, Sergeant Troy reaches there and sincerely addresses her as the queen of the corn-market. He praises her with his full-throated ease and says again and again that she is the most beautiful woman he has ever seen on the earth and in whole of England. After a prolonged love-dialogue that ensues between the both, Troy gives a golden watch to Bathsheba as a present, which she returns when he withdraws from the field. In fact, Troy, is a reckless, cunning soldier. He says so many things in the praise of Bathsheba, and makes so many pledges and oaths that ultimately Bathasheba, being a perfect romantic lady, is trapped. Troy says to her that he will go to another place just within one month and he will like to talk to her continuously. He also seeks her permission to let him work in her fields so that he can find time to meet and talk her. Bathsheba succumbs to her romantic moods and allows him all such liberties. In a word, Troy overpowers her with a more arresting and captivating personality than her own. To Oak and Boldwood, she paid no heed, but to Troy she had to yield.

In the latter part of June, one day Bathsheba is busy hiving the bees in her garden. She is all alone in her house, even Liddy is out that day. She has dressed the hive with herbs and honey, has also fetched a ladder, brush, and crook for the purpose. But while she is busy, she finds Troy standing before him. She is rather taken aback, but Troy wants to help her in the bee-hiving. No sooner does he come and meet her than he starts praising the beauty of Bathsheba. But Bathsheba asks him to put on the veil and gloves or the bees will sting him fearfully. But he wants Bathsheba's help in fixing them on his body properly. While Troy was busy sweeping and shaking the bees from the tree, Bathsheba looks on at him from the ground, holding up the hive with the other hand for them to fall into. After the work is over, Troy mentions to her that he is equally good at the sword-exercise. Being a romantic girl, she likes such bodily acrobatics very much. She had already heard about Troy's dexterity in sword-exercise. So she wants to see the sword exercise for herself to be performed by Troy. The place chosen for this is the hollow pit amidst the ferns in the hill situated just opposite Bathsheba's dwelling place. It is almost a mile off, into an uncultivated tract of land, dotted with tall thickets of brake fern, plump and diaphanous from recent rapid growth. It is evening summer-sun light that both meet each other in the hollow pit. Troy is already waiting for her there and he helps her to descend the slope. The pit is a saucer-shaped concave, naturally formed, with a top diameter of about thirty feet. Troy demonstrates the sword-exercise with so much skill and dexterity that Bathsheba feels completely enchanted. In such a fit of enchantment, Troy cuts a lock from her hair and preserves it as a permanent remainder of their love. When the game ends, Bathsheba develops a very strong liking for Troy. Now she feels her weakness in unnecessarily allowing Oak and Boldwood to love her. In the end, when they depart, Troy passionately kisses her, to which she does not resist — perhaps the first of her warm kisses.

One evening, Bathsheba goes for a short walk by a path through the neighbouring cornfield. In the way, she meets Oak, who now advises her to be careful from bad characters. In referring to bad characters, he refers to Sergeant Troy, but Bathsheba does not pay any heed to his advice. Then he refers to Boldwood and his love to her. But she rejects Boldwood and is not prepared to listen anything against Troy. Oak, who actually knows a lot about Troy's character, again advises her to be away from Troy, but she refuses. As a matter of fact, she is strongly infatuated by Troy's personality and is not prepared to listen anything against him. At last, she asks Oak after a long argument to go back. To his great surprise, Oak finds on his returning a few yards, that a shape arises from a nearby field and meets Bathsheba. It was Troy, for whom she is used to take such short evening walks.

Both Bathsheba and Troy talk a lot lovingly. Troy comes to leave her to the very door of her house. Now he says that he will not come for 2 days, as he will go to Bath for an urgent piece of work. He puts a warm kiss on her cheeks and goes away. She then writes a big note to Farmer Boldwood rejecting his love advances at all. Liddy, her maid servant, comes to know of Bathsheba's love for Troy. Bathsheba takes her into confidence, and instructs her not to divulge this secret to anybody. She has mentally prepared herself to marry Troy at all costs, finding no defect or weakness in him. The next evening, Boldwood meets her. By now, he has also come to know of her liking for Troy. He also knows through rumours in the neighbourhood that Bathsheba is thinking of marrying Troy at the earliest. So he is beyond himself with rage and anger. Being frustrated in love already once, he does not like to fail this time. A heated argument regarding their love for each other takes place between the both. Boldwood is tactless in love matters, though he is more earnest and more reliable than Troy. Ultimately, Bathsheba says almost *No* to him, which makes him mad. Boldwood is a man of very furious temperament. He does not brook any of his rivals, He, therefore, determines to murder Troy and swears in the very presence of Bathsheba that he will certainly kill Troy. This makes Bathsheba fearful of her future.

Bathsheba is now worried about Troy's safety. She, therefore, herself goes to Bath to inform him of the developments that have taken place. Since she has not informed anybody of his visit to Bath, where Troy has already gone to, there is a great commotion in the house. Liddy, Gabriel Oak and Coggan are all worried. But when all of them see Bathsheba herself riding in the cart, everybody is taken aback. Their suspicion is all the more matured now to notice how Troy has been attached to her, of late. She passes a week at Bath without sending any information back to the house. Then a note is circulated by Maryann to all that her mistress (Bathsheba) may be detained by important work there at Bath. Another week also passes, but Bathsheba does not come. Coggan reports back to all after his return from Bath that he saw Bathsheba and Sergeant Troy meeting, talking and loving to each other and that Bathsheba was dressed in a shining gold-colour silk gown trimmed with black lace. Oak now concludes that they might have married and that she might be worried because of Troy's safety from Boldwood. One evening Bathsheba and Liddy return to their house in a gig. After sometime, Boldwood comes to meet her, but she asks Liddy to tell him that she does not want to talk to him. He is very sad and upset and instead of going to his house, he wanders to and fro the lower part of Weatherbury. After sometime, he sees that Troy comes and goes to the chamber of Bathsheba. While Troy comes out of her house, Boldwood catches hold of him and threatens him to forget Bathsheba. Boldwood reminds him of his attachment to Fanny Robin. Troy feels somewhat nervous, but he plays a trick upon him. In order to put him off, he says to Boldwood that he cannot marry Bathsheba as he is poor. At this, Boldwood promises to pay him fifty pounds, if he marries Fanny Robin. He will pay him fifty pounds more if he leaves Weatherbury at once and forgets Bathsheba for ever. To this suggestion, Troy very cleverly says that it is not he but Bathsheba who has asked him to marry her. He then takes fifty pounds from Boldwood. But at the same time Bathsheba comes and when Boldwood is standing afar, Troy talks to her in a tone that is all audible to her. Both start talking to each other about their love. Boldwood now feels convinced that Bathsheba does not love him. She is only making a fool of him. His anger gives way to sympathy; his envy to love. He regards himself unfit for Bathsheba and instead of killing Troy allows him to carry on his love with her. Boldwood offers his money to Troy to enable him to marry Bathsheba rather quickly. On the 17th instant, at St. Ambrose's Church, Bath, Troy and Bathsheba are married to each other. Boldwood plunges into unhappiness and pessimism thereafter. Troy and Bathsheba now live together and Oak, as a man of courage and tolerance, accepts this as a reality of life.

One night, at the end of August, when Bathsheba's experiences as a married woman are still new, it so happens that while Troy is busy in drinking and dancing in a party hosted by him to celebrate his marriage, there is a very heavy rain. The stackyard of Weatherbury Upper Farm is largely damaged. There are five wheat-ricks in this yard, and three stacks of barley. A total of about seven hundred and fifty pounds of money is involved in this damage. While Troy is revelling and sleeping carelessly, it is Oak who tries his best along with others to save the stackyard from damage. Bathsheba herself supervises the action in the stackyard. She is unhappy with Troy for his carelessness and for the first time she realises her folly in not marrying Oak, who is still devoted and honest in his actions.

One day, both Oak and Boldwood meet together and both talk to each other for long. They also talk about the strange behaviour of Bathsheba in deceiving them both. Boldwood seems to be much pained whereas Oak does not think he has been wronged much. He only thinks that a man should endure what he cannot cure. He believes in the theory that a man should try his best to adapt himself to his changing circumstances.

One Saturday evening in the month of October, while Bathsheba and Troy are returning from the market, they meet a woman in the way at *Yalbury Hill*. Her name is Fanny Robin, whom Troy has loved and has now deserted. She is a poor lady and is pregnant now. She is in utter need of money and has come to meet Troy. A wicked fellow as Troy is, he now acts in such a clever manner that he does not allow Bathsheba to know Fanny's whereabouts. He gives Fanny some money and asks her to meet him on Monday morning at ten exactly on Grey's Bridge. On Bathsheba's insistence, he only admits that he knows the woman and nothing more. She becomes suspicious of the character of Troy and is now prepared to believe what others in the neighbourhood use to say of him. But now onwards, a sort of unpleasantness begins in the behaviour of Bathsheba for Troy.

One day Troy demands twenty pounds from Bathsheba. Actually, he needs this money to help Fanny, but he does not tell this thing to her. Somehow, he prevails upon Bathsheba and is successful in extracting money from her. She now believes that 'her romance has come to an end'; and that 'all romances end at marriage.'[24] Troy goes to meet Fanny, but before that, Bathsheba further insists on knowing more about the other lady. When he is putting a brown curl of Fanny in his watch, Bathsheba sees it and does not tolerate it. She requests him to burn that lock of hair, which he does not listen to. He then admits that he has a special relationship with Fanny. Instead of telling her that Fanny is about to give birth to a child, he merely says that he is particularly related to her.

When Bathsheba is very much perturbed over what has happened to her luck, she listens to the talk of Oak, Boldwood and Joseph in the field. Joseph informs that Fanny is dead. In a way, Fanny is related to Boldwood, so it is being informed to all that he will fetch the dead body of Fanny. Bathsheba gets some relief in the heart of her hearts, but she feels sympathised towards the dead and she herself want to send her own waggon in order to bring the dead body of Fanny.

In the meantime, Troy comes there. He does not meet Fanny and, as the ill-luck would have it, he is unable to give money to her. After giving birth to a baby, she dies. Troy is very unhappy and disturbed to see Fanny and her baby who are now dead. He immediately gets two separate stones prepared as reminders of their memory. He kneels again and again to the coffin and sees the dead face and kisses it. Bathsheba feels jealous of it. Ultimately, Fanny is buried.

Troy and Bathsheba feel displeased and unhappy in the company of each other. Troy is a romantic mind and he does not, therefore, feel at ease at Bathsheba's indecent conduct. He wants to go to the shore and decides to spend some days at Budmouth. Coming to the southward direction of the Pacific, he descends to a small basin of sea enclosed by cliffs. Troy's nature freshens within him; he thinks he will rest and bathe here before going farther. He undresses himself and plunges into it. No sooner does he plunge into the deep waters of the sea, than the strong waves carry him along the other side. He is unable to swim in the whirlpool of water. Many bathers see him being carried to another shore and many take him to be dead in Lulwin Cove.

News is brought to Bathsheba of Troy's possible drowning in the sea. She feels extremely repentant and regards, perhaps for the first time, that life is really a big burden. In the meantime, Oak is promoted to the post of bailiff by Bathsheba, who waits for some time for Troy in the hope that he may still come. Oak now acts as a go-between Bathsheba and Boldwood. Boldwood is still infatuated by the beauty of Bathsheba. He is hopeful of winning over her. Bathsheba now returns from a two months' visit to her old aunt at Norcombe and on her return, through Liddy, he renews his proposal of marriage to her. But initially, Bathsheba decides not to marry at least for six years. However, she does not ignore him completely and has got a soft corner for him.

Gradually, Boldwood and Bathsheba come closer and closer, till it is a rumour quite rife in the neighbourhood that Bathsheba is going to marry Boldwood. On one occasion, Troy, is seen by some in a sheep fair, but he also comes to know of the rumour of the possible marriage between Boldwood and Bathsheba. Actually, Troy is not drowned; he is only taken to be drowned. While one day, Bathsheba is returning from Casterbridge Market, she is being escorted in the gig by Boldwood. After talking for long on a variety of topics, both enjoy the travel. Soon Boldwood asks simply if she will marry him some day. Bathsheba now admits that she still loves him and respects him. She also tells him that she may marry him at some appropriate time. Oak also encourages Bathsheba to marry Boldwood and assures her of

Boldwood's fidelity and sincerity towards her. Bathsheba also repents over what she has done in the past.

Boldwood makes Bathsheba agreeable to the proposal that she will come to a party he will arrange on the eve of Christmas. Bathsheba, after great hesitation agrees to it. Boldwood wants to make his party a grand success and it is the big talk in Weatherbury. Boldwood arranges the party on a grand scale. He is extremely happy that day. He gets a new suit prepared for this occasion and at the appointed day wears it with a radiance on his face. Bathsheba dresses herself well and along with Liddy goes to the party at the appointed time, where Boldwood is impatiently waiting for her. After some wait, she comes and Boldwood receives her too warmly to describe. There is a lot of dance and drink at the party. Boldwood, during the course of these joyous hours, puts a ring on one of the fingers of Bathsheba, which she hesitates initially. After enjoying for about an hour or so, Bathsheba asks Liddy to get ready for departure from the party. Somehow, she is feeling perplexed and slightly disturbed at the prospect of Troy's being still alive.

In the meantime, Troy also reaches there. He is wearing such a dress as can easily hide his real identity. Troy comes to know of the very purpose of this party being arranged by Boldwood. Troy now enters the main hall and there is a deadly silence on looking at Troy still alive. Some notice Troy, but Boldwood is still unable to identify him. Bathsheba is pale and horrified. In the end, Troy is being recognised by Boldwood. Then, Troy turns to Bathsheba, whose mouth is now blue and dry, and her vacant eyes are fixed on him. Troy now says to Bathsheba that he has come to take her away with him. While Troy is pulling the arm of Bathsheba, Boldwood shoots Troy dead with his gun out of anger and anguish. Troy falls on the ground. After that, Boldwood comes out of the house and goes away. A petition is addressed to the Home Secretary advancing the circumstances which appear to justify a request for the consideration of Boldwood's sentence. In the end, he is not saved.

Now Oak is the only person who survives the trials of life. Gradually, Bathsheba finds in him the perfect specimen of a husband. She starts taking interest in him. Oak also takes over the farm of Boldwood and now he supervises both the farms in a collective and combined way. One day, Bathsheba goes to Oak, while he is sitting outside his house ruminating over his past, and proposes to him to marry her. Oak agrees to it in the end, and both live as husband and wife. Bathsheba has had sufficient experience of life, and she, therefore, makes compromises with it. Oak and Bathsheba start realizing that marriage is a bond of lasting faith and friendship. Thus the novel comes to an end with a philosophic note.

II

The Victorian Age is an age of ideological fermentation and innovative experimentation. Thomas Hardy, the man, is known for his ideological fermentation and Thomas Hardy, the novelist, earned laurels for making innovative experiments in fiction writing. Whereas from Darwinism, he drew the idea of Unconscious Will, he borrowed the concept of Immanent Will from Schopenhauer. For his concept of Cosmic Consciousness, he rummaged through the oriental literature particularly the *Bhagavadgita*.

For innovative experimentation, he represents the late Victorian Age almost as forcefully through his novels as Charles Dickens does the early Victorian age. One of the major movements during the nineteenth century was the movement of science and Hardy's reaction to and approbation of this movement are as powerful and moulding as those of George Meredith. In fact, during the Victorian Age, different scientific theories came into evidence, but the evolutionary theory, of which Darwin, was the chief harbinger, swayed almost all other theories; and in order to understand Hardy's concept of Darwinian Unconscious Will, it is prudent to develop some idea about Darwinism.

Darwinism is the collection or amalgamation of evolutionary theories propounded by Charles Darwin and others which powerfully influenced almost every domain of man's activity. Of the historical landmarks, such as Darwin's *Origin of Species* (1859), *The Descent of Man* (1871); Herbert Spencer's *First Principles* (1862); Huxley's *Man's Place in Nature* (1863); John Leckey's *History of Rationalism* (1865); John Tyndall's *The Imagination in Science* (1870); Wallace's *Darwinism* (1889); Taylor's *Primitive Culture* (1871); Matthew Arnold's *Literature and Dogma* (1873); and Leslie Stephen's *The Science of Ethics* (1882) opened up new vistas of scientific inquiry into man's mind and heart including his origin and evolution. It led to the gradual decline of well-entrenched values and beliefs. The spirit of agnosticism which looked askance at everything untested and unexperimented further deepened.

The doctrine of evolution propounded by Darwin, Wallace, Spencer and Huxley banished, in one stroke, God from Nature, Life and even from Soul, compelling the evolution of the Unconscious Will, or a Blind Power to control the Universe. This view of God led to an abrupt decay in orthodox Christian faith in a Benevolent Almighty. In educational field, the Test Act of 1871 brought about a significant change : for, both Oxford and Cambridge Universities were liberated from the dominance of the Church : even history, philosophy and physical science found a place alongside of humanities and mathematics in these famous Universities, especially in Oxford University. This may partly be ascribed due to the decline of economy and industry, religion and morals, but largely owing to the movement of science, especially the impact of evolutionism.

In such a changed socio-political situation spawned by Darwinism, Hardy was almost baffled like other novelists of the age. He was at a loss to understand as to how he should strive to synthesise what is old and what is yet to be established as the actual source of will in human body. The great voices of the age — Dickens, Trollope, Thackeray, Gaskell, Gissing, Moore, Butler, Meredith — were equally baffled to see mighty transmogrifications taking place all around, but their consternation and bafflement were confined to certain particular socio-political developments. It was Hardy who, first of all, tried to deliberate on a serious aspect of Human Will.

In fact, whereas Meredith, his coeval, tried to reconcile on the baffling issue of human will by taking recourse to a creative evolutionism approximating to the creative evolution of the Bergsonian, of the Tagorean stamp, which entails faith in intuition, Hardy adopts a three-pronged approach. For physical evolution, he drew inspiration what is known as Darwinism, for emotional evolution he takes help of the Biblical Monotheism and for spiritual evolution, he seeks succour and sustenance from the basic teachings of *The Bhagavadgita*. His Darwinian Unconscious Will of the physical evolution is the Schopenhauerian Immanent Will of the spiritual evolution. Again, Hardy's Immanent Will is as creative as Darwinian postulate of evolution through struggle for existence. Shorn of any specific nomenclature, Hardy's Immanent Will or Unconscious Will or Cosmic Consciousness is as Omnipresent as *The Bhagavadgita's* Brahma. Not only this, Hardy's Immanent Will is as creative and as indestructible as *The Bhagavadgita's Parama Brahma*. Bocke and Spinoza talked of Necessity which philosophically suggested Cosmic Consciousness. *The Bhagavadgita* propounds the theory of Cosmic Consciousness and Hardy's Immanent Will in the *Dynasts* is another form of Cosmic Consciousness.

Darwinism, in essence, lays down five stages of evolution. The first stage of evolution is the stage when the doctrine of Struggle for Existence applies. By this, the general inference is that the stronger as well as the weaker species struggle for existence, in which only those survive which are the fittest. As the stronger species of fish eat the weaker ones, likewise the weaker kinds of mankind gradually become extinct. But for this physical existence, a kind of strong will power is needed for proper adaptation. Herein lies the involvement of some creative urge to survive, which in pure biological sense is a type of Will which the Darwinian enunciation suggests to be called by the name of Unconscious Will. The second stage of evolution as laid down by the Darwinism is the principle of domestication and the third stage is the stage of mutation. In both these stages the role of Unconscious Will is quite significant. The next stage is the stage of reproduction, which demands more strivings and urges. But these strivings and urges are not merely biological or physical; for, they involve the mind and soul also.

According to the Biblical version, God created man in His own image. But the Darwinian principles altogether banish this divine tinge from the life of a man. Hardy, being a true Christian, has not digested the idea that God should altogether be banished from the life of man. However, he has not doubted the rational explanation of the evolution of man. In this baffled situation, Hardy laid stress on the essential goodness of man quite irrespective of the fact whether there is God in Heaven or not. His loud proclamation in *Tess* that there was not God in Heaven and all was not right with the world is specifically suggestive of the proverbial Victorian gloom from which he was suffering like other writers of the age. For Hardy, inner urge for doing good in life is more important than worshipping a deity. Hence, Hardy has immense faith in a kind of Will, which keeps every man alive.

Hardy accepts Darwinism in so far as it explains the biological evolution of man; nowhere does he present a world bereft of noble virtues or noble visions. Often even the landscape is obscured by the heavy mist of doubt, the mortals who wander about this landscape appear to be governed by cruel chance that gives them no option, as to the direction of their wanderings. No doubt, he often implies that there is some kind of governing power beyond and behind the material universe, but there is no fixed belief in any kind of the Meredithian compensation of spirit. Again, whatever power there be behind, the universe is obviously so no utilitarian value : the claims of Christianity as a world-religion seem preposterous to him. He is, therefore, as absolute a pagan as though all religions are alike imperfect to him. This is why, he has often been called a materialist or atheist; whereas in fact, he is neither of these : because Eustacia rises above all materialism — she will not break her sacred marriage vows for Demon Wildeve, because she has a soul to save : and again, her belief in Heaven persists till the end though Heaven is accused of cruelty for devising tortures for her.

Hardy's Darwinism manifests itself in his novels in one another form of determinism also, which is yet a sort of ripened form of Unconscious Will. According to Hardy, human action is not free but determined by motives, which are regarded as external forces acting on the Will. The characters, therefore, would appear to be helpless; and yet the tragic characters do not appear to be mere puppets jerked by a malicious fate. Were it so, they would miss an essential condition of tragedy. A towering and laudable desire may be doomed to be brought level with futility, but one profoundly enjoys the brave quality of the assertion of desire; a life abject in sorrow is nothing enjoyable and, therefore, nothing tragical. A tragic character, who endures the most pitiless destiny is never in the least abject.

Hardy's Unconscious Will is the Darwinian creative or evolving energy or an inner urge, which is responsible for the self-development and self-movement. Oneness and immanentia are inseparably bound together, each is a necessary corollary and consequence of the other and both are of equal importance; and this inner force has a number of characteristics. Here Hardy's concept of Unconscious Will is different from Meredith's; for, in Meredith's novels, the struggle for existence occurs under the providence of a God that repays and regards good and punishes bad. Those who struggle for existence on the lines of goodness, virtue and fine intuition, they are better evolved species not only physically but also spiritually. They live longer than those living by the sheer force of reason and logic. Hardy's acceptance of Darwinism gives a rational explanation of the development of man, so does Meredith's; but Hardy does not go beyond the physical evolution, and places both intuition and free will at the mercy of natural causation, which Meredith, of course, rejects. Meredith's explanation of the creative will and godly intuition is above Hardy's explanation of logic and reason in the light of scientific evolution. Hardy's Darwinism, therefore, connotes his acceptance of the biological evolution plus his faith in the Biblical

Monotheism : whereas, meredith's is his acceptance of the biological evolution plus his faith in a benevolent God. Man struggles in Meredith's world for existence in order to glorify good and enhance virtue, and finally to make this world a heaven of Gods; whereas in Hardy's, man struggles for existence for mere existence's sake; good deeds as preached by the Christian religion; are a superadded pleasure and calm to it. Nonetheless, Hardy's concept of the struggle for existence involves the full play of the Immanent Will.

For a proper understanding of Hardy's concept of Cosmic Consciousness, let us have a little bit of deeper probing into what *The Bhagvadgita* propounds about Human Will. In the *Dynasts*, Hardy lets us know his mind about the Unconscious Will, Immanent Will and the Cosmic Consciousness and the basic difference between the three types of inner urges or creative energies.

Thomas Hardy made a tall claim to have discovered the idea of Unconscious Will of the universe in his correspondence dated March 22, 1904 to Edward Clood and dated June 2, 1907 to Edward Wright respectively.[25] But the fact remains that Hardy derived the idea of the Immanent Will from Schopenhauer,[26] who himself was greatly influenced by the teachings of the *Upanishads*[27] and the *Bhagavadgita*. Schopenhauer treats nature as the objectification of the Will; life as an essentially painful and futile striving; and detached attitude as the only panacea to be released from the imperious demands of the Will.[28] Professor Ledger Wood and Frank Thilly find ascetic living as the best way to total negation of the Schopenhauerian Will. It is tantamount to the Christian humanism or the resignation and Will-lessness as practised by the Buddhist saints. Schopenhauer profoundly read Plato, who believed in the immortality of soul and its transmigration. The Schopenhauerian world as idea and will are the different manifestations of the Platonic ideas. Schopenhauer attributes different *gunas* to his concept of powerful will, which Hardy calls the Immanent Will, and which the *Bhagavadgita* too attributes :

> ...that the will, of which human life, like every phenomenon, is the objectification, is a striving without aim or end. We find the stamp of this endlessness imprinted upon all the parts of its whole manifestation, from the most universal form, endless time and space, upto the most perfect of all phenomena, the life and efforts of man. We may theoretically assume three extremes of human life, and treat them as elements of actual human life. First the powerful will, the strong passions (*Radscha-Guna*). It appears in great historical characters; it is described in the epic and the drama. But it can also show itself in the little world, for the size of the objects is measured here by the degree in which they influence the will, not according to their external relations. Secondly, pure knowing, the comprehension of the *Ideas*, conditioned by the freeing of knowledge from the service of will; the life of genius (*Satva-Guna*). Thirdly and lastly, the greatest lethargy of the will, and also of the knowledge attaching to it, empty longing, life-benumbing languor (*Tama-Guna*).[29]

In the *Bhagavadgita* (Chapter 18), the theory of *gunas* with their proper divisions, *viz.*, *Satvic, Rajas* and *Tamas*, has been propounded. The Satvic guna has been explained as :

> नियतं संङ्गरहितम् रागद्वेषतः कृतम्।
> अफलप्रेप्सुना कर्म यत्त्वासात्त्विकमुच्यते।।[30]

The Rajasic action has been explained as :

> यत्तु कामेप्सुना कर्मः साहंकारेण वा पुनः।
> क्रियते बहुलायासं तद्राजसभुदाहृतम्।।[31]

And the Tamasic action has been explained as :

> अनुबन्धम् क्षयं हिंसामनवेक्ष्य च पौरूषम्।
> मोहादारभ्यते कर्मः यत्तत्तामसमुच्यते।।[32]

In Chapter II, the *Bhagavadgita* propounds the idea of action without desire and fruit is the duty of everyone, which Schopenhauer finds the best course for the release from the imperious demands of will :

> कर्मण्येवाधिकारस्ते मा फलेषु कदाचन।
> मा कर्मफल हेतुर्भूर्गा ते सङ्गोऽस्त्वकर्मणि।।[33]

John Holloway's interpretation of Hardy's philosophy as natural living is the Schopenhauerian release of the imperious demands of will and is also tantamount to the way as enunciated by the *Bhagavadgita*. *The Mayor of Casterbridge* is a study of this idea. The more the paralysis of the Immanent Will, the more the tragic struggle is there. Henchard succumbs to the powerful paralysis of the Immanent Will. Donald Farfrae keeps up a seemingly detached attitude and so does Elizabeth Jane. Susan fails to lead a will-less and resigned life, so she meets a tragic doom. Hardy himself writes in the preface that "the story of *The Mayor of Casterbridge* is more particularly a study of one man's deeds and character, perhaps, any other of those included in my Exhibition of Wessex life."[34] Under the fit of his *Tamsic* guna, Henchard sells his wife Susan to Newsan which is certainly a paralytic attack in the Immanent Will :

> "I'll tell ye what — I won't sell her for less than five," said the husband, bringing down his fist so that the basins danced, "I'll sell her for five guineas to any man that will pay me the money, and treat her well; and he shall have her for ever, and never hear aught O' me. But she shan't go for less. Now then — five guineas — and she's yours. Susan, you agree?"

She bowed her head with absolute indifference.[35] Henchard's character is a study of the different dimensions and manifestations of the Immanent Will; his failures and successes are interlinked with the effectiveness and non-effectiveness of the Immanent Will.

The following is the most oft-quoted passage in *The Mayor of Casterbridge* where Henchard perhaps appears to be most detached in the sense of the detached deeds of the *Bhagavadgita* :

> And thus Henchard found himself again on the precise standing which he had occupied a quarter of a century before. Externally there was nothing to hinder his making another start on the upward slope, and by his new lights achieving higher things than his soul in its half-formed state had been able to accomplish. But the ingenious machinery contrived by the gods for reducing human possibilities of amelioration to a minimum — which arranges that wisdom to do shall come *pari passu* with the departure of zest for doing — stood in the way of all that. He had no wish to make an arena a second time of the world that had become a mere painted scene to him.

Very often, as his hay-knife crunched down among the sweet-smelling grassy stems, he would survey mankind and say to himself : "Here and everywhere be folk dying before their time like frosted leaves, though wanted by their families, the country, and the world; while I, an outcast, an encumberer of the ground, wanted by nobody, and despised by all, live on against my will."[36]

Deeds, gunas, immanent will, character and fate are closely interlinked in Hardy's novels. Henchard becomes the Mayor of Casterbridge by dint of his hard work and perseverance; from an itinerant drunkard and hay trusser, he becomes the wealthiest corn-merchant of the town. He makes a firm resolve not to touch wine for twenty years and rises to newer heights. But the moment he takes to drinking again he declines and touches the nadir. His capacity to work dwindles; his fate deceives him; his deeds fade into rituals; his gunas grow tamsic and ultimately he dies a tragic death. So is the case with Wildev and Giles Winterbourne. Alec and Jude, Sergeant Troy and Bathsheba Everdene also get happiness and unhappiness, success and failure, mirth and gloom in accordance with their virtues and vices, deeds and gunas. In juxtaposition of this category of characters of extreme good and bad, is the category of those characters who are neither too passionate nor too indifferent, but those who try to do good deeds. Precisely, thcy arc more given to temperance, which the *Bhagavadgita* also stipulates for a happier living. Fancy Day, Elfride Swancourt, Gabriel Oak, Diggory Venn, Donald Farfrae, Fitzpiers and Angel Clare are such characters who practise temperance and lead comparatively a happy life. Even the *ex-cathedra* comment with which *Tess of the D'Urbervilles* concludes that "Justice was done and the President of the Immortals in Aeschylean phrase had ended his sport with Tess"[37] reflects upon the Hardyian belief in the essential goodness of human nature which by implication is the essential nobleness of Hardy's characters even in moments of their ruin.

In the *Bhagavadgita* (Chapter XI), Lord Krishna shows to Arjun that the whole universe is concealed in Him and everything in the world is already fixed and determined :

त्वमक्षरं परमं वेदितव्यं
त्वमस्य विश्वस्य परं निधानम् ।
त्वमव्ययः शाश्वतधर्मगोप्ता
सनातनस्त्वं पुरुषो मतो मे ।।[38]

(You are the supreme Indestructible worthy of being realized; you are the ultimate resort of this universe. You are the protector of external Dharma; I consider You to be the external imperishable being.)

Hardy's determinism is similar to the above concept as enunciated in the *Bhagavadgita*. Again, as in the *Bhagavadgita*, the concept of *Samskara* evolves as human life, a fixed and determined concept of spiritual evolution, so in Hardy's novels, the Christian humanism does wholly help grow a man higher and higher both physically and spiritually. It is true that Hardy accepts the whole concept of the Darwinian evolution of man, but his total belief in the cardinal virtues of the Christian religion does good a man for spiritual evolution and perfection.

According to Hardy, human action is not free but determined by motives, which are regarded as "external forces acting on the will."[39] The characters, therefore, would appear to be helpless, and yet the tragic characters do not appear to be mere puppets jerked by a malicious fate. Were it so, they would miss an essential condition of tragedy. A towering and laudable desire may be doomed to be brought level with futility, but one profoundly enjoys the brave quality of the assertion of desire; a life abject in sorrow is nothing enjoyable, and therefore, nothing tragical. But the tragic characters who endure all the vicissitudes and odds of life with patience turn out to be more perfect, as in the *Bhagavadgita*, a man with good deeds forms good samskaras and ultimately grows more perfect. External pressure or coincidence is always there in Hardy's novels, yet the internal conflict, the conflict of good and bad outweighs in the end. Angel Clare, for instance, does appear to be a puppet in the hands of fate, yet external compulsions are far less predominant on him than internal ones. His getting more and more detached to crystallise his vision of the world, the society and ultimately of Tess is remarkably underlined as and when he grows internally.

Hardy's Immanent Will is the Darwinian creative or evolving energy, which is responsible for self-development and self-movement. Oneness and immanentia are inseparably bound together; each is a necessary corollary and consequence of the other and both are of equal importance. This inner force has five characteristic features : first, the Will is one and Immanent like the *Bhagavadgita's* Brahma, for it is represented as the one and the only source from which all life and activity are flowing : secondly, the Will is autonomous, determining everything, it is itself determined by nothing and human events are but the manifestations of its mysterious designs. No earthly power can swerve the bias of its power which governs all things by its clock-wise laws. Thirdly, the Will is unconscious, viewless and voiceless and lastly, it is indestructible, endless like the *Bhagavadgita's* Lord Krishna or Parama Brahma. Conditioned by this Immanent Will, man in Hardy's novels is often a willing, surrendering being, completely ruled by the fixed mysterious inclinations of his nature. The Will within him urges him on, often against his better judgment. It is, for instance, some inexplicable power that draws together Eustacia and Wildev; Alec and Tess; Farfrae and Lucetta; Jude and Sue.

Whereas the evolution of man in the *Bhagavadgita* is thus wholly spiritual, Hardy's is a combination of science say Darwinism plus his complete faith in the Biblical Monotheism. Hardy's man struggles for existence in the Darwinian sense of the term and his physical existence is meaningless without his faith in the sterling virtues of life, the basis of the Christian humanism and which exactly corresponds to the spiritual evolution of man as enunciated in the *Bhagavadgita*.

In the *Bhagavadgita*, Lord Krishna says to Arjun "whenever there is decline of righteousness, and unrighteousness is in the ascendant, then I body myself forth for the protection of the virtuous, for the destruction of evil-doers, and for establishing

Dharma (righteousness) on a firm footing, I am born from age to age" :

यदा यदा हि धर्मस्य ग्लानिर्भवति भारत।
अभ्युत्थानमधर्मस्य तदाऽऽत्मानं सृजाम्यहम्।।
परित्राणाय साधूनां विनाशाय च दुष्कृताम्।
धर्मसंस्थापनार्थाय सम्भवामि युगे युगे।।[40]

This is Hardy's view of Cosmic Consciousness which approximates to Bucke's and also Spinoza's view of *Necessity*. By inference it means that whenever there is a collapse of good, the Immanent Will, though often irresponsible and blind, yet grows into self-consciousness and ultimately assumes the form of Cosmic Consciousness. In the *Dynasts*, the same concept of Cosmic Consciousness or the theory or Necessity of Expediency has been explained by Hardy. When Hardy's critics fell hard upon him, finding too many philosophic abstractions in the *Dynasts*, Hardy wrote to his friend Pretor, Fellow of St. Catherine College, Cambridge, explaining his view of Freewill versus Necessity. Pretor understood Hardy's point of view well and wrote back to him :

> "My thanks for your tremendous new statement in *The Dynasts* of the world-old problem of Freewill versus Necessity. You have carried me on to the mountain with Jesus of Naizareth and viewing with Him the great conflict below, one chooses with Him to side with the spirit of the Pities, in the belief that they will ultimately triumph; and even if they do not we at least will do our little to add to the joy rather than to the woe of the world.... The spirit of the Pities is indeed young in comparison with the Years, and so we must be patient.... Your conception of the Immanent Will — irresponsible, blind, but possibly growing into self-consciousness, was of great significance to me, from my knowledge of Dr. Bucke's theory of the Cosmic Consciousness."[41]

In fact, Hardy's ameliorism is inevitably bound to suggest various improvements and his pessimism to paint a real picture of things. He is, therefore, often misconstrued to banish God from Heaven or to tarnish the image of God with a bitter coat of malignancy. Were it so his Henchard, Tess, Jude, Gabriel Oak and others would prove to be the most despised human beings.

But it is not so. His providence is wholly conscious and not malignant. In his correspondence to Mr. Edward Wright, Hardy writes :

> That the unconscious Will of the Universe is growing aware of Itself I believe I may claim as my own idea solely — at which I arrived by reflecting that what has already taken place in a fraction of the whole (*i.e.*, so much of the world as has become conscious) is likely to take place in the mass; and there being no Will outside the mass — that is, the Universe — the whole Will becomes conscious thereby; and ultimately, it is to be hoped, sympathetic.[42]

Hardy's Cosmic Consciousness is, therefore, the Nature in her primordial form which is bound to grow into perfection. Here his views approximate to the concept of Prakrti as enunciated in the *Bhagavadgita* :

> मम योनिर्महद्ब्रह्म तस्मिन्गार्भ दधाम्यहम्।
> संभवः सर्वभूतानां ततो भर्वात भारत।।[43]
>
> [My Prakrti or Nature in her primordial, undeveloped state is the womb of all creatures; in that I place the seed (of consciousness). The birth of all beings follows from this combination of Matter and Spirit.]

Florence Emily Hardy has authentically rebutted the charge of Hardy's postulating a malignant and fiendish God on the ground that whatever Hardy propounded was in perfect consonance with the Christian values and his concept of Immanent Will is the driving, birth-giving force to good. It ennobles us to meet perfection what Einstein and Spinoza say in their scientific terminology or what evolutionary principles too underline, "In connection with this subject (Cosmic Consciousness) it may be here recalled, in answer to writers who now and later fond of charging Hardy with postulating a malignant and fiendish God, that he never held any view of the sort, merely surmising an indifferent and unconscious force at the back of things 'that neither good nor evil knows'. His view is shown, in fact, to approximate to Spinoza's — and later Einstein's — that neither Chance nor Purpose governs the universe, but Necessity."[44]

From the points enumerated above, an effort has been made to steer clear of a number of controversies about Hardy's concept of Immanent Will. Let us now have some glimpses of his pragmatic uses and applications with proper analytic observations of the Immanent Will through his famous novels. In fact, Hardy's universe is a dwelling place where ultimate causes are inscrutable, where man's destiny is predestined and predetermined by an indifferent and nonchalant Providence; where man suffers miserably at the iron hands of a cruel and merciless destiny. "Rather must I apprehend," he writes, "that man, in some inconceivable way, may at his best moments represent a principle darkly at strife with that which prevails throughout the world as known to us."[45] In this fierce strife, Immanent Will plays an important role in so far as it goads a man on to keep up his spirits high and enlivened. The weaker the Immanent Will, the lesser will be the chances of survival. In the Darwinian sense of the term, this spirit of fierce struggle is the basic instinct which governs and operates the principle of survival of the fittest. This spirit of fierce struggle may be termed as Cosmic Consciousness in the sense the *Bhagavadgita* enunciates.

But whereas the spirit to survive in the Darwinian sense is purely biological, the same in the Christian religion becomes tantamount to the Cosmic Consciousness. Hardy may see this spirit or urge to be or not to be a part of God or a Blind Power, he does not doubt at all the overall impact of good and the degenerating effect of evil. Purity of action is its own reward, whether the presumed God or the feigned hypocritical air of religiosity vouchsafes purity to be worthy of any reward. "Of all the theological systems," Hardy asserts, "most convincing is the Manichaeism, which, of course, under another name, was held by the Puritans themselves."[46] In fact, the Manichaeism systems of the universe seem to have confirmed Hardy's view that man should constantly endeavour to glorify good without the least expectation of its being rewarded. With this spirit, he exhorts a tiny human being to achieve what may appear to be impossible. In the purity of action, the purity of love works wonders. The last lines of *Far From the Madding Crowd* explicitly carry this strong message. "Where, however," writes Hardy, "happy circumstance permits its development, the compounded feeling proves itself to be the only love which is strong as death — that love which many waters cannot quench, nor the flood drown, beside which the passion usually called by the name is evanescent as stream."[47]

Hardy's exhortation to do good despite failure and wrath by God is a superhuman advice. But Hardy is incorrigibly optimistic and finds an absolute conviction while glorifying good. His Unconscious Will of the Darwinian stamp, his Cosmic Consciousness of the schopenhauerian imprint and his Free Will of the Maredithian cast are one and the same creative force and energy. Nervous breakdowns are no doubt frequent, yet the final message is the same. Even the famous paralytic fit of the Immanent Will in *The Mayor of Casterbridge* seems to glorify good. "But the ingenious machinery," exclaims Henchard so magnificently, "contrived by the Gods for reducing human possibilities of amelioration to a minimum — which arranges that wisdom to do shall come *pari passu* with the departure of zest for doing — stood in the way of all that. He had no wish to make an arena of a second time of the world that had become a mere painted scene to him."[48]

The above outburst by Henchard is the outcome of the paralytic fit of his resolute Will. If Henchard, the tragic hero of immense potential, has the will to denounce the world by terming it a "painted scene", the same man has the absolute will to pardon her love and endure what his prudence dictates at the moment. "He schooled himself," Hardy graphically sketches Henchard, "to accept her will, in this as in other matters, as absolute and unquestionable. He dreaded lest an antagonistic word should lose for him such regard as he had regained from her by his devotion, feeling that to retain this under separation was better than to incur her dislike by keeping her near."[49]

Tess, the heroine of *Tess of the D'Urbervilles*, has a resolute will to oppose and dislike Alec knowing the fact that he was her seducer. Notwithstanding the grave end awaiting her, she feels extremely determined to enjoy Clare's company for ever. She prefers death to separation from Clare. The type of happiness she gets with Clare is the type of happiness she has never derived in her life from any source. She does not fear God, not even the society, which criminally hurled labels of a lewd woman, an impure maiden, on her. Hardy himself presents her rather philosophically in such a tone as to attract everybody's attention. Probably, the kind of role attributed to the Immanent Will as the *ne plus ultra* of tragic intensity is even greater than Shakespeare's. The end of the novel epitomises this spirit : "Justice was done, and the President of the Immortals, in Aeschylean phrase, has ended his sport with Tess. And the d'Urbervilles knights and dames slept on the tombs unknowing. The two speechless gazers bent themselves down to the earth, as if in prayer, and reminded thus a long time, absolutely motionless : the flag continued to wave silently. As soon as they had strength they arose, joined hands again, and went on."[50]

Hardy's Immanent Will often errs in properly guiding his characters. That is why because "God's not in his heaven : all's wrong with the world!"[51] A mortal goes astray despite his best judgment and discretion. The constancy of the Immanent Will is broken and paralysed. "In the ill-judged execution of the well-judged plan of things," Hardy philosophically advises, "the call seldom produces the comer, the man to love rarely coincides with the hour of lover. Nature does not often say, 'See!' to her poor creature at a time when seeing can lead to happy doing; or reply 'Here!' to a body's cry of 'Where!' till the hide-and-seek has become an irksome, outward game."[52] Whenever the Immanent Will, in the guise of the dictate of the typical Hardyian mould, operates it absolutely ceases to distinguish and demarcate as to what is to be destroyed and what to be preserved, whether the worthy must by rewarded and the unworthy be punished. Hardy himself is at a loss to understand this mysterious working of the Blind Power and its Immanent Will. "Why it was," Hardy again philosophises, "that upon this beautiful feminine tissue, sensitive as a gossamer, and practically blank as snow as yet, there should have been traced such a course pattern as it was doomed to receive : why so often the coarse appropriates the finer thing the wrong man the woman the wrong woman the man, many thousand years of analytical philosophy have failed to explain to our sense of order."[53] This haphazard scheme of things where good does not get its reward and bad goes unpunished has, of course, no moral, ethical and religious moorings. It is, indeed, a chance causation, a sheer coincidence that decides matters. In the true Darwinian sense, this is the kernel of evolution, and an off-shoot of Unconscious Will — a forceful creative urge which enables Gabriel Oak, Clare, Farfrae to survive and Boldwood, Alec and Henchard to die. Tess's existence, her happiness, and unhappiness — are just a matter of chance. The overall operative force is just a fraction of the Immanent Will, having nothing to do with her joys and woes. In the midst of storm, Tess is rarely protected by a Benevolent God. "Darkness and silence," Hardy again writes in a despondent mood, "ruled everywhere around. Above them rose the primeval yews and oaks of the Chase, in which their poised, gentle roosting birds in their last nap; and about them stole the hopping rabbits and hares. But, might some say, where was Tess's guardian angel? Where was Providence of her simple faith? Perhaps, like that other god of whom the ironical Tishbite spoke, he was talking, or he was pursuing, or he was in a journey, or he was sleeping and not to be awaked."[54]

Being perplexed too much to see any clear light of hope, Tess, like any hapless man, feels bewildered even to the extent to neglect whatever spiritual, moral or religious is ever left in her. That is why, Hardy believes in the Omnipresence of a Mind and Intelligence throughout the Universe to which no name can so fittingly be applied as God. Elizabeth's powerful instinct to survive is perhaps the type of mind Hardy refers to again and again, which in the Darwinian sense of the terms may be treated as the Hardyian way of adaptation or the natural living, on which even the Immanent Will attacks less fiercely. "To keep in the rear,"

Hardy makes Elizabeth speak, "of opportunity in matters of indulgence is as valuable a habit as to keep abreast of opportunity in matters of enterprise.... Her triumph was tempered by circumspection; she had still that field — mouse fear of the coulter of destiny despite fair promise, which is common among the thoughtful who have suffered early from poverty and oppression.

> "I won't be too gay on any account," she would say to herself. "It would be tempting Providence to hurl mother and me down, and afflict us again as he used to do."[55]

While lying on his death bed, he preferred to listen to the lines from the *Rubaiyat of Omar Khayyam* full of agnosticism and reminding of the Blind Power :

> Oh! Thou, who Man of baser Earth didst make,
> And ev'n with Paradise devise the Snake :
> For all the Sine wherewith the Face of Man
> Is blacken'd — Man's forgiveness give — and take![56]

is ever left in her. "In the daylight, indeed," Tess feels "her terrors about her soul to have been somewhat exaggerated; whether well-founded or not she had no uneasiness now, reasoning that if Providence would not ratify such an act of approximation she for one, did not value the kind of heaven lost by the irregularity — either for herself or for her child."[57] "I don't quite feel easy," Tess says to herself, "all this good fortune may be scourged out of me afterwards by a lot of ill. That's how heaven most does. I wish I could have had common banns."[58]

Often it is debated whether nature, chance, fate and other natural phenomena work in unison with the Immanent Will or not. To some, the answer is yes, but for others, no. Nonetheless, the fact remains that in Hardy's novels, there appears a sort to togetherness of all these forces working together. To all these forces, a man's existence is of no consequence, and a man becomes as helpless before them as flies before the wanton boys :

> As flies to wanton boys are we to the gods.
> They kill us for their sport.[59]

The Immanent Will, if it really wills, is a great destroyer. With Tess, this will is not satisfied till her complete destruction. The scene of her being caught sleeping by the police to be hanged for ever is the one which Hardy could ever write elsewhere with the utmost force and sincerity of tragic intensity. Here, the Immanent Will has its full circle and probably the last stage of effect :

> 'It is no use, Sir,' he said. 'There are sixteen of us on the Plain, and the whole country is reared.'
>
> 'Let her finish her sleep!' he implored in a whisper of the men as they gathered round.
>
> When they saw where she lay, which they had not done till then they showed no objection.... Soon the light was strong, and a ray shone upon her unconscious form, peering under her eyelids and waking her.
>
> 'What is it, Angel?' she said, starting up.
>
> 'Have they come for me?'
>
> 'Yes, dearest,' he said, 'They have come.'
>
> 'It is as it should be,' she murmured,' Angel,
>
> I am almost glad — yes, glad! This happiness could not have lasted. It was too much. I have had enough; and now I shall not live for you to despise me![60]

Hardy like Butler, however, does not approve of Darwin's undue insistence on natural selection as the wholesome agency of evolution. Hardy's Immanent Will is, therefore, allied to an Unconscious Memory in living organisms, by virtue of which a man solves vital problems by intelligent strivings rather than by uninspired weeding out by natural selection.

In *The Dynasts*, Hardy poses the question, "What of the Immanent Will and its designs?"[61] and the Spirit of the Years answers :

> It works unconsciously, as heretofore,
> Eternal artistries in Circumstance,
> Whose patterns, wrought by rapt aesthetic rote,
> Seem in themselves Its single listless aim,
> And not their consequence.[62]

The Chorus of the Pities further exclaims :

> Still thus? Still thus?
> Ever unconscious?

An automatic sense
Unweeting why or whence?
Be, then, the inevitable, as of old,
Although that so it be we dare not hold![63]

To this, the Spirit of the Years further answers :

Hold what ye list, fond unbelieving Spirits,
You cannot swerve the pulsion of the Byss,
Which thinking on, yet weighing not Its thought,
Unchecks Its clock-like laws.[64]

The Spirit of the Pities further makes meaningful, queries about the Immanent Will :

Why doth It so and so, ever so,
This viewless, voiceless Turner of the Wheel?[65]

To this query, the Spirit of the Years answers thus :

As one sad story runs, It lends Its heed
To other worlds, being wearied out with this;
Wherefore Its mindlessness of earthly woes,
Some, too, have told at whiles that rightfully
Its warefulness, Its care, this planet lost
When in her early growth and crudity....[66]

The Spirit of the Pities further says :

Meet is it, none the less,
To bear in thought what though Its consciousness
May be estranged, engrossed afar, or sealed,
Sublunar shocks may wake Its watch anon?[67]

This is again answered by the Spirit of the Years :

Nay. In the Foretime, even to the germ of Being,
Nothing appears of shape to indicate
That cognizance has marshalled things terrene,
Or will (such as my thinking) in my span...

* * *

The Will has woven with an absent heed
Since life first was; and ever will so weave.[68]

The Spirit Sinister then concludes :

Hence we've rare dramas going — more so since
It wove Its web in that Ajaccian womb![69]

The Spirit of the Years dittoes this :

Well, no more thus on what no mind can meet
Our scope is but to register and watch

By means of this great gift accorded us —
The free trajection of our entities.[70]

This, the Spirit of the Pities, also okays :

On things terrene, then, I would say that though
The human news wherewith the Rumours stirred us
May please they temper, years, 'twere better far
Such deeds were nulled, and this strange man's career.[71]

Not only this, even the Shade of the Earth simply terms herself to be the shade of the Immanent Will :

They may come, will they. I am not averse,
Yet know I am but the ineffectual Shade
Of her the Travailler, herself a thrall
To it; in all her labourings curbed and kinged![72]

The Spirit of the Years also shows her helplessness before the Immanent Will :

Mercy I view, not urge; — nor more than mark
What designate your titles Good and Ill,

* * *

But only through my centuries to behold
Their aspects, and their movements, and their mould.[73]

The Spirit of the Pities also says so :

They are shapes that bleed, mere mannikins or no,
And each has parcel in the total Will.[74]

Hardy's Immanent Will is so powerful that even the Spirit Sinister says to herself that whatever might awful appears all around is but a manifestation of It (Immanent Will) :

Limbs of Itself :
Each one a jot of It in quaint disguise?
I'll fear all men henceforward![75]

In *The Dynasts*, the wars happened, are already predestined by the Immanent Will. The Spirit of the Years is ordered to let the human cruelty take place in the guise of fierce fighting :

Open and chant the page
Thou'st lately writ, that sums these happenings,
In brief reminder of their instant points
Slighted by us amid our converse here.[76]

And, in fact, first of all, it is the Recording Angel, who reads out its decree :

Now mellow-eyed Peace is made captive,
    And Vengeance is chartered
To deal forth its dooms on the Peoples
    With sword and with spear....[77]

In her conversation with Semichorus I and II of Rumours, the Spirit of the Years feels sympathetic about the meaningless strivings of Napoleon and other warriors ready to wage war : for, the Spirit already knows as to what the Immanent Will has in store for them :

Methinks too much assurance thrills your note
On secrets in my locker, gentle sprites;...

*   *   *

Forgetting the Prime Mover of the Gear,
As puppet watches him who pulls the strings;[78]

The dimensions of force of the Immanent Will have been portrayed by the Spirit of the Pities :

Amid this scene of bodies substantive
Strange waves I sight like winds grown visible,
Which bear men's forms on their innumerous coils,
Twining and serpentining round and through.[79]

The Spirit of the Years, likewise, makes a vivid presentation of this Blind Power :

These are the Prime Volitions, — fibrils, veins,
Will tissues, nerves, and pulses of the Cause,
That heave throughout the Earth's compositure,
Their sum is like the lobule of a Brain....[80]

Hardy's Immanent Will is, therefore, Omnipotent. Semichorus II dittoes this view :

The Immanent Will, that urgeth all,
Rules what may or may not befall?[81]

Semichorus I also confirms whatever Semichorus II says :

Ere systemed suns were globed and lit
The slaughters of the race were writ.[82]

Even wars, either on land or elsewhere are reported to be preordained by the Immanent Will :

And wasting wars, by land and sea,
Fixed, like all else, immutably![83]

A man's entire life, even the vast space and the limitless time move or unmove by the dictates of the Immanent Will :

> So the will heaves through Space, and moulds the times,
> With mortals for Its fingers! We shall see
> Again men's passions, virtues, visions, crimes,
> Obey resistlessly
> The mutative, unmotived, dominant Thing
> Which sways in brooding dark their wayfaring![84]

The Spirit Sinister, too, is scared of the Immanent Will :

> Come, sprite, don't carry your ironies too far, or you may wake up the Unconscious Itself, and tempt It to let all the gory clockwork of the show run down to spite me ![85]

So does the Spirit of the Years draws a very terrific picture of the working of the Immanent Will :

> ...Men pass to dark corruption, at the best,
> Ere I can count five score : these why not now?
> The Immanent Sharper builds Its beings so
> Whether ye sigh their sighs with them or no!
> The night fog enwraps the isle and the dying English army.[86]

A number of lines from *The Dynasts* have purposefully been quoted in order to prove that Hardy systematised his philosophical views on the Immanent Will much later to be fully expressed in this epic-drama of the war with Napoleon. In all the three parts, nineteen acts and one hundred and thirty scenes that this epic-drama contains, Hardy's views on the Immanent Will are recurrent phenomena. However, the tragic view he presented in his novels is almost the same as expressed by Hardy in *The Dynasts*. Hence, the scheme of treatment of the Immanent Will in the foregoing pages is that Hardy's novels have been given preference to this epic-drama. In fact, in shaping Hardy's concept of the Immanent Will, the teachings of Darwin, J.S. Mill, Spencer, Huxley and of others played a very vital role. From Clodd, he derived the idea of the Unconscious Will. "His sense of a Will other and more compulsive than man's was deepened by his study of the Greek tragedians, as the novels attest; he knew these long before he became acquainted with Schopenhauer and Hartmann."[87] "Possibly he had Hartmann's ideas in mind, that life is not worth living and the only sane plan is to lay it down, when he wrote *Jude the Obscure*."[88]

In summation, this discussion may be concluded by what Thomas Hardy himself wrote to Edward Wright on June 2, 1907, "...The will of a man is...neither wholly free nor wholly unfree. When swayed by the Universal Will...he is not individually free; but whatever it happens that all the rest of the Great Will is an equilibrium the minute portion called one person's will is free, just as a performer's fingers are free to go on playing the pianoforte of themselves when he talks or thinks of something else and the head does not rule them."[89]

REFERENCES

1. Marshal, Percy : *Aspects of the Novel*, Edward Arnold & Co., London, 1970, p. 80.
2. Stevenson, Lionel : *The English Novel*, Constable & Co., London, 1960, p. 88.
3. Lever, Katherine : *The Technique of the Novel*, Harper & Co., New York, 1908, p. 145.
4. *Far From the Madding Crowd*, p. 22.
5. *Ibid.*, p. 29.
6. *Ibid.*, p. 35.
7. *Ibid.*
8. *Ibid.*, p. 36.
9. *Ibid.*, p. 40.
10. *Ibid.*, p. 97.
11. *Ibid.*, p. 110.
12. *Ibid.*, p. 112.
13. *Ibid.*, p. 139.
14. *Ibid.*, p. 140.
15. *Ibid.*, p. 142.
16. *Ibid.*
17. *Ibid.*, p. 144.
18. *Ibid.*, p. 161.
19. *Ibid.*, p. 175.
20. *Ibid.*, p. 176.
21. *Ibid.*, p. 178.
22. *Ibid.*, p. 198.
23. *Ibid.*, p. 199.

24. *Ibid.*, p. 277.

25. "When *The Dynasts* was published (Part I in 1904, Part II in 1906, Part III in 1908), Hardy's friends began writing to him about 'It', pointing out that a neuter *It* could not logically be conceived of as possessing volition. 'The Will', therefore, is (they thought) a contradiction in terms. To Edward Clodd, Hardy wrote on March 22, 1904 : 'What you say about the Will is true enough, if you take the word in its ordinary sense. But in...a secondary sense...that of effort exercised in an...unconscious manner.' Hardy thought the word permissible. To Edward Wright he wrote (on June 2, 1907) : 'I quite agree with you...that the word Will does not perfectly fit the idea to be conveyed — (that of) a vague... urging...force'; but he again defended his use of the word and claimed that his theory about the Will 'settled the question of Free-Will (hyphenated) *vs.* Necessity'. He accordingly had made the Spirit of the Pities declares :

We hold that thy unscanted scope Affords a food for final Hope."

(Weber, Carl J : *Hardy of Wessex : His Life and Literary Career*, Routledge & Kegan Paul, London, 1940, p. 246).

26. "In saying this, Hardy ignored, or forgot, the book he had bought for five shillings back in 1889 or 1890 — a copy of Mrs. Karl Hillebrand's translation of Schopenhauer's doctoral dissertation at Gottingen, *On the Four-fold Root of the Principle of Sufficient Reason* (London, Bell, 1889; the first publication of this work in English). Hardy's use of the term 'the Immanent Will' in *The Dynasts*, of course, made many a reader think that Schopenhauer was its source, but Hardy was always inclined to be evasive on that point. When Helen Garwood earned a Ph.D. degree at the University of Pennsylvania with a dissertation on *Thomas Hardy, an Illustration of the Philosophy of Schopenhauer* (1911) and sent Hardy a copy of it, he replied, somewhat cryptically : "My pages show — harmony of view with Darwin, Huxley, Spenser, Hume, Mill and others, all of whom I used to read, more than Schopenhauer". *Ibid.*, pp. 246-47.

27. "In Schopenhauer's writings, it is possible to detect influences from the systems of Plato, Kant and the *Upanishads*, all of which he studied at the Universities of Gottingen and Berlin." [Hartman, James B. (ed.) *Philosophy of Recent Times*, McGraw Hill Book Co., New York, 1967, Vol. I, p. 82.]

28. "Schopenhauer's voluntaristic system established the primacy of the Will in the position of the Kantian thing in itself. Starting from the phenomenalistic view of the world as Idea, he supposed that nature everywhere should be regarded as a blind, unconscious force underlying all aspects of change and development and manifesting itself in various immutable types from lowest matter to man. Schopenhauer developed this notion of an irrational, objectless Will in the area of moral

philosophy and described life as an essentially painful, selfish, futile striving. Release from the imperious demands of the Will he believed to be possible only in the detached attitude of the artistic, philosophical, or religious ascetic." *Ibid.*, p. 82.

29. *Ibid.*, p. 119.
30. *The Bhagavadgita,* Chapter XVIII, Shloka 23.
31. *Ibid.*, Chapter XVIII, Shloka 24.
32. *Ibid.*, Chapter XVIII, Shloka 25.
33. *Ibid.*, Chapter II, Shloka 47.
34. *The Mayor of Casterbridge,* pp. v-vi.
35. *Ibid.*, pp. 18-19.
36. *Ibid.*, p. 313.
37. *Tess of the D'Urbervilles,* p. 517.
38. *The Bhagavadgita,* Chapter II, Shloka 18.
39. Elliot, A.P. : *Fatalism in the Novels of Thomas Hardy*, p. 110.
40. *The Bhagavadgita*, Chapter IV, Shlokas 7 and 8.
41. Hardy, Florence Emily : *The Life of Thomas Hardy*, p. 337.
42. *Ibid.*, p. 335.
43. *The Bhagavadgita,* Chapter XIV, Shloka 3.
44. *Op. cit.,* p. 337.
45. *Letters,* p. 200.
46. *Ibid.*, p. 280.
47. *Far From the Madding Crowd,* p. 469.
48. *The Mayor of Casterbridge,* p. 313.
49. *Ibid.*, p. 298.
50. *Tess of the D'Urbervilles,* p. 446.
51. *Ibid.*, p. 292.
52. *Ibid.*, p. 53.
53. *Ibid.*, p. 91.
54. *Ibid.*, p. 90.
55. *Ibid.*, p. 115.
56. *Ibid.*, p. 235.
57. *Ibid.*, Preface, p. 23.
58. *Ibid.*, pp. 443-44.
59. *The Mayor of Casterbridge,* p. 92.
60. Hardy, Florence Emily : *The Life of Thomas Hardy* (quoted), Macmillan, London, 1965, p. 446.
61. *The Dynasts*, Macmillan & Co., London, 1948, p. 1.
62. *Ibid.*
63. *Ibid.*

64. *Ibid.*,
65. *Ibid.*, p. 2.
66. *Ibid.*
67. *Ibid.*
68. *Ibid.*
69. *Ibid.*
70. *Ibid.*
71. *Ibid.*, p. 3.
72. *Ibid.*
73. *Ibid.*, p. 4.
74. *Ibid.*
75. *Ibid.*
76. *Ibid.*
77. *Ibid.*, p. 5
78. *Ibid.*, p. 6.
79. *Ibid.*, p. 7.
80. *Ibid.*
81. *Ibid.*, p. 53.
82. *Ibid.*
83. *Ibid.*
84. *Ibid.*, p. 191.
85. *Ibid.*, p. 245.
86. *Ibid.*
87. Baker, E.A. : *The History of the English Novel*, Vol. IX, Barnes & Noble Inc., New York, 1936, p. 86.
88. *Ibid.*
89. Hardy, Emily Florence : *The Life of Thomas Hardy*, Macmillan & Co., London, 1965, p. 335.

   • Also published in *VFSNA*, Delhi, 2002, pp. 26-64.

7

Scientific Impact on Dickensian School of Novelists — Mrs. Elizabeth Gaskell, Anthony Trollope, W.M. Thackeray and George Eliot

THE OFT-CITED conversation replete with despondency and scepticism between Boldwood, the farmer, and Gabriel, the shepherd, in Hardy's *Far From the Madding Crowd*,[1] and the famous repartee, permeated with scientific curiosity and ignorance between Lady Constance, the novice, and Tancred, the instructor, in Disraeli's *Tancred*[2] virtually demarcate the magnitude and quantum that the scientific thought had left on the early as well as on the late Victorian fiction. The stream of scientific thought, on having meandered through the initial stages of the Victorian period till having reached its late spectrum, had influenced, during the earlier part, the physical existence of man in particular, and the mental and spiritual existence in general; but during the later part, it had influenced almost every domain of thought. Boldwood's dialogue with Gabriel sufficiently illustrates this conviction that the 'gourd' of science had really 'smitten the prophet' in man :

> O, Gabriel! I am weak and foolish, and I don't know what, and I can't fend off my miserable grief! ...I had some faint belief in the mercy of God.... Yes, He prepared the gourd to shade me, and like the prophet I thanked Him and was glad. But the next day He prepared a worm to smite the gourd and wither it; and I feel it is better to die than to live.[3]

This is a picture of the total collapse of faith in God by the end of the nineteenth century that Hardy has delineated in his works : it is the size and depth of the impact of scientific thought on the late Victorian fiction that he has perspicuously drawn, being the most representative novelist of his age.

Tancred exhorts Lady Constance to read the latest books on science, and by apparently alluding to *The Origin of Species*, he asserts the paramountcy of scientific thought over common beliefs and convictions of the day :

> Oh ! but it is all proved; you must not argue on my rapid sketch; read the book. It is impossible to contradict anything in it. You understand, it is all science; it is not like those books in which one says one thing and another the contrary, and both may be wrong. Everything is proved : by geology, you know. You see exactly how everything is made; how many worlds there have been; how long they lasted; what went before, what comes next. We are a link in the chain, as inferior animals that preceded us...this is development we had fins; we may have wings.[4]

Of course, the tale of scientific advent from the early to the late Victorian period is the tale of our having fins in the earlier part and the possibility of our having wings in the latter part of our evolution. The early Victorian fiction has expressed the scientific dominance in different ways from the late Victorian fiction : the former is, in a word, physical, material and wordly",[5] whereas the latter, is absolutely "mental, spiritual and intellectual."[6] The industrial revolution, the movement of democracy, the cry for reform, the revolt against faulty educational methods, the growing rift between the rich and poor, the decline in religious faith, and the growth of urbanization — all were "the apparent scientific repercussions physical, material and worldly"[7] — "seen palpably reflected through"[8] the works of those novelists belonging to the earlier part of the age. The spirit of scepticism, the deep-rooted pessimism and despondency, the complete vacillation of faith in God, "the shattering of the Papal authority under the crumbling feet of intellect and science",[9] and finally, the helpless cry of man asking — is life at all worth-living? — these were the candid repercussions — mental, spiritual and intellectual — seen reasonably answered by the novelists belonging to the later part of the Victorian period. While noticing the scientific impact, we have to demarcate its nature and quantum also, and in doing so, it will naturally appear that some common characteristics and movements, which came into evidence during the earlier stages, continued even up to the very end of the Victorian age, and, thus, it gives rise to a discernible overlapping and intermingling of many literary tendencies in fiction. However, a very precocious discrimination will place the novelists of the early period on a much different and easily recognizable footing, and that will enable us to note the quantum and nature of scientific impact on their novels.

"It would be fallacious to believe"[10] that it was all of a sudden that the scientific impact during the Victorian period become so wholesome and mighty : whereas, the fact is that the stream of scientific thought had gradually been flowing through various centuries, preparing a fertile background for such a mighty impact only during this period. As the Renaissance period witnessed "an abrupt approval of man for science,"[11] the same instant approbation of man for "the miraculous sway of scientific throught"[12] was evidently felt during the Victorian period and, all the novelists, therefore, yielded and succumbed to it. The Copernican belief of universe more or less tallied with Newton's or Darwin's only with the exclusion and exception of the miraculous interposition of heavenly bodies; Thomas Diggies, an Elizabethan-Copernican, very little differs from Thomson, a Newtonian-Augustun or from Hardy, a Darwinian-Victorian[13] only with their qualitative approbation of God. One inference is obvious : the scientific curiosity was goading every artist on to penetrate deeper into the forbidden layers of life, of religion, and of superstitions in order to answer more comprehensively all those enigmas, which had enshrouded human existence since long in various mysteries. During the Victorian period, "this bold experiment"[14] for unfolding mysteries of life was conducted, and herein lies the greatness of the Victorian novelists, because they made their best efforts to traverse into the forbidden literary regions now explored by scientific theories.

Now, 'this bold experiment' in the field of fiction, of unravelling the mysteries of life as well as of delineating the contemporary life in conformity with the scientific doctrines is to be analysed from two distinct standpoints — *viz.*, the matter of science,[15] which is the central theme of the present and the following chapters; and the method of science,[16] which will be the main theme of this Chapter. The matter of science invaded the fictional art of the late Victorian age as also that of the method of science more powerfully than the early Victorian age; and this impact, therefore, has different shapes and sizes, often even confusing to be clearly labelled, yet always recognizable in "its varying hues and embers."[17]

One of the great movements of paramount significance during the Victorian period was the industrial revolution, a reference to which has already been made in Chapter 2, and which was the direct consequence of the abrupt development of physical sciences, the impact of which on fiction was proportionate to its impact on contemporary social life. As a result of this movement, "big industries got installed in big industrial towns by big businessmen through big investments"[18] of their ill-earned capital : the exploitation of the ill-fed labour, swarmed around industrial places in stinking slums by the millionaires, came into evidence : the rift between the rich and poor became all the more widened : and, as a corollary, this movement started yielding to various insoluble social riddles in its wake, making the life of the day more given to physical comforts and luxuries, on the one hand, and deepening the spirit of restlessness even among the hoi-polloi, the rank and file, on the other.[19]

Of the various ramifications of fiction during the Early Victorian period, the most significant one which truly reflected the spirit of the industrial movement and that of democracy and of reform was the Dickensian school, which comprised of such eminent novelists as Charles Kingsley, Charles Reade, Walter

Besant, James Rice, and Richard Whiteing, in whom the social purpose is conspicuously dominant. This period also witnessed a big crowd of women novelists, the chief among them were — M. Russell Mitford, Mrs. Bray, Mrs. Clive, Mrs. Marsh, Mrs. Trollope, The Brontes, Mrs. Gaskell, George Eliot, Mrs. Henry Wood, Mrs. Craik, Charlotte Yonge, Mrs. Oliphant, Mrs. Lynn Lynton, M.E. Braddon, Miss Ramee, Rhoda Broughton and Edna Lyall. There were also such independent and trend-settler novelists as Thackeray, Disraeli, Trollope and Butler. While Thackeray and Trollope wrote intellectual novels through satire, Disraeli and Butler wrote political novels. Of the women novelists, some followed Dickens and the humanitarian group, and others followed George Eliot and Mrs. Gaskell. Thus, there were different kinds of fiction-schools during the early Victorian period, the chief being — the Dickensian school, the Gaskell-school, the George Eliotian school, the Thackeray-school, and the Trollopean school of fiction writing. On the minor novelists of these schools, the impact of scientific thought has been not so conspicuous and stringent as on the major novelists, because the minor novelists failed to react so nicely and logically to this impact as the major ones. It is why, this impact is to be studied and analysed by making a survey of the novels of the major novelists. It is, therefore, thought prudent to trace the scientific influence through the study of the novels of Dickens, Charles Reade, Charles Kingsley, Mrs. Gaskell, Walter Besant, James Rice, Richard Whiteing, Trollope, Thackeray and George Eliot, because all of them represent their respective schools and age in a very comprehensive way, and all of them favourably responded to and reacted against scientific impact.

Charles Dickens stands to the early Victorian period almost the same relation as Thomas Hardy to its later part in fiction; or as Chaucer to the fourteenth century and Shakespeare to the Elizabethan period in poetry. As such, "Dickens's novels epitomise the contemporary life"[20] with all "its crotchets and prejudices,"[21] "virtues and frailties,"[22] and "reactions and revolts,"[23] apportioning severally the quantum of social and literary changes and their fermentation. Being a truly representative novelist, "Dickens gleefully responded to and reacted against"[24] all these changes — social, economic, political and cultural, brought forth by the onward march of science, which, being proportionately added and abetted by man's inquisitive tempter and curiosity, in fact, of the Renaissance rationalism and of the Newtonian science, still continued unabashed with an added vigour through the Dickensian period. Its apparent manifestations were the industrial revolution, the commercial revolution, the democratic revolution, and the urban revolution, which were triumphantly depositing many outworn shibboleths of the day into an abyss of despair.

In Dickens's novels, there is "the discernible impact of industrial revolution,"[25] which was closely connected with the impact of scientific movement, a great movement of the Victorian period, indeed. The aftermath of this revolution were — "the impoverishment of the labour class,"[26] the increase of the slums, the widening of the gap between the rich and the poor, the problem of unemployment, of sanitation, and of the decline in agricultural conditions. Persons financially well-entrenched amassed wealth so "mercilessly and thoughtlessly"[27] by exploiting the workers in chimney-factories that money became the summum bonum, the final goal of their life. "Children of very tender age"[28] were employed in factories, and there they starved because of more work and less wages; woman laburers also get very "meagre wages in lieu of their day's hard work;"[29] men workers, too, were meted out "an inhuman treatment,"[30] because they were required to work for longer hours than the stipulated ones; and, they lived in unhygienic conditions, "dingy cells and dark alleys :"[31] suffocated in dirty surroundings and whiled away their time in lethargy and squalor. In *Pickwick Papers* and *David Copperfield*, instances of the prevalent wide gulf and disparity between the rich and the poor, the high and the low are numerous, particularly that singular one in the latter, where David earns only seven shillings a week in a factory doing quite a trite job, and faces starvation by going empty-stomach on the seventh day of the weak. Dickens's grim cry against and appalling description of David's hard days and starvation touches *ne plus ultra* when he narrates David's arranging his food into different packets and a day passing without food, which is really reminiscent of the identical with thousands of such innocent workers and their miserable existence of the day.[32]

In *David Copperfield*, again, the sociologist in Dickens rancorously pours out his vials of wrath by creating David, the immortal child hero, and making his misfortunes almost identical with the huge lot of labourers, rendered destitute by industrial revolution and many other social problems that this revolution brought about in its trail of destruction. David becomes, at the age of ten, "a little labouring hind in the service of Murdstone and Grinby,"[33] whose trade *inter alia* was "the supply of wines and spirits to certain ships,"[34] which "made voyages both to the East and West Indies."[35] David, like many other men and boys, employed in the factory to examine "empty bottles against the light, and reject those that were flawed, and to rinse and wash them,"[36] gets excruciating pains to keep his body and soul together, while pasting labels on full bottles, or fitting corks to them, or putting seals upon the corks, or packing finished bottles in casks, because he gets very meagre wages, and also because he, like Mick Walker and Mealy Potatoes, the other workers in the factory, has to work for longer hours than the stipulated ones. On having discovered that Mealy has not been christened, and that Mick Walker has long been suffering from poverty, David, the fondest child of Dickens, comes to grief, and here the sociologist in Dickens, as elsewhere in other novels at various places, points accusingly at the society :

> There were three or four of us, counting me. My working place was established in a corner of the warehouse, where Mr. Quinion could see me, when he choose to stand up on the bottom rail of his stool in the counting-house, and look at me through a window above the desk. Hither, on the first morning of my so auspiciously beginning life on my own account, the oldest of the regular boys was summoned to show me my business. His name was Mick Walker, and he wore a ragged

> apron and a paper cap. He informed me that his father was a barge-man, and walked, in a black velvet headdress, in the Lord Mayor's Show. He also informed me that our principal associate would be another boy whom he introduced by the — to me — extraordinary name of Mealy Potatoes. I discovered, however, that this youth had not been christened by that name, but that it had been bestowed upon him in the warehouse, on account of his complexion, which was pale or mealy. Mealy's father was a waterman, who had the additional distinction of being a fireman, and was engaged as such at one of the large theatres, where some young relation of Mealy's — I think his little sister — did Imps in the Pantomimes.[37]

Dickens's novels are, indeed, an authentic replica and repository of the industrial revolution and its attendant repercussions on the social, economic and political life of the early Victorian England. In *Martin Chuzzlewit*, for instance, "the dark no-thoroughfares near Todgers's", "the gloomy court-yards," and "the belated wayfarers" are reminiscent of thousands of the metropolitan changes that the industrial revolution brought forth in its wake with its innumerable attendant evils :

> There were gloomy courtyards in these parts, into which few but belated wayfarers ever strayed, and where vast bags and packs of goods, upward or downward bound, were for ever dangling between heaven and earth from lofty cranes. In the throats and maws of dark no-thoroughfares near Todgers's, individual wine-merchants and wholesale dealers in grocery-ware had perfect little towns of their own; and, deep among the foundations of these buildings, the ground was undermined and burrowed out into stables, where cart-horses, troubled by rats, might be heard on a quite Sunday rattling their halters.... But the grand mystery of Todgers's was the cellarage, approachable only by a little back door and a rusty grating : which cellarage within the memory of man had had no connection with the house, but had always been the freehold property of somebody else, and was reported to be full of wealth : though in what shape...was a matter of profound uncertainty and supreme indifference to Todgers's, and all its inmates.[38]

Congested, shabby, haphazard, impenetrable, irrational, and withal utterly humanized, the visible and palpable presence of a complex civilization and its history, "eccentric, elaborate, thick, various, outlandish,"[39] absurd, Todgers's is the central item in Dickens's own list of "Epsoms and Ascots,"[40] and which Dickens, the sociologist, delineates from the stand-point of a detached onlooker, diagnosing the social malady with the interest and spirit of a scientist.

In *Oliver Twist*, Dickens, the sociologist, presents a world where child labourers are doomed to decay in the midst of chill penury and pain, and where Oliver, like many unfortunate children, is born only to be sent to the gallows :

> The Board were sitting in solemn conclave, when Mr. Bumble rushed into the room in great excitement, and addressing the gentleman in the high chair, said,
>
> 'Mr. Limbkins, I beg your pardon, Sir! Oliver Twist has asked for more!'
>
> There was a general start. Horror was depicted in every countenance.
>
> 'For more!' said Mr. Limbkins. 'Compose yourself, Bumble, and answer me distinctly. Do I understand that he asked for more, after he had eaten the supper allotted by the dietary?'
>
> 'He did, Sir,' replied Bumble.
>
> 'That boy will be hung,' said the gentleman in the white waistcoat. 'I know that boy will be hung.'
>
> Nobody controverted the prophetic gentleman's opinion. An animated discussion took place. Oliver was ordered into instant confinement; and a bill was next morning pasted on the outside of the gate, offering a reward of five pounds to anybody who would take Oliver Twist off the hands of the parish. In other words, five pounds and Oliver Twist were offered to any man or woman who wanted an apprentice to any trade, business, or calling.[41]

The sociologist, the psychologist, and the economist combine all together in Dickens's in *Bleak House*, "which even Chesterton thought to be the best of Dickens's novels,"[42] and which, a famous critic, named Churchill, too, finds to be "among the best of the world-novels."[43] Besides an epitome of social, economic and industrial conditions in this novel, as in *Hard Times, Little Dorrit, Our Mutual Friend, Dombey and Son* and in other novels, there is "the combination of diverse qualities"[44] of social gloom, of sentimental melodrama, and of symbolism that evidences the existence of a sociologist, of an economist, and of a psychologist collectively in Dickens. The portrait of Skimpole in this novel singularly sticks to our memory like a leech, particularly his treatment of the man who comes to arrest him; his economically slipshod condition reminiscent of thousands of poor; his proverbial gloom of life reminding innumerable workers' pitiable living; and his wistful optimism recalling hundreds of thousands of labourers humbugged by political mountebanks. The processes of sociology and psychology work together in the character of Skimpole, the moment he sees the man who has come to arrest him for debt :

> 'Keep your temper, my good fellow, keep your temper' Mr. Skimpole gently reasoned with him, as he made a little drawing of his head on the fly-leaf of a book. 'Don't be ruffled by your occupation. We can separate you from your office.... We are not so prejudiced as to suppose that in private life you are otherwise than a very estimable man, with a great deal of poetry in your nature, of which you may not be conscious....
>
> 'But when you come down here...it was a fine day. The sun was shining, the wind was blowing, the lights and shadows were passing across the fields, the birds were singing.'
>
> 'Nobody said they weren't, in my hearing....'
>
> '...you didn't think...to this effect. "Harold Skimpole loves to see the sun shine, loves to hear the wind blow; loves to watch the changing lights and shadows; loves to hear the birds, those choristers in Nature's great cathedral. And does it seem to me that I am about to deprive Harold Skimpole of his share in such possessions, which are his only birthrights!" You thought nothing to that effect?'
>
> 'Very odd and very curious, the mental process is, in you men of business!' said Mr. Skimpole thoughtfully.[45]

In *Hard Times*, as in *Pickwick Papers*, *Great Expectations*, *A Tale of Two Cities*, and *Little Dorrit* and in other novels, too, Dickens, the social reformer, is pained to the core of his heart to see countless child labourers ruthlessly doomed to decay. His child heroes — Oliver in *Oliver Twist*, Smike in *Nicolas Nickleby*, Little Nell in *Old Curiosity Shop*, Dombey in *Dombey and Son*, and Jo in *Bleak House* — all suffer from the pangs of poverty, and all have to face untold trials and tribulations of life.

His other famous characters — Barkis, Traddles, Trootwood, Uriah Heep, Micawber, Peggotty, Betsy, Buzfuz, Pecksniff, and many more such other portraits in other novels, too, are the lively transcripts of reality of an age copiously deformed by the onwards march of science in the guise of industrial revolution. Places and cities once the abodes of saints in pre-industrial age, have now been converted into sophisticated abodes of impostors in post-industrial period :

> Let us strike the key-note, Coketown, before pursuing our tune. It was a town of red brick, or of brick that would have been red if the smoke and ashes had allowed it.... It was a town of machinery and tall chimneys, out of which interminable serpents of smoke trailed themselves for ever, and never got uncoiled.... It contained several large streets all very like one another, and many small streets still more like one another.... You show nothing in Coketown but what was severely workful...the jail might have been the infirmary, the infirmary might have been the jail, the town-hall might have been either.[46]

The Dickensian school of novelists followed their mentor in one way or the other with regard to their reactions against the impact of science : while some more or less remained almost unaffected by this great movement of science, others like Charles Reade, Charles Kingsley, Mrs. Elizabeth Gaskell, Walter Besant, James Rice and Richard Whiteing favourably responded to and reacted against this movement.

Charles Reade, "a great novelist of the humanitarian group,"[47] showed an appreciable awareness of scientific attitude and temper in his novels. In *Hard Cash, Peg Woffington*, and *Christie Johnstone* "the glimpses of medical knowledge"[48] and "seafare technicalities"[49] are the recurrent phenomena, and one would like to remember "the gifted practitioner Sampson,"[50] who is the champion to slay Goliath and who gives prescriptions in full Chinese language with even "burlesque translation"[51]: crowds of doctors figure, especially alienists. Medical profession has its quacks who amass wealth through unscrupulous means : David Dodd goes mad after being swindled out of his fourteen thousand, and one of his accomplices also suffers from long mental aberration because of his being treated by a quack : Alfred Hardie, quite sane and mentally alert, is imprisoned in three different institutions : old Maxley becomes a raving idiot and being absolutely disillusioned and frustrated kills Hardie's sister. The apex of the story and also of the medical farce, in the guise of its being altruistic framework for human survival is beautifully discernible when Dodd and his would-be son-in-law find themselves in the same madhouse, and in the same apartment when the place is on fire; and Dodd's stalwart son, now a fireman, rescues both, pouring out vials of wrath on the medical profession. "The sarcastic medical reformer Sampson," the Negro Vespasian and his chum Yankee Fullalove typify many of the salient features of the money-minded quack doctors of the day, for whom "the canons of altruism and philanthrophy"[52] were nearly meaningless, absolutely hollow, and completely devoid of all professional ethics.

Charles Reade, as a psychologist, studying the mind and heart of men and women belonging to different sections of the society in the way in which a modern psychiatrist with his up-to-date scientific paraphernalia would be expected to, appears to the fore in his famous novel *Griffith Gaunt or Jealousy* (1866). The process of unravelling the deepest layers of the mind as well as heart in a psychological method of Griffith, Mercy Vint, Kate and Mercy Leicester is no less significant than that of a pathologist : Griffith Gaunt's "offering himself to poor Mercy Vint in a treacherous way ignoring his wife Kate"[53] : the tempest in Griffith's soul afterwards : "the jealousy and envy"[54] between Kate and Mercy — all remind of George Eliot's description of psychological reality, and George Meredith's interpretation of modern psychiatry. The same psychological approach comes true of Reade's another novel named, *The Cloister and the Hearth*, in which the psychologically studied characters of Gerard, the assumed father of Erasmus, his partner Denys, his sometime servitor, the merry vagabond Cul de Jatte, and the much-enduring Margaret, do not look like figures painfully exhumed from books and broadsheets, but full-scale psychological studies. The best illustration, that sticks to memory like a leech, of psychological feat, in Reade's *A Terrible Temptation : A Story of the Day*, is where Richard vehemently goads on Sir Charles, the magistrate,"[55] to "commit Lady Basset's son to prison,"[56] and, where the Lady makes this dramatic revelation that the youth is his own flesh and blood :

> When they were gone Mary turned to Richard Bassett, and said, "Why do you want him sent to prison? to spite Sir Charles here, to stab his heart through his son?"
> Sir Charles groaned aloud.
> The woman heard, and thought of things. She flung herself on her knees, and seized his hand. "Don't you cry, my dear old master; mine is the only heart shall bleed.
> He is Not Your Son."
> "What!" cried Sir Charles, in a terrible voice.
> "That is no news to me", said Richard. "He is more like the person than Sir Charles Bassett."
> "For shame! for shame! cried Mary Meyrick. "Oh, it becomes you to give fathers to children — when you don't know your own flesh and blood. He is Your Son Richard Bassett."
> "*My son*!" roared Bassett, in utter amazement.
> "Ay, I should know, For I am his Father."
> This astounding statement was uttered with all the majesty of truth; and when she said, "I am his mother," the voice turned tender all in a moment.
> They were all paralysed, and, absorbed in this strange revelation, did not hear a tollering footstep; a woman, pale as a corpse, and with eyes glaring large, stood amongst them all in a moment, as if a ghost had risen from the earth.
> It was Lady Bassett.[57]

Reade shows his interest in engineering and technological sciences in his novel, named *Put Yourself in his Place*. While padding out his descriptions with documentary evidences on the huge and expensive installations of machinery in satanic mills and factories, Reade infers in an inductive method of a modern scientist how these gigantic implements and tools exploit the labourers involved in appalling poverty and how, as a protest, the discontented operatives intervene the running of the factory-machinery. The hero, in the novel, is the workman of mechanical genius in advance of his time, and who exhibits his calibre and acumen of a man really embedded in scientific temper; "earns three times as much as his comrades."[58] The spirit of heart-burning, as is naturally expected of such an inequality, makes his "comrades band together to destroy"[59] his tools and even his life. The collapse of a dam due to a catastrophic flood reflects upon Reade's knowledge and task of an engineer; and its construction and utility, as explained by Jael Dence,[60] is reminiscent of a student studying Civil Engineering science at a higher stage. The possibilities of its collapse, of the water-exit capacity and the estimated loss in the event of its being dilapidated, which have convincingly been explained in the novel, constitute an official report from an engineer to his department for approbation and confirmation.

Reade's knowledge of navigation, of sea-life, and of its pleasures and privileges seems to be authoritatively remarkable in his novel, named *Foul Play*. Ship-knackers and "the wicked business in coffin ship"[61] come up for discussion in this novel : "the scuttling of ships,"[62] indeed, for the sake of the insurance money is a topic calculated to bring out all Reade's powers of melodrama and also to show his expert knowledge of seafare. Ships have been described as getting under way, and steering across "the Pacific from Sydney, homeward bound."[63] A lady goes into raptures over the method of finding latitude and longitude by the chronomcter in mid-ocean. This is the year of panic in the City (1866), and the suspension of payment by Overend and Gurney,[64] which, of course, does not escape Reade's attention. His scientific tempter is, thus, apparently clear from his description of sea-life. In another novel, *Love Me Little, Love Me Long*, "simple chivalrous sailor David Dodd and the Diana — like Lucy Fountain"[65] enjoy voyage and sea-life, enduring, thrilling fights with the pirates, and often demonstrate their skill and knowledge relating to the modern science of navigation. Reade is, therefore, well ahead of his times in this respect, because this scientific temper of his places him above Collins and Kingsley.

Charles Kingsley, a Devon man, son of the rector of Clovelly; "a lover of nature,"[66] with "scientific training to write excellent elementary works on natural history and geology,"[67] and with sufficient scholarship to acquit himself to the satisfaction of his time as Professor of Modern History at Cambridge; a man with practical views on agriculture; a stimulating preacher, under the influence of "the Carlylean principle of induction,"[68] involving as a primary process, the patient accumulation of facts — a principle palpably seen even in the works of modern historians and "the Bucklean coterie of writers;"[69] who endeavour to understand the psychology of the races — he gleefully struggled for the enlightenment and the social betterment of the languishing labourers residing in industrial slums, while adopting the programme of Christian socialism which Frederick Denison Maurice had tried to put in action during his stay in London; establishing his approximation to Ludlow, Vansittart Neale, Thomas Hughes besides Maurice and his followers, in founding the Society for the Promotion of Working Men's Associations (1849). In his periodical contributions to *Politics for the People* (1848), and to *The Christian Socialist* (1850-51), he "waged a relentless war against the Mammonism"[70] that the industrial revolution and "scientific march brought in their wake"[71]; and strongly made an appeal for reasonable and legitimate compassion and sympathy, like the humanitarian group of novelists, especially like that of Dickens, for the victims of industrial greed and unlimited competition, denouncing the orthodox political economy of the day.

In *Yeast*, which first appeared in *Fraser's Magazine* (1848), to be separately published in 1851, Kingsley espouses the Christian rationalism with the accuracy and observation of a scientist by making the novel "a forceful manifesto :"[72] in *The Saint's Tragedy* (1848), which, of course, made a social drama out of the story of Elizabeth of Hungary, he attacks the Romish priest-craft the doctrine of celibacy"[73] with the force of the Carlylean method involving scientific principle of induction : in *Alton Locke* (1850) and other published volumes of sermons, he appears as the scientist, eulogizing country life, and "a forceful hater of slums,"[74] the apostle of social hygiene in all senses of the term, and also, as a disciple of the idealism of Coleridge and Carlyle, a fierce Protestant, and as the declared adversary of Pusey and Newman. His *Hypatia* (1853) with its sub-title as *New Foes With An Old Face* is "a subtle exposition of the social and spiritual doctrines in the style of a scientist :"[75] it is an astonishing portrayal of the mental and moral qualms of the day with all the modern paraphernalia of love of a dissipated scientific temper "at cross-purposes and complicated intrigues :"[76] his *Westward Ho*! (1855) and *The Heroes, or Greek Fairy Tales For My Children* (1856), both the products of the Crimean War period when the muscular novel was struggling to eulogize the Muscular Christianity even through such utterances as of Tennyson, the Poet Laureate (1850) by now, of Lawrence, and of Maurice, is a clarion call of a scientific adventurer to invigorate the muscles of men's bodies, and the endurance of their hearts, to make them rejoice in their strength bereft of which, even great Mechanics' Institutes would finally end in intellectual priggism and the Christian Young Men's Societies in that of religious Pharisaism.

Mrs. Elizabeth Gaskell's period is one, as she depicts in her novels, when scientific doctrines were gradually swaying upon the literary imagination, or "rather forcing it to reconcile with their fundamental principles."[77] Newton and Einstein applied the theory of gravitation, and of relativity respectively on physical sciences, prognosticating thereupon the resultant other scientific laws indispensable, of course, for all times to come. In literature "the fundamental spirit of such scientific doctrines"[78] has meaningfully been applied on 'fictional art"[79] by Mrs. Gaskell. She convincingly theorizes that "every deed however implicit and of serious nature has its after-effects."[80] It suggests, therefore, that every action has its reaction : every act has its repercussion; and, it purposefully "approximates to the law of Nemesis in religion"[81] or the poetic justice in the literature of the past, the glimpses of which are traceable in Shakespeare's *Macbeth*, where the hero,

Macbeth hesitates to assassinate Duncan knowing it well that it will have its indispensable and inevitable repercussions. But in fiction, the experiment of this type leading to psychological thrust on characters has been enunciated only by Mrs. Gaskell. In *Mary Barton, a Tale of Manchester Life*, Mary Barton, Esther, Jem Wilson and John are convincing psychological studies : upon Mary's father "driven to frenzy by the wrongs of his class and her lover being charged with the murder offence;"[82] her love with Jem Wilson and upon her being intervened by her aunt Esther — all these situations give rise to mental and ethical questions to be solved with the insight and acumen of a psychologist.

In *Moorland Cottage*, Edward, Maggie Brown and Cousin Phillis; in *Ruth*, Ruth; in *North and South*, Higgins, Robert Moore, Jack, John Thornton, Margaret Hale and Lennox; in *Cranford*, Lady Ludlow, Miss Matty, Cousin Phillis, Molly Gibson, Holbrook, Peter, Lady Glenmire and Miss Jenkyns; in *Wives and Daughters*, Gibson, Squire Hamley, Lord Cumnor, Preston, and Cynthia Kirkpatrick — all are memorable psychological studies; and one feels convinced, after going through these life-like portraits, of Mrs. Gaskell's penetrating insight into the heart and mind of her characters. Some of the actions and episodes belonging to these characters have their psychological phobia regarding ethical theory of retribution, and the characters, therefore, seem to suffer from the psychological fear that their actions have been watched over by some unseen force and they shall recoil upon them — giving birth to a unique blend of psychology and religion in her fiction, practised, first of all, only by Mrs. Gaskell. Of the episodes and situations giving glimpses of the fusion of this unique intermingling of psychological ethics, there are some readily countable and reasonably amusing. Ruth, for instance, "a seduced girl,"[83] being innocently "duped and deceived by a political mountebank,"[84] is miserably forced to suffer from "ethical, psychological and social complexes :"[85] Mary Barton, a poverty-stricken labour girl, and her father's outcry during the strike period; Higgins's "calculated atheism";[86] Miss Matty's "love-episode with Holbrook,"[87] a burglar scare and the return of Peter as the Aga Jenkyns — all give rise to many points of serious study in psychology, religion, and ethics.

Lady Ludlow's association with her "feudal compassions,"[88] with all her "wisdom, prejudice, shrewdness and obstinacy";[89] Mr. Gray's impressive devotion and moral courage with his persistence of district-visits in spite of a bad cough, for which the ladies send him gruel and bottles of medicine; Mr. Horner's reservedness, which makes him gallant while sacrificing his life as a martyr to duty, obviously because he has no woman to look after him; Miss Galindo's frank views on the institution of marriage; Daniel Robson's strikingly didactic humour at the procrastinating Corney; Philip Hepburn's love-affair with Sylvia, a creature of such charm and spirit as it detracts nothing from her beauty, or from her dignity, that she can neither read nor write; Preston's plausible melodramatic actions; Cynthi Kirkpatrick's love-affairs and her "reprehensible, delicate and delectable feminine squeamishness"[90] — all these and many such more segments of fictional narratives are "psychologically wholesome analyses"[91] that have become "rather truer and scientifically approved"[92] by "the modern advances of pathology and medical sciences on literature."[93]

Mrs. Gaskell's factory novels evidence her claims to be "a celebrated sociologist"[94] through her fiction : the sociologist, in her, touches upon "a volley of searching questions ranging from social vices to social amelioration via class-conflict,"[95] from human struggles to individual liberation via social-conflict. "The pathetic rendering of the industrially revolutionized slums and street-alleys;"[96] the appalling poverty "reckoning sacrifice"[97] by the poor to the voracity of the rich; and, in it the large multitude of the labourers depressed mentally and socially under the crumbling and defiant dictates of the rich — are some of the pertinent social aspects that the social scientist in Mrs. Gaskell endeavours to study; and thereby formulating a set of philanthropic and altruistic measures to alleviate the social disorder; and in this way, she seems to avow herself to be a humanitarian whose heart is thoroughly suffused with the milk of human kindness.

Gaskell saw the year of the Reform Act, while she was married to the Rev. William Gaskell, Unitarian Minister and a Professor at the training college, at Manchester, at the age of twenty-two; she saw the year of the beginning of the industrial revolution; and also, the year of distress and discontent raging in all the manufacturing districts, of which "Manchester was the most afflicted."[98] The Gaskells were the leading workers among the poor, labouring on the spot in the cause for which "Sadler, Ashley, and their comrades were fighting in Parliament."[99] It was the phase, of course, of sternest social fermentation, in which the Chartist agitation swayed the public mind; and Mrs. Gaskell realised its full implications. Her feelings were all the more crystallized and became tragically sharper on the loss of her dear little child; and more so, when she found the miserable state of the toiling classes in a city, "where housing was neglected to a degree now almost incredible,"[100] and which she has depicted in her novels in "harrowing colours;"[101] and also, where feeling between the employers and the factory-hands was at a boiling point. Mrs. Gaskell's sympathy and compassion for the cause of the labourers was founded on her being an eye-witness : and, in this respect, she is superior to Disraeli and Dickens, both the noted sociologists in the realm of fiction; because the former in his *Sybil* which appeared in 1845, becomes a doctrinaire and abstract commentator; whereas, the latter in his *Hard Times* which appeared a year after, misfires the reality of the case, and also, because both of them lacking an on-the-spot-case-study.

Ruth, her best sociological novel, is a predicament of "a socially betrayed woman."[102] Ruth is that woman, who is cunningly seduced like many simple, innocent inhabitants of Manchester, by a fraudulous minister; who is later on found out, and who brings on his head obloquy and even material retribution. Ruth is socially damned : she is almost treated as an outcast. But the seemingly looking minister with sermonic garb is nothing to lose on that count. Mrs. Gaskell has rightly demanded the same moral standard for men and women, and has inevitably raised her outcry from "the Pharisees, who saw in the charitable conduct of the minister only an aggravation of the offence;"[103] as one witnesses the same from Trollope's Dr. Thorne and Hardy's Tess.

In *Mary Barton, a Tale of Manchester Life*, the unfairness and injustice of the industrialists lustily busy in stretching the doctrine of competition to its fatal logical extremes against the poor toiling labourers living in stingy dungeons half-fed and ill-treated, evidence Mrs. Gaskell's social awareness, and her study of contemporary reality as a sociologist. In content and presentation, it is what can always be expected of a behavioural scientist. Its telling effect heightens when Mrs. Gaskell, "the sociologist,"[104] presents the case of Mary : and of her father who "commits a crime at the behest of the workers committee," because he is driven to frenzy, and becomes "a mentally aberred chronic patient of paranoia,"[105] fit to be settled in a lunatic asylum, because of certain wrongs of his own class. The cycle of the social crime moves on : Mary's lover is wrongly charged with murder : "remorse preys upon John's mind,"[106] and after an affecting interview with the father of his victim he dies : the man shot is one of the employing class, who has been pursuing Mary Barton, though she is deeply in love with Jem Wilson : and finally, Mary's "self-consistency is sacrificed",[107] in the end, because of her poverty and low birth. The wheel of justice keeps on moving until the poor Mary and her entire life are completely ruined. It is, of course, not the pathetic tale of the struggle and of ruin fighting against various social odds, of one Mary; it rather points towards many such helpless women, indeed.

Mrs. Gaskell's persuasive appeal and reconciliatory pleading for amicable reproachment and wider understanding between the capital and labour are evidenced in her another sociological novel named *North and South*. It is, of course, a tale told by Mrs. Gaskell, the social historian by drawing a contrast between the patriarchal landed gentry of the agricultural south and the aristocrats of money in the industrial north. In Robert Moore, therefore, one finds Mrs. Gaskell's "philanthropic industrialist"[108] who is thoroughly conscious of his social obligations, if he has any claims of his "property rights"[109] : in John Thornton, Mrs. Gaskell conceives of one not given to "one's self-aggrandisement,"[110] and of one who is always meditating "to cement the gulf between the employer and the employed;"[111] quite reminiscent of negotiatory sermons of Dickens's in *Hard Times* and of Charles Reade's in *Put Yourself in his Place*. Viewing from the standpoint of a sociologist, this novel has all possible segments of a particular run of society to be studied analysed and universalized. But the most telling one is the outcry of a poor father during the strike ruminatingly hinting at five shilling a week, the cumulative effects of whose pathos is really beyond description :

> It's no use, Higgins. Hoo cannot live long a' this'n. Hoo's just sinking away — not for want o' meat hersel' — but because hoo cannot stand th' sight o' the little ones clemming. Ay, clemming! Five shilling a week may do well enough for thee, wi' but two mouths to fill, and one on 'em a wench who can welly earn her own meat. But it's clemming to us. An' I tell thee plain — if hoo dies, as I'm fear'd hoo will afore we've getten th' five per cent. I'll fling th' money back i' th' master's face, and say, 'Be domned to yo'; be domned to th' whole cruel world o' Yo'; that could na heave me th' best wife that ever bore childer to a man!' An' look thee, lad, I'll hate thee, and th' whole pack o' th' Union. Ay, an' chase Yo' through heaven wi' my hatred — I will, lad! I will — if yo're leading me astray i' this matter. Thou saidst, Nicholas, on Wednesday sennight — and it's now Tuesday i' th' second week — that afore a fortnight we'd ha' the masters coming a — begging to us to take back our work, at our own wage — and time's nearly up — and there's our lile Jack lying a — bed, too weak to cry, but just now and then sobbing up his heart for want o' food — our lile Jack, I tell thee, lad! Hoo's never looked up sin' he were born, and hoo loves him as if he were her very life — as he is — for I reckon he'll ha' cost me that precious price — our lile Jack, who weakened me each morn wi' putting his sweet little lips to my great rough fou' face, a — seeking a smooth place to kiss – an' he lies clemming.[112]

Indeed, Jack, dying of hunger, in this novel reminds us of many such poverty-stricken and socially-exploited helpless labourers whom industrial revolution rendered almost destitute, and who were, indeed, as are traceable, in plenty, in Mrs. Gaskell's other social tales — *Cranford, Mr. Harrison's Confessions, Wives and Daughters* and *Sylvia's Lovers*. In fact, Mrs. Gaskell anatomizes social life in all its perspectives, ever expected of a novelist.

Walter Besant and James Rice, two other prominent novelists of the humanitarian group, whose chief exponent was Charles Dickens, individually as well as in collaboration did "the Yeoman's service to the down-trodden stratum of society"[113] by delineating the chill penury and appalling illiteracy that existed in it, and also by suggesting reasonable measures to be adopted to ameliorate its lot in a manner involving scientific rationalism and accuracy of detail with a scientific attitude of mind. Many of their "scientific reasonings give place to points in biology, psychology and pathology :"[114] often they enunciate views having conformity with and influence of Herbert Spencer and of Comte. Besant in his admirable little volumes on *Westminster* and *London*, and James Rice in his thought-provoking *All Sorts* and *Conditions of Men* describe London life with almost as humanitarian vigour and "scientific precision."[115] as Dickens and Charles Reade did; indeed, withal these Dickensian and Readean imitation of 'London Life', there is something more arresting and more captivating in them, *viz.*, an undercurrent or spirit of revolt that may endanger future social set-up into crumbling pieces of scepticism and pessimism; and that arresting force shook the complacency of the apathetic middle class; and, finally proved a powerful ally to supplement the work of such reformers as "Wilberforce, Ashley, Oastler and Robert Owen,"[116] whose sincere endeavours further stimulated and invigorated the works of Bernard Shaw and John Galsworthy.

Equally important novelist in whose novels scientific attitude of mind prognosticates many succeeding, fast emerging evolutionary doctrines and in whose novels the humanitarian note constitutes the central deponent protest against the self-complacency, the apparent smugness and the feigned cant, like those of Walter Besant's and James Rice's, is Richard Whiteing. With "a stringent questioning note in a scientific spirit,"[117] he attempts to probe deeper into the sordid living of the industrial labour and lights up their sufferings in an honest way as forcefully as William Rathborne Greg and William Cobbett did in the case of the agricultural poor. He espouses their cause in his novel, *No. 5, John, Street* in the days of social unrest and political fermentation with the same balanced reasoning and scientific spirit as a scientist analyses his experiment. In fact, he "dittoes much of political doctrines of Francis Place,"[118] a noted democrat who rendered Yeoman's service to the industrial population of the city; and he, therefore, teaches on the similar lines on which earlier than him, John Howard thought for prison reform or on the same pattern, Bentham and Romilly thought to purify the criminal laws. On ameliorative footing, his enthusiasm for moral resurrection and "rational thinking is emulative of the men like the Wesleys"[119] and of "the forward-looking thinkers like Herbert Spencer and Huxley."[120]

By the time we reach Anthony Trollope, "The Victorian society witnessed much social fermentation,"[121] an upsurge of multitudinous movements which had their tremendous repercussions on the social moorings. "This transition-stage impelled social scientists to study all movements"[122] in their of a universe that we do not know. Trollope has, therefore, studied a quiet world, "a society of semi-public character."[123] The clerical and the higher lay-society of Barsetshire, with the De Courcys, Greshams, Thornes, Luftons, and Grantlys as prominent as the bishops and deans, is everybody's study,[124] like politics or the leading events of the London season. "Everyone knows everyone else;"[125] and such affairs as "the jilting of Lily Dale;"[126] the corporeal punishment inflicted on Mr. Crosbie or Mr. Moffat; Mr. Crawley's supposed theft; Lady Glencora's love-affair; or the disappearance of Lizzie Eustace's diamonds — are all public property. Other things that Trollope is good at catching are professional mannerisms and the stamp of groups and sects; his parsons and lawyers and lawyers' clerks have all the marks of their orders, "which may cut across other social distinctions,"[127] and, at the same time, are balanced discerningly with the more general human instincts and the more personal motives. But Trollope's interest in "the class system"[128] is not that of a sociologist; he relishes it for its effects on character, and for the comedy it provides. His social perspective is a great deal wider than those of the Brontes', Mrs. Gaskell's or Charlotte Yonge's; but "it had nothing like the scope of Dickens's and Thackeray's."[129]

Trollope ignores many other "classes of society,"[130] since they do not provide "material for his fictional art"[131] or they do not amuse him. He conceives of "classes as collections"[132] of interesting individuals whose manners and ways of living are "fairly uniform,"[133] "aspects of minor interest to the sociologist."[134] Caprice or idiosyncrasy either of a race or of an individual always provides amusement to Trollope. For instance, when Frederic Harrison remakes upon the thorough knowledge of the organism of English society which specially distinguishes Trollope, he is little misleading; organisms and organizations are the main concern of the sociologist, not of Trollope. One elementary method of the sociologist, a primary and indispensable act, is to classify : Trollope is less of a classifier than Thackeray or even Dickens. Though he is fond of bestowing appellations, which are labels rather than names, upon the undistinguished crowd, such as Miss Gushing, Major Fiasco, Sir Abraham Haphazard, Dr. Fillgrave, Mr. Bold, Mr. Love and Mr. Kissing — who especially affords the Commissioners their little joke that Kissing, they feared, went by favour, and that love would still be lord of all, — the lawyers Fidus Neverbend and Gitemthruet, or the election agents, Mr. Nearthewinde, Mr. Closerstil, and Mr. Reddypalm — all indicate a clear sign that there are generic specimens rather than odd individuals or eccentrics, nevertheless, his more mature and far significant characters are, indeed, more superb than these mere variations of a few breeds. His characters, such as Mr. Harding, John Eames, Mr. Proudie, Dr. Thorne, Miss Dunstable, Grace Crawley, Mary Thorne, Archdecon Grantly, Plantagenet Palliser, or the Signora Neroni — all are "the classifications of individuals,"[135] who cannot be categorised so flatly "as saints, snobs, fortune-hunters, flirts, wiseacres or nincompoops, or mere eccentrics"[136] like those of Dickens's caricatures and Thackeray's snobs. He does not present a classified world like theirs, on the contrary, Trollope wishes to show off the infinite differences and the inexhaustible comedy of "men's peculiarities of temperament,"[137] mentality and selfish or generous outlook. He is, therefore, all for differentiating between people whether of the same sex, station, and type, or otherwise. It is why, there is always a good variety of people in his novels even amongst his snobs, rogues, lovers, parsons, politicians, or other representatives of parts, vices, professions, or social orders, always suffused with a sense of individuality; and in this regard, of course, Trollope really surpasses "all other novelists and sociologists."[138]

The psychologist in Trollope is even more powerful than the sociologist, because he seems to be capable of answering more problems through his psychological analyses than through sociological studies. Ranging from the ordinary revelation of the depth of heart and mind to even unaccountable motives affecting bizarre relationships between people, complicated natures and temperaments and faults of the common order — all have been psychologically probed into. *Orley Farm, Can You Forgive Her?*, *Phineas Redux, The Claverings*, and *He Knew He Was Right* — all are Trollope's remarkably seasoned psychological attempts in the field of fiction-writing. Violet Effingham, Phineas Finn, Lord Chiltern, Lady Laura, Madame Max Goesler, and the Duke of Omnium — all are fine character-studies in the annals of psychology. Of the situations of psychological import, in *He Knew He Was Right*, is the one where Trollope offers an analytical study of "the chill remorseless marital tyranny of Robert Kenneby,"[139] and "the rancorous, though unconfessed and half-conscious jealousy :"[140] the another in *Phineas Redux*, where Phineas and Lady Laura try to be confidants, yet they have their sincere doubts about each other :[141] the third, in the same novel where the rivalry of Chiltern and Phineas is prolonged due to Violet Effingham's rejection and these lovers and her receiving them now as dear family friends.[142] In *Orley Farm*, Lady Mason's culpability and her sham offer material for deeper and more tragic psychological studies; in *Can You Forgive Her*? the unhappy imbroglios of Lady Glencora and her husband imply a serious psychological dent : in *The Belton Estate*, and *The Claverings*, the quandary of one more or less in love with two persons constitutes the psychological study. Clara Amedroz, for instance, is in a quandary not to conclude as to who of the two suitors — Captain Aylmer, "the cold-hearted and conventional,"[143] and Will Belton, "the rough diamond, the bluff and impulsive"[144] is worthy of her. Belton Castle's inheritance and the Clara — Mrs. Askerton scandal — complicate the issue further. In the end, Clara rejects Will Belton, being secretly in love with the captain, until she finds him a cold-blooded fish of a man, who thinks of nothing in the world but being respectable and Will's temptation in vengeance :

> Captain Aylmer, when he heard the hearty tone of the girl's answer, already began almost to doubt whether it was wise on his part to devote the innermost ben of his cellar to wine that was so cheap. Not that he had any idea of receding. Principle, if not love, prevented that..."when you asked me, I could but tell you the truth," she said, smiling at him. The truth is very well, but he would have liked it better had the truth come to him by degrees.[145]

"When the humorists and humanitarians abandoned," rightly observes W.L. Cross, "cathedrals and ruined castles for London slums and the factory towns of north England, they let the novel down from the picturesque heroic to the matter of contemporary life."[146] In Thackeray's novels "the matter of contemporary life"[147] is depicted through "intellectual realism" not to create "an atmosphere of false sentiment,"[148] but to "detect latent absurdities"[149] in social life. Thackeray's interpretation of realism is based on sound intellectual probing into it : it requires a mental strain, a scientific rationalism to appreciate. It is so because Thackeray regards novel not merely "a representation," not merely a literary transcript of reality : "but also as an interpretation of life,"[150] like that of Fielding. For Thackeray, life is a complicated activity to be viewed and commented dispassionately and objectively : it is rather the unbiased report of facts reproduced by an intelligent scientist. Thackeray's intellectual realism is, therefore, one presented by that scientist of human behaviour, who unveils sentiments from genuine feelings; and who definitely knows that he is buying vanity in the fair of life. Thus the impact, on Thackeray's fiction, of scientific thought is to be interpreted in his endeavour to portray intellectual realism rather than in those already enumerated and traced in the preceding novels.

In *The Book of Snobs*, Thackeray anatomizes the science of "snobography" : the variety of hypocrites and cajolers with all their cunning, makes him a certified "social anatomist;"[151] and, so does the social anatomy in another novel *Vanity Fair* through "the snobbery-incarnate Amelia,"[152] Dobbin, Rawdon Crawley, Lieutenant Osborne, and Becky Sharp.[153] In *Pendennis*, this social anatomy of snobbery has been discreetly performed through such "remarkable snobs"[154] as Major Pendennis, Blanche Amory and Colonel Altamount : in *Henry Esmond*, through the delineations of Esmund himself, Beatrix and Marlborough : in *The Virginians*, through the characters of General Lambert, Theo, Hetly Lambert, Sampson and Lord Castlewood. The art of snobbery practised by Clive, Colonel and Ethel New come in *The New Comes*; "the cunning of hypocrisy"[155] evidenced through the deeds of Philip, Caroline, Dr. Firmin and Mrs. Talbot in Philip; "the idiosyncratic motives"[156] of Barry and Frederick in *Barry Lyndon* — are manifest proofs to entitle Thackeray to be a first-rate social anatomist.

Thackeray's intellectual view concerning worldly realism, as expressed through the triteness of commonplace affairs of life, prose being a medium, is really far-reaching and more significant than it may appear to be so at a cursory glance, because to study the common pretences of life, the inborn feelings of hatred, jealousy and love, the imposture, snobbery and dissimulation; and also the struggle between *what is* and *what is not* with a philosophic sneer-*what should be*, on the lines of social and medical anatomy, the two distinct advanced disciplines of modern sciences, naturally entails a wider view of practical realism of life on the part of a novelist.

From Thackeray's and Trollope's novels onwards, the scientific impact on fiction becomes perceptible, but in George Eliot's novels, as it will be seen in the ensuing discussion, this impact forms an important segment of fiction-writing, which afterwards in the hands of Meredith and Hardy got *ne plus ultra.* In George Eliot's novels, the impact of scientific thought is as manifest and various as her contacts and intimacy were with the leading luminaries of scientific movement of the day. She has accepted Erasmus Darwin's doctrine of change and evolution, but there is also a proof, as recorded by George S. Haight, her biographer, to substantiate that she does not approve of Darwin's unscientific spiritualism; rather she terms his religious revelation as most unscientific; and, she strongly feels that spiritualism was not a "degrading folly, imbecile in the estimate of evidence, or else impudent imposture :"[157]

> Spiritualism was becoming a resource of many (even intelligent) people whose faith in religious revelation had declined. The Erasmus Darwins arranged with a professional medium named Williams to conduct a seance at their house on 16 January, 1874, which the Leweses attended. The Charles Darwin family was there, the Litchfields, Hensleight Wedgwood, Fred Myers, Galton, Mrs. Bowen, and others, seated about a large dining table. But Lewes, regarding the medium's insistence on complete darkness as unscientific, 'was troublesome and inclined to make jokes and not play the game fairly and sit in the dark in silence', wrote Mrs. Litchfield. After a few of the usual 'manifestations', he and George Eliot left in disgust. She saw nothing to change her opinion that spiritualism was either 'degrading folly, imbecile in the estimate of evidence, or else impudent imposture.'[158]

George Eliot's view of God and spirit, world and vice is more or less the same as that of George Meredith's, with the only significant difference that she does not insist too much on "intuition,"[159] and thereby approximating it to "conventional religion."[160] As a matter of fact, the seed of *Daniel Deronda* got sprouted on January 16, 1874, when George Eliot dined with the Darwins and when she disbelieved in toto the spiritualism bereft of sterling virtues of Christian humanity. In this novel, spiritualism has been "tempered with science"[161] in such a way that the feigned controversy between the science and religion is considerably minimized and widely accepted.

George Eliot's intimacy with Auguste Comte, "an exponent of the positivist science,"[162] is of a curious nature; for, it is "more scholarly than worldly"[163] and it is, therefore, more of a moulding impact than of others; and, it is via John Chapman, a leading theologian of the time. In October, 1851, John Chapman arrived at Rosehill with Robert William Mackay, "a bachelor of forty-seven."[164] Both Chapman and Mackay believed that both the moral and the physical elements were subject to the same "inexorable law of consequences";[165] and that human duty was comprised in the earnest study of that law and obedience to its teaching. Following Creuzer, Mackay traced the origin of all divinities to nature-cults in his book — *The Progress of the Intellect as Exemplified in the Religious Development of the Greeks and Hebrews,* in which he took recourse to those ways of divine revelations which Casaubon adopted to solve theological controversies; and, he accepted Strauss's view of the mythical character of the Bible. Since John Chapman got Mackay's book published, and since Mackay was the singular theologian to accept Strauss's view of the theology, it was but natural that Chapman should ask the translator of Strauss's, *i.e.,* George Eliot, to write an article on the book, which she accepted as an editor of *The Westminster Review.* In this review, she made a comprehensive analysis of Comte's view of the positivist science and there are, therefore, certain evident glimpses of Comte's scientific theories in her novels, especially in the

Middlemarch, Daniel Deronda, and *Romola.* Besides her own deep-rooted interest in and liking for Comte's philosophy, it was her own husband Lewes, who too, took much pains in revising and reading proof of Comte's *Philosophy of the Sciences;* and, George Eliot also read the Comte proofs and was zealous in promoting the book on Lewes's account. Chapman had published Harriet Martineau's abridgement of Comte's *Positive Philosophy* a few weeks after John brought out Lewes's book, *Comte's Philosophy of the Sciences,* and though they were very different in scope, reviewers naturally tended to draw comparisons. Marian had tied vainly to get someone to write an article on Comte for the *Westminster Review*; when Alexander Bain, refused, "the books were left to Huxley to treat in his science summary, January 1854."[166] As the last proof-sheets were going through her hands, Marian wrote to ask Chapman not to send Huxley's article to the printer till he discussed it with her. In it, Huxley, after warm praise of Miss Martineau's work, attacked Lewes as a mere "book scientist"[167] in a contemptuous manner. George Eliot made every effort possible to defend her husband and published two articles in the *Leader* two weeks later to give a correct interpretation of "Comte's view of positivist science."[168] In her novels, the Comte view of life and world has been naturally evidenced; but, the *Prelude* to *Middlemarch* has very beautiful and meaningful lines which are universally acclaimed; for, they bear a close resemblance to Comte's vision of life and world, on the one hand; and George Eliot's modification of Comte's philosophy approximating it, with due accompaniment of scientific tempering to the Wordsworthian concept of human solidarity, the unity of man, the oneness of faith, on the other :

> The passions that build up our human soul,
> Not with the mean vulgar works of man,
> But with high objects, with enduring things —
> With life and nature, purifying thus,
> The elements of feeling and of thought,
> And sanctifying, by such discipline,
> Both pain and fear, until we recognize —
> A grandeur in the beating of the heart.[169]

Herbert Spencer's influence on George Eliot is also reflected through her novels; and, it is the impact of the former that largely determines the role of free will and evolutionary processes in the life of her significant characters. She saw Spencer's doctrine of evolution growing through different stages from very close quarters; for she was introduced to him in August, 1951, while she was in London with the Brays to see the exhibition at the Crystal Palace, and after her return to the Strand in September, 1951, she saw him there frequently. One night she went with Spencer to the Lyceum to see *The Chain of Events,* a play in eight acts, adapted by Lewis from the French :

> It was a very long chain and drags rather heavily (she told Charles Bray). No sparkle, but a sort of Dickens — like sentimentality all through — in short, I think it might please you. As a series of tableaux I never saw anything equal to it. But to my mind it is execrable moral taste to have a storm and shipwreck with all its horrors on the stage. I could only scream and cover my eyes. It was revolting to hear the cheers and clapping of the audience. But perhaps all that was pure philosophy, and they were so thoroughly imbued with your beloved optimism that they felt more than ever reconciled to the scheme of things.[170]

Spencer often had tickets for Covent Garden and sometimes asked her to go with him. "I had two offers last night," she wrote to Clara, "— not of marriage, but of music — which I find it impossible to resist. Mr. Herbert Spencer proposed to take me on Thursday to hear William Tell, and Miss Parkes asked me to go with her to hear the Creation on Friday."[171] As the spring days grew warmer, she and Spencer would walk on the terrace of Somerset House, to which Chapman had a key; in those days before the Thames Embankment was built only a balustrade separated it from the river. There, with no noise but the gulls and the passing streamboats, they would pace backwards and forwards for hours, discussing a variety of subjects. To his friend Edward Lott, Spencer wrote on April 23, 1852 about :

> Miss Evans, whom you have heard me mention as the translatress of Strauss and as the most admirable woman, mentally, I ever met. We have been for some time past on very

> intimate terms. I am frequently at Chapman's, and the greatness of her intellect conjoined with her womanly qualities and manner, generally keeps me at her side most of the evening.[172]

But to Marian, Spencer seems very soon to have made it clear that his admiration was of her mental qualities only, for she wrote to the Brays on April 27, 1852 : "We have agreed that we are not in love with each other and that there is no reason why we should not have as much of each other's society as we like. He is a good, delightful creature and I always feel better for being with him."[173] Of course, their liking for each other was of a permanent nature : for, they sang together at the Chapman's evening parties, and he helped her make copies of the resolutions to be offered at the book-sellers meeting. "My brightest spot next to my love of old friends," she wrote to Cara, "is the deliciously calm new friendship that Herbert Spencer gives me. We see each other every day and have a delightful Camaraderie in everything. But for him my life would be desolate enough now, with poor Mr. C. so occupied and so sad — but he runs away with a great deal of my time."[174] On many fine days, they made longer excursions to the Chiswick Flower Show or to Kew Gardens, discussing possible articles for the *Westminster.* "I went to Kew yesterday," she wrote to Sara Hennell on June 29, "on a scientific expedition with Herbert Spencer, who has all sorts of theories about plants — I should have said a proof-hunting expedition. Of course, if the flowers didn't correspond to the theories, we said, 'tant pis pour les fleurs.'"[175]

From Herbert Spencer, Eliot drew much inspiration to crystallize her knowledge of the Greek and other literatures and to put her readings in a scientific mould of opinion. She had finished reading the *Odyssey* before she wrote in her *Journal 13,* June, 1855 : "I began the second book of the *Iliad* in Greek this morning :"[176] in December, 1855, she was reading Sophocles in a new edition of the *Antigone,* which she reviewed for the *Leader* : and, she referred to the Greek drama in different issues, for example, the *Ajax* in September 22, 1856; the *Oedipus trilogy* in February 14, 1857; the *Electra* in August 12, 1857; the

Philoctetes in October 25, 1857; the *Aeschylus* trilogy followed in the *Agamemnon* in December 6, 1857; the *Choephori* in January 7, 1858; and the *Eumenides* in February 8, 1857. She continued the practice of reading Greek and moulding her knowledge of this language in a scientific temper, even after coming into closer contacts with Spencer and Huxley. R.C. Jebb, meeting her at Cambridge in 1873, recalled her saying that Sophocles had influenced her most by his "delineation of the great primitive emotions."[177] Vernon Rendall, the editor of *Notes and Queries,* in a series of interesting articles on *George Eliot and the Classics,* remarked about her fondness for Sophocles :[178] her first published story — *Amos Barton,* quoted a couplet from the *Philoctetes,* and in subsequent works, she went on, says Rendall, "to a garland of Greek which I have not seen equalled in the writings of any other author, inside or outside fiction."[179] Her knowledge of Latin, which was considerably wider, was equally tempered in scientific spirit : Horace she naturally quoted most frequently : but Virgil, Cicero, Persius, Livy, Tacitus, Plautus, Quintilian, and Pliny are some of the others who came easily to her mind. Indeed, her knowledge of the classics was more solid than that of Thackeray which he got at Charterhouse and Cambridge, probably wider than that of Trollope which he got at Harrow and Winchester; and which she proportionately mixed and used with scientific accuracy and intenseness; and which made Huxley remark sneeringly about George Eliot that she was merely a "pseudo-scientist,"[180] which equally amazed Lewes, who later on defended George Eliot by writing many articles. However, Huxley's theory of evolution impressed her, except that there should be a respectful place for the divine agency, which controls our mortal world. As a matter of fact, Huxley refused to admit any place for divinity of the Christian religion and reproached the authority of the church to adhere to such a religious conception of divine agency. George Eliot accepted Huxley's physical evolution without any hesitation like Hardy, but like George Meredith, again, her conception of good and bad is essentially Christian.

All these influences went together in moulding the outlook of George Eliot : and, in her novels, one finds a significant impact of science to the extent that her novels are literally termed as novels of ideas; because, there are ideas to discuss : there are isms to ponder over : there are approaches to psychology, sociology, pathology and psychiatry, which are closely linked with particular disciplines of modern sciences. Rather, they are an intermingling of science, literature and realism of modern life with an interpretation of values whereby one can at least put aside the dross and squalor of the present milieu.

In George Eliot's novels, the theme is commonplace, yet the treatment is "scientifically real and life-like :"[181] her protagonists are very commonplace people; yet she "invests them with tragic dignity of the lowliest, the most prosaic, the least attractive person."[182] They show, of course, the astounding power of seeing through "shams and pretentious airs"[183] or the reverse of modest worth to the real truth of things, of revealing what ordeals and agonies are rankling in the hearts of those who show an impassive exterior or are too humble to open their bosom to the world. Amos Barton is "too complacent and too obtuse"[184] to see through "the wiles of the pampered foreign countess,"[185] who sponges on his overworked wife. The faithful Milly, the hail-fellow-well-met parson Mr. Gilfil, and the angry Caterina are the characters, who talk of the reality of life exactly in a scientific manner. In her other novels too — *Adam Bede* (1859), *The Mill on the Floss* (1860), *Silas Marner* (1860), *Romola* (1863), *Felix Holt* (1866), *Middlemarch* (1871-72) and *Daniel Deronda* (1876) — the scientific treatment of the commonplace things is quite evident. In *Adam Bede,* the basis of the plot is a story, told to her by Mrs. Evans, the Methodist aunt, of the girl hanged for child-murder; in *The Mill on the Floss,* the basis of the plot is the household friends, who may be conceived as forming the rustic chorus to the tragic drama with the most remarkable practical sense of Maggie; in *Silas Marner,* the theme is based on her Warwickshire memories in the form of an idyll, mingling tragedy and comedy proportionately. "Poor misshapen Silas,"[186] his faith in God and the reliance of an infirm and diffident nature on his fellow-beings shattered by "the false accusation of theft,"[187] migrates from his home somewhere in the industrial north, "to the village of Raveloe,"[188] and there carries on his trade of a weaver, but keeps himself aloof from his neighbours, being left with no object in life but to save and hoard and count his money. "One night the treasure disappears,"[189] and the old miser rushes frantically into "the parlour at the Rainbow Inn"[190] to tell the company gathered there of his loss. And then, as he wakes out of one of his epileptic fits, the first thing his eyes fall upon is a child's golden hair, and he instantly thinks that his gold has been restored. The little foundling who has crept into his cottage becomes the instrument of his redemption : in *Romola,* George Eliot has approximated more and more to the Comtist definition of a work of art, the concrete realization of philosophic ideas : in it, she, first of all, explored the dimmer regions of consciousness, to trace the inner phenomena, of which characters and deeds are the outward manifestations. In *Felix Holt,* the plot is concerned mainly with the people George Eliot had once known quite familiarly in the Midlands, involving a retrospect, the period being that of the agitation for reform in the thirties : in *Middlemarch,* which is supposed to be her ripest and fullest exposition of mind and philosophy, there is the scientific treatment of the complex life of a provincial town at the middle of the century, bringing on the scene half-a-hundred separate characters, of whom nearly a dozen are analysed to the depths, and shown developing or deteriorating, as they face circumstances honestly and discerningly or succumb to the internal weakness which corrupts motive and paralyses will; it is, in a way, a study of the doctrine of determinism of positivist science : and finally, in *Daniel Deronda*, the basic theme is the psychological and scientific study of the laws of human life : it is rather a sardonic treatise on life than a mere compendious commentary on social manners. Deronda is a pure idealization, the visionary *Mordecai* pure literature : it is only "on Gwendolen Harleth and her struggles with her baser self"[191] and the recalcitrance of the world that the old genius pours itself out again : Gwendolen has resemblances to Maggie and Romola and even Dorothea, with more of "the human admixture of weakness and error."[192]

The major novelists of the age influenced their disciples in different ways, for instance, the school of Thackeray in fiction-writing finds its support in the works of Benjamin Disraeli, but unlike Thackeray, Disraeli is more concerned with the political life of the age than either with the psychological or the intellectual study of the social beings. He shows an apparent awareness of scientific developments of the age, but his chief concern is to uphold the supermacy of a new Tory Democracy. His famous novels — *Vivian Grey, Coningsby, Tancred* and *Sybil* — all deal with the political life of the age, of the mid-Victorian in particular, with a forceful satire. In reformative spirit, Disraeli heralded that unbounded and unflinching faith in social reforms as in the novels of Mrs. Gaskell and Charles Kingsley; in political acumen, he prognosticated the work of Lord Lytton, and in humanitarian spirit, he followed the Dickensian school of novelists, because his *Sybil* alone, which deals with the life of the labourers subsequent to the first Chartist riots, entitles him to be one of their groups. In his *Tancred*, Disraeli implicitly refers to *The Origin of Species,* yet he is not as concerned with and disturbed by the Darwinian principle of evolution as the novelists belonging to the later part of the age, such as Meredith and Hardy, were. It is why, his novels lack the psychological strain of George Eliot and George Meredith, who were immensely influenced by science.

The psychological strain of George Eliot is also significantly missing in the novels of many women novelists belonging to the early as well as the mid-Victorian period, though the strains of domesticity and that of romantic adventure are "pleasantly blended"[193] in their works. Emily Bronte's *Wuthering Heights*; Anne Bronte's *Agnes Grey* and *The Tenant of Wildfell Hall*; and Charlette Bronte's *The Professor, Jane Eyre, Shirley* and *Villette* are the prominent works in which the elemental passion with an unruly revolt against conventions, for woman-emancipation, against formalism and hypocrisy is more predominant than any other strain of psychological fiction. There is a conspicuous paucity of scientific impact on Miss Mitford's *Our Village*; Harriet Martineau's *Deerbrook*; Mrs. Clive's *Paul Ferrol,* Mrs. Henry Wood's *East Lynne*, Mrs. Craik's *John Halifax, Gentleman,* and Miss Charlotte Yonge's *Heir of Redcliffe.* Women novelists of lesser genius such as Mrs. Gore, Mrs. Marsh, Mrs. Trollope and Mrs. E. Lynn Linton delighted more in the presentation of emotional situations and passionate feelings with their characteristic strain of the primal forces of woman nature than in intellectual and psychological study of and approach to human nature. The direct impacts of the Darwinian evolution, the Spencerian Synthetic Philosophy and the Chambersian Uniformitarianism hardly stirred their imagination to write novels on the psychological pattern of George Eliot.

Then, there are novelists belonging to the early as well as the mid-Victorian period in whose works only the promiscuous strain of romance is more predominant than any other strain. In William Carleton's *Autobiography,* Gerald Griffin's *The Collegians,* Samuel Lover's *Handy Andy,* Charles Lever's *Jack Hinton*, James Grant's *The Romance of War,* Marryat's *Jacob Faithful,* and Michael Scott's *Tom Cringle's Log,* the strain of romance is so powerful that it carries the beauty and charm of Sir Walter Scott's novels. The same romantic tradition with an equal flavour for natural objects is copiously seen in the works of Theodore Hook, James Morier, and Samuel Warren. In Lord Lytton's novels named *The Caxtons, My Novel, Pelham* and *Paul Clifford,* the romantic strain is mixed with the satiric strain; because he talks of urban fashion in *Pelham* and of political hypocrisy in *Paul Clifford* and shows sufficient knowledge of the political system as he had been a liberal member of the Parliament for some time. The romantic strain in Henry Kingsley's *Ravenshoe,* John Whyte Melville's *Gladiators,* and John Galt's *The Entail* is often unalloyed but it sometimes cuts across the strain of domesticity and that of social revolt in fiction. Thus, the romantic strain, during the early and mid-Victorian period has three distinct forms — pure romantic strain, mixed strain of romance plus domesticity, and romantic strain with a satiric touch.

Thus, the impact of scientific thought on Dickens, Charles Reade, Charles Kingsley, Mrs. Elizabeth Gaskell, Walter, Besant, James Rice, and Richard Whiteing has been reflected through the industrial movement and its attendant evils and other repercussions, whereas the same impact on Anthony Trollope through that of sociological interpretation and psychological studies : on Thackeray through intellectual reality, whereas on George Eliot, through that of scientific positivism. It is true that in Dickens's novels as well as in the novels of those belonging to the humanitarian group of novelists, the spirit of science has influenced less penetratingly and less stringently than in those of Trollope, Thackeray and Eliot, because by the time Eliot got published her *Adam Bede* in 1859, the evolutionary theory of Darwin had sufficiently been confirmed by such pre-Darwinian evolutionists as Chambers, Lyell, Wallace, Herschel and Dr. W.C. Wells and many more such eminent scientists; and because on the publication of Darwin's *Origin of Species* in 1859, the same year in which *Adam Bede* was published, the Darwinian theory of evolution was laboriously and intelligently popularized by Spencer and Huxley. Trollope got published his *Barchester Towers* in 1857, and Thackeray, his *The Virginians* in 1859 — both the years conspicuously noted for the scientific theories and their meteoric impact, on the one hand, and the religious decline *vis-a-vis* the debatable pithecoid origin of man, on the other. In such circumstances, it was but natural for Thackeray, Trollope and Eliot to be influenced more by the impact of science than those novelists belonging to the Dickensian school of fiction-writing.[194]

NOTES AND REFERENCES

1. *Far From the Madding Crowd*, pp. 300-03.
2. *Tancred*, pp. 141-45.

3. *Far From the Madding Crowd*, p. 302.
4. *Tancred*, p. 144.
5. Bush, Douglas : *Science and English Poetry*, p. 104.
6. *Ibid.*, p. 105.
7. *Ibid.*, p. 106.
8. *Ibid.*
9. Henkin, L.J. : *Darwinism in the English Novel* 1860-1910, p. 174.
10. Whitehead, A.D. : *A History of the Warfare of Science with Theology*, p. 73.
11. *Ibid.*, p. 74.
12. *Ibid.*, p. 75.
13. Irvine, William : *Apes, Angels and Victorians*, p. 215.
14. Oliphant, J. : *Victorian Novelists*, p. 29.
15. Compton-Rickett, Arthur : *A History of English Literature*, p. 406.
16. *Ibid.*
17. Ford, F.M. : *The English Novel*, p. 109.
18. Rees, J.F. : *Social and Industrial History of England 1815-1918*, p. 273.
19. Young, G.M. : *Victorian England*, pp. 147-50.
20. Leavis, F.R. : *The Great Tradition*, p. 47.
21. Hughes, J.L. : *Dickens as an Educator*, p. 10.
22. Crotch, W.W. : *Charles Dickens : Social Reformer*, p. 201.
23. Gissing, G. : *Charles Dickens : A Critical Study*, p. 102.
24. Engle, M. : *The Maturity of Dickens*, p. 19.
25. Butt, J. and Tillotson, K. : *Dickens at Work*, p. 95.
26. Cruikshank, R.J. : *Dickens and Early Victorian England,* p. 36.
27. House, Humphry : *The Dickens World*, p. 39.
28. Fielding, K.J. : *Charles Dickens : A Critical Introduction*, p. 127.
29. Jackson, T.A. : *Charles Dickens : The Progress of a Radical*, p. 34.
30. *Ibid.*, p. 35.
31. Crotch, W.W. : *Charles Dickens : Social Reformer*, p. 194.
32. *David Copperfield*, p. 194.
33. *Ibid.*, p. 148.
34. *Ibid.*
35. *Ibid.*
36. *Ibid.*, p. 148.
37. *Ibid.*, pp. 148-49.
38. *Martin Chuzzlewit,* p. 164.
39. Marcus, Steven : *Dickens from Pickwick to Dombey*, p. 257.
40. *Ibid.*

41. *Oliver Twist*, pp. 27-29.
42. *Charles Dickens,* p. 81.
43. *A Guide to English Literature : From Dickens to Hardy,* Vol. VI, p. 134.
44. *Ibid.*
45. *Bleak House,* pp. 276-77.
46. *Hard Times,* pp. 56-7.
47. Turner, A.M. : *The Making of the Cloister and the Hearth*, p. 17.
48. Tolles, W. : *Tom Taylor and the Victorian Drama*, p. 102.
49. Phillips, W.C. : *Dickens, Reade and Collins : Sensation Novelists*, p. 96.
50. Sutcliffe, E.G. : 'Fact, Realism and Morality in Reade's Fiction' in *Studies in Philology,* XLI, p. 23.
51. Haines, L.F. : 'Reade, Mill and Zola : a Study of the Character and Intention of Reade's Realistic Method' in *Studies in Philology*, XI, p. 37.
52. *Ibid.,* p. 38.
53. *Griffith Gaunt or Jealousy*, p. 9.
54. *Ibid.*, p. 11.
55. *Terrible Temptation* : *A Story of the Day*, p. 27.
56. *Ibid.,* p. 37.
57. *Put Yourself in his Place,* p. 43.
58. *Ibid.,* p. 44.
59. *Ibid.,* p. 55.
60. *Foul Play,* p. 34.
61. *Ibid.,* p. 35.
62. *Ibid.,* p. 38.
63. *Ibid.,* p. 43.
64. *Love Me Little, Love Me Long,* p. 20.
65. Kendall, G. : *Kingsley and His Ideas*, p. 134.
66. Marmo, M. : *The Social Novels of Kingsley*, p. 210.
67. Marriott, J.A.R. : *Charles Kingsley : Novelist*, p. 18.
68. Kaufmann, M. ; *Charles Kingsley : Christian Socialist and Radical Reformer*, p. 57.
69. Matthew, B. : *Charles Kingsley*, p. 63.
70. Northland, F. : *Social Strain in Charles Kingsley*, p. 43.
71. Martin, R.B. : *Life of Charles Kingsley*, p. 83.
72. *Ibid.*, p. 94.
73. Marmo, M. : *The Social Novels of Kingsley*, p. 115.
74. *Ibid.*, p. 116.
75. *Ibid.*, p. 117.

76. Wright, Edgar : *Mrs. Gaskell*, p. 185.
77. Pollard, A. : *Mrs. Gaskell*, p. 160.
78. Haldane, E. : *Mrs. Gaskell and Her Friends*, p. 89.
79. Sharps, J.G. : *Mrs. Gaskell's Observation and Invention*, p. 97.
80. *Ibid.*, p. 98.
81. *Mary Barton, a Tale of Manchester Life,* p. 109.
82. *Ruth,* p. 43.
83. *Ibid.*, p. 96.
84. *Ibid.,* p. 92.
85. *North and South,* p. 126.
86. *Cranford,* p. 90.
87. *Ibid.,* p. 37.
88. *Ibid.,* p. 64.
89. *Wives and Daughters,* pp. 27-28.
90. Arberry, A.J. : *Mrs. Gaskell's Novels*, p. 19.
91. *Ibid.*, p. 21.
92. *Ibid.*, p. 28.
93. Hopkins, A.B. : *Life of Mrs. Gaskell*, p. 237.
94. *Ibid.*
95. *Ibid.*, p. 238.
96. *Ibid.*, p. 239.
97. *Ibid.*, p. 303.
98. *Ibid.*, p. 384.
99. French, Y. : *Life of Mrs. Gaskell*, p. 127.
100. *Ibid.*, p. 130.
101. *Ruth*, p. 32.
102. Ayres, M. : *Mrs. Gaskell's Novels*, p. 38.
103. *Mary Barton, a Tale of Manchester Life*, p. 51.
104. *Ibid.*, p. 53.
105. *Ibid.*, p. 129.
106. *Ibid.,* p. 130.
107. *North and South,* p. 32.
108. *Ibid.,* p, 93.
109. *Ibid.,* p. 103.
110. *Ibid.,* p. 201.
111. *Ibid.,* p. 285.
112. Wright, M. : *Political Radicalism and Victorian Novelists*, p. 78.
113. *Ibid.*, p. 79.
114. Savin, M. : *The Victorian Novelists*, p. 115.

115. *Ibid.*, p. 161.
116. Winwar, F. : *Richard Whiteing : a Victorian Novelist*, p. 57.
117. *Ibid.*, p. 63.
118. Preston, K. : *Life of Richard Whiteing*, p. 215.
119. *Ibid.*, p. 216.
120. Sadleir, M. : *Trollope : a Commentary*, p. 179.
121. Bowen, E. : *Trollope : a New Judgment*, p. 201.
122. Nicolas, S. : *Anthony Trollope's Novels*, p. 37.
123. *Ibid.*, p. 39.
124. *Ibid.*, p. 47.
125. Escott, T.H. : *Life of Anthony Trollope*, p. 242.
126. *Ibid.*, p. 262.
127. *Ibid.*, p. 301.
128. Escott, T.H. : *Life of Anthony Trollope*, p. 301.
129. Winwar, R. : *Fictional Technique of Trollope*, p. 34.
130. *Ibid.*, p. 35.
131. *Ibid.*
132. Ransome, F. : *Trollope : A Critical Study*, p. 121.
133. *Ibid.*
134. Savin, M. : *Trollope : His Novels and Society*, p. 21.
135. *Ibid.*, p. 29.
136. Cunliffe, W. : *Trollope's Mind and Art*, p. 104.
137. *Ibid.*
138. *He Knew He Was Right*, p. 40.
139. *Ibid.*, p. 57.
140. *Phineas Redux*, pp. 77-80.
141. *Ibid.*, pp. 114-18.
142. *The Claverings*, p. 114.
143. *Ibid.*
144. *Ibid.*
145. Cross, W.L. : *The Development of The English Novel*, p. 197.
146. Baker, E.A. : *The History of English Novel*, p. 382.
147. Cross, W.L. : *op. cit.*
148. *Ibid.*, p. 198.
149. Baker, E.A. : *op. cit.*
150. *Ibid.*, p. 355.
151. *Vanity Fair*, p. 73.
152. *Ibid.*, pp. 83-86.
153. *Pendennis*, p. 23.

154. *Philip*, p. 105.
155. *Barry Lyndon*, p. 216.
156. Haight, S. Gordon : *George Eliot — A Biography*, p. 469.
157. *Ibid.*
158. Hardy, B. : *Novels of George Eliot*, p. 279.
159. Haldane, E.S. : *George Eliot and Her Times : A Victorian Study*, p. 127.
160. Bullett, Gerald : *George Eliot*, p. 167.
161. Hanson, L. & E. : *Mary Ann Evans and George Eliot*, p. 135.
162. Stephen, L. : *George Eliot*, p. 121.
163. Thale, J. : *Novels of George Eliot*, p. 26.
164. Haight, G.S. (ed.) : *A Century of George Eliot Criticism*, p. 39.
165. Olcott, C.S. : *George Eliot : Scenes and People in Her Novels*, p. 11.
166. Crompton, M. : *Life of George Eliot*, p. 251.
167. *Ibid.*, p. 257.
168. *Prelude to Middlemarch*, p. 34.
169. Haight, S. Gordon : *George Eliot—A Biography*, p. 112.
170. *Ibid.*
171. Spencer, Herbert : *Autobiography*, pp. 394-95.
172. Haight S. Gordon : *op.cit.*, p. 113.
173. *Ibid.*
174. *Ibid.*
175. *Ibid.*, p. 195.
176. *Ibid.*
177. *Ibid.*
178. *Ibid.*
179. *Ibid.*
180. Hardy, B. : *The Novels of George Eliot*, p. 134.
181. *Ibid.*
182. Haldane, E.S. : *George Eliot and Her Times : A Victorian Study*, p. 151.
183. *Amos Barton*, p. 23.
184. *Ibid.*, p. 25.
185. *Silas Marner*, p. 32.
186. *Ibid.*, p. 34.
187. *Ibid.*, p. 37.
188. *Ibid.*, p. 62.
189. *Ibid.*, p. 63.
190. *Daniel Deronda*, p. 15.
191. *Ibid.*, p. 19.
192. Compton-Rickett, A. : *A History of English Literature*, p. 549.

193. *Ibid.*

194. Published in *ISTVF,* Delhi, 1994, pp. 71-112; 'Anthony Trollope : the Sociologist, was presented at the XXVI session of AIETC held at Bombay on November 28-30, 1975; 'Self-seeking in *David Copperfield*,' was presented at the XXIII session of AIETC held at Chandigarh on December 28-31, 1967; also published in *VFSNA*, Delhi, 2002, pp. 66-102.

8

Walker Percy : Christianity and Humanism and Women Perspectives in *The Second Coming, The Moviegoer, The Last Gentleman, The Lancelot* and *Love in the Ruins*

WALKER PERCY hates the application of scientific humanism to relieve mankind of its drudgery and boredom, what he precisely terms as modern-day malaise. From Kaufmann, Soren Kierkegaard, Jean-Paul Satre and Albert Camus, Walker Percy drew his existential vision. Nonetheless, he rejects Kierkegaard's total emphasis on individual experience, inwardness, possibility and subjectivity.

Walker Percy told Ellen Oglethrope way back in 1981 that he did not understand woman nature. Nevertheless, Allen, Moira, Lola, Kitty, Mrs. Vaught etc., are his remarkable portrayals of women nature. Whereas the first part of this chapter deals with Walker Percy's Christianity and humanism *vis-a-vis* his existential vision, the second part deals with the women perspectives in his major novels.

I

In an interview with Jan Nordby Gretlund in 1981, Walker Percy has propounded his philosophy of Catholicism *vis-a-vis* Christianity. On being asked about Sutter Vaught in *The Last Gentleman* and his atheism and unbelief, Walker Percy makes it sufficiently clear that knowledge in God and faith in God are two different issues and both should not be confused. Whereas

Kierkegaard does not treat knowledge as an act of faith; it is Thomas Aquinas who regards faith as a form of knowledge. For Percy, faith is a form and knowledge both — the form is God Himself and the knowledge is the self-realization or the faith that God creates man in his own image.[1] Walker Percy is mainly concerned with the spirit of Christianity and not with its forms. He expects of a truly Christian an unbounded capacity of reform and reaffirmation. Though in his novels, "Percy does not evangelize, his novels end with some form of epiphany."[2] "In the tradition," says Jac Tharpe, "of the prophets and moralists, he threatens that reform is urgent before the time is too late in "these dreaded latter days" of *Love in the Ruins*, and he may even at times suggest that the 'second coming' is at hand. He does not argue for asceticism; rather, he displays a high regard for nature, in which man was made to live and enjoy the world."[3]

Percy prefers Roman Catholicism to Christianity for the simple reason of the former's being more open to reform and reaffirmation than the latter. A Roman Catholic has immense potentiality to improve, to move to the upward stage of religion, which Kierkegaard terms as "a religious consonance" more than a Christian. A Roman Catholic has a creed, whereas a Christian has a ritual. Percy's novels are deeply rooted in the Catholic faith, notwithstanding the apparent touch of non-religiosity over them. *The Moviegoer* has a protagonist in Binx Bolling who is endowed with a natural proclivity of self-realization. From sex-indulgence to rolling in wealth, he traverses a vast track of sin, but ultimately like a true Roman Catholic he listens to his inner voice. The protagonist in *Love in the Ruins* returns to the Church in the end. Percival in *Lancelot* makes no show of his religious faith and Will Barrett in *The Second Coming* appears as a person of renewed faith.

But Percy, like Kierkegaard, makes a lot of difference between Christianity and Christendom. For Percy, "Christianity is the uncluttered central body of Christian doctrine, with its concept of God's grace and individual salvation through a personal savior. Christianity is a way of living and a concept of eternal life.

Christendom is the geographical area, the realm of Christianity, as opposed to that of Islam or Buddhism, which has nourished the fantastic institution that has formed in association with Christianity, without regard for Christian doctrines. Christendom is characterized especially by its great moral failure."[4]

Percy treats moral failure of Christendom as akin to political tyranny. He is also of the view that Christendom restricted natural growth of the ideals of Christianity partly due to European politics and largely due to the new concept of forgiveness to a bad conduct. Moreover, Christendom employs all outdated and obsolete symbols, especially church edifices.

For instance, in *The Second Coming*, on his way to play golf, "Will Barrett passed the Christian Church, the Church of Christ, Church of God, Church of God in Christ, Church of Christ in God. Assembly of God, Bethel Baptist Church, Independent Presbyterian Church, United Methodist Church, and Immaculate Heart of Mary Roman Catholic Church."[5]

Percy considers America to be a great land of believers in Christian religion. But notwithstanding all rituals, gaudy shows of wealth in the performance of Christian festivals, the Americans have utterly failed to practise the true doctrines of Christianity in their life. The obvious symptoms of their failure are *inter alia*, the sexual unrestraint and compromise with cheap fundamentalism, inhuman treatment with the blacks. Commenting on moral failure of the USA in the guise of following Christianity, as has been evidenced in Percy's novels, Jac Tharpe has rightly elaborated the theme, "In the United States, obvious indications of Christendom's moral failure are sexual unrestraint and compromise with cheap fundamentalism, mistreatment of blacks, and the indication to stomach any combination of abstractions on the theory that a man has a right to his beliefs. Compromise with fundamentalism takes the form of drawing the sweet Jesus into everyday life with such ideas as Jesus Christ the greatest pro of them all (*Love in the Ruins*) the invisible golfer at the country club in Paradise Estates."[6]

The Last Gentleman is Percy's best elaboration of the moral failure of the Christendom : for, Williston Bibb Barrett, the protagonist, passes through the worst sort of moral trauma. Vaught, the patriarch in the novel, the wealthiest owner of the world's second largest Chevrolet agency, also does not find solace and contentment despite his masquerading as a great devotee of Christianity. Vaught's wife, "whose flashing pince-nez is brighter than her mind,"[7] too, is equally unhappy notwithstanding her rich prayer offerings and routine rituals. Kitty, a twenty-one-year old girl "resembling a Georgia peach"[8] is ultimately reunited to Will, despite their initial differences. Tita and Val are only the two characters in the novel who truly represent Christian values through their deeds. Sutter, a doctor in the novel and "who calls himself a pornographer"[9] and who has all the ostentatious conduct of a typical Christian, ultimately submits himself to the faithful observance of the Christianity.

In an interview with John Carr, Percy himself admitted that "*The Last Gentleman* is nothing but a journey." Certainly, his journey is the religious journey of Will Barrett from vice to virtue, from unbelief to belief, from unfaith to faith in Roman Catholicism, Barrett feels disillusioned with the ritualistic mode of Christianity and consequently he turns to Roman Catholicism. In the beginning he embarks upon his journey as a sick man, as a man too much given to moral depravity and to the lust of money, but in the end, his returning to Alabama to be reunited with Kitty is a happy sign of his restoration of faith in true Christian religion. "This young man," admits Percy, "Will Barrett, was both a great deal worse off than Binx and better off. He was worse off because he was sick; he was really sick.... He really existed in what Kierkegaard would call the religious mode.... The abyss was always yawning at his feet. The book is nothing but a journey. The question, you see, is whether it is better to be a drowning man, or alive and well in East Orange."[10] The Kierkegaardian mode of religion is tantamount to the Percyian passionate pilgrimage, which he attributes to Barrett. The concealed meaning of "passionate pilgrimage" of Barrett is obvious — his willingness to be reformed. Percy considers this stage of willingness to be reformed an essential condition to embrace Roman Catholicism. In another interview with Brown, Percy elaborates the meaning of "passionate pilgrimage" through the character of Barrett and defends his point of view that Barrett is certainly the "sane pilgrim in a mad world." "Barrett, on the other hand," argues Percy, "has a passionate pilgrimage that he must follow, and he is looking for a father-figure. His symptoms are ambiguous, however, and he could go in various directions. The ambiguity is deliberate. The reader is free to see him as a sick man among healthy business men or as a sane pilgrim in a mad world."[11]

But Sutter in *The Last Gentleman* is a case in isolation, who treats sex as essential precondition for passing from the transcendent to the immanent. Sex keeps him "sane" or at least wise enough to keep his relationship intact with the earth. Sutter also considers "sexual indulgence necessary for intellectuals in a highly technological society where they so rarely have to endure ordeals associated with daily living and are therefore free to devise and attempt to realize any generalization or abstraction."[12] Sutter attaches too much importance to sex-indulgence because "between religion and science, Christendom and heathenism, the soul is so distrait that only the body's indulgence in sex avails for experiencing the real world. Alienation is such that only sex offers pleasure in the world."[13] But despite all this, Sutter doubts if, in reality "purity and life can only come from eating the body and drinking the blood of Christ."[14]

In *Love in the Ruins*, love is the theme and the unromantic wastelands of Christendom are the ruins.[15] Tom More, the protagonist, in the novel, watches shooting at Tom's house by a member of an ill-organized group of Bantus led by a rabid Ph.D., from Ann Arbor. Tom has grown into a "bad Catholic" by losing his religion. His daughter Samantha has died and his wife runs off with a heathen Englishman. He attempts suicide in utter despair. He is saved on the Christmas eve by a female musician named Lola, whom he loves. Tom develops scientific humanism to gauge the sickness of the sundered man of the West. His attempt to replace God as physician-saviour wins him Nobel prize and he ultimately rebels against God. Percy himself has made comments about Dr. More's behaviour, and through him, has echoed the pangs of the ailing humanity, "Dr. More was a diagnostician. He knew something was wrong but he full victim to pride, was reduced by the devil. Immelmann was the devil, of course, who showed Dr. More how to cure. It worked for a while.... The big mistake was in him, that he could believe he could treat a spiritual disease with a scientific device however sophisticated."[16] In the same interview with Abadi-Nagy, Percy further elaborates the point, "The view of Pascal and some others who were interested in the human condition was that there is something wrong with mankind. So it is always undecided in my novels. This is the main question of the novels. Here is a hero who is afflicted, shows malaise, dislocation, and he is surrounded by apparently happy and sane people, particularly Dr. More, who lives in paradise Estates. So who is crazy, the people apparently happy or those radically dislocated characters?"[17] By contrasting between angelism and bestialism, between transcendence and worldiness, Percy has tried to solve this tangle. Tom's strong individuality and inordinate lust have discordant urges for him : for, the urge to have faith in God comes in him in the end, "I believe in God and the whole business but I love women best, music and science next, whiskey next, God fourth, and my fellowman hardly at all."[18] Percy offers a solution — a balance between body and soul : for body he prescribes love and for soul, the doctrines of Christianity. This prescription is typically Percyian borrowed from Kierkegaard. Too much indulgence in sex is as bad as too much alienation and abstraction. Both are extreme limits and are, therefore, pernicious and devastating to human beings. A scientific device invented to teach humanism as in *Love in the Ruins* is not only preposterous but also laughable. All scientific and mechanical feats of excellence demonstrated through abrupt and explosive developments in various fields of knowledge are half-truths. One of the champions of scientific humanism in *Love in the Ruins* is a biologist, who, notwithstanding his tall claims, himself has "no idea how to get on with the simple business of reproduction. He even asks for an artificial organ because his own natural organ will not perform."[19]

"*The Second Coming* is," remarks Jac Tharpe, "yet another attack on Christendom, in the most religious town, in the most religious state, in the most religious section of the most religious country in the world."[20] In fact, Percy juxtaposes two priests in order to demonstrate the well-entrenched old values and the ramshackle and fleeting new values. Jack Curl, the Episcopal priest represents old values but he has no confession to make that he believes in God. Father Weatherbee represents the new values, who has done sufficient evangelical and missionary work of the church for years in North Carolina in the countryside of Mindanao. Both Jack Curl and Father Weatherbee virtually stand poles apart in their faiths, convictions and religious outlooks. Whereas Jack Curl is "in the tradition of the fat friar, with revised liturgy, reform and social welfare"[21] trying to extend Christendom by establishing love communities and retirement villages in the midst of such idiot performers as Tod and Tannie, Father Weatherbee is confident of liberating his followers, the simple islanders of Mindanao from all possible sense of guilt. Precisely, Percy adopts a different method of attack on Christendom in *The Second Coming*. In place of juxtaposing Christian and Catholic believers as in *Lancelot* and in *The Moviegoer*, he takes up the dialectic of the believers and the non-believers as he does in *The Last Gentleman*. The tone of the dialectic is calm and quiet as in *Love in the Ruins*. Will, the protagonist, a retired law practitioner, makes his intense search for God not in the way Jack Curl suggests but, on the other hand, in the way Father Weatherbee shows. Till the first two hundred and fifty pages of the novel, Will intends to commit suicide because he wants God to reveal Himself before him. Later on he gives up the idea of committing suicide and sacrifices the rest of his life for his own followers. In fact, all the main characters of *The Second Coming* — Will, Allison and Marion have an incorrigibly religious proclivity notwithstanding their having suffered from some physical ailment or deficiency.

The most remarkable aspect of *The Second Coming* is its epiphany — *God appears*. As a general rule Percy concludes all his novels rather unexpectedly with a sense of revelation. For example Binx becomes suddenly religious : Jamie's death reveals the miracle of baptism and salvation : Tom confesses, takes Eucharist and celebrates God's presence. After *Lancelot's* raving about meaninglessness, Percival offers the alternative of eternal life, and Will awakes to deeper knowledge.[22]

Percy hinges his quest for true Christianity on three major issues, namely the question of love, the rift in body and soul and the queerness of unhappy man in good environments. In the last three sections of *The Second Coming*, the typical Percyian resolution is quite obvious : for, Will manages three old men in section 10 of the novel to go to work for him and Allison; Father Weatherbee performs the religious marriage ceremony and thirdly, and perhaps more importantly, Will finds good environment in the company of a happy man. Will and Allison both are blessed by Father Weatherbee in section 11 of the novel which is the summation of elevated human souls. Section 12 begins, "Father Weatherbee sat behind Jack Curl's mahogany desk with its collection of Russian ikons in bleeding Mexican crucifixes."[23] This is truly epiphanic which precisely means that through reunion of souls, revelation of God is possible. Father Weatherbee's exclamation before the poor villagers in Mindanao is another instance of this revelation, "They believed me! They believed the Gospel whole and entire, and the teachings of the church. They said that if I told them, then it must be true or I would not have gone to so much trouble."[24]

Will admits of priest's authority in the end of the novel realizing that through his divine agency, revelation of God is possible. His outlook is completely changed and he accepts Allison open-heartedly just as a gift of God quite differently from *Lancelot's* accepting Margot. The end of the novel which is in itself a kind of divine revelation is the quintessence of the Percyian teachings of Christianity :

> What do I want of him, mused Will Barrett.... Will Barrett thought about Allie in her green house, her wide grey eyes, her lean muscled boy's arms, her strong quick hands. Her heart leapt with a secret joy. What is it I want from her and him, he wondered, not only want but must have? Is she a gift and therefore a sign of a giver? Could it be that the Lord is here, masquerading behind this simple silly holy face? Am I crazy to want both, her and Him? No, not want, must have. And will have.[25]

Walker Percy regards that "life is a mystery, love is a delight. Therefore I take it as axiomatic that one should settle for nothing less than the infinite mystery and the infinite delight, *i.e.*, God. In fact I demand it. I refuse to settle for anything less."[26] Will, the protagonist, in *The Second Coming* does not accept less than a meaningful revelation of God. Jac Tharpe is justified to term his novels as "edifying discourses urging the main Roman Catholic doctrine about faith, good work, marriage and family."[27] God's revelation comes to Percy's protagonists as a great fascination. Sartre treats fascination as an essential condition to realize one's own self. Percy's fascination is another name for wonder which itself is revealed through the processes of *watching*, *waiting* and *immense curiosity*. In *The Moviegoer*, Binx lays "dozing yet wakeful and watchful."[28] While seeing Red river, Binx feels "the first faint stirrings of curiosity about the particular seat I was in."[29] Ever since he had an experience of unconsciousness in the army, he says he is wakeful, asking himself, "What is this that is going to happen? Clearly nothing. Yet there I lie, wakeful and watchful as a sentry."[30] Later, he says, "Instead of trying to sleep I try to fathom the mystery of this superb at dawn."[31]

Wonder and search, though appear to be distinct courses of reaching the ultimate truth, they, nevertheless, meet each other in very ordinary and routine affairs of life. In *The Second Coming*, the narrator says that this is a "world of endless wonders,"[32] where a man seeks his existence. Similarly in *The Moviegoer*, Binx says, "The search is what anyone would undertake if he were not sunk in the everydayness of his own life. This morning, for example, I felt as if I had come to myself on a strange island."[33] In the *Lancelot*, the immense curiosity comes to the fore in a more heightened way than in other novels. In *The Last Gentleman* wait and watch are akin to immense curiosity. The following dialogue between Will and David is worth quoting :

> 'What I'm going to do!' cried David.
> 'Do like me,' said the engineer seriously.
> 'Watch and wait. Keep your eyes open.'[34]

While writing *The Moviegoer*, Percy wanted to create a character like Crusoe : for, Crusoe had immense curiosity and is a lifelong pathfinder. As such, Crusoe is a favourite symbol for Percy, used also to elucidate his theories of epistemology. The wonder or the miracle or the divine revelation comes through the physical contacts with objects bit by bit. Crusoe watched and waited throughout his life : the more Percy's characters wait and watch, the more they advance nearer their salvation : "Watch ye therefore and also wait. For ye know not the day and the hour wherein the sign of man cometh."

Walker Percy's last novel named *The Thanatos Syndrome* is mainly designed to testify the endurance of those who have unflinching faith in the doctrine of Roman Catholic religion. It goes without saying that each of Percy's novels is one step in the direction of reaffirmation in Catholicism. For example, if *The Moviegoer* is just the germinal phase for Catholicism, the resurrected believer in *The Second Coming*, namely Will docs not question the whys and wherefors of the forms of God. Traversing the religious ground till *The Thanatos Syndrome*, Walker Percy's tone and tenor is not of a religious seeker but of a person already highly religious and who wants to test his faith and strength. John Edward Hardy pertinently treats *The Thanatos Syndrome* as a Catholic novel designed mainly "to test faith and the strength of those who pretend to seek it, not directly to sustain."[35] All the chief characters in the novel named Eve, Van Doran, Donna, Lucy, Lipscomb, Comeaux and Mickey LaFaye — are not only worldly wise but also full of immense endurance and patience. Kierkegaard treats knowledge of evil as a necessary precondition to realize the existence of goodness. Similarly Walker Percy considers knowledge of evil, reality of sin and of death as a necessary precondition of faith. Walker Percy also treats guilt as a perennial source of pride. The *Thanatos Syndrome* has, therefore, been written in a slightly different religious tone and that is why this novel has a very elderly priest in Father Smith who delivers long sermons emphasizing the importance of the ten commandments of the *Bible*. John Edward Hardy considers this novel more Catholic than a mere Christian revision of Freudian thinking on death instinct.[36] The notion of redemption or salvation is certainly a salient feature of this novel which makes it more distinct than other novels.

Walker Percy's *Love in the Ruins* "is a dystopia designed to reveal the deficiencies in humanistic attempts at building utopias and possibly even those with God at the centre."[37] A utopia is an ideal place or society where everything good and worth-while takes place. In the Western world, a number of writers have attempted to create a utopia, an ideal world where there will be no human suffering, no poverty, no want : for, the men will do no wrong. But such utopias have hitherto been not materialized. *Love in the Ruins* is therefore a dystopia, an anti-utopia, which demonstrates the ills in a utopia based on scientific humanism. Science, having touched the *ne plus ultra* of triumph over man in almost every domain of his thought in the modern times, now claims to create a utopia whereby promising human being all comforts, even salvation ascertaining face-to-face encounter with God. The believers in the Christianity have tempted many an unbeliever into this utopia, but Percy exposes all such claims as sheer sham and religious hypocrisy. The entire theme of love and that of religious faith in *Love in the Ruins* weaves a dystopia through the life of Tom More, the protagonist, which fully exposes the tall claims of the followers of the Christianity of ascertaining human salvation through scientific humanism.

Percy is opposed to the idea that scientific humanism can change the behaviour, conduct and outlook of men and that it can cultivate inborn qualities in them. Percy considers this claim as a simple farce. He also rejects the idea that scientific humanism can replace both the Christianity and the Roman Catholicism. A controlled behaviour and a sort of regimented conduct both in family and society may be ushered in by gradual application of scientific humanism is the obvious thesis put forth by many distinguished men of science and religion in the West. This synthesis of science and religion has been made operative in the Western countries with full gusto and enthusiasm. But Walker Percy sees no end of human misery. Still, the negro problem is there; still the dichotomy, the hiatus between the whites and the blacks is persisting in the USA. In hospitals, the number of the neurotics does not decrease. The war threats still hover over the world as the Sword of Democles. These symptoms are the obvious symptoms of an ailing society, of a world still suffering from want and miseries. *Love in the Ruins* exposes all these pseudo-claims of scientific humanism to the full view of those who want to substitute scientific humanism for either Christianity or Roman Catholicism.

Walker Percy considers the apparent fissures even in Catholic religion as unfortunate : for, instead of bringing about salvation of America, it will reckon misery :

> Our Catholic church here split into three pieces : (1) the American Catholic Church whose new Rome is Cicero, Illinois; (2) the Dutch Schismatics who believe in relevance but not in God; (3) the Roman Catholic remnant, a tiny scattered flock with no place to go.
>
> The Roman Catholic Church, which emphasizes property rights and the integrity of neighbourhood, retained the Latin mass and plays *The Star-Spangled Banner* at the elevation.
>
> The Dutch schismatics in this area comprise several priests and nuns who left Rome to get married. They threw in with the Dutch Schismatic Catholics. Now several divorced priests and nuns are importuning the Dutch cardinal to allow them to remarry.
>
> The Roman Catholics hereabouts are scattered and demoralized. The one priest, an obscure curate, who remained faithful to Rome, could not support himself and had to hire out as a fire-watcher. It is his job to climb the fire tower by night and watch for brushfires below and for signs and portents in the spies.[38]

Tom More himself is a bad Catholic : for, his conduct is ostentatious, but his heart is not pure. Outwardly, he can perform all the rituals which a Catholic is expected to perform, but he can hardly help others. For him, physical comforts, wine and woman are the greatest gifts of God. Notwithstanding his masquerading as a great believer in God, his actions are not in consonance with his hypocritical conduct. He believes in the Holy Catholic Apostle and Roman Church, in Jesus Christ, in anything that claims revelation of God to him. But he cannot believe his fellowmen :

> I am a Roman Catholic, albeit a bad one. I believe in the Holy Apostle and Roman Church, in God the Father, in the election of the Jews, in Jesus Christ His Son our Lord, who founded the Church on Peter his first vicar, which will last until the end of the world. Some years ago, however, I stopped eating Christ in Communion, stopped going to mass and have since fallen into a disorderly life.... Generally I do as I please. A man, wrote John, who says he believes in God and does not keep his commandments is a liar. If John is right, then I am a liar. Nevertheless, I still believe.[39]

Tom invents scientific devices to enhance humanism, but his own fear is that he himself will not be cured of his own deficiencies. He claims to develop faculties to gauge depths of human mind and soul, but he is not sure if scientific humanism will further increase or decrease :

> My article, it is true, is an extremely important one, perhaps even epochal in its significance. With it, my little invention, in hand, any doctor can probe the very secrets of the soul, diagnose the maladies that poison the wellsprings of man's hope. It would save the world or destroy it — and in the next two hours will very likely do one or the other — for as any doctor knows, the more effective a treatment is, the more dangerous it is in the wrong hands.[40]

Percy propounds, through the mouth of the protagonist, the philosophy of purity of deeds and of conduct in a religion irrespective of the specificity of its kind. A Christian, a Roman Catholic or for that matter any person having faith in a particular religion has to conform to the purity of actions in his conduct. Without purity of deeds and conduct, a believer turns himself automatically into a non-believer. No religion worth the name ever teaches its followers hollowness in respect of conduct and deeds. A non-believer in Christian religion is as good or as bad as a believer in Roman Catholic religion only in its rituals but with hollowness in actions :

> The scientists, who are mostly liberals and unbelievers, and the businessmen, who are mostly conservative and Christian, live side by side in Paradise Estates. Though the two make much of their differences — one speaking of "outworn dogmas and creeds," the other of "atheism and immorality," *et cetera et cetera* — to tell the truth, I do not notice a great deal of difference, between the two. Both sorts are generally good fellows, good fathers and husbands who work hard all day, come home at five-thirty to their pretty homes, kiss their wives, toss their rosy babes in the air, light up their charcoal briquettes, or perhaps mount on their tiny tractor mowers. There are minor differences. When conservative Christian housewives drive to town to pick up their maids in the Hollow, the latter ride on the back seat in the old style. Liberal housewives make their maids ride on the front seat. On Sundays Christian businessmen dress up and take their families to Church, whereas unbelieving scientists are apt to put on their worst clothes and go bird-watching. As one of my behaviorist friends put it, "my Cathedral is the blue sky and my pilgrimage is for the ivory-billed woodpecker." The fabulous and lordly bird that some say still inhabits the fastness of the swamp.[41]

Walker Percy believes in the gradual evolution of man's inner being namely the spiritual, the angelic part of man. The bestiality in man is a manifestation of his physical strength or the animal strength, which needs sublimation to his higher urges. In this respect, Percy's approach is similar to that of George Eliot and George Meredith. George Eliot's thesis of Nemesis is Meredith's spiritual evolution of man. Eliot has propounded the theory that if we do good, its reaction will be good, and likewise, if we do wrong, its reaction will naturally be bad. All her novels are, therefore, based on the theme of struggle between good and bad. Similarly, George Meredith's novels are based on the theme of the struggle between the physical and the spiritual urges in man. In the end, it is the spiritual urge which negates the physical urges and turns them into a state of nothingness. In Thomas Hardy's novels, whether the main protagonists believe in God or not, they are, nevertheless, believers in good conduct of life. His Henchard and Tess may be tiny human beings with their puny human endeavours, they are, nonetheless, great believers in good human conduct. Walker Percy's protagonists initially appear to be non-believers but ultimately they end up as great believers in Roman Catholic religion, which they consider the only repository of every kind of wisdom that humanism can teach the mankind. Here Percy's approach appears as sublime and lofty as we find in *The Tempest*, in which Prospero's forgiveness assumes a universal appeal.

Percy treats humanism in its pure form as the quintessence of all religions including Christianity and Roman Catholic religion. He, therefore, regards both humanism and Christianity as identical and as just the two sides of the same coin. But he is against any scientific approach to humanism claiming a wholesome cure to all the ills of humanity. As such, he is against any such scientific humanism which the experts in the modern century claim to have devised as a patent cure to all the ills of mankind. Percy rejects all such scientific devices, if found viable at all, as a counterfeit propaganda to divert the attention of the simple people. At best, he considers them to be the figment of imagination of a few religious snobs and political mountebanks to dupe and deceive the gullible.

Percy has summed up his thesis of Roman Catholicism versus scientific humanism in the concluding part of *Love in the Ruins*, where the protagonist, though initially hesitant to confess his sins before the priest thinking his scientific achievements as superior to religion, turns into a person with profound faith in Roman Catholic religion. He then treats his mechanical devices as inconsequential and is, hence, whole-heartedly prepared to confess his sins :

> "Meanwhile, forgive me but there are other things we must think about : like doing our jobs, you being a better doctor, I being a better priest, showing a bit of ordinary kindness to people, particularly our own families — unkindness to those close to us is such a pitiful thing — doing what we can for our poor unhappy country — things which, please forgive me,

> sometimes seem more important than dwelling on a few middle-aged daydreams."
> "You are right. I'm sorry," I
> say instantly, scalded.
> "You're sorry for your sins?"
> "Yes. Ashamed rather."

"That will do. Now say the act of contrition and for your penance I'm going to give you this."

Through the little window he hands me two articles, an envelope containing ashes and a sackcloth, which is a kind of sleeveless sweater made of black burlap. John XXIV recently revived public penance, a practice of the early Church.

While he absolves me, I say an act of contrition and pull the sackcloth over my sports coat.

> "Go in peace. I'll offer my mass for you tonight."
> "Thank you," I say, dumping the ashes in my hair.[42]

II

Walker Percy himself clearly admits, "But to me, a normal woman is a mystery. I can only understand her if she is as neurotic as I am."[43] Talking of Ellen Oglethrope, Percy acknowledges his feigned ignorance about women except women from Georgia, "Ellen Oglethrope, I think is a...she is drawn from my Georgia background. Part of my family comes from Georgia. My mother's family were Georgia Presbyterian girl. And she is not neurotic, she knows exactly what she wants. She may not be very deep; I wasn't too interested in her, I just wanted to have her there — I plead ignorance, I don't know enough about women."[44] Similarly, while refuting the charge of treating women with harshness, Percy asserts, "What about Allie in *The Second Coming*? She is crazy, but she is pretty normal. And what about Aunt Emily in *The Moviegoer?* She is not only normal, but normative. As normative as Marcus Aurelius."[45] On Gretlund's query as to why girl characters in his novels are mentally unstable, Percy replies, "We, that go back to device I use consciously, namely, to arrange the placement of the hero and the heroine so that it is always a question : who is crazy? Whether he is crazy and the rest of the world is sane — or, he is sane and the rest of the world crazy. It is supposed to be a delicately balanced issue, so that many people can read it and say : well, I am also crazy. Allison is a crazy woman living in a sane world, or may be she seems crazy because she is reacting sanely to an insane world. Someone like Allison, who is beginning a new life, starting afresh, even creating a new language — may be she is on the track of sanity. It is not difficult to make out a case that the world is mad."[46]

Percy also admits that the women characters in *The Last Gentleman* get a "harsh treatment,"[47] but of the women characters in *The Moviegoer,* Percy is not sure if he had been mild or harsh with them, "I don't know whether that is anti-feminism on my part, or the difficulty for a male novelist to create a woman. Good women writers have an easy time creating men. But, how many women did Hemingway create?"[48] Percy also justifies the thesis of R.D. Laing who creates neurotic or psychotic women characters, "Right this is, of course, the thesis of R.D. Laing, the psychiatrist, that schizophrenics in their own way are sane. I think that most psychiatrists disagree, and they may be right in that Laing takes it to an extreme, but for literary purposes it is a convenient thesis. A Schizophrenic may be on the track of sanity; he finds the world unbearable, show that the world is, indeed, unbearable. And that there are certain strategies you have to take to live in it, and there are persons who are entitled to have a psychotic reaction."[49]

But notwithstanding all the above denials and confessions, Percy has embellished his novels by delineating a number of unforgetable women characters who in themselves offer a virgin ground for a deeper psycho-analytical study. For example, in *The Moviegoer,* Sharon and Aunt Emily stand poles apart from each other not only in experience and age but also in mental temperament. In *Lancelot,* Lucy, Magot, Raine and Anna constitute a variety of lewd and sexy women characters. In *The Last Gentleman,* Kitty, Jamie, Rita, Val, Mrs. Vaught and Myra Thigpen are major women characters of absorbing interest. In

The Second Coming, Allison is a memorable woman character. In *Love in the Ruins,* Ellen, Moira and Lora are remarkable women characters offering deeper psychoanalysis. In *The Phanatos Syndrome,* Mrs. Brunette and Mrs. Cheney offer complexity and variety of woman nature. Percy juxtaposes his female and male characters, often a neurotic female contrasting with a normal male character and often also the *vice-versa* in so many cases. For instance, in *Love in the Ruins,* Tom, whose first love is woman and who has lost his daughter and whose wife also deserts him, is juxtaposed with Ellen, 'the sturdy keeper of keys' and ultimately both are married, having gone through almost all the cycles of revolution and evolution of human development. Moira, in the same novel, is a dumb blonde, a thorough pleasure seeker not interested in a family life and Percy has juxtaposed her against Tom, though she deserts him, too. Lola is equally unstable, and is a complete embodiment of sensual potential. She also deserts Tom and she has, therefore, been juxtaposed with Tom.

Take, for instance, another situation from another novel named *The Last Gentleman,* where Williston Bibb Barrett (abbreviated as Barrett) and Kitty have been juxtaposed. Other female characters such as Jamie, Rita, Val and Myra Thigpen do appear in the scheme of juxtaposition but in a very inconsequential way. Lucy and Lancelot in the novel named *Lancelot* come together and other characters such as Magot, Raine and Anna do emerge as lively figures but their comparison and contrast with their counterpart male characters are negligible. *The Second Coming* presents Will and Allison in contrast and probably it is Allison who convinces more than other female characters.

Before embarking upon to categorize Percy's women characters, let us be quite clear about one very important factor which formed his view of woman character. As has been discussed elsewhere, Percy is mainly concerned with a man's inner and outer Being as Kierkegaard, Sartre, Camus and Marcel, the major harbingers of the Existentialist School, were obsessed with the idea of the Consciousness and Being. As such, these great existentialists openly express dissatisfaction with the way male and female characters were drawn by taking help of external details of physique, society and nature. They are mainly concerned with the psyche of their characters. Consequently, they fix their characters in certain situations — the real life situations and then they want to analyse his or her behaviour, conduct and thinking associated with the problem of being alive or remain alive in the present. Herein, they openly advocate for a departure from the traditional style of studying the psyche of characters. Percy is an existentialist in respect of practising the fictional art of studying the psyche of his characters the way Kierkegaard and Marcel do. While postulating his philosophy of character-drawing in his fictional art, Percy admits :

> I write about women from the exclusive point of view of hero or anti-hero. As such, the view of women or anyone else may be limited by the narrowness of the vision. The nature of the narrowing, however, I would hope to be significant. If Binx Bolling tends to see people oddly. Accordingly, there is no attempt to flesh out female characters — or any other characters — in the style of the nineteenth-century novel.... What interests me is not how it feels to be...that particular woman, but how it feels to be a particular consciousness, male or female, set down in the world the way it is."[50]

Percy denies having followed the French anti-novelist school, where a complete de-emphasis on characters takes place to highlight objects and settings. "My Characters are," he asserts, "not like the French anti-novels where there is a complete de-emphasis on the characters. Actually, the writers of the anti-novelist school in France are more interested in objects and things. They spend five pages describing a tea cup, or at least how a man sees a tea cup, all the details of his consciousness of a cup. So I certainly don't place myself in that school."[51] Percy considers twentieth century a fragmented or broken age, and as such, fictional art employed to delineate characters during the nineteenth century as was done by many celebrated novelists such as Tolstoy in his *magnum opus War and Peace,* has been virtually rendered ineffective these days. Percy also treats nineteenth century as an established one in comparison to the modern times. He, therefore, dittoes the John Barthian view that "it was no longer possible to write nineteenth-century novels, a novel which has the usual characters, where the characters interact, where there is a story line, a development of plot, a resolution — a classical novel.... I think that the nineteenth-century novel would reflect a rather intact society, an intact culture, where people understood who they were and what they were doing; whereas, now, the world is much more fragmented, people don't understand themselves as well as or what they are doing as well. And to the degree that a novel reflects life, I think that the modern novel has become much more fragmented, without a strong and conventional plot and all that."[52] Percy also defends his stand of not crowding his fictional canvass with a number of female characters. His standpoint is that a psychoanalytical approach to the woman psyche in a certain place at a certain time is the best way to understand the Being of a female character. He admits, "...my feeling is — to write from one point of view of one consciousness located in a certain place at a certain time. Maybe it's because of a breakdown in communications that hear so much about now. Maybe writers, both poets and novelists, are much more locked into themselves, and because of that, perhaps a creative work is more apt to be written from the perspective of a single consciousness seeing the world around him. The classical novel took place on a great stage which the reader watched more or less unself-consciously. In the modern novel, the perspective backs up. What is being presented now is not so much the action on the stage as the experience of the spectator in the privacy of his box."[53]

With this background of framework within which Percy creates his women characters, let us now categorize them on the basis of their individual traits. Jac Tharpe divides Percy's women characters into three groups, with several possible variants.[54] The first group is of those, "depressing and opressive"[55] old ladies, cousins, aunts and aquired hangers on noted for their longevity and survival, attached by kinship or other association to Southern families.[56] Though Jac Tharpe considers Aunt Emily in *The*

Moviegoer as outside the ken of this category, yet with due emphasis on her inborn quality of stoicism, she may be included into this classification. The second group is of those women characters who are "revellers"[57] and who thoroughly lend themselves to the hump and grind of the beastly machine, with full indulgence in worldly and physical pleasures. Doris, Margot and Lucy are representatives of this category. The third group is consisted of those women characters who are "nondescript"[58] and often "ill-treated."[59] The only redeeming feature of these women characters is that they turn out to be highly faithful and committed life-partners in the long run.

In *The Moviegoer,* the most forceful character is that of Aunt Emily, whose surmonizing tone is awe-inspiring. She persistently preaches rather sardonically the importance of sticking to one's duty and also to decent human conduct. She acts as a guiding force to the Binx family. Of the Roman Catholicism, she eloquently speaks to anybody at any odd hour. Her sermons to Binx and Lonnie are worth remembering. Probably Walker Percy has delineated no other lively and forceful character as Aunt Emily in his succeeding novels. William Percy, under whose tutelage Percy, the novelist, passed a long span of his formative life, appears again and again in the character of Aunt Emily. Speaking of Aunt Emily's generosity, Binx says of her :

> My Aunt has done a great deal for me. When my father was killed, my mother, who had been a trained nurse went back to her hospital in Biloxi. My Aunt offered to provide my education. As a consequence much of the past fifteen years has been spent in her house. She is really my great aunt.[60]

Percy feels proud of Aunt Emily as he feels proud of every woman belonging to the South. "I believe," the narrator says in *The Moviegoer,* "the South has produced more high-minded women, women of universal sentiments, than any other section of the country except possibly New England in the last century."[61] The narrator in the same novel is proud of having six living aunts in the South well-known for their qualities of kindness, tolerance and prudence. "Of the six living aunts," tells the narrator in *The Moviegoer,* five are women of the loftiest theosophical pan

Brahman sentiments. The sixth is still a Presbyterian."[62] Percy has endowed Aunt Emily with inborn qualities of niceness and generous feelings in particular and the Southerner women in general. The narrator watches a programme on TV and watches a play named 'This I belive,' in which women have been shown as paragons of courage, tolerance and forgiveness. Aunt Emily is one such representative character who has unique understanding of men and manners. Talking of generous feelings and niceness of six living aunts (Aunt Emily being one of them) in New Orleans, the narrator in *The Moviegoer* remarks, "If I had to name a single trait that all these people shared, it is their niceness. Their lives are triumphs of niceness. They like everyone with the warmest and most generous feelings. And as for themselves : it would be impossible for even a dour person not to like them."[63] And, in fact, there is none who does not like Aunt Emily in *The Moviegoer.*

Aunt Emily feels jittery and despondent because she does not approve of Binx's inconsistent moral conduct. Her joy knows no bounds when Binx and Kate are finally married. Binx winds up business in Gentilly and comes to North Carolina alongwith her. Binx's duck club is purchased by Sartalamaccia for twenty-five dollars and Sharon, now Mrs. Stanley Sharmoun, lives in a shotgun cottage previously owned by Nell Lovell and independently handles business. All these developments, Aunt Emily considers to be happy signs of peace and prosperity in Binx's life. She, therefore, revises her opinion about Binx, who hitherto was considered to be a worthless scion of an illustrious family by her. Binx himself admits a major change in Aunt Emily's outlook towards him. "My aunt," he remarks, "has become fond of me. As soon as she accepted what she herself had been saying all those years, that the Bolling family had gone to see and that I was not one of her heroes but a very ordinary fellow, we got along very well. Both women (Aunt Emily and Kate) find me comical and laugh a good deal at my expense."[64]

The second category of Percy's women characters is of those who are pleasure-seekers and revellers, too much given to physical comforts and sex-indulgence. Most of them enjoy prosperity and they have all the cunning of experienced religious mountebanks. They are healthy, beautiful and regardless of what others consider them to be. Many of them treat themselves as paragons of virtue and masquerade them as different from and better than others. But their moral snobishness is soon exposed and their real character comes to the fore to be detested by their own companions *ad nauseum.* Jac Tharpe terms them as fully replete with the spirit of bestialism. They "lend themselves to the hump and grind of the "beastly" machine, the rape and thump that is sexual intercourse and the process of life."[65] Lucy, Lancelot's first wife, Doris, Tom's lost wife and Margot are but representatives of the category of revellers or pleasure-seekers. They, in fact, consider sex to be something to be enjoyed and women are entitled to enjoy sex. The *ne plus ultra* of the shamelessness on the part of Margot really shocks the protagonist in *Lancelot,* who considers himself highly scheming and artful in love-making, "She undressed without bothering to turn out the light (as quickly as in the Texaco restroom in Odessa: zip! zip! naked!). She stood naked before the mirror, hands at her heir, one knee bent, pelvis aslant. She turned to me and put her hands under my coat and in her funny way took hold of a big pinch of my flank on each side. Gollee. Could any woman have been as lovely? She was like a feast. She was a feast. I wanted to eat her. I ate her."[66]

Raine in *The Moviegoer* is all sex : for, no life with full enjoyment of sex is meaningless for her. Looking at Sheron in the same novel, Binx is unable to restrain himself from indulging in sex with her later on, whom he considers as fresh and beautiful as Bama peach from Georgia. Binx says of her rather hypnotically, "She is beautiful and brave and chipper as a sparrow. Son of a bitch, it is enough to bring tears to your eyes. I don't know what is wrong with me. She smiles at me, then cocks her head."[67] Binx and Sheron enjoy the beach site and Sheron comes out of water. Binx sees her fairly closely and is hypnotised by her beauty. In fact, it is Binx who often provides necessary framework for consideration of Percy's women falling into the category of pleasure-seekers and revellers. Binx treats sex for indulgence and women to be seduced and enjoyed. He does not despise or feel shy of Sheron's naked figure emerging from the beach-side. He rather feels elated at Sheron's naked appearance treating this as a major precondition to enjoy married life :

> Her suit is of a black sheeny stuff like a swim-meet suit and skirtless. She comes out of water like a spaniel, giving her head a flirt which slaps her hair around in wet curl and stooping, brushes the water from her legs. Now she stands musing on the beach, leg locked, pelvis aslant, thumb and forefingers propped along the iliac crest and lightly, propped lightly as an athlete. As the salt water dries and stings, she minds herself, plying around the flesh of her arm and sending fingers along her back.[68]

Kate in *The Moviegoer* likes to enjoy sexual life more than other gifts of God. On Binx's becoming a bit religious and remorseful, she chides him and, subsequently in a mood of love, her conduct with Binx approximates to that of a whore :

> Kate moans and clings to me. "I feel awful.
> Let's go to your roomette."
> "It's been made up."
> "Then we'll lie down."
> We have to lie down : the door opens onto the bed. Feeling tender toward her, I embrace her and tell her that I love her.
> "Oh now," says Kate and takes hold of me coarsely. "One of that, bucko."
> "None of what?"
> "No love, please."
> I misunderstood her and pull away.
> "No no. Don't leave either," she says,
> holding me and watching me still.
> "All right."
> "Just don't speak to me of love, bucko."

Kate, like Binx treats money as "good counterpoise to beauty."[69] Without money, the quest of beauty is meaningless. Money and love, sex and beauty go hand in glove with each other. She confesses it to Binx, "Yes. It may be the noblest way of living, but it is one way. It is my way! Oh dear sweet old Binx, what a joy to discover at last what one is. It doesn't matter what you are as long as you know."[70]

Margot in *Lancelot* is highly sexy and lustful. She is "unfaith from the beginning"[71] and "her marriage and premarriage"[72] are aspects of "abiding lust"[73] and sinful conduct. Lancelot's first wife also betrays him, and now even Margot proves most unfaithful and morally depraved. Percy has investigated into the inner being of other female characters of this novel particularly all scions as well as progenitors of Margot's family. Percy seems to have written this novel in order to highlight the issue of moral depravity and also that of sex indulgence in America as a whole. The Margots in the USA are the typical women thriving on the gullibility of a number of Binxes. Percy infers as keen psychiatrist and learned anthropologist that Margot's mother too was "either unfaithful or gave the impression so strongly as to make the truth unimportant."[74] Not only this, Lancelot's daughter Lucy is "ready for corruption."[75] Even in Siobhan, a seven year old child, Lance finds signs of sex already appearing.[76] In the same novel, there is yet another woman character named Raine, who is nothing but a thorough sexual character. Probably, in no other novel, Percy has been so harsh and frank in the treatment of women characters *vis-a-vis* sex and moral depravity as in *Lancelot.*

Of Lucy and Margot, Lancelot says :

> Lucy I loved too, but Lucy was a dream, a slim brown dancer in a bell jar spinning round and round in the "Lime-light" music of old gone Carolina long ago. Margot was life itself as if all Louisiana, its fecund oil-rich dark greens and haunted twilights, its very fakery and money-loving and comicalness, had all been gathered and fleshed out in one creature. It meant having her and not being haunted holding all of gold green Louisiana in my arms. She was a big girl.[77]

Percy himself has used the following triangles in order to substantiate Margot's being faithless, always ready to be corrupted in all respects and never capable of love except sex-indulgence. In the first triangle, she concentrates her lustful eyes on Merlin and in the second, on Jacoby :

Merlin vanishes. Margot droops and is still, like a puppet hung from its string.

It is a triangle. At first I thought I was part of the triangle, the losing angle, so :

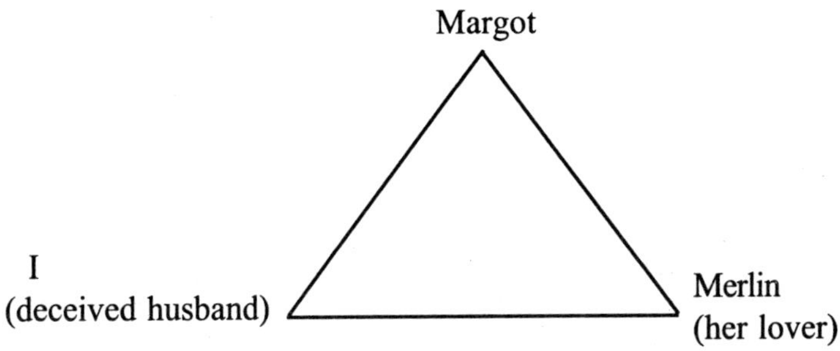

Then I see they are not talking about me at all, that it is a different triangle :

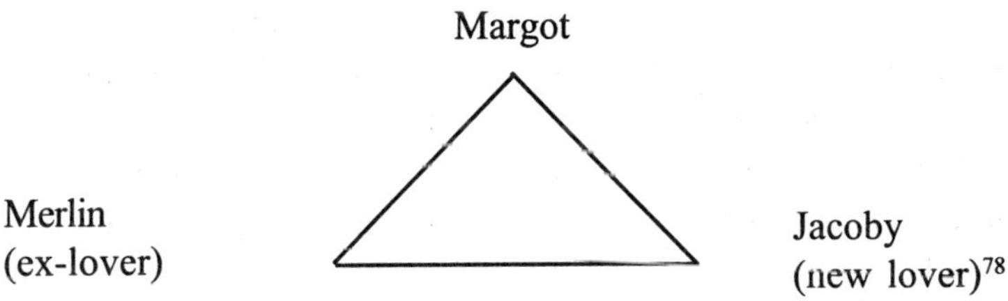

Lucy, Dana and Raine are all sexually mad women characters. Percy considers them insane patients and, with the help of a swastikaed triangle, elaborates their mania for sex-indulgence :

Lucy is like a patient. Certain operations are being performed on her.... Raine is slim and swift, moving so fast her body leaves etoplasm behind. Dana stands naked....

The three lie together. Their bodies fuse but their arms move like a six-arm Shiva.

Now they are doing something else. Dana kneels in a horizontal plane, takes Lucy's head in both hands, and guides it towards him.

Raine moves much more quickly. Her sleek head flies off and burrows into Lucy's stomach.

The figures make a rough swastikaed triangle :

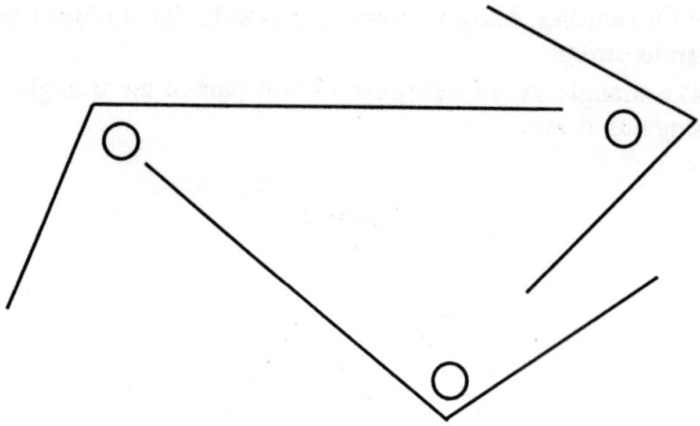

> Elgin is right. The sound track is poor. No words are audible except near the end an unrecognizable voice which is neither clearly male nor female seems to come from nowhere and everywhere — and only fragments at that....[79]

"Callie has been Judge Jomes's mistress for twenty years"[80] in *Lancelot.* Miss Irma and Mrs. Jenny James in the same novel have" a certain reputation from the past."[81] Anna, again in the same novel, is gang raped, sexually abused and morally wronged. Lance consoles Anna on her being raped by philosophizing that sexual indulgence is a sort of evolutionary sign of mankind. "The great secret," he says, "of the ages is that man has evolved, is born, lives, and dies for one end and one end only : to commit a sexual assault on another human or to submit to such an assault."[82] On the doctrine of Original Sin, Lance does not blame man but God Himself. "You were," he says, "onto it with your doctrine of Original Sin. But you got it exactly backwards. Sin is not something man did to God but something God did it to man, so monstrous that to this day man cannot understand what happened to him."[83] Justifying rape as a step towards evolution, Lance theorizes, "Ah, sweet mystery of life indeed indeed yes, exactly, yes indeed that is what it is : to be rammed, jammed, stuck, stabbed, pinned, impaled, run through, in a word : Raped."[84] Lance thinks that with the idea of sexual liberation dawning upon women, a new revolution of love and sex in America has set in. "After all, he emphatically remarks, "the facts are elementary. They are as every biology student knows : of the three million species on earth the human female is the only one capable of living in a state of constant estrus; of having an orgasm; of making love face to face with her mate.... She is the only creature on earth on perpetual heat."[85] "Eye to eye," he further says, "face to face, belly to belly, breast to breast, day in and day out, in heat the year round — there is the omega point of evolution! A comedy isn't it, women trying to escape that? That's like a hen wanting to be a hawk. A lioness, yes, a lioness can do it, for she is a lion most of the time, fighter and hunter, and only periodically hikes her tail."[86] Lance further makes outrageous remarks about sex-indulgence of the Americans in general, "...The pornography of American life is not the work of evil men. No, it is the sensible work of clever men who have at last fathomed God's design for man.... By the way it is not true that Americans are by nature the most pornographic people on earth. The Russians and the Chinese are simply behind times, busy catching up."[87] Lance also makes certain apt comments which certainly go a long way off to theorize about the Percyean type of women characters. For instance, he thinks that man is entitled to practice violence on a woman and a woman is made to endure it. "God's secret design," he comments, "for man is that man's happiness lies for men in men practising violence upon women and that woman's happiness lies in submitting to it."[88] He further elaborates his point, "The secret of life is violence and rape, and its gospel is pornography."[89] The moot point behind the above comments of Lancelot is that he has used them in order to diagnose the moral depravity and mental proclivity to sex-indulgence in modern America, which are in a very horrifying stage and which Percy himself terms as a big disease.

In *The Last Gentlemen,* men have been shown as either gentlemen or fornicators and women as either ladies or whores.[90] The charge of Panthea Reid Broughton against Percy's *The Last Gentleman* is that despite his objection to dualism of scientists, he himself has presented the concept of dualism in this novel. Broughton is doubtful of the veracity of Percy's angelism versus bestialism; immanence versus transcendence; and body versus soul.[91] But, whatever element of dualism Percy injects into the body of his major characters in *The Last Gentleman,* the fact remains that they have fully been drawn in consonance with his concepts of love, sex and human nature. His women characters are varied and worth deeper psychoanalytical attempts. Kitty, for instance, is a twenty-one year old beauty in the novel, who has virtually become a siren being well aware of the enticing value of her appearance. She has, of course, immense capacity to give and take pleasure. She is, in a word, sex-incarnate. Though she is not married to an excellent sex-performer, she is ready to indulge in sex with anyone who can offer her sufficient money. She has no qualms of moral conscience left in her. Will adores her either as a lady or as a whore. In the same novel, Rita is another woman character, who is Sutter's divorced wife. Val is Vaught's daughter, who embraces Roman Catholic religion. Mrs. Vaught is a nondescript. Jamie, a sixteen year old girl, dies early. Myra Thigpen is Mr. Vaught's daughter who he begets from his first wife. Now, all these women characters are sex-maniacs in one way or the other.

Sutter's reflections in his case diary deal, in some details, with the mania of sex and of other discordant feelings of love, which usually characterize the conduct of women in his novels and also the possible causes of the modern malaise of perverted sex in America :

> Women, of course, are the natural pornographers today, because they are not only dispossed by science of the complexes of human relations (all but the orgasm) but are also kept idle in their suburban houses with nothing to do but read pseudo-science articles in the Reader's Digest and dirty novels (one being the natural preamble of the other). U.S. culture is the strangest in history, a society of decent generous sex-ridden men and women who leave each other to their lusts, the men off to the city and conventions, abandoning their wives to the suburbs, which are the very home and habitation of lewd dreams. A dirty deal for women, if you ask me.[92]

Rita, in the same novel, suffers from lust, fear, despair, spitefulness and a number of similar other diseases, which are the natural corollary of the so-called sex-revolution, "Don't be too hard on Rita. She is peeved, not perverted. (The major discovery of my practice : that there are probably not such entities as "schizophrenia" and "homosexuality," conceived as Platonic categories, but only peevishness, revenge, spitefulness, dishonesty, fear, loneliness, lust, and despair — which is not to say we don't need psychiatrist. You people don't seem to be doing too well, you know.)[93]

Sutter considers lewdness and paltriness to be two basic defects in American character as opposed to the Russians who are sexually modest.[94] Lewdness and paltriness render Americans un-Christians, "Americans are the most Christian of all people and also the lewdest. I am no match for them! Do you know why it is that Russians, who are atheists, are sexually modest, whereas Americans, the most Christian of peoples, are also the lewdest?"[95]

In *Love in the Ruins,* Ellen is Tom's nurse and then wife and also 'the sturdy keeper of keys.' Moira is a dumb blonde, a pleasure-seeker, who deserts Tom and is not ready to undertake any difficulty for embracing a family life. Lola is another woman character in the same novel, who is an incarnate of sexual potential. She also deserts Tom and is given to sexual pleasures. Like Moira, she, too, hates to lead a well-settled family life. But Tom dreams of all the women at the same time to live with. He fansies, "My heart melts with love and my brain sings in the musical-erotic sulcus when I think of Lola and Moira. How lovely are the dauthters of men! If I live and love Moira, who is to love Lola and how can I tolerate it? Same with Lola — Moira. And will Ellen stand for it in either case? Only one solution : I must live with all three."[96]

The end of *Love in the Ruins* reunites Tom and Ellen, because Tom now appears to have kept faith in polygamy. Nevertheless, some of Tom's mental aberrations are noteworthy and have an apparent bearing on Percy's view of woman :

> Knowing, not woman, said Sir Thomas, is man's happiness.
>
> Learning and wisdom are receding nowadays. The young, who already know everything, hate science, bomb laboratories, kill professors, burn libraries.

> Already the monks are beginning to collect books again....
> Poor as I am, I feel like God's spoiled child. I am Robinson Crusoe set down on the best possible island with a library, a laboratory, a lusty Presbyterian wife, a cozy three house, an idea and all the time in the world.[97]

In the *Second Coming,* the women characters are more appealing and more enchanting than those in other novels. As a matter of fact, in this novel Allison is the most dominant woman character and she belongs to the third category of Percy's women characters. As has been made clear in the beginning, Percy's women characters of the third category prove to be much simpler and more God-fearing. They prove trustworthy life-partners. Despite the fact that they are ill-treated in life by their own kiths and kins, they nonetheless, enjoy happy married life. In this novel, Percy "appears to have found a good woman for his good man and a man worthy of her."[98] Allen, though mistreated by her own mother is ultimately married to Tom, who, too, finds a good woman in Allen and re-start a happy married life with renewed faith in Christianity. Women characters in *The Thantos Syndrome,* too, treat purity of sex as the basis of married life. Mrs. Cheney is happy because she believes this simple fact in life. But Donna is unhappy and repentent because of her sexual behaviour. Probably the most appropriate illustration of woman-man relationship in *The Second Coming* is where the protagonist and his beloved have nothing to express in words but their conduct has a thorough rythm with no ifs and no buts :

> They kissed again. Her mouth was sweet and tart. His tongue went in her. Her tongue, surprised, was taken aback, then ventured forward, partly his lips slyly. Kissing her was entering a new and happy land.
> "What have you been eating?" he asked her.
> "Pawpaws. They're best after a frost."
> "Let me taste."
> They kissed again. They were sitting now. He noticed that no matter how they kissed, standing or sitting, her body somehow fronted and flew against me.
> "Kissing you is a delight but not a rounded and closed-off delight," she said.

"No?"

"No, it is an opening-out delight and wanting. Kissing is like now fine, more is better, and what about it?"

"I know."

"Your tongue is welcome but you, that is, the salient you, would be even more so."

"I know, I know."...[99]

This is, in deed, a great revelation of permanent bliss through love. Percy's women characters belonging to the third category are really blessed by the spark of love, and they are really capable of enjoying the pilgrimage of life treating themselves to be fortunate human beings. They also don't seem to suffer from the pangs of the typical American malaise of sex-mania and money-madness.

REFERENCES

1. Jan Nordby Gretlund : "Laying the Ghost of Marcus Aurelius", *South Carolina Review*, 13 (Spring 1981), pp. 3-12.
2. Jac Tharpe : *Walker Percy* (Boston : Twayne Publishers, 1983), p. 18.
3. *Ibid.*
4. *Ibid.*, p. 19.
5. *The Second Coming,* p. 13.
6. Jac Tharpe : *op. cit.*, p. 20.
7. *Ibid.*, p. 65.
8. *Ibid.*
9. *Ibid.*
10. John Carr : p. 328.
11. Brown, p. 7.
12. Jack Tharpe : *op. cit.*, p. 71.
13. *Ibid.*
14. *The Last Gentleman,* p. 282.
15. Jac Tharpe : *op. cit.*, p. 78.
16. Abadi-Nagv, p. 17.
17. *Ibid.*, p. 16.
18. *Love in the Ruins*, p. 6.
19. *Ibid.*
20. Jac Tharpe : *op. cit.*, p. 106.
21. *Ibid.*, p. 107.
22. *Ibid.*, p. 119.

23. *The Second Coming,* p. 356.
24. *Ibid.*, p. 359.
25. *Ibid.*, p. 360.
26. Eric Voegelin : *The Ecumenic Age* (Baton Rouge : Louisiana State University Press, 1974), p. 73.
27. Jac Tharpe : *op. cit.*, p. 122.
28. *The Moviegoer*, p. 88.
29. *Ibid.*, p. 75.
30. *Ibid.*, p. 84.
31. *Ibid.*
32. *The Second Coming,* p. 189.
33. *The Moviegoer,* p. 13.
34. *The Last Gentleman,* p. 226.
35. John Edward Hardy : *The Fiction of Walker Percy* (Chicago : University of Illinois Press, 1987), p. 269.
36. *Ibid.*, p. 269.
37. Jac Tharpe : *op. cit.*, p. 81.
38. *Love in the Ruins*, pp. 5-6.
39. *Ibid.*
40. *Ibid.*, p. 7.
41. *Ibid.*, p. 15.
42. *Ibid.*, p. 399.
43. Jan Nordby Gretlund : "Laying the Ghost of Marcus Aurelius," *South Carolina Review,* 13 (Spring 1981), p. 3.
44. *Ibid.*, p. 4.
45. *Ibid.*, p. 3.
46. *Ibid.*, p. 5.
47. *Ibid.*
48. *Ibid.*, p. 6.
49. *Ibid.*, p. 9.
50. Carlton Cremeens : "Walker Percy, The Man and the Novelist : An Interview," *Southern Review,* NS. 4 (Spring 1968), p. 284.
51. *Ibid.*, p. 285.
52. *Ibid.*
53. *Ibid.*, p. 290.
54. Jac Tharpe : *Walker Percy* (Boston : Twayne Publishers, 1983), p. 27.
55. *Ibid.*
56. *Ibid.*
57. *Ibid.*
58. *Ibid.*

59. *Ibid.*
60. *The Moviegoer,* p. 26.
61. *Ibid.,* p. 108.
62. *Ibid.*
63. *Ibid.* (The narrator further remarks, "Everyone on this I Believe believes in the uniqueness and dignity of the individual. I have noticed, however, that the believers are far from unique themselves, are in fact alike as peas in a pod," p. 109.)
64. *Ibid.,* p. 237.
65. Jac Tharpe : *op. cit.*, p. 27.
66. *Lancelot,* pp. 170-71.
67. *Ibid.,* pp. 130-31.
68. *Ibid.,* p. 131.
69. *Ibid.,* p. 196.
70. *Ibid.*
71. Jac Tharpe : *op. cit.*, p. 28.
72. *Ibid.*
73. *Ibid.*
74. *Ibid.*
75. *Ibid.*
76. *Ibid.*
77. *Lancelot,* p. 119.
78. *Ibid.,* p. 189.
79. *Ibid.,* p.192.
80. *Ibid.,* p. 210.
81. *Ibid.*
82. *Ibid.,* p. 222.
83. *Ibid.*
84. *Ibid.*, p. 223.
85. *Ibid.*
86. *Ibid.*
87. *Ibid.*, p. 224.
88. *Ibid.*
89. *Ibid.*
90. This phrase generally belongs to Panthea Reid Broughton, "Gentlemen and Fornicator : *The Last Gentleman* and a *Bisected Reality*," in *The Art of Walker Percy : Strategems for Being*, ed. Panthea Reid Broughton (Baton Rouge : 1979), pp. 96-114; Panthea Reid Broughton further writes, "Percy uses sexual matters as convenient illustrations of Cartesian dualism. But he fails to see in them a means for overcoming that split, since sex, even for a married gentleman, is still fornication. In the biblical

sense, fornication means idolatry or mistaking the profane for the sacred; thus the terms supposes a dualism. The Dionysian life, should, however, transcend dualism. Eros should conjoin the secular and the sacred, the flesh and the spirit, in a union which is ineffable and transcendent," p. 113.

91. *Ibid.*, p. 96. [Broughton further argues, "In everything he writes, Walker Percy protests against doubleness. In "A Theory of Language," for example, Percy criticizes the linguists for perpetuating a "somewhat decrepit mind-body dualism" (MB, 300); in "Culture : The Antinomy of the Scientific Method" he insists that scientists must instead "forgo the luxury of a bisected reality" (MB, 242). And yet that very dualism for which he chides linguists and scientists seems to be a habit of mind with Walker Percy. That is, even as Percy protests against dualism, he presents in his fiction alternatives which tend to be either/or choices : either body or mind, bestialism or angelism, immanence or transcendence."]
92. *The Last Gentlemen*, p. 281.
93. *Ibid.*, p. 282.
94. *Ibid.*, p. 292.
95. *Ibid.*
96. *Ibid.* (Elaborating this point further, Sutter graphically paints a dismal picture of perverseness of sex in America : "Main Street, USA. = a million dollar segregated church on one corner, a drugstore with dirty magazines on the other, a lewd movie on the third, and on the fourth a B-girl bar with condom dispensers in the gents' room. Delay-your-climax cream. Even our official decency is a lewd sort of decency. Watch a soap opera on TV where everyone is decent….

    Soap opera is overtly decent and covertly lewd. The American theatre is overtly lewd and covertly homosexual. I am overtly heterosexual and overtly lewd. I am therefore the only sincere American."), pp. 292-93.
97. *Love in the Ruins,* p. 304.
98. Jac Tharpe : *op. cit.,* p. 30.
99. *Love in the Ruins*, p. 328. (Percy further writes, "Similarly and moreover…. Do you feel a smiling ease with me as well as a sweetness for me in the deep regions?" "Yes, in the deep regions, a sweetness, as well as the smiling ease."), p. 328. 'Walker Percy's Novels : Christianity and Humanism', Proceedings ABI 1993 Conference, 19, pp. 125-31, 'Walker Percy: The Making of the Novelist,' JCC, 12, pp. 35-67.

9

Science and Late Victorian Fiction

"PASSING FROM the vernal woods"[1] of the early Victorian period to the later one, one naturally comes across the fictional productions which entirely seem to be the pabulum of science. Science of the early Victorian milieu, of Dickens and Trollope became the science of the late milieu, of Meredith and Hardy. The innocent faith of the masses in the Christian religion of the scientific days of the early 40's of the nineteenth century gave way to the vacillating agnosticism, energized by Darwinism, of the late 80's and 90's of this period, bringing the century to a close. Science swayed, sustained, and superintended as far as possible, "every sophisticated and well-trained outlook"[2] — giving some the gloomy vision, the tragic phenomenon of the universe; and to others, by compulsion or otherwise, a more sombre and sedate view of life and world. However, no one how so great he might be the voice of the age, could escape the impact of science. Meredith accepted it as "a great challenge,"[3] and Hardy, too, embraced it as a great reality of life; to the former, it strengthened a vision where man evolves towards highest spiritual perfection; to the latter, it strengthened a gloomy and tragic vision of life and world.

But, since all the scientific theories during the Victorian age, such as uniformitarianism as propounded by Chambers, and Naturalism as enunciated by Herschel, were largely dominated by Darwinism, which was originated by Darwin and perfected by Herbert Spencer, T.H. Huxley, Tyndall and John Lecky; and since Darwinism swayed every domain of thought, the impact of scientific thought both on Meredith and Hardy, as on other minor novelists of the age, is to be studied and analysed in the light of their acceptance of and reactions against the Darwinian theory of evolution and its impact on the contemporary life. Since Meredith and Hardy represent the late Victorian age "in a much wider and truer sense,"[4] and since both of them accept Darwinism "in their own characteristic ways,"[5] it has been thought prudent to study the impact of Darwinism on them in detail. But, besides Darwinism, they were also influenced by the much-talked-about common scientific opinions of the age, such as Lyell's theory of the formation of earth, Hugh Miller's "principle of cosmos,"[6] Martineau's unitarianism and Spencer's naturalism, as also the other novelists like Richard Jefferies, Rutherford, George Gissing, George Moore, M.E. Braddon and Miss Ramee, though novelists of less recognition and acclaim of the age — were powerfully influenced. Of the multitude of novelists, and of the variety of fiction that this age produced, the most affected by the scientific impact were only those "who watched the advent of new scientific theories with an open mind,"[7] without the bias of parochial feelings, and in this respect, Meredith and Hardy "proved themselves to be the worthiest of all."[8] In "extending the frontiers of the psychological novel,"[9] that came into existence with "George Eliot's treatment of intellectual reality"[10] during the mid-Victorian period; of the sociological novel, that came in vogue through the sincere efforts of Dickens and his disciples, of Charles Kingsley, of Charles Reade, and the Bronte Sisters; and the regional fiction, that got maturity through Scott's novels and through those of his followers; *inter alia* other schools of fiction-writing, such as sentimental novel, domestic novel, romantic novel, and impressionic novel; the contribution of Meredith and Hardy is, of course, epoch-making. While Meredith applied the Spencerian psychology on fiction, Hardy used the Darwinian evolution on it : the former extended the scope of psychological fiction by evincing faith in the social philosophy of the Unitarians, the latter "added big dimensions to the scope of regional and sociological fiction"[11] by anticipating Agnosticism of the many noted members of the Metaphysical Society of the eminent Victorians. In between Meredith and Hardy, there are very few novelists worth the name who ever displayed any remarkable independence as original novelists, and who could powerfully reacted and responded to the scientific advent. However, there is a group of novelists comprising of such novelists as Richard Jefferies, Rutherford, George Gissing, George Moore, Miss Braddon, and Miss Ramee, who, though not as prolific and representative novelists as Meredith and Hardy, have effectively responded to and powerfully reacted against the advent of science.

It is, of course, true that the psychological and sociological fiction, besides "other fictional ramifications of the age,"[12] got further momentum due to Spencer's and Huxley's psychological and sociological interpretations. During the late Victorian age, their new interpretations in the field of psychology, sociology and other such behavioural sciences, got an instant confirmation in Meredith's and Hardy's novels, which was still in the doldrums, during the early Victorian period, despite the best efforts by Thackeray and Trollope in this regard. The great majority of the novelists, especially the romancers and many amongst the women group of novelists, "remained more or less unaffected by the advent of science,"[13] partly because of "their limited range of experience and temperament,"[14] but largely because of "their dormant and docile artistic talents."[15]

It is in this historical perspective that we have to study only those novelists belonging to the late Victorian period, who have faithfully represented the impact of scientific thought in their novels; and from this point of view, as otherwise too, from that of chronology, Meredith's and Hardy's novels, which are the epitome of the age, deserve greater attention than those of others. Since between Hardy and Meredith, the former is chronologically nearer to us than the latter, Meredith deserves priority of treatment over Hardy, but because Meredith does not feel fatigued to encounter the forceful onward march of science and since his acceptance of Darwinism is less cent per cent and less complete than that of Hardy, it is prudent that Hardy the scientist, the sociologist, the psychologist, the geologist, and finally, the Darwinist, should be studied prior to Meredith, the scientist, the psychologist, and finally, the Darwinist of the Bergsonian stamp, even ignoring the chronological order, in order to see their greater spirit of involvement in the scientific movement of the Victorian age.

During the late Victorian age, we come across a huge congregation of novelists, who either followed Meredith or Hardy, the two most prominent and most representative novelists of this age, or imitated some chief novelists of the early Victorian age, such as Dickens, Charles Reade and Mrs. Gaskell. There were romancers, such as William Ainsworth, Wilkie Collins, George Macdonald, William Sharp, Richard Blackmore, William Black, John Henry Shorthouse, and Stevenson who wrote novels with a romantic strain, and who showed little awareness of scientific temper in their fiction. Then, there were novelists of social and domestic life, such as John Watson, George Douglas Brown and George Gissing, who tried to display their interest in social problems with somewhat scientific curiosity, and amongst them all, George Gissing favourably reacted to scientific impact. There were also such novelists as George Burrow, Laurence Oliphant and Richard Jefferies, in whose novels the vagrant note is predominant, and adhering to no school of fiction-writing, there are often very interesting characteristics traceable in their novels. However, all of them have largely been represented by Richard Jefferies, because he favourably responded to and reacted against scientific impact. Thus, there were many schools of fiction-writing prevalent during the late Victorian period, the chief among them being — the Meredithian school, the Hardyian school, the George Gissing school, the Moorean school, and the Miss Rameean school. Since the schools of Hardy and Meredith dominated others with regard to their favourable reaction to scientific impact, it is wise to study this impact first in their novels.

Science affected Hardy's works more than the novels of any other novelist of the Victorian period; he appears in his novels as the most conscious scientist to apprehend the immutability of nature, the mutability of human life; the bigness of nature, the littleness of man; the inexorable character of natural laws, and the puny struggles of human beings. It is often an agricultural scientist in him detailing many things of deeper interest burgeoning on science of agriculture; often a veterinary scientist suggesting various professional skills; and, often an ecologist and pathologist treating nature and its other phenomena with the interest and care of a professional. Besides his overall picture of life and universe immensely being affected and influenced by science, his novels have various illustrations where different scientists engaged in their different disciplines of knowledge are actively busy in furthering their knowledge and skill in related fields.

In *Far From the Madding Crowd*, for instance, the astronomer in Oak speaks, when he is being carried along the road at a rate rather considerable for a vehicle without springs, and under circumstances of physical uneasiness, to listen to the conversation of Billy Smallbury and Master Poorgrass :

> Charles's Wain was getting towards a right angle with the Pole Star, and Gabriel concluded that it must be about nine O'clock — in other words, that he slept two hours. This small astronomical calculation was made without any positive effort, and while he was stealthily turning to discover, if possible, into whose hands he had fallen.[16]

While describing Norcombe Hill and its surroundings, the astronomer in Hardy details stars and sky with the authority and authenticity of a skilled professional :

> The sky was clear — remarkably clear — and the twinkling of all he stars seemed to be put throbs of one body, timed by a common pulse. The North star was directly in the wind's eye, and since evening the Bear had swung round it outwardly to the east, till he was now at a right angle with the meridian. A difference of colour in the stars — often read of than seen in England — was really perceptible here. The sovereign brilliancy of Sirius pierced the eye with a steely glitter, the star called Capella was yellow, Aldebaran and Betelgueux shone with a fiery red.[17]

Again, when Oak retires to his hut and wants to ascertain the time of night from the altitudes of the stars, Hardy's knowledge of and interest in astronomy is evident :

> The Dog-star and Adlebaran, pointing to the restless Pleiades, were half-way up the Southern sky, and between them hung Orion, which gorgeous constellation never burnt more vividly than now, as it soared forth above the rim of the landscape. Castor and Pollux with their quiet shine were almost on the meridian : the barren and gloomy Square of Pegasus was creeping round to the north-west; far away through the plantation Vega sparkled like a lamp suspended amid the leafless trees, and Cassiopeia's chair stood daintily poised on the uppermost boughs.[18]

Gabriel Oak's surgery of sheep demonstrates Hardy's knowledge of veterinary sciences. The type of surgery that Oak performs is one that a modern histologist is expected to perform :

> Gabriel was already among the turgid, prostrate forms. He had flung off his coat, rolled up his shirt-sleeves, and taken from his pocket the instrument of salvation. It was a small tube or trochal, with lance passing down the inside and Gabriel began to use it with a dexterity that would have graced a hospital-surgeon. Passing his hand over the sheeps' left flank, and selecting the proper point, he punctured the skin and rumen with the lance as it stood in the tube; then he suddenly withdrew the lance, retaining the tube in its place. A current of air rushed up the tube, forcible enough to have extinguished a candle held at the orifice.[19]

Out of total number of 57 sheep involved in injury, Oak could survive 49; four sheep died, three recovered without any operation and one also missed his surgical magic :

> Forty-nine operations were successfully performed. Owing to the great hurry necessitated by the far-gone state of some of the flock, Gabriel missed his aim in one case, and in one only — striking wide of the mark, and inflicting a mortal blow at once upon the suffering ewe. Four had died; three recovered without an operation. The total number of sheep which had thus strayed and injured themselves so dangerously was fifty-seven.[20]

Hardy shows his knowledge of agricultural implements in his novels, and often prognosticates like an agricultural-engineer, assigning different roles and functions to different agricultural implements. In *Tess of the D'Urbervilles*, there are various such illustrations listing his knowledge of agricultural implements; but an oft-quoted passage that very readily comes to memory in *The Mayor of Casterbridge*, is one where Hardy elaborately speaks of a variety of such implements used in the modern farming :

> Scythes, reap-hooks, sheep-shears, bill-hooks, spades, mattocks, and hoes at the ironmonger's; beehives, butter-firkins, churns, milking stools and pails, hay-rakes, field-flagons, and seed-lips at the cooper's; cart-ropes and plough-harness at the saddler's; carts, wheel-barrows, and mill-gear at the wheelwright's and machinist's; horse-embrocations at the chemist's; at the glover's and leather-cutter's, hedging-gloves, thatchers' knee-caps, ploughmen's leggings, villagers' patterns and clogs.[21]

Hardy, the Civil Engineer, and the architect, is always present in his novels in one form or the other. Innumerable are the passages in his novels to testify to his knowledge of architectural sciences. One instance of his profound knowledge of architecture, which is often quoted, is his scientific measurement of the Ring at Casterbridge locally termed as the finest Roman Amphitheatre in *The Mayor of Casterbridge* :

> The Amphitheatre was a huge circular enclosure, with a notch at opposite extremities of its diameter north and south. From its sloping internal form it might have been called the spittoon of the Jotuns. It was to Casterbridge what the ruined Coliseum is to modern Rome, and was nearly of the same magnitude. The dusk of evening was the proper hour at which a true impression of this suggestive place could be received. Standing in the middle of the arena at that time thereby degrees became apparent its real vastness, which a cursory view from the summit at noonday was apt to obscure.[22]

Or, the architectural designs of the house of Bathsheba Everdene in *Far From the Madding Crowd* :

> Fluted pilasters, worked from the solid stone, decorated its front, and above the roof the chimneys were panelled or columnar, some coped gables with finials and like features still retaining traces of their Gothic extraction. Soft brown mosses, like faded velveteen, formed cushions upon the stone tiling, and

> tufts of the houseleek or sengreen sprouted from the eaves of the low surrounding buildings. A gravel walk leading from the door to the road in front was encrusted at the sides with more moss — here it was a silver-green variety, the nut-brown of the gravel being visible to the width of only a foot or two in the centre. This circumstance, and the generally sleepy air of the whole prospect here, together with the animated and contrasting state of the reverse facade, suggested to the imagination that on the adaptation of the building for farming purposes the vital principle of the house had turned round inside its body to face the other way. Reversals of this kind, strange deformities, tremendous paralyses, are often seen to be inflicted by trade upon edifices — either individual or in the aggregate as streets and towns — which were originally planned for pleasure alone.[23]

One of the great disciplines of modern researches engaging attention of the behavioural scientists is the study of sociology: because with the advance of atom and nuclear civilization, the social complications have put multifarious responsibilities on the shoulders of a sociologist. The social scientist in Hardy always presents social problems in his novels, and the best ones become those which offer a far-reaching and deeper analysis of social problems of their contemporary milieu. Even a cursory glance over his novels will testify to this great fact that his novels are specimens of convincing social studies. *The Mayor of Casterbridge*, for instance, studies the problem of drinking, when Michael Henchard, the hero, sells his wife Susan to a navigator named Newson for default of payment of wine in the inn publicly; and when he resolves not to touch wine for full twenty-one years, and pledges to work hard as a way to atone for his wrong doing :

> I, Michael Henchard, on this morning of the sixteenth of September, do take an oath before God here in this solemn place that I will avoid all strong liquors for the space of twenty-one years to come, being a year for every year that I have lived. And this I swear upon the book before me; and may I be strook dumb, blind, and helpless, if I break this my oath![24]

But, alas! Henchard, an envy of his cruel fate and indifferent destiny, is found addicted to wine again after suffering heavy losses in his corn-trade, and after being reduced to a pauper, having been completely defeated by Farfrae, his rival in every field of life — whether be it business, or love, or social prestige. Despite his efforts for amelioration in feelings and habits, the poor fellow is mocked at by his superior Gods :

> But the ingenious machinery contrived by the Gods for reducing human possibilities of amelioration to a minimum — which arranges that wisdom to do shall come *pari passu* with the departure of zest for doing — stood in the way of all that. He had no wish to make an arena a second time of the world that had become a mere painted scene to him.[25]

The problem of drinking also appears in *Tess of the D'Urbervilles*, where Tess's father John Durbefield, having come to know of his high ancestral connections and reputed forefathers, drinks so heavily as to forget his ordinary routine affairs of life and sends Tess, with her brother, to perform his own duties, which proves to be the starting point of tragedy in her life. In *Jude the Obscure*, Jude Fawley, a South-Wessex villager, filled with intellectual aspirations and passions for learning, takes to drinking, when he gets frustration in his love-affair, first with Arabella Donn, and then with Sue; and particularly, when his intellectual and scholarly ambitions remained unfulfilled. Thus, Hardy, the sociologist, is not unaware of the problem of drinking and its attendant evils in his novels, similar illustrations of which can be cited in abundance from his other major novels to substantiate this point of view.

"Being a novelist of the rural life,"[26] Hardy is also aware of the problem of poverty and economic backwardness of villagers in his novels. Tess's tragedy in life begins with poverty and ends with it, without an end to this social evil. Her compulsion to meet Alec is purely a monetary one; for, her parents fondly hope to see her matrimonial alliance with Alec, a rich man's son, despite their poverty, only on the basis of their respectable ancestry which they have lately discovered. But Alec, a morally lax fellow, entraps her, with the result that the poor innocent creature becomes the mother of an illicit baby to face unimaginable social condemnation at the hands of the so-called custodians of the society. She then comes in contact with Angel Clare and marries him only to suffer from further buffets of life : and, lastly, comes to Alec again to be finished for ever by her President of the Immortals. The entire story "seems to be woven into the fabric of poverty and cruelty of fate."[27]

In *Far From the Madding Crowd*, "the pangs of poverty"[28] and its resultant repercussions from social view-point are no less stringent than the one just referred to. Gabriel Oak wishes to marry Bathsheba, but the former is poorer than the latter, and the result is obvious — a constant struggle for indifferent existence with innumerable ups and downs of life of a graver import. Boldwood also loves Bathsheba, but the poor fellow also meets the same frustration and dejection. Serjeant Troy wins Bathsheba with his elemental approximation to her, but it all ends with the transience of a bubble of water. Oak and Bathsheba now decide to live as husband and wife, because they come out as triumphant in the struggle for existence, and because they fully recognize what the social evil of poverty has in its store to wreck a happy reunion of two creatures.

Hardy, "being the last great novelist of the Victorian age,"[29] saw all changes brought about by science in the life of the people : he witnessed "a variety of transitional processes"[30] stealthily but gradually becoming well-settled and firmly-entrenched. He was "sore to see agricultural decline"[31] in the wake of industrialization, the neglect of the toiling class in the name of urbanization, "the ostracization of simple", innocent pleasures of life in the guise of civilization, and also the agnosticism born of Darwinism. Being faced with a volley of pertinent queries as to the insignificance of human life, God and universe, in the world controlled by automatic processes of natural laws in the light of new developing scientific and evolutionary principles, Hardy's essentially tragic vision of life, and universe grew severer and more tragic in his novels. Finding man's existence no better than the life of helpless flies in the hand of a wanton boy, seeing man a puny prey in the hands of his cruel fate, witnessing how Gods mock at man's innocent acts,

Hardy lost all sympathy for the unseen divine and sought, in turn, to recompensate this loss of faith by emphasizing the importance of cardinal virtues in life. His stories are, therefore, replete with this noble content of life : his characters are noble at heart and try to reach the height of goodness through their good deeds. Henchard, Tess, Angel, Gabriel Oak, Boldwood, Jude — all have the essential goodness of nature and faith in the sterling values of life, does not matter all of them become extinct unceremoniously in the world founded on scientific principles, completely devoid of a benevolent God and soothing supernatural agencies. But even in this presentment of scientific world, the Hardyian man — of virtue and of goodness, is truly Christian.

Hardy, the sociologist, asks a number of questions from his readers so as to stir their self-complacency and the social acceptance of certain faulty and irreligious values. Tess's child dies "unbaptized with the appalling horror of inhumanity :"[32] she does not disclose the identity of her illicit and stolen-love, because she knows it fully well that the society, the chief villain in the rustic life, will not pardon her guilt, though committed without any wrong intentions. Tess tolerates it and accepts the total blame as her own : Alec, the seducer and the corrupter of her innocent and inexperienced youthful beauty, does not get any social punishment for his wrong doings. For the same quantum of social guilt, disproportionate punishment is meted out, the heaviest one to Tess, and nothing at all to Alec. Again, after marriage with Angel Clare, there is "a double standard of measurement of ethical and moral lapses"[33] from social and ethical point of view in the life of Tess. Angel insists on Tess to narrate her past life, after he himself tells her of his own amorous-affair with a woman before marriage. Tess, in the fond belief that she would be pardoned for telling her past guilt, narrates it to Angel Clare, though she revealed it earlier through a letter of confession, which, by a freak of coincidence, did not reach him in time, before marriage. No sooner does Angel listen to it, than he becomes impatient to desert her, and Tess's misery in life again begins. For the same social guilt, it has double standard to inflict punishment; and, Hardy, the sociologist, meliorist, and, the psychologist presents this problem enchantingly and convincingly so as to give it "a universal tinge to be asked perpetually even today."[34]

Meredith, like Hardy, was "fully aware of the multifarious changes"[35] brought about by science in many aspects of life; and, also of those "set in motion by many scientific theories"[36] of the day. He was fully cautious of "the total damage"[37] that Darwinism brought forth in its wake to the old orthodox Christian religion and faith; of the colossal waste of simple pleasures of human life brought about by "the mechanical civilization"[38] with its *uberrima fides* in the competitive urbanization : and finally, of the stupendous exploitation of the toiling class caused by the capitalist class in its trail of voracious urge for unending industrialization. Meredith welcomed the onward march of science : applauded evolution with his full-throated ease : and, highly eulogized the champions of science; but, like Hardy, he would have noted "the plethoric growth of knowledge simultaneously with the stunting of wisdom."[39]

But still deeper and more pragmatic approach of a scientist appears in Meredith's novels when he interprets and applies the scientific ideas to the conduct of life rather than studying them in external and physical world. His *Richard Feverel* is the perfect application of scientific ideas to the life of its characters, especially to the characters of Sir Austin Feverel and Richard. Sir Austin's pleading before Egeria, Lady Blandish, not to reject his son's love seems to be as scientific and psychologically true as an engineer prepares an accurate report on the construction of a dam, with the only distinction that here Meredith discusses the process of feelings instead of brick, stone, iron or cement, necessary for such a report :

> When the experiment appeared to have failed, all humanity's failings fell on the shoulders of his son.... The young man had plotted this. From step to step Sir Austin traced the plot. Manichaen tendency, from which the sententious eulogist of

> nature had been struggling for years (and which was partly at the bottom of the system), now began to cloud and usurp dominion of his mind. As he sat alone in the forlorn dead-hush of his library, he saw the devil.... There by the springs of Richard's future, his father sat; and the devil said to him : "Only be quiet : do nothing : resolutely do nothing : your object now is to keep a brave face to the world, so that all may know you superior to this human nature that has deceived you. For it is the shameless deception, not the marriage, that has wounded you."
>
> "Ah!" answered the baronet, "the shameless deception, not the marriage; wicked and ruinous as it must be; a destroyer of my tenderest hopes! my dearest schemes! Not the marriage — the shameless deception!" and he crumpled up his son's letter to him, and tossed it into the fire.[40]

Or, the passage reporting on Richard's becoming the father, and his feeling "a revelation mounting obscurely to his brain :"

> A pale grey light on the skirts of the flying tempest displayed the dawn. Richard was walking hurriedly. The green drenched weeds lay all around in his path, bent thick, and the forest drooped glimmeringly. Impelled as a man who feels a revelation mounting obscurely to his brain, Richard was passing one of those little forest-chapels, hung with votive wreaths, where the peasant halts to kneel and prey. Cold, still, in the twilight it stood, rain-drops pattering round it. He looked within, and saw the Virgin holding her child. He moved by. But not many steps had he gone ere his strength went out of him, and he shuddered. What was it? He asked not. He was in other hands. Vivid as lightning the Spirit of Life illumined him. He felt in his heart the cry of his child, his darling's touch. With shut eyes he saw them both. They drew them from the depths; they led him a blind and tottering man. And as they led him he had a sense of purification so sweet he shuddered again and again.[41]

Or, the one remarkable passage in *Vittoria*, where Carlo bids farewell to the women who have loved him :

> Carlo smiled.... "The Brescians are up : that's an hour that has struck, and there's no calling it to move a step in the rear. Brescia under the big Eastern hill which throws a clock on it at sunrise! Brescia is always the eagle that looks over Lombrady! And Bergamo! You know the terraces of Bergamo. Aren't they like a morning sky? Dying there is not death; it's

> flying into the dawn. You Romans envy us. Come confess it, you envy us. You have no Alps, no crimson hills, nothing but old walls to look on while you fight. Farewell, Merthyr Powys. I hear my servant's foot outside. My horse is awaiting me saddled, a mile from the city. Perhaps I shall see my wife again at the door below, or in heaven. Addio! kiss Luciano for me. Tell him that I knew myself as well as he did, before the end came. Enrico, Emilio, and the others — tell them that I love them."[42]

Thus, the most important impact of science of Meredith's novels is in the form of psychological thrust, a kind of experiment in fiction that had been set in motion by George Eliot, in particular, and other exponents of the intellectual realism such as Thackeray and Trollope, in general. In fact, Meredith regards fiction-writing as a part of science, and the study of psychology therein as a gateway of knowledge relating to human nature. Being much influenced by Herbert Spencer's synthetic philosophy, Meredith endeavoured to apply psychology on fiction. What Spencer did for science at large, Meredith achieved it in the narrower domain of fiction : the former gave a wider application of psychological truths in his synthetic philosophy, the latter gave a wealth of illustrative material of psychology in his novels. In all his novels — *The Ordeal of Richard Feverel* (1859), *Evan Harrington* (1861), *Emilia in England* (1864) afterward changed to *Sandra Belloni, Rhoda Fleming* (1865), *Vittoria* (1867), *Harry Richmond* (1871), *Beauchamp's Career* (1876), *The Egoist* (1879), *The Tragic Comedians* (1880), *Diana of the Crossways* (1885), *One of Our Conquerors* (1890), *Lord Ormont and His Aminta* (1894), and *The Amazing Marriage* (1895), the psychological strain remains conspicuously more preponderant than other strains; and that is why, Trevelyan regards his novels as "penetrating psychological studies of the later milieu of the Victorian age."[43]

The psychologist in Meredith makes him declare : "At present, I am aware, an audience impatient for blood and glory scorns the stress I am putting on incidents so minute, a picture so little imposing. An audience will come to whom it will be given to see the elementary machinery at work; who, as it were, from some slight hint of the straws, will feel the winds of March when they do not blow."[44] Even to life during the Victorians, when people did not know how to react to 'the winds of March', Meredith gave the clarion call to taste those novels in which "the invisible life"[45] of characters has been psychologically studied; in which the events of life have been made the subtle points, through the exposure of characters, of logic; and where the rendering of the entire treatment as a fine piece of psychology and "scientific spirit in literature."[46] Shibli Bagarag, Richard, Evan Harrington, Harry Richmond, Rhoda, Dahlia, Edward Blancove, Camilla, Carlo, Ottilia, Beauchamp, Clara Middleton, Laetitia Dale, Vernon Whitford, Diana, Lord Dannisburg, Lady Dunstane, Victor Randor, Nataly, Anastasia Robinson, Lady Charlotte Eglet, Fleetwood, Lord Loverllier, and Carinthia, and a host of such other characters constitute the best psychological studies. In them, one wonderfully finds a whole world inhabited by different kinds of persons with their multiplied psychology and temperaments. In this respect of psychological fiction, Meredith, therefore, deserves the same status as Spencer and Huxley in their own fields of specialization.

Of the multiplied illustrations of psychological study with which every page of Meredith's novels abounds, the one very lively and interesting that readily comes to mind is one where Wilfrid and Emilia are sitting by Wilming Weir at evening, and where their love — psychology has very evidently and artistically been studied by Meredith. Here only a few sentences would throw a flood of light on the working of psychology of love :

> 'You are my own, are you not Emilia?'
>
> 'Yes; I am,' she answered simply.
>
> 'That water seems to say "for ever,"' he murmured; and Emilia's fingers pressed upon his.
>
> Of marriage there was no further word. Her heart was evidently quite at ease; and that it should be so without chaining him to a date, was Wilfrid's peculiar desire. He could pledge himself to eternity, but shrank from being bound to eleven O'clock on the morrow morning."[47]

The sociologist, besides the psychologist, in Meredith makes him write social novels on the pattern of George Eliot and Thomas Hardy. Meredith, being influenced by Carlyle, Mill, Ruskin, Cotter Morison, Leslie Stephen, James Thomson, Hyndmann, John Morley, York Powell, G.W. Foote, and Edward Clodd,[48] has dealt with various social problems, "as they were prevalent and tantalizing those days the mind of the common men,"[49] in his novels. But his treatment of the social problems is different both from Eliot's and Hardy's. While Eliot feels fatigued in her defence against social solutions, and while Hardy feels pessimistic in his prescription of social ailments, Meredith takes the social problem as a natural course of evolution. It is his view that society itself would evolve for being converted into an ideal one; as it is also his conviction that man's evolution is not only Darwinian, it is spiritual also. Whether or not, society and men will turn into heaven and angels, one vital fact is certain, that Meredith's concept of the spiritual evolution in fiction atleast redeemed a lot of botheration and ennui of the contemporary Victorian life. So Meredith is a sociologist of the Herbert Spencerian stamp, whose cosmic and ethical processes of psychology aim, like Meredith's, at the spiritual evolution of society and its inhabitants.

The soil science is one of the most advanced studies of agricultural sciences of today, and in every agricultural University, now-a-days, the agricultural scientists have brought about a green revolution through their expertise and skill of soil experiments. Meredith's love for the soil or the earth is the love of an agricultural scientists or a modern farmer, who sees a closer propinquity of and love for the earth both from the point of view of utility and congenial influence. In his novels, nature, which is an ally to earth, is a living, developing and divine part, and it always enables man to do good deeds in life. Meredith had read with interest Lyell and Chambers, both the popular botanists and geologists of the day; he had also known Herschel's theory of naturalism. As such, his approach to nature is the approach of that agricultural scientist who sees a lot of bounty and prosperity hidden in its womb, and a huge mass of congenial influence concealed in its treasure to make human beings truly good human beings. His nature, therefore, has neither the Wordsworthian brooding spirit in it nor the Shelleyian swift-winged spirit of love; neither the Tennysonian nonchalant spirit nor the Browningian joyful comradeship. Meredith's approach to nature and earth is out and out the most scientific.[50]

Of the three most famous scientific theories of the late Victorian period, *viz.*, uniformitarianism, Darwinism and naturalism, it was Darwinism which dominated other theories; and Meredith, the Darwinian evolutionist, deals with the concept of evolution explicitly or implicitly almost in his every major novel. He, like Hardy, accepted the whole theory of Darwinism as a rational explanation of the development of life. But "his is not merely a biological evolution like that of Thomas Hardy;"[51] on the contrary, his is the spiritual evolution. For Darwin, and his disciples, mind, intuition, free will and individuality have no separate entities; for Hardy, too, these things had no isolated significance; and through reason and through the principle of natural selection and that of the survival of the fittest, the evolution of the whole mankind may be justified. But for Meredith, reason is inferior to intuition, and the theory of natural selection, too, cannot annihilate individuality and thc importance of free will and of spontaneity. Thus, Meredith, the Darwinian evolutionist, and also Hardy, the Darwinian disciple, have sufficiently represented through their novels, the most effective scientific theory of the day, which naturally forms the major impact on their novels, for which, it has been thought prudent, to devote a full one chapter separately for its proper study and appreciation.

Besides influencing the great novelists of the Victorian age, the principles of struggle for existence and natural selection also influenced other minor and less known novelists of the day. Richard Jefferies, for instance, who was eight years Hardy's junior, in *The Dewy Morn* (1884), shows his interest in the natural working of the universe in a Darwinian sense, where there is the survival of the fittest, where only the most capable ones survive. Jefferies presents a universe in which the Darwinian principles operate constantly for human evolution; in which every human being is put to the toughest trial for existence; but his is the universe different from Darwin's and Hardy's in one sense, *i.e.*, there is the existence of a Christian God — both benevolent and loving. He himself has admitted this fact and joyously proclaimed, "This wondrous loveliness (purity of nature) purified and freed his soul from the grossness of material existence."[52] Jefferies has regarded human existence as a doleful tale like Hardy, his mentor; yet unlike him, he does not leave human beings at the mercy of a cruel fate. The oneness of Felise, the sombre view of Rosa helped them keep their spirits cheerful throughout, despite the scathing criticism and social humiliation they suffered while encountering various odds in life. In his another novel, *The Story of my Heart* (1883), Jefferies seems to be influenced by the Meredithian concept of spiritual evolution, and as such, it is "man's intelligence,"[53] his virtuous living and intuitive creative energy, "despite nature's sporadic attempts at stultifying man's aspirations,"[54] that a universe full of intuitive awareness has been presented. In *After London, or Wild England* (1886), and *Amaryllis at the Fair* (1887), Richard Jefferies presents "the Hardyian nature"[55] with the "soothing touch of the Meredithian earth,"[56] infusing "physical comforts"[57] and "the joyous happiness of soul together;"[58] evincing, thus, to be fully conscious of the scientific developments and theories of the day together with their wider implications and repercussions.

Hardy's gloom characterizes the novels of Rutherford, George Gissing and George Moore, though this arises out of different causes. Mark Rutherford peeps deeper into the drab, ugly aspects of life : and, he therefore, feels indignant at human existence; Gissing transcribes the reality of life which is, of course, appalling in its ultimate analysis; and, he, therefore, regards life as a serious phenomenon; whereas, Moore feels fatigued to understand the inner meaning of a new civilization founded on atoms and other deadly weapons. Over and above this gloom, however, on these three novelists, there is an immeasurable impact of science to be analysed and studied in different forms and dimensions.

In Mark Rutherford, the scientist, "impels him to study the mind and heart of his characters"[59] as minutely and accurately as experiments are carried out in big laboratories. In *The Autobiography* and *Deliverance*, "the effort at enunciating the psychological novel is praiseworthy,"[60] because "one finds every approach to the mental study and analysis"[61] on the part of the novelist in accordance with "the fundamental principles"[62] of "modern psychology."[63] It is, perhaps, in this spirit that E.A. Baker regards these novels as epoch-making efforts at the inclusion of psychological element in English fiction. "And, taken together," writes he, "the two books form an introspective history heralding the modern psychological novels. For it is on the adventures and agonies of a soul that Mark Rutherford is always intent; even the commonest story — and those of Mark and Miriam and Zachariah are far from common — is given the depth and intensity of tragic life."[64]

Mark regards his act of devoting many hours of prayer to God as no better than "a horrible hypocrisy,"[65] because it is his avowed belief that "direct appeal to God can only be justified when it is passionate."[66] Wasting time on religious books as well as on prayer to deities, well-entrenched in the niche of cathedrals and churches, Mark regards as of no significance and treats it as an act of senseless sham. While at College, he preferred the *Lyrical Ballads* to the *Bible*, because it brought about a change in him "only to be compared with that which is said to have been wrought on Paul himself by the Divine apparition."[67] He finds in its passionate study a benevolent divinity of Wordsworth, "substituting a new and living spirit for the old deity, once alive, but gradually hardened into an idol."[68] But this hardening process is gradually deepened because of the callous modern civilization, where persons lead a dual life, very difficult to be studied even by a psychologist, as in the case of Snale, the draper and his wife, both a psychologist's despair :

> Both were daubs, but curiously faithful in depicting what was most offensive in the character of both the originals, Mr. Snale's simper being preserved, together with the peculiarly hard, heavy sensuality of the eye in Mrs. Snale, who was large and full-faced, correct like Mr. Snale, a member of the church, and cruel, not with the ferocity of the tiger, but with the dull insensibility of a cartwheel, which will roll over a man's neck as easily as over a flint.[69]

Mark Rutherford's Deliverance is the exposition of the Darwinian concept of the struggle for existence : the brilliant character of Theresa is the niece of the Darwinian bookseller, Wollaston : the original character of Miss Leroy is purely a scientific product of the modern hypochondriac complex civilization : the London in which they inhabit is truly a "City of Dreadful Night;"[70] a place of the Thomsonian setting where

> The world rolls round for ever like a mill;
> It grinds out death and life and good and ill;
> It has no purpose, heart or mind or will.[71]

But the purposelessness and meaninglessness of the London city corrupted by the onward march of science is redeemed by Mark Rutherford's tranquillity and calm of the Meredithian stamp : the stoic character his soul of the Spinozian and the Marcus Aureliusian echo.

The same conflict of ideas and ideologies wrought by science is traceable in his other works : *Miriam's Schooling, Michae Trevanion, Catharine Furze, Clara Hopgood, John Inglesant*, and *Robert Elsmere* — all of which constitute to be good studies, entailing scientific impact on modern minds, particularly from the point of view of psychology. They open up new layers of mind and heart, even wider than those written by George Eliot, Meredith, and Hardy; and, they, therefore, herald a new direction to modern novels of psychology, especially those of the stream of consciousness.

George Gissing "approximates Hardy"[72] in his "outlook towards God and universe"[73] and the place of man "in a vast world,"[74] being controlled by a blind and powerful force : he dittoes "Thomas Love Peacock in his outlook towards science."[75]

As to the first approach, he regards "universe as an inhabitation,"[76] where "ultimate causes are inscrutable :"[77] where man's destiny is pre-determined by an indifferent and nonchalant Providence : where man suffers miserably at the cruel and merciless destiny. "Rather must I apprehend," he writes, "that man, in some inconceivable way, may at his best moments represent a principle darkly at strife with that which prevails throughout the world as known to us."[78] The Manichaeism system of universe seems to have confirmed his view that man should constantly endeavour to glorify good without the least expectation of his being rewarded; and, in this advocacy for the good for its own sake, he conveniently tallies the Puritanic conception of virtue. "Of all theological system, "he writes, "the most convincing is the Manichaeism, which, of course under another name, was held by the Puritans themselves."[79]

Science, he regards, as "the remorseless enemy of mankind."[80] In science, he sees, the end of "all the beauty of the world;" an approach typically Peacockian in substance, who, too, regards science as the most powerful virus which gradually eats into the vitality of human life; and who in his famous novels — *Headlong Hall, Melincourt, Crotchet Castle Gryll Grange, Maid Marian, The Misfortunes of Elphin*, and *Nightmare Abbey* enunciates the philosophy of scientific agnosticism through such immortal characters of his as Mr. Forster, "the perfectibilian," Mr. Escot, "the deteriorationist," Mr. Jenkinson, "the status-quo-ite," and the Reverend Doctor Gaster.[81] Gissing finds in new civilization, based on science the roots of barbarism, the callousness of heart, and the seeds of all beastly conflicts. Science, for him, is not an ennobling force or a soothing balm or a blessing fairy, it is rather a demon bent on creating "a blood-drenched chaos"[82] in mankind. "I see," he passionately argues against science, "it destroying all simplicity and gentleness of life, all the beauty of the world; I see it restoring barbarism under a mask of civilization; I see it darkening men's minds and hardening their hearts; I see it bringing a time of vast conflicts, which will pale into insignificance "the thousand wars of old", and, as likely as not, will whelm all the laborious advances of mankind in blood-drenched chaos.[83]

This evident distrust for science is copiously traceable in George Gissing's novels : in *Demos* (1886), Kingcote, "the refined, sensitive and pessimistic"[84] prototype of the novelist himself, "tortured with jealously is Isabel's apparent lightness,"[85] and "a demagogue of the working-classes,"[86] typifies Gissing's scientific objectivity with a hostile reaction to it. In *Thyrza* (1887), Thyrza, a factory-girl imbued with the Ruskinian teaching, vehemently reacts to the scientific impact on modern life, and regards industrialization as a bane on human happiness, because her love, meandering through serpentine ways of modern civilization, ends in renunciation and death. In *A Life's Morning* (1888), James Payn transmogrifies her simple pleasures of life into a tragic one, because it is science which is wholly responsible for it. In another famous novel, *The Nether World* (1889), Gissing presents a sharp reaction to scientific march, because it has caused a gloomy panorama of misery, of squalor, and of savagery in the modern life. In *New Grub Streets* (1891), Gissing curses science and its world, in which even authors are forced to struggle in an environment of garrets and basements, often too poor to afford a fire, and slaving daily at the British Museum for an uncertain pittance. In *Born in Exile* (1893), Gissing presents the inner history of a man whose integrity, rather than his happiness, has been affected by science. *In the Year of Jubilee* (1894), *Eve's Ransom* (1895), and *The Whirlpool* (1897), both present Gissing's scientific approach to study the effects of the socialistic programme on different characters and their capacities : Rolfe's uncertainty, in *The Whirlpool*, for example, shows the gist of all these works, namely, whether or not to welcome the onward march of science, the revolt against "The softness and sweetness of civilization,"[87] and he is, ultimately, forced to recognize "the brute savagery of it,"[88] "the very lingo,"[89] "the tongue of Whitechapel blaring lust of life in the track of English guns;"[90] and prognosticates further that the complex social life will prove a curse to the posterity.

But despite an apparent hostile attitude towards science, Gissing prefers to be known as a scientific artist;[91] and, in fact, it is almost a truism to pronounce that it has been his avowed aim, like George Moore's, to write fiction on scientific lines. There is, of course, "a scientific impartiality,"[92] as, for instance, when he explains Mutimer, he draws up what he calls "a tabular exposition of the man's consciousness,"[93] and sets forth the motives impelling or restraining his ambitious democrat, who is on the point of breaking with Emma Vine, the girl of his own class, and marrying the genteel Adela. Such type of scientific objectivity and analysis entitles him to the rank of a scientific novelist, despite his distrust in and hatred against scientific principles; and, in any serious attempt at tracing this positive influence of science on him, even an iota of doubt cannot be raised against his being not a true scientific novelist.

Like George Gissing's, George Moore's temper is highly scientific, as it is his famous statement that "the idea of a new art based upon science, in opposition to the art of the old world that was based on imagination, an art that would explain all things and embrace modern life in its entirety, in its endless ramifications."[94] Moore's is, in fact, an art with "endless ramifications," as were his sources of influences, and science being one of them. To his plastic, receptive nature, he attributes a variety of influences, acknowledging that :

> My soul, so far as I understand it, has very kindly taken colour and form from the many various modes of life that self-will and an impetuous temperament have forced me to indulge in. Therefore I may say that I am free from original qualities, defects, tastes etc., what is mine I have acquired, or, to speak more exactly, chance bestowed, and still bestows, upon me. I came into the world apparently with a nature like a smooth sheet of wax, bearing no impress, but capable of receiving any; of being moulded into all shapes. Nor am I exaggerating when I say I think that I might equally have been a Pharaoh, an ostler, a pimp, an archbishop, and that in the fulfilment of the duties of each a certain measure of success would have been mine.[95]

In fact, "science has been one of the many influences,"[96] moulding and shaping "his plastic nature,"[97] and that compelled him to seek propinquity with many celebrities of fiction in the modern world for evolving his style and craftsmanship as a novelist. It is with this background that we can notice the influence of such naturalists as Flaubert, the Goncourts, and Zola on the works of his first literary phase which witnesses the publication of *A Modern Lover* (1883), *A Mummer's Wife* (1885), *A Drama in Muslin* (1886), *Spring Days* (1888), and *Esther Waters* (1894). But, Balzac's influence is also apparent in *Esther Waters*, and *The Confessions of a Young Man* (1888), and "of the decadent aesthetes, of Pater, of Synge"[98] in his later novels.

In *Avowals*, Moore declares that "my only affectation is complete naturalness."[99] His long training, and the Paterian principle of art, enabled him to evolve a purified and perfected form of the primeval mode of story-telling, essentially the oral mode, which could be used both in epic narrative and in a more transparent and more spontaneous kind of mental analysis than he had been able to realize in the introspective study of Evelyn Innes. In his effort at "the approximation to a sustained kind of naturalness,"[100] with the self-consciousness which was "the correlative to the missing ego,"[101] Moore was succeeding in his life-long effort at "self-creation,"[102] at establishing a "scientific projection of personality of his own."[103] In the *Confessions, Memoirs of my Dead Life* (1906), Hail and Farewell! (1911-14), and *Avowals* (1919), Moore has essayed to project his personality on scientific lines with their various recessions : they are, therefore, the novel — kind of biographical fiction, weaving his recollections of life in a most methodical way with the apparent Proustian stamp.

The analyst in Moore is always at work, and it is the observant eye of the analyst in him that makes his novels highly pregnant with a scientific sense. Moore seems to have dittoed Harding's assertion that the naturalist school of novelists choose trite events of life and put them on the rigorous test of scientific scrutiny and observation before letting them pass off as artistic :

> We do not always choose what you call unpleasant subjects, but we try to go to the roots of things; and the basis of life being material and not spiritual, the analyst inevitably finds himself, sooner or later, handling what this sentimental age calls coarse.... The novel, if it be anything, is contemporary history, an exact and complete reproduction of (the) social surroundings of the age we live in. The poem, on the other hand, is an idealization, and bears the same relation to the novel as the roast beef does to the rich, ripe fruit which you savour when your hunger is satisfied.[104]

The position of Samuel Butler recalls the typical Peacokian relation to two significant ages, *viz.*, the Romantic and the Victorian; to the former, whose associations were as deeper and long-lasting as to the latter. Butler's *Erewhon* was published in 1872; his second important novel *Erewhon Revisted* in 1901, a year terminating the great Victorian age into another; and, his third novel *The Way of all Flesh* began in 1873, finished in 1884 and published in 1903, a year after his death, practically falls into the purview of the modern age from the standpoint of literary chronology. Thus, Butler *sine dubio* bridges two important ages, *viz.*, the Victorian and the Modern; to the former, his associations are as indicative of his ingrained *uberrima fides* in Darwinism as they are of his deep-rooted belief in scientific positivism of the latter. Even greater and more powerful than Meredith's and Hardy's are Butler's reactions to Darwinism; for he admires Darwin's work, and like Meredith and Hardy accepts it with certain reservations; he aims at correcting Darwin's undue insistence on natural selection as the wholesome agency of evolution; and in many passages in his three famous novels, *viz.*, *Erewhon, Erewhon Revisted* and *The Way of all Flesh*, as well as in his other critical works namely, *Alps and Sanctuaries of Piedmons* (1881) and *Ex Voto* (1888), Butler illustrates with both "lambent wit and dialectical skill"[105] his opposite doctrine of "an unconscious memory in living organisms,"[106] by virtue of which they solve their vital problems, and so, by "intelligent striving"[107] rather than "the uninspired weeding-out by natural selection,"[108] progress in complexity and variety.

In all his major novels, Butler deals with many of the Darwinian principles of evolution and their wider repercussions on human life. In *Erewhon*, Ernest Pontifex inculcates a refined Laodiceanism as the wisest rule of life, believing in the omnipresence of a mind and intelligence throughout the universe to which no name can be so fittingly applied as God. According to him, it is true that we may not always know very clearly what is meant by God, and things may not always work together for the particular kind of good that we desire; but there is 'a something' as yet but darkly known which makes right right and wrong wrong, and no man can ultimately fail who obeys the dictates of that voice which we can all hear within us if we will but listen to it. He, therefore, anticipates a spiritual view, unlike Darwin, of the world, since he maintains that life is not the sport of chance and natural accidents, but self-determined — an affair of self-development, of ultimate realization of all the possibilities inheriting in the germ. The universe in itself is instinct with the mind of God : the mind of God is in all that has mind throughout all worlds. If we speak ill of God in our ignorance, it may be forgiven us, but if we speak ill of His Holy Spirit indwelling in good men and women it may not be forgiven us.

In *Erewhon Revisted* and *The Way of all Flesh*, Butler enunciates his doctrine of evolution on the basis of Darwinism, but his evolution is the spiritual evolution of Meredith; though it hardly matters that his God should specifically be identified with, even more definitely than he had done in *Erewhon*, where he maintains that there is no God but the universe, and man in this world is His prophet. He does not seem content with the idea of the Spirit and the Life which creates, governs, and upholds all living things, or a single Being or Animator : his God, being a person, must have a body, must be corporeal, else he does not imagine Him as existent.

The evolutionary belief in Butler enables him to delineate psychologically perfect human portraits : the biologist in him makes his analysis of human mind and heart more logical and scientific. As he always insists that the mental phenomena that matter are commonly not those which leave plain traces on the surface, he explores the instincts, the temperamental dispositions, likes and dislikes, obstinate impulses, of which the individual himself is not more than half aware. He pays more attention to the unconscious than to the conscious realm of mind and motive; it is there, he believes, that the decisive conflicts are fought out, and insignificant events lead ultimately to failure or success, misery or happiness, or rather, as he puts it, to disease and sickness or health and vigour. He considers in a word, a human being to be a moral entity or character with pathological effects; there is a continual insistence on heredity and on every early influence : a character's life is traced from childhood to puberty, to its collision with the facts of sex, and to crime much oftener than will average out in ordinary life. A favourite case has been the 'inferiority complex' in *The Way of all Flesh*, evidencing influence of Freud and Jung and Adler on Butler, and Butler's influence on his disciples and admirers, such as H.G. Wells, Somerset Maugham, Bernard Shaw, J.D. Beresford, Oliver Onions, Frank Swinnerton, Gilbert Cannen, May Sinclair, Clemence Dane, E.M. Delafield, Dorothy Richardson and Virginia Woolf, with the only exception of D.H. Lawrence, who stands apart as possessed of, or possessed by, an innate and almost mystical clairvoyance.

The brilliant luminaries of the scientific movement during the Victorian era not only influenced the major novelists of the day, they also left significant impact on many minor novelists. Lyell, the geologist; Hugh Miller, the biologist; Robert Chambers, the evolutionist; Spencer, the engineer; Huxley, the naturalist; Tyndall, the physicist; Martineau, the unitarian; and Clifford, the scientist — all exerted their profound influence even on the minor novelists of the day. Three main scientific theories, *viz.*, Darwinism, uniformitarianism and naturalism, the first, propounded by Darwin, Spencer and Huxley in main, the second, by Chambers, and the third, by Herschel and others — all left an indelible impact on the novelists. Besides these theories, the influence of the Metaphysical Society, which was founded in 1869, ten years after *The Origin of Species*, and "which consisted both of Gnostics and Agnostics,"[109] such as, of statesmen — Gladstone, Lord Selborne and the Duke of Argyll; of churchmen — Dean Stanley and F.D. Maurice; of Unitarians — Martineau; and of the poets — Tennyson and Browning etc., has also been profound on some minor novelists of the Victorian period, though they have not given as sustained and elaborate manifestation of this scientific impact as the major novelists like Meredith and Hardy have given through their novels.

Such minor novelists during the late Victorian period, of the group of women novelists, are M.E. Braddon (Mrs. Maxwell, 1837-1915), and Ouida (Miss Louisa de la Romee, 1840-1908). Both these women novelists have had the opportunity to meet some members of the Metaphysical Society, and as a result of their occasional meetings with such eminent scientists of the Society as Martineau and Dr. W.G. Ward, these novelists were influenced by the Gnostic as well as Agnostic current of thought of the period. Miss Braddon finds evolutionary principle of the development of life unconvincing until the Meredithian concept of spiritual evolution is added to it. Like many churchmen, such as F.D. Maurice and Duke of Argyll, who were the prominent members of the Metaphysical Society, Miss Braddon regards evolutionary theory as propounded by Darwin and his protagonists as only "one-sided explanation of physical existence of man,"[110] and "it is", she, again, opines, "as lacking in foundation as body without soul."[111] She, therefore, follows the Meredithian evolution of man and not that of the Darwinian one. In her famous novel *Vixen and Ishmael*, though a sensational novel, she has given sporadic references to illustrate his viewpoint regarding man's existence on earth. Secondly, her depth and insight of human psychology, as revealed through her characters, is as remarkable as that of George Eliot.

Miss Ramee, who called herself 'Ouida', is more prolific a novelist than Rhoda Broughton and Edna Lyall, the other women novelists of the day, and even more popular than Miss Braddon. She does not approve of Darwinism as it is; like Miss Braddon, she regards evolution of physical side of man, completely bereft of spiritual element as unsatisfactory. Her concept of evolution is, therefore, more or less Meredithian. In her famous novels *Two Little Women Shoes, Pascarel, Trincotrin* and *Moths*, she has given stray examples of evolutionary process of man, but everywhere, she has taken support from the Meredithian concept of man's evolution, and consequently, she has given due weightage to man's spiritual side and its development. Her social novel *Moths* is characteristically psychological in the sense that there is the psychological study of characters with the psychological insight of George Eliot and Meredith. Her delineation of "certain moods of sexual emotion"[112] is really superb, and "can only be equalled in the pages of George Sand."[113] Her love of nature recalls Wordsworth's and her presentation of its beauty that of Hardy's. Her description of the natural phenomena especially the earth is, in essence, almost Meredithian, and her love of its atmosphere is reminiscent of the Pre-Raphaelite school of artists and poets. But her treatment of the contemporary scientific theories is not as sustained and systematic as that of Meredith's and Hardy's; she seems rather content with their occasional and sporadic allusions to specific discussions only.

Thus, from the foregoing discussion, it becomes sufficiently clear that the spirit of science gradually deepened towards the end of the Victorian period, and by the time Hardy got full public acclaim, Darwinism had become one of the powerful scientific impacts not only on the most aware minds, but also on the minds of the *hoi-polloi*, the rank and file. Meredith and Hardy, both being the most representative novelists of the late Victorian age interpreted Darwinism in their own ways, and since both of them variously applied the Darwinian theory of evolution in their novels, which none of their disciples could ever apply, their treatment of Darwinism requires a separate study in the following chapter.[114]

NOTES

1. Ford, F.M. : *The English Novel*, p. 80.
2. Pritchett, V.S. : *The English Novel*, p. 102.
3. Wright, W.F. : *Art and Substance in George Meredith*, p. 23.
4. Henkin, L.J. : *Darwinism in English Novel 1860-1910*, p. 117.
5. *Ibid.*
6. Smalley, F. : *Science and Nineteenth Century*, p. 158.
7. Howell, W.D. : *Criticism and Fiction*, p. 206.
8. Fox, R. : *The Novel and the People*, p. 16.
9. Stang, Richard : *The Theory of the Novel in English*, p. 50.
10. Williams, Harold : *Two Centuries in English Novel*, p. 192.
11. Chew, S.C. : *Thomas Hardy : Poet and Novelist*, p. 72.
12. Muller, H.J. : *Modern Fiction : A Study of Values*, p. 39.
13. Johnson, R.B. : *Women Novelists*, p. 59.
14. *Ibid.*, p. 60.
15. *Ibid.*
16. *Far From the Madding Crowd*, p. 48.
17. *Ibid.*, p. 9.
18. *Ibid.*, p. 13.
19. *Ibid.*, pp. 162-63.
20. *Ibid.*, p. 163.
21. *The Mayor of Casterbridge*, p. 36.
22. *Ibid.*, pp. 76-77.
23. *Far From the Madding Crowd*, pp. 80-81.
24. *The Mayor of Casterbridge*, p. 25.
25. *Ibid.*, p. 313.
26. Abercrombie, L. : *Thomas Hardy : A Critical Study*, p. 151.
27. Weber, C.J. : *Hardy in America*, p. 25.
28. Cecil, D. : *Hardy the Novelist*, p. 62.
29. Elliott, A.P. : *Fatalism in the Works of Thomas Hardy*, p. 40.
30. *Ibid.*
31. Brown, D. : *Thomas Hardy*, p. 90.
32. MacDowall, A.S. : *Thomas Hardy : A Critical Study*, p. 34.
33. *Ibid.*, p. 50.
34. Guerard, A.J. : *Hardy : The Novels and Stories*, p. 140.
35. Priestiley, J.B. : *George Meredith*, p. 21.
36. Bailey, E.J. : *The Novels of George Meredith*, p. 80.
37. Sassoon, S. : *George Meredith*, p. 27.
38. Photiades, C. : *George Meredith*, p. 84.

39. *The Dynasts*, Preface, p. iii.
40. *The Ordeal of Sir Austin Feverel,* p. 77.
41. *Ibid.,* p. 101.
42. *Vittoria,* p. 20.
43. *The Poetry and Philosophy of George Meredith,* p. 73.
44. Quoted, Curle, R.P.H. : *Aspects of George Meredith*, p. 62.
45. *Ibid.*, p. 258.
46. *Ibid.*
47. *Emilia in England*, p. 54.
48. Ellis, S.M. : *Life of George Meredith*, pp. 275-77.
49. *Ibid.*, p. 301.
50. Sencourt, R.E. : *Life of George Meredith*, pp. 179-81.
51. Henkin, L.J. : *Darwinism in the English Novel 1860-1910*, p. 55.
52. *The Dewy Morn*, Preface, p. iii.
53. *The Story of my Heart,* p. 74.
54. *Ibid.,* p. 75.
55. Thomas, E. : *Jefferies*, p. 19.
56. Thom, A.F. : *The Life Worship of Richard Jefferies*, p. 104.
57. Salt, H.S. : *Richard Jefferies : A Study*, p. 50.
58. Looker, S.J. (ed.) : *The Worthing Cavalcade*, p. 39.
59. Maclean, C.M. : *Life of Richard Jefferies*, p. 207.
60. Merton, E.S. : *The Autobiographical Novels of Mark Rutherford*, p. 29.
61. Stone, W. : *Life of Richard Jefferies*, p. 182.
62. Stock, I. : *William Hale White*, p. 49.
63. Roberton, M. : *Richard Jefferies : a Critical Study*, p. 63.
64. Baker, E.A. : *The History of English Novel*, Vol. ix, pp. 89-99.
65. *The Autobiography*, p. 10.
66. *Ibid.*
67. *Ibid.*, p. 25.
68. *Ibid.*
69. *Ibid,* p. 29.
70. *Mark Rutherford's Deliverance,* p. 23.
71. *Thomson's Poems,* p. 105.
72. Ward, A.C. : *George Gissing*, p. 125.
73. Swinburton, S. : *George Gissing the Novelist*, p. 90.
74. Harrison, A. : *George Gissing*, p. 26.
75. Gapp, S.V. : *George Gissing : Classicist*, p. 62.
76. Donnelly, M. : *Gissing, Grave Comedian*, p. 13.
77. Bjorkmann, E. : *Voices of Tomorrow*, p. 73.

78. *Letters*, p. 200.
79. *Ibid.*, p. 280.
80. *Ibid.*, p. 268.
81. *Headlong Hall,* p. 4.
82. *Letters,* p. 269.
83. *Ibid.*, pp. 268-69.
84. *Demos,* p. 17.
85. *Ibid.*, p. 19.
86. *Ibid.*
87. *The Whirlpool,* p. 13.
88. *Ibid.*, p. 19.
89. *Ibid.*
90. *Ibid.*
91. Swinburne, Frank : *George Gissing : a Critical Study*, p. 10.
92. Baker, E.A. : *The History of English Novel*, vol. IX, p. 135.
93. *Demos*, p. 21.
94. *Confessions of a Young Man*, p. 7.
95. *Ibid.*, p. 9.
96. Brown, M.J. : *Moore : a Reconsideration*, p. 61.
97. Sechler, R.P. : *George Moore : a Disciple of Walter Pater*, p. 113.
98. Hone, J.H. : *Life of George Moore*, p. 70.
99. *Avowals*, p. 115.
100. Brown, M.J. : *Moore : a Reconsideration*, p. 81.
101. *Ibid.*, p. 83.
102. *Ibid.*
103. Hone, J.H. : *Life of George Moore*, p. 187.
104. *A Mummer's Wife*, p. 39.
105. Baker, E.A. : *The History of the English Novel*, Vol. X, p. 256.
106. *Ibid.*
107. *Ibid.*
108. *Ibid.*
109. Compton-Rickett, Arthur : *A History of English Literature*, p. 593.
110. *Vixen and Ishmael*, p. 14.
111. *Ibid.*
112. Compton-Rickett, Arthur : *op. cit.*, p. 533.
113. *Ibid.*
114. 'Scientific Outlook of Thomas Hardy in His Novels' was presented at the XXIV session of the AIETC held at Ajmer on December 27-29, 1978; 'Science and the Trio of RGM' was presented at the XXX session

of the AIETC held at Madras on November 27-30, 1979; Thomas Hardy's Fictional Art' was presented at DSC, PCBCH (AUA) on 2-10-1969; 'Impact on Science on Late Victorian Fiction' and '*Far From the Madding Crowd* : A Fictional Feat in Story-Telling' were delivered as Invited Lectures at the Academic Staff College, Lucknow University, Lucknow (India) during 1992; 'Scientific Thought and Late Victorian Fiction' was also published in *ISTVE*, Delhi, pp. 113-44; also published in *VFSNA,* Delhi, 2002, pp. 105-32.

10

Darwinism in the Novels of George Meredith and Thomas Hardy

GEORGE MEREDITH was twelve years senior to Thomas Hardy in age : the former was thirty-one years of age, while the latter was only nineteen at the time of the publication of *The Origin of Species* — the scientific landmark to put a considerable awareness on the literary minds of the day; and, to divide, with a sharp-edged weapon of questioning tendency, the early Victorian milieu from the latter one. Both Hardy and Meredith were immensely influenced by Darwinism : rather, both were sustained and nourished on Darwinian pabulum more enduringly and logically than perhaps all their predecessors and coevals; because both accorded their approbation and consent to Darwinism as it was basically enunciated by Darwin himself and subsequently modified with the possibilities of wider implications by his noted protagonists and admirers — Spencer, Huxley, Lecky, John Morley, Leslie Stephen and other followers. Both manifested their acceptance of Darwinism through their novels : both accepted the movement of the advance of science, evolution being one of its branches of knowledge : "both recognized the vital fact that Darwinism could offer many reasonable and logical answers to many insoluble conundrums of life and religion."[1] Both recognized "evolution in itself absolutely unarmed with any other ethical or moral succour"[2] as sufficiently a rational explanation of the development of life. Both regarded Darwinism as the logical corrective to the contemporary religious superstitions : both recommended and applauded a scientific bent of mind to inquire into the corruptible layers of different creeds and dogmas. Both acknowledged the sway of the Darwinian dictate on the contemporary thought.

But there are subtle and distinguishing points in their acceptance of Darwinism "that vertically cleave their belief to be manifested in their novels."[3] In fact, Hardy accepted the whole theory of evolution without any iota of doubt, even that of "natural selection"[4] as the causative agency : whereas Meredith kept his unflinching faith in intuition, in spontaneity, and in free will, pleading that reason, as its frontiers are circumscribed, and its sphere limited, it cannot explain every enigma of life; he unlike Hardy never allowed himself to become obsessed with the idea of the inexorable working of natural laws : he repudiated, unlike Hardy again, any contention and plea that mind and conduct were equally at the mercy of a system of causation, a notion that would undermine and annihilate individuality.

Meredith believes in creative evolution which "practically connotes"[5] the spiritual evolution of R.N. Tagore and Aurobindo Ghosh of India; of Bergson and Schopenhauer of France. Meredith's faith in intuition, spontaneity and free will corresponds with the belief in the immortality and pre-existence of soul of the Hindus; of the Buddhists; of the Pharisees among the Hebrews; of the Assyrians; and of the Babylonians. The Alexandrian Jews, imbued with the doctrine of an individual intuition, and the Schopenhauer palingenesis, soaked in indestructible existence of free will, have much in common with the Meredithian concept of intuition, a concept beyond the Hardyian acceptance of the physical evolution of Darwinism.

In fact, Hardy draws succour and support from Darwinism "to make and rationalize a way of life — a tragic and pessimistic vision of the world,"[6] which he crystallizes and shapes all the more "with the touchstone of the evolutionary principles of the day."[7] Hardy's view of life, as presented in his novels, is a view devoid of soul or intuition : it is a view that is highly scientific and full of the preponderance of good : it is rather the Biblical Monotheism which makes him believe that the retribution of good is good; of bad, bad, in a typical Christian tone. On the contrary, Meredith accepts Darwinism to the extent in full to which it offers scientific explanation to the development of life; but fully realizing that science has its limitations and that it can hardly solve the inner creative puzzles, Meredith goes much deeper to explain man's soul and intuition leaving reason only at the gateway of science. In a word, Hardy's position is one of a Sufi among the Mohammedans; a Palestinean Jew among the Hebrews; a Herodotus among the Egyptians; a Pythagoras among the Hellenes; who believes in intuitive sense of good and bad, who has a strong predilection for essential goodness in human nature; but who does not accept the principle of intuition and of creative process of soul which, of course, drives life towards perfection simply because it is not explained by reason; simply because it transcends much higher than the range of bestial reason.

Meredith's faith in an intelligence transcending the reason, and in a power within man and not outside and beyond him corresponds with Hardy's supreme will controlling all things, sentient as well insentient : but his faith in such intuitions as those of an unconscious memory, of a vital impulse, and of a creative energy, urging the living creatures forward, and of an insight solving difficulties as they arise and evolving finer organs to cope with new emergencies, smacks of the Bergsonian philosophy of creative evolution, and makes him entitled to the appellation of a Bergsonian before Bergson; of a creative evolutionist before modern evolutionists. With Meredith the hereditary transmission theory or the cellular transmission theory of Darwin is a source of inspiration : it is not the end of his creative evolution. The tabula rase belief seems to cut no favour with him : it is, at its best, a stepping-stone to jump over to some higher intuitive creation, where reason and science have their significant roles to play, and where they do not become the separate entities to dominate the overall picture of life. With Hardy, it is so; for him reason and science have formed a particular view of life, which he incessantly presents in his novels. Even his higher vision of life is conditioned by the limits of scientific reason, on the contrary :

> Or is it that some high plan betides,
> And yet not understood,
> Of Evil stormed by Good,
> We the Fornlorn Hope over which Achievement Strides?[8]

In fact, Hardy is apparently moved by the scientific impact of the day, especially of Darwinism, and he is as "spontaneous of prey"[9] to the contemporary Victorian agnosticism and proverbial scepticism as many of his coevals and successors were, such as Swinburne, James Thomson, John Davidson, Lord de Tabley, W.E. Henley, Stevenson, Richard Jefferies and Francis Thompson — to name only a few luminaries who reacted against the impact of science in their own ways. Hardy, like Swinburne, has revolted against man's inhumanity for man; voiced against human limitations and celestial injustice; and has vociferously presented a real plight and predicament of human beings in his tragedies : like James Thompson, he has visioned the gloom of a universe, out of suicidal despair, in which there is nothing real but man's hopelessness; and, also imagined a world on scientific lines, which ultimately grows conscious in human mind — "Glory to man in the highest! for Man is the master of things;"[10] like, John Davidson, he has prognosticated much earlier the abyss of stark materialism where there is no need of Gods as they were man's mistake and, hence, a fallacious imagination worth sinking into oblivion, reversing the age-old maxim that God made man in His own image to Man has created the gods in his own image, asking, therefore, to ostracize Jupiter, Apollo, Pluto, Jehovah and Thor : like Tabley, he has challenged divine justice indignantly;[11] like Henley, he has defied 'Divine Artificer' with a distinguishable force of stoicism;[12] like Stevenson, he has shown an unflinching faith in the essential goodness of human nature despite its reduction to a meaningful causative agency : like Richard Jefferies, he has exhorted us to accept the unparalleled and colossal disaster of death with a mystical yearning for an intenser and more scientific communion with and appreciation of an illimitable cosmos of thought : like Francis Thompson and other decadent literary artists of the concluding part of the age, the *fin-de-siecle*, he has resolved to wage of ruthless war against the social cruelty and injustice "to derive the maximum pleasure and consolation that life can ever offer to human beings."[13] These manifestations of Darwinism or the evolutionary principles through the works of the contemporary artists were quite obvious; and, amongst them all, Hardy has manifested them in his tragedies and comedies, perhaps even more systematically and logically than others. One or two of the salient features of Darwinism — such as the principle of domestication, of mutation, of struggle for existence, of natural selection are traceable in the works of the above-mentioned luminaries : but in Hardy's novels, a balanced and more elaborate picture of Darwinism is copiously and logically traceable. In Meredith's novels, there is an elaborate depiction of the evolutionary tendencies plus the intuitive searching "for immortalizing human soul,"[14] for glorifying man's good deeds by drawing a close resemblance that many religions and philosophies of the world have done, especially the Hindus amongst the Indians, and the Pharisees amongst the Hebrews.

With the acceptance of Darwinism, Hardy was invested with an accurate, or rather say, almost the mathematical vision of a neutral world, in which the soulless mechanism operates constantly and ruthlessly but evenly, producing good or evil, crushing evil or good, without bias one way or the other. Nature for him therefore, appears just like a vast engine, run by a blind impulsion, a Will that knows not why it acts : it is "only able to work by Law."[15] Science made him exclude the supernatural, ignore the individual : it would regard a creative will, especially one that was unconscious and controlled by something else, as an absurdity : but his essentially religious bent of mind goads him on to an approximation of a 'Divine Artificer,'[16] a source of energy, a poetic semblance of the Biblical Monotheism.

The Hardyian vision is thus basically swayed by Darwinism : it gave a vehement jolt to his well-entrenched orthodox Christian view of 'God' and world; so far he held sacrosanct in various ways of life. Hardy now recognized how Darwinism could crumble the pillars of the majestic edifice of the Evangelical theology, Christian religion and mythology : and, with the acceptance of the wider implications of Darwinism, further, the remainings of the vacillating supremacy of ramshackle religion got another "nerve-shattering blow,"[17] which naturally shook every great voice of the age in his divine belief.

This mental vision of Hardy is systematically to be traced in his pastoral extravaganzas, miscellaneous novels, pastoral comedies, pastoral romances and pastoral tragedies. His pastoral extravaganza, *i.e.*, *The Well Beloved* (1897), published serially as *The Pursuit of the Well-Beloved* in 1892; his pastoral romances, *i.e.*, *Under the Greenwood Tree* (1872), *Far From the Madding Crowd* (1874), *A Pair of Blue Eyes* (1875), *The Trumpet Major* (1880), and *The Woodlanders* (1887) present his world "set in a Darwinian Conception :"[18] there is the acceptance of "the physical side of evolution :"[19] there is "the study of environment and surroundings to fit in on the basis of struggle and natural selection."[20] Darwinism, as a whole, on certain characteristic components of this theory, such as the principle of natural selection, the theory of domestication, the principle of mutation; and finally, the principle of struggle for existence — can be traced in various manifestations in his novels of these two classifications.

Hardy's comedies fully manifest Darwinism : his novels of ingenuity, though they lack the intensity and death of the total acceptance of Darwinism as in his ripened and more perfect tragedies; yet in the acceptance of biological evolution in relation to the surroundings and environment, rather the essential prelude to the bigger drama of Darwinism — these comedies such as *The Hand of Ethelberta* (1875), *A Laodicean* (1881), and *Two on a Tower* (1882) become finer and more artistic than even his tragedies.

Hardy's tragedies are, in a way, the Darwinian enunciation of Evolution : [21] for, the chief tenets of Darwinism are copiously traceable in them. *The Return of the Native* (1878) propounds *inter alia* the basic concept of Darwinism — the theory of natural selection; *The Mayor of Casterbridge* (1886), the theory of Immanent Will as later improved upon by Darwin's supporters and protagonists such as Herbert Spencer and T.H. Huxley; *Tess of the D'Urbervilles* (1891), the theory of struggle for existence alloyed with the Biblical Monotheism; and, *The Simpletons* and *Hearts Insurgent*, published serially in 1894 and 1895, revised and issued as *Jude the Obscure* (1896), the theory of domestication, of mutation plus the overall tragic vision soaked in pessimism with the characteristic Sophoclean and Aeschylean stamp.

Between *Far From the Madding Crowd* and *The Return of the Native*, Hardy wrote *The Hand of Ethelberta, The Trumpet Major, Two on a Tower, A Laodicean, The Well Beloved*, and *Desperate Remedies*, which he termed as the '*Novels of Ingenuity*', in which there is a combination of romances, fantasies, and extravaganzas plus Darwinism of purely a theoretical nature : and in them, Hardy's brain lies fallow to digest various principles of Darwinism and its wider implications. The young astronomer of *Two on a Tower* watches the stars with a frightening sense of the incommensurable magnitude of the stellar universe in a Godless Darwinian world; and puts his senior darling and himself — the two insignificant and tiny human beings in juxtaposition to the big stars with no protection with the mock-providence, the President of the Immortals of Tess; and finally, outcries to visualize his deep despondency, helplessness and meaninglessness of life on a globe, where the machine is automatically moving, and where the clogs of the machinery are the lives of men dearly wishing to live in the world; and where the meaning of life is conspicuously missing. St. Cleeve's nightmare is the "plethoric growth of knowledge"[22] of science, but equally formidable and haunting, like Hardy's himself, is his ghost of science terrifying "simultaneously with the stunting of wisdom."[23] One notices the impact of Darwinism even in the nightmares of the astronomer :

> It is the terrors of the sky that thrill and fascinate St. Cleeve, and sometimes give him nightmares : "if...you are restless and

> anxious about the future, study astronomy at once. Your troubles will be reduced amazingly. But your study will reduce them in a singular way, by reducing the importance of everything. So that science is still terrible, even as a panacea. It is quite impossible to think at all adequately of the sky — of what the sky substantially is, without feeling it as a juxtaposed nightmare.[24]

One of the cardinal tenets of Darwinism is the struggle for existence culminating in the survival of the fittest : the stronger species or genus annihilate by way of eating or destruction or otherwise the weaker ones : the smaller fish is engulfed by the bigger one because it is a natural law of evolution. In the struggle for existence only the stronger ones survive : the weaker species automatically become extinct; and in their stead the existing ones evolve further to get their comfortable adjustment to their natural surroundings and environment. Amongst the lower species this struggle is not so complicated and complex as it is in the higher species. Amongst human beings, this struggle for existence is rather more complex and intenser than animals. Hardy accepts this aspect of Darwinism *in toto*; and in his tragedies, there is the fullest manifestation of this principle more than his comedies; and it is why, John Holloway terms his philosophy, as enunciated through his tragedies, as "the philosophy of natural living."[25]

In *Far From the Madding Crowd*, all the chief characters — Gabriel Oak, Bathsheba Everdene, Serjeant Troy and Boldwood, besides the minor ones such as Henry, Bottom, Poorgrass, Jan Coggan and Fanny — struggle for existence, in which only the stronger ones survive. Oak emerges triumphant with a strong sense of finality, because of his unswerving endurance and limitless capacity to encounter all trials and tribulations of life. He suffers loss of his sheep-herding even while he is not a wealthy and effluent shepherd, but he endures this cruel buffet of fate very calmly : afterwards, his heart is broken due to flirtations of Bathsheba : then various public insults are hurled upon him by Serjeant Troy and Boldwood : but ultimately, Boldwood and Troy as well as Bathsheba — all succumb to their elemental passions of love, jealousy and hatred, because it was all their hereditary possession, and there was no escape for them from their surroundings and environment.

Boldwood, who is the traditional calm, self-disciplined nature stung to infatuation by a woman's capricious blandishments; Troy, who is the rake in a military tunic, selfish and cynical, though not quite unfeeling, a trifle histrionic, and irresistibly debonair; and Bathsheba, who is a raw piece of elemental passions — all succumb to their nature that they got by inheritance from their ancestors. They fail to move with their changing nature : they lack the skill to live naturally. Even Hardy's protestation that "God was palpably present in the country, and the devil had gone with the world to town,"[26] could not save them from their final decay thought they lived in the country of God, and not in the town of devil. Even amidst the "flossy catkins of the later kinds, fern-sprouts like bishops' crosiers, the square-headed moschatel, the odd cuckoo-pint" — looking "like an apoplectic saint in a niche of malachite, — snow-swite ladies' — smokes, the toothwort, approximating to human flesh, the enchanter's night-shade, and the black-petaled doleful-bells"[27] — all these fully evolved natural objects properly nourished by and timely superintended after by Hardy's President of the Immortals, Boldwood, Bathsheba and Troy — all do not know to evolve naturally : they find themselves misfit in their surroundings and environment : they fail to struggle for existence for long and are, ultimately, defeated. On the contrary, Gabriel Oak continues to live naturally : he does not suffer from the paralysis of will; rather, he fights against the Immanent Will or destructive snares of his bodily elements. He succeeds in the end, because he endures all trials and tribulations, because nature selects him to be the fittest one, because he proves himself to be the strongest species.

In *The Return of the Native*, the principle of the struggle for existence predominates the entire action : Wildeve, Clym, Diggory Venn, Eustacia and Thomasin — all struggle for existence in accordance with the inner forces and external challenges. Wildeve and Eustacia die by way of drowning because of their elemental passions, because they find themselves unable to adjust to their surroundings and environment. Clym and Thomasin partly survive owing to their partial adjustment to their environment : it is only Diggory Venn who successfully survives to the last on account of his total acceptance of and adaptability to his surroundings.

In *The Mayor of Casterbridge*, Henchard, Farfrae, Newson, Susan, Elizabeth Jane and Lucetta — all have to struggle hard for their existence. Henchard is destroyed by the unusual fit of the paralysis of an Immanent Will : Farfrae comparatively survives more : Susan and Lucetta die miserably : but Elizabeth survives more. In *Tess of the D'Urbervilles*, Tess, Alec and Angel — all struggle hard for existence. Tess is destroyed, so does Alec : Angel survives though with broken and delighted hopes. In *Jude the Obscure*, Jude Fawley, Phillotson, Arabella Donn and Sue — all struggle for existence; but all, finding themselves unable to adjust according to their surroundings and environment, die and are no more remembered and worshipped; rather they become as naturally extinct as the stuff of a dream.

Thus, Darwinism made Hardy express in his novels a set vision of the world which is governed by a force neither good nor bad but indifferent to man's feelings : human individuality and his desires always being in conflict with such an indifferent power. "Happiness is," he writes in *The Mayor of Casterbridge*, "but the occasional episode in a general drama of pain."[28] His men and women, therefore, struggle for it, and are always snatching at happiness, striving to express and to fulfil themselves and breaking themselves against a power that takes no heed of them. For this disproportion between moments of happiness and sorrow — the Hardyian proverbial pessimism, he has a double-edged vision of life and world to set. If he sees the littleness of life, he also sees the greatness of it : there being no contempt for human will, endurance and passion. Since all is not futile, and since all is not hateful, Hardy's world has something to struggle for, not merely for pessimism, but also for glorifying at least the cardinal virtues of life.

Hardy accepts Darwinism in so far as it explains the biological evolution of man : nowhere does he present a world bereft of noble virtues or sombre visions. Often even the landscape is obscured by the heavy mist of doubt, the mortals who wander about this landscape appear to be governed by cruel chance that gives them no option, as to the direction of their wanderings. No doubt, he often implies that "there is some kind of governing power beyond and behind the material universe,"[29] but there is no fixed belief in any kind of the Meredithian compensation of spirit. Again, whatever power there be behind, the universe "is obviously of no utilitarian value :"[30] the claims of Christianity as a world-religion "seems preposterous to him."[31] He is, therefore, as absolute a Pagan as though he had written from thousand years before Christ, because all religions are alike imperfect to him. It is why, he has often been called a materialist or atheist; whereas, in fact, he is neither of these : because Eustacia rises above all materialism — she will not break her sacred marriage vows for Damon Wildeve, because she has a soul to save; and again, her belief in Heaven persists till the end though Heaven is accused of cruelty for devising tortures for her.

Hardy's Darwinism manifests itself in his novels in one another form of determinism also. According to Hardy, "human action is not free but determined by motives,"[32] which are regarded as "external forces acting on the will."[33] The characters, therefore, would appear to be helpless; and yet the tragic characters do not appear to be mere "puppets jerked by a malicious fate."[34] Were it so, they would miss an essential condition of tragedy. A towering and laudable desire may be doomed to be brought level with futility, but one profoundly enjoys the brave quality of the assertion of desire : a life abject in sorrow is nothing enjoyable and, therefore, nothing tragical. The tragic characters, who endure the most pitiless destiny are never in the least abject : this destiny, however, this destroying or levelling or assimilating power, is not merely external to the characters who contend with it : that would be precluded by Hardy's characteristic conception of necessity. There is certainly a good deal of external compulsion in the working of his plots, and it sometimes takes the form of coincidence : but the external pressure or coincidence is always far less important to the significance of the whole than the conflict in the minds of the characters, which constitutes his tragic apprehension or vision of the world.

It appears that in Hardy's novels, it is the intellect which predominates the whole action, whereas in Meredith's novels, it is the heart which virtually triumphs the whole action. About God, Hardy is indifferent, whereas Meredith is full of reverence. Meredith does not consider any human activity without heavenly order, but for Hardy, it is not essential that the dictate of God should always, interfere. 'The President of the Immortals' of Hardy's *Tess* is indifferent to human actions and a man is killed by this unseen force just for its own pleasure. But this attitude of Hardy to God is not, in any way, obstructive to his being an incorrigible optimist about the essential goodness of man. Like a true Christian, he has a very strong belief in the fundamentally positive fine nature of all the human beings. Yes, it is altogether a different matter that a human being has to struggle incessantly to strive perfection in life.

"Hardy's Immanent Will is the Darwinian creative or evolving energy or an inner urge,"[35] which is "responsible for self-development and self-movement."[36] "Oneness and immanentia are inseparably bound together :"[37] each is a necessary corollary and consequence of the other and both are of equal importance; and this inner force has five characteristic features : first, the Will is one and Immanent, for it is represented as the one and only source from which all life and activity are flowing and its "patterns underlie all mundane phenomena :[38] secondly, the Will is autonomous, determining everything, it is itself determined by nothing : human events are but the manifestations of its mysterious designs : and with no earthly power can swerve the bias of its power which governs all things by its clock-wise laws : thirdly, the Will is unconscious, viewless and voiceless, the turner of the wheel works unconsciously in an automatic sense unwearyingly why or whence, and like a hunter its drowsed fingers dance with skilled unmindfulness : fourthly, the Will is aimless. Thinking on it does not weigh its thought and no answer is given to the question — why does it so and so and ever so? And if it has any aim at all, it is a listless aim. Lastly, the Will is indestructible : endless like the wheel of Destiny; it turns, it works eternal artistries in circumstances; it has woven with an absent head since life first was, and ever will so weave. It is then the Immanent Will or God which is the supreme power, governing the whole world, all life, and all affairs. It is an abstract power and is "utterly indifferent to life of man,"[39] and, it therefore, works like "a powerful automatic machine rolling on its own predestined way."[40]

Conditioned by this Immanent Will, man in Hardy's novels is "a willing rather than a thinking animal,"[41] and he is ruled not by reason but by "the mysterious inclinations of his nature."[42] The Will within him urges him on, often "against his better judgment."[43] It is some inexplicable power that draws together Eustacia and Wildeve : Alec and Tess : Farfrae and Lucetta : Jude and Sue. Lovely specimens of humanity like Eustacia and Tess are crushed bitterly, idealists like Clym and Oak are fatigued in their hopes, and bounty is scattered in the path of the undeserving like Wildeve and Clym and Troy. So the secret of Hardy's tragic power and tragic intensity lies in the opposition between the blind unconscious operation of circumstances and the passionate consciousness of man.

In Meredith's novels, there is "the struggle for existence,"[44] but it occurs "under the providence of a God"[45] that "repays and rewards good and punishes bad."[46] Those who struggle for existence on the lines of goodness, virtue and fine intuition, they are better evolved species not only physically but also spiritually; they live longer than those living by the sheer force of reason and logic only. Darwinism confirms their biological evolution, and intuition their spiritual one. Hardy's acceptance of Darwinism gives a rational explanation of the development of man, so does Meredith's; but Hardy does not go beyond the physical evolution, and places both intuition and free will at the mercy of natural causation, which Meredith, of course, rejects. Meredith's explanation of the creative will and godly intuition is above Hardy's explanation of logic and reason in the light of scientific evolutionary theories of the period. Hardy's Darwinism, therefore, connotes his acceptance of the biological evolution plus his faith in the Biblical Monotheism; whereas, Meredith's is his acceptance of the biological evolution plus his faith in a benevolent God. Man struggles in Meredith's world for existence in order to glorify good and enhance virtue, and finally to make this world a heaven of Gods : whereas, in Hardy's, man struggles for existence for mere existence's sake; good deeds as preached by the Christian religion are a superadded pleasure and calm to it. Hardy's universe is inhabited by helpless, tiny human beings with their puny endeavours; whereas, Meredith's is inhabited by persons of ennobling creative forces : in one, the gloom of life is predestined, in another, it is self-made and self-created.

Even a cursory glance over Meredith's novels will reveal the fact that in his universe, man's struggle for existence, and even his natural selection, the two cardinal principles of Darwinism have "a noble effect :"[47] it will be seen how man's trials and tribulations leave him "a better evolved species"[48] both from the point of view of biology and spirituality. The barber, Shibli Bagarag, in *The Shaving of Shagpat*, with his winged emprise by oracular prophecy, dauntlessly encountering sorceresses and jinness, baffling illusions and paralysing enchantments; the imposter Shagpat, with the Peacockian stamp, and the magician Bhanavar with the traditions of Thessalian magic, which Meredith's father-in-law, Thomas Love Peacock, found in Apuleius and Petronius; Sir Austin Feverel in *The Ordeal of Sir Richard Feverel*, with his intellectual load of a scientist and psycho-analyst; Richard, the son, with his worldly inexperience and falling into the toils of a siren, bribed by a villainous rival, for Lucy; Richmond Roy in *Evan Harrington* with his sombre vision of good and bad; Even Harrington, with his impersonation of youth; Rhoda and Dahlia in *Rhoda Fleming* with their feminine psychology; Nevil Beauchamp in *Beauchamp's Career* with worldly involvements and political acumen; Sir Willoughby in *The Egotist* with his egotistical pronouncements; Mrs. Caroline Norton in *Diana of the Crossways* with her romantic bent of mind — all struggle for existence in their own ways, and all achieve not only the physical evolution, but also the spiritual one, or at least, justify their decay or evolution, according to their quantum of goodness or evil. They, therefore, testify to the Meredithian Darwinism which in not wholly divested of divinity.

In Meredith's novels, the principles of struggle for existence and that of natural selection operate in a process which has its own ethical gravitation. Unlike Hardy, his universe has some ethical value and magnitude, and his characters accordingly evolve and perish. The appalling tragic gloom of Hardy, in the Meredithian world, intensifies not because the Immanent Will suffers from a paralytic hit, or because the President of the Immortals has ended his sports with the poor and tiny human beings. It all happens because his characters repay their deeds; the law of Nemesis overtakes them; the principle of poetic justice testifies to their doings. Even the bad has a grain of good, and it is not repressed with any reason under the triumphant gloom of Death forthwith. Richard Feverel, for instance, despite his selfishness and headstrong youth struggles for a happy existence under the benevolent protection of God :

> When we have gone out and seized it in the highways, certain inscrutable laws are sure to be at work to bring us to the criminal bar sooner or later.... Richard Turpin wanted both — singing 'Money or life' to the world : Richard Feverel has done the same, substituting 'happiness' for money, frequently synonyms. He was just as much as highway robber as his fellow Dick, so that those who have failed to recognize him as a hero, may now regard him in that light. Meanwhile the world he has squeezed, looks exceedingly patient and beautiful.[49]

Despite Meredith's acceptance of Darwinism like that of Hardy's, his vision of life ever remains sombre and sane : he never regards life as a cup of poison or as a vale of tears, rather he regards it as a cup of ale enduringly to be enjoyed and consumed to its full. Meredith's characters, even after facing a lot of trials and tribulations in life, even after enduring various buffets, turn out to be finely evolved species of good nature. They are neither repressed by the wickedness of their fellows, nor are they pessimists owing to the nonchalance of the cruel governance of the universe : rather they prove, in the end, stout persons of sombre vision, of essential goodness; because Meredith himself regards virtuous living as superior to anything else in life :

> Philosophy bids us to see that we are not pretty as rose-pink, not so repulsive as dirty drab; and that instead of everlastingly shifting those barren aspects, the light of ourselves is wholesome, bearable, fructifying, finally a delight.... And imagine the celestial refreshment of having a pure decency in the place of sham; real flesh; a soul born active, wind-beaten, but ascending. Honourable will fiction then appear; honourable, a fount of life, an aid to life, quick with our blood.... Worse than that alternative dirty drab, your recurring rose-pink is rebuked by hideous revelations of the filthy foul; for nature will force her way, and if you try to stifle her by drawing, she comes up, not the fairest part of her uppermost.[50]

In Meredith's novels, the struggle for existence is not hastened to a final destination being proportionately added and abetted by nature and its agents, as in Hardy's novels. Nature 'red-in-tooth-and-claw,' frightening the tiny, helpless human being, scoffing and violently laughing at his miserable lot, of the Hardyian setting is conspicuously absent in Meredith's novels. Indeed, Hardy's Darwinism strips nature of its essential compassion for man; whereas Meredith's does not do so, rather it invests nature with a strong sense of sympathy and pity for him. However, it is not to be construed that the Meredithian nature has the romantic transcendentalism : for him, nature is not a brooding spirit of peace as for Wordsworth, nor the swift-winged spirit of Love as with Shelley : nor, on the other hand, is merely an exquisite mechanism, unmoral if not immoral, as with Tennyson — nor a cheery, amusing, joyful comrade as to Browning.[51] The most effective component of nature, *i.e.*, the earth, to Meredith is a kind, though Spartan mother — who attracts us to her by those elemental bonds that tell us that we come from her, yet repels us because she has nothing but silence or grim rebuffs and reproaches for our desperate and often wanton hopes and high aspirations.[52] Man :

May entreat, aspire,
He may despair, and she has never heed,
She drinking his warm sweat will soothe his need —
Not his desire.[53]

Hardy's Darwinism excludes nature as of inconsequential phenomenon; whereas Meredith's Darwinism includes nature as of vital significance, because man cannot, do, according to Meredith, without the rough, yet needful education of this great mother — something of what we may learn from her. Meredith gives us, in Melampus (the physician naturalist), the natural treasure as the gateway to knowledge :

For him the woods were a home,
And gave him the key of knowledge.[54]

But the Meredithian joy in earth as a source of inspiration and strength is a corollary to his conception of man's spiritual evolution and intuitive maturity. Meredith conceives nature as something supplementary to man's evolution from the point of view of inner-perfection : it is not an ally to soulless universe of Hardy to put a dampening effect on man's evolving personality. Even the splendour and rapture of the physical side of his nature, the magic of Spring in *Love in a Valley* have a more sombre and ennobling impact on man's drooping spirits than Hardy's nature of the Valley of Blackmoor on Tess and Alec. The oft-quoted lines from *The Lark Ascending* ennoble every individual even with the worst drooping spirits of defeatism, instead of heightening their gloom :

He rises and begins to round :
He drops the silver chain of sound,
Of many links without a break
In chirrup, whistle, slur, and shake :[55]

Or

All intervolve and spreading wide,
Like water-dimples down a tide,

Where ripple, ripple overcurls
And eddy into eddy whirls.[56]

Hardy's acceptance of Darwinism with its wider implications cancels individuality, because taking reason and science as the distinct and final touchstones to measure the depth of human existence, he sees nothing beyond them; whereas, Meredith's acceptance of Darwinism together with its all possible paraphernalia, does not goad him on to dub the conception of an irresistible human individuality. Consequently, Meredith has a deep-rooted faith in and fondness for an indelible individuality of man inexplicable even in terms of reason and science. He regards individuality as firmly based on intuitive energy and, hence, supremely above reason and logic. On this bifurcating point between reason and intuition, much of a distinguishing nature of Hardy's Darwinism and that of Meredith's comes to the fore, evidencing much proof to be put for and against each of them. It is why, Meredith has a very strong sense for individuality : he is always full of life, ebullient life. A born fighter, and a lover of inner-conflict, as Meredith was, he holds that "nothing the body suffers, the soul may not profit by"[57]; and also that "resolution is a form of light; our native light is this darkened world."[58] But Meredith's individuality is not entirely another name of self-confidence or self-assertion of the egotistical nature. Meredith does not accord his approbation to self-conceit or self-dependence founded on unripe faith or unreasonable belief. He, therefore, recommends a moderate approach to nature tempered with rationality is the real beginning for wisdom : a passion spun and plotted unreasonably is the beginning of self-betrayal and self-defeat :

Our life is but a little holding
Lent to do a mighty labour.[59]

Or

In tragic life God wot, no villain need be!
Passion spin and plot;
We are betrayed by what false within.[60]

Or

> Fools run jabbering of the theory of
> Fate, to escape the annoyance of
> tracing the cause.[61]

Meredith's view of individuality has the power "to drag human beings upward :"[62] it has the power "to goad every man on to face the challenges of life."[63] With this power, Meredith contends that life, a very hard business as it is, also becomes in itself an enchanting task. Like Browning, Meredith wants to see every human being wishing and cherishing incessantly to come to this life again with the strength and repository of experience of previous life, so that he may evolve further and, at one stage, may claim approximation even to the divine powers. A born fighter, as he was, there is no maunderings for him to weaken his confirmed vision of life and world : unlike Ibsen and Tolstoy, he does not despair of his age — or content himself with nothing "the bad potatoes", or denying the physical side of life : he shares, on the contrary, the Greek quality of temperance, avoiding asceticism and sensuality, dittoing modern hedonism and recommending the Tolstoyian approach. It is all because his view of individuality taught him to be so, because he wanted the world to be so spiritually and physically evolved, where heaven might be brought down on earth.

Meredith believes that the physical evolution leads to the spiritual evolution : without body the spirit cannot be conceived of. It is through the realm of physical or biological evolution that a man can enter the next realm of the spirit. Without one the other is defunct and in the scheme of life, therefore, each is desirable. "We do not get," writes Meredith, "to any heaven by renouncing the Mother we sprang from, and when there is an eternal secret for us, it is best to believe that Earth knows, to keep near her even in our utmost aspiration."[64] It is through the nature that we learn discipline — the very process of further evolution from biological to spiritual : from passion to intellect. "Through Nature", he argues, "only can we ascend : St. Simon saw the Hog in Nature, and took Nature for the Hog."[65] It is why, with this approach to nature, Meredith would neither bid us, like the elder

Nature poets, find our chief inspiration and consolation in Nature; nor, like the town-lovers, plunge us into the stimulus of crowds :

> Not where the troubled passions toss the mind,
> In turbid cities, can the key be bare,
> It hangs for those who hither thither fare,
> Close inter threading nature with our kind.[66]

In the Meredithian world, the Darwinian struggle for existence has a sombre aspect : in it, there is no tooth and claw struggle : in it, man's evolution is not perfect and final without altruistic feelings, because without them, we decay and rot. In Meredith's novels, the higher the aim is, the richer the intuitive power will be : the more the tragic and gloomy the aspect of life is, the more sombre and enjoyable the result will be. After all, the most tragic thing is not death nor pain, but 'an unteachable spirit.' What man needs is — blood, brain and spirit; each acting in co-operation :

> Blood — and brain and spirit — three...
> Join for true felicity —
> Are they parted, then expect
> Someone sailing will be wrecked.[67]

And a love of the light within will lead us through the darkness of life :

> Overhead, overhead,
> Rushes life in a race,
> As the clouds, the clouds chase;
> And we go,
> And we drop like the fruits of the tree
> Even we — Even so.[68]

In fact, Meredith reaches the highest echelon of perfection as a novelist when Matthew Arnold's animadversions about science were beginning to be heard with a note of caution : Meredith's *Richard Feverel* being exactly contemporary with Darwin's *Origin of Species*. Sir Austin's best-remembered stricture that "Man is a self-acting machine,"[69] yet he like his creator, *i.e.,* Meredith, himself accepts later evolution as a hypothesis that casts a flood of light on human history, and by enabling man to organize his life for attainable ends provides a basis for morality. For what may lie beyond, man must have faith in the wider incidence of all that is revealed. Swinburne's *Hertha,* The *Hymn of Man* and *Pilgrims* propound a different creed from that in *Earth and Man*; because Swinburne's symbolical interpretation of Kantian metaphysics is different from Meredith's and far different from Hardy's; and, because Meredith's cosmology is a bold speculation on the facts of existence, confirmed by what he feels to be his true communion with Nature, his mother, having close resemblances like that of Butler's. Like Hering and Butler, Meredith's works reveal the intrinsic working of instinct and obscure impulse and of an occult responsiveness to the influences of external nature; but it is not so in Hardy's interpretation of the tenets of Darwinism.

In *Diana of the Crossways*, Meredith confirms "the speeding of us, compact of what we are, between the ascetic rocks and the sensual whirlpools, to the creation of certain nobler races, now very dimly imagined."[70] For the incessant and continuous process of evolution, there is no terminus : for the goal of strife is in the illimitable distance; it is not an end, but a direction. Evolution, the survival of the fittest, or the progress through blood and tears, is the law of being; man will attain health and holiness only in its devout acceptance : the real direction lies ahead of us to be found out only at the behest of Nature and evolutionary process :

> She can lead us, only she,
> Unto God's footstool, whither she reaches;
> Loved, enjoyed, her gifts must be,
> Reverenced the truths she teaches,
> Ere a man may hope that he;
> Ever can attain the glee
> Of things without a destiny.[71]

In *Hymn to Colour*, Meredith sings of a divine direction to be trodden on for an overall spiritual perfection, which is always conspicuously absent in the works of Hardy. Darwinism, in the Merédithían novels is imperfect without the glory of God, interlinked with the glory of a benevolent nature and earth :

> This way have men come out of brutishness,
> To spell the letters of the sky and read

A reflex upon earth else meaningless,
With thee, O fount of the Untimed! to lead;
Drink they of thee, thee eyeing, they unaged.
Shall on though brave wars waged.

More gardens will they win than they lost;
The vile plucked out of them, the unlovely slain,
Not forfeiting the beast with which they are crossed,
To stature of the Gods will they attain,
They shall uplift their Earth to meet her Lord,
Themselves the attuning chord![72]

Meredith has less expectation of Shelley's millennium, the myth of perfectibility, than even what Browning had, yet his doctrine of incessant spiritual evolution is, in a way, a kind of modification on Darwin's biological evolution. In him, there exists the scientist who sacrifices all to the quest of truth; the philosopher who seeks to penetrate into the veil of the absolute; the artist fashioning an image of supernatural beauty; and the poet and novelist engaged on the loftiest service within the compass of his powers. But it is not to be inferred from all this that he applies "science of Theometry" in Rossetti's sarcastic phrase, even on God and His process of working. Meredith is, as far, on the one hand, from a formal pantheism, as, on the other, from the assured theosophy of Blake, who identified the prophetic mind, "called by mortals the Imagination," with the Logos, and accepted it as the infallible intermediary between man and the divine. Meredith's *uberrima fides* is, therefore, in the moral elements, in the preponderance and predominance of good; sins, he regards as transgressions of natural laws, and hence, they are bound to bring their corresponding chastisement; goodness is attained through obedience; and, to require definite certainties in us, unfaith, the scepticism of doubting Thomas are to be put apart; for —

These are our sensual dreams;
Of the yearning to touch, to feel
The dark Impalpable sure,
And have the unveiled appear.[73]

Preaching the religion of evolution, Meredith bids us kneel with him to the God's Providence, where Spirit ennobles us :

She being spirit in her clods
Footway to the God of Gods,
The Great Unseen, nowise the Dark Unknown.[74]

Meredith's spirit is, in a word, a part of his Darwinism, because it is very near to him; whereas, Hardy's Darwinism is absolutely devoid of it; and, it explains the fundamental difference between the both :

I neighbour the invisible
So close that my consent
Is only asked for spirits masked
To leap from trees and flowers.

And this because with them I dwell
In thought, while calmly bent
To read the lines dear Earth designs
Shall speak her life on ours.[75]

NOTES

1. Henkin, L.J. : *Darwinism in the English Novel, 1860-1910*, p. 100.
2. *Ibid.*
3. Seward, A.C. : *Darwin and Modern Science*, p. 205.
4. *Ibid.*
5. *Ibid.*
6. Guerard, A.J. : *Hardy : The Novels and Stories*, p. 23.
7. *Ibid.*
8. *Wessex Poems* (*Nature's Questioning*), p. 58.
9. MacDonald, A.S. : *Thomas Hardy : a Critical Study*, p. 139.
10. Baker, E.A. : *The History of English Novel*, Vol. IX, p. 83.
11. *Ibid.*
12. Weber, C.J. : *Hardy in America*, p. 19.
13. Elliot, A.P. : *Fatalism in the Works of Thomas Hardy*, p. 101.
14. Braybrooke, P. : *Thomas Hardy and His Philosophy,* p. 70.
15. *Later Years*, p. 226.
16. Baker, E.A. : *op. cit.*, p. 84.
17. Guerard, A.J. : *op. cit.*, p. 91.
18. Henkin, L.J. : *op. cit.*, p. 67.
19. *Ibid.*
20. *Ibid.*, p. 69.
21. Brown, D. : *Hardy the Novelist*, p. 59.
22. *The Dynasts*, preface, p. iv.
23. *Ibid.*

24. *Two on a Tower*, p. 104.
25. *Thomas Hardy*, p. 39.
26. *Far From the Madding Crowd*, p. 164.
27. *Ibid.*, pp. 164-65.
28. *The Mayor of Casterbridge*, p. 327.
29. Rutland, W.R. : *Life of Thomas Hardy*, p. 351.
30. *Ibid.*, p. 362.
31. *Ibid.*, p. 370.
32. Elliot, A.P. : *op. cit.*, p. 110.
33. *Ibid.*, p. 115.
34. *Ibid.*, p. 116.
35. Henkin, L.J. : *op. cit.*, p. 172.
36. *Ibid.*
37. *Ibid.*, p. 179.
38. *Ibid.*
39. Abercrombie, L. : *Thomas Hardy : A Critical Study*, p. 55.
40. *Ibid.*
41. Blunden, E. : *Life of Thomas Hardy*, p. 195.
42. *Ibid.*
43. *Ibid.*, p. 201.
44. Lindsay, J. : *Life of George Meredith*, p. 340.
45. *Ibid.*
46. *Ibid.*
47. Henkin, L.J. : *op. cit.*, p. 95.
48. *Ibid.*, p. 97.
49. *Ordeal of Richard Feverel*, p. 74.
50. *Diana of the Crossways*, p. 21.
51. Compton-Rickett, Arthur : *A History of English Literature*, p. 538.
52. *Ibid.*
53. *Earth and Man*, p. 79.
54. *Ibid.*
55. *Vittoria*, p. 49.
56. *Ibid.*
57. *Ibid.*
58. *Ibid.*
59. *Ibid.*, p. 81.
60. *Modern Love*, p. 17.
61. *Meditation Under Stars*, p. 21.
62. *Galland, R. : George Meredith*, p. 39.

63. *Ibid.*
64. *Sandra Belloni,* p. 11.
65. *Ibid.*
66. *Earth's Secret,* p. 39.
67. *Woods of Westermain,* p. 19.
68. *Dirge in Woods,* p. 7.
69. *Richard Feverel,* p. 71.
70. *Diana of the Crossways,* p. 113.
71. *Ode to the Spirit of Earth in Autumn,* p. 3.
72. *Hym to Colour,* p. 4.
73. *A Faith on Trial,* p. 7.
74. *The Four Zoas,* p. 119.
75. *Outer and Inner,* p. 19.

Also published in *ISTVF*, Delhi 1993, pp. 145-68; 'Evolutionism in Thomas Hardy's Novels' was also presented at the XVII session of the AIETC held at Hyderabad (India) on November 22-25, 1966; also published in *VFSNA*, Delhi, 2001, pp. 133-54.

BIBLIOGRAPHY

Beja, Morris. *Psychological Fiction.* Illionis : Scott Forestman and Co., Glenview, 1971.

Bode, Carl (ed.). *The Young Rebel in American Literature.* London : Heinemann, 1959.

Brombert, Victor (ed.). *Hero in Literature.* New York : Fawcett publications Inc., 1969.

Browne, Fishwick and Marsden. *Heroes of Popular Culture.* Bowling Green, OHIO: Bowling Green University, Popular Press, 1972.

Butler, Bill. *The Myth of Hero.* London : Rider & Company, 1979.

Campbell, Joseph. *The Hero with a Thousand Faces.* New York : Princeton University Press, 1973.

Carr, E.H. *International Relations Between the Two World Wars 1919-1939.* London : Macmillan & Co., 1950.

Cather, Willa Sibert. *One of Ours.* New York : Knopf, 1922.

Chase, Richard. *The American Novel and its Tradition.* London : Boll, 1958.

Cohen, Henning (ed.). *Landmarks of American Writing.* Madras : Higginlothams (P) Ltd., 1971.

Commager, Henry Steele. *The American Mind.* New Heaven : Yale University Press, 1950.

Cornillon, Susan K. (ed.). *Images of Women in Fiction : Feminist Perspectives.* Ohio : Bowling Green, 1972.

Cunliffe, Marcus. *The Literature of the United States.* Middlesex : Pelican Book Ltd., 1967.

Doren, C.V. *The American Novel.* New York : The Macmillan Co., 1960.

Edgar, Pelham. *The Art of the Novel : From 1700 to the Present Times*. Now York : Macmillan, 1933.

Erikson, Erik H. *Identity Youth and Crisis*. New York Inc. : W.W. Norton & Co., 1950.

Feidelson, Charles & Paul Prodtkorb. *Interpretation of American Literature*. New York : Oxford University Press, 1968.

Fiedler, Leslie A. *Love and Death in the American Novel*. New York : Criterion Books, 1960.

Flugel, J.C. *Man, Morals and Society*. Middlesex : Penguin Books, 1962.

Forster, E.M. *Aspects of the Novel*. New York : Harcourt Brace, 1955.

Frohock. W.M. *The Novel of Violence in America* : *1920-1950*. Boston : Beacon Press, 1964.

Galloway, David D. *The Absurd Hero*. Austin & London : University of Texas Press, 1974.

Gardiner, Harold C. (ed.). *Fifty Years of the American Novel* : *A Christian Appraisal*. New York : Scribner's, 1952.

Goldhurst, William. *F. Scott Fitzgerald and His Contemporaries*. World Publishing Co., 1963.

Gross, Theodore L. *The Heroic Ideal in American Literature*. New York : The Free Press, 1971.

Gurko, Leo. *Heroes, Highbrows and the Popular Mind*. Freeport, New York : Books for Libraries Press, 1971.

Hale, Nancy. *The Realities of Fiction*. London : Macmillan & Co., 1963.

Hardy, John Edward. *Man in the Modern Novel*. Seattle & London : University of Washington Press, 1974.

Hicks, Granville. "The Thirties, a Reappraisal," *The Saturday Review of Literature*, 46.30, March 1963.

Hock, Sidney. *The Hero in History* : *A Study in Limitation and Possibility*. Boston : Beacon Press, 1962.

Hoffman, Frederick, J. *The Modern Novel in America, 1900-1950*. Chicago : Henry Regnery Company, 1967.

——. *The Twenties : American Writing in the Post-war Decade*. New York : The Free Press, 1965.

Jones, Peter G. *War and the Novelist : Appraising the American War Novel*. New York : Columbia University Press, 1941.

Josipovici, Gabriel. *The World and the Book : A Study of Modern Fiction*. Stanford, California : Stanford University Press, 1971.

Jung, C.G. *Modern Man in Search of Soul*. London : Routledge & Kegan Paul Ltd., 1961.

Karl, Frederick Robert. *The Existential Imagination*. Greenwich : Fawcett Premier, 1963.

Ketelbey, C.D.M. *A History of Modern Times From 1789*. London : George G. Harrap & Co., 1958.

Lewis, Windham. *Men Without Art*. London : Carsell, 1934.

Lidell, Robert. *Robert Lidell on the Novel*. Chicago : University of Chicago Press, 1969.

Litz, A. Walton (ed.). *Modern American Fiction Essays in Criticism*. New York : Oxford University Press, 1970.

Lubbock, Percy. *The Craft of Fiction*. London : Jonathan Cape. Paperback, 1965.

Mannheim, Karl. *Diagnosis of Our Time*. New York : Oxford University Press, 1944.

McCarthy, Harold T. *The Expatriate Perspective American Novelists and the Idea of America*. Rutherford, Madison, Teaneck : Fairleigh Dickinson University Press, 1974.

McCornick, John. *American Literature 1919-1932*. London : Routledge & Kegan Paul, 1971.

Mizener, Arthur. *Twelve Great American Novels*. London : The Bodley Head, 1968.

Morehead, Albert H. and Blum, Harold J. *100 Great American Novels*. New York : The New American Library, 1966.

Muir, Edwin. *The Structure of the Novel*. New York : Harcourt Brace & World, 1969.

Muller, Hurbert J. *Modern Fiction : A Study of Values*. New York: McGraw Hill Book Co.

O'Faolain, Sean. *The Vanishing Hero*. London, 1956.

Quinn, Arthur Hobson. *American Fiction : An Historical and Critical Study*. New York : D. Appleton-Century Company, 1964.

Robertson, Esmonda, M. (ed.). *The Origins of the Second World War*. London : Macmillan & Co., 1971.

Sands, Maurice. *An Outline of the Modern American Novel*. Boston, Mass : Student Outlines Co., 1963.

Snell, George. *The Shapers of American Fiction : 1798-1947*. New York : Cooper Square, 1961.

Spiller, Robert, E. *The Cycle of American Literature*. New York : The New American Library, 1956.

Springer, Mary Doyle. *Forms of the Modern Novella*. Chicago : University of Chicago Press, 1975.

Thomas, McCormack. *Afterwards : Novelists on Their Novels*. New York : Harper and Row, 1969.

Torgovnick, Marianna. *Closure in the Novel*. Princeton : Princeton University Press, 1981.

Trilling, Lionel. *The Liberal Imagination*. New York : The Viking Press, 1951.

——. *The Experience of Literature*, New York : Holt, Rinehart and Winston, 1967.

Tuttleton, James W. *The Novel of Manners in America*. Chapel Hill : The University of North Carolina Press, 1972.

Wagenknecht, Edward C. *Cavalcade of the American Novel*. New York : Holt, 1952.

Waith, Eugene M. *The Herculean Hero*. New York : Columbia University Press, 1962.

Walcutt, Charles Child. *American Literary Naturalism : A Divided Stream*. Minneapolis : University of Minnesota Press, 1966.

Wasserstorm, William. *Heiress of All the Age : Sex and Sentiment in the Genteel Tradition*. Minneapolis : University of Minnesota Press, 1959.

Way, Brian. *F. Scott Fitzgerald and the Art of Social Fiction*. London : Edward Arnold Ltd., 1980.

Wheelis, Allen. *The Quest for Identity*. New York : W.W. Norton & Co., 1981.